HOW TO BAKE

Also by Nick Malgieri

———

NICK MALGIERI'S PERFECT PASTRY
GREAT ITALIAN DESSERTS

HOW TO BAKE

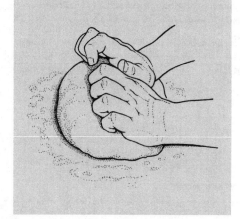

NICK MALGIERI

PHOTOGRAPHY BY TOM ECKERLE

HarperCollins*Publishers*

HarperCollins books may be purchased for educational, business, or sales promotional use. For information please write: Special Markets Department, HarperCollins Publishers, Inc., 10 East 53rd Street, New York, NY 10022.

FIRST EDITION

DESIGNED BY JOEL AVIROM

DESIGN ASSISTANT: JASON SNYDER

ILLUSTRATIONS BY LAURA HARTMAN MAESTRO

PHOTOGRAPHY BY TOM ECKERLE

PROPS BY CECILIA GALLINI

FOOD FOR PHOTOGRAPHS PREPARED BY ANDREA TUTUNJIAN

Library of Congress Cataloging-in-Publication Data

Malgieri, Nick.
     How to bake : the complete guide to perfect cakes, cookies, pies, tarts, breads, pizzas, muffins, sweet and savory / Nick Malgieri. — 1st ed.
          p.   cm.
     Includes bibliographical references and index.
     ISBN 0-06-016819-6
     1. Baking.   I. Title
TX765.M33   1995
641.8'15—dc20   95-32231

95 96 97 98 99 ❖ /RRD 10 9 8 7 6 5 4

In Memory of Peter Kump

ACKNOWLEDGMENTS

A book this size necessarily has many hands that contribute work in many different ways and I hope to thank them all. First of all, Susan Friedland, my editor, was there every step of the way, advising and prodding, and was involved with every phase of producing this book. Also special thanks are due to my agent, Phyllis Wender, who is always there when I need her. Nancy Nicholas provided her unerring editorial insight and unfailing sense of humor in the work she did on the manuscript. My thanks to her, to Carol Siegel, the copy editor, and to associate editor Jennifer Griffin.

Joel Avirom provided a wonderful design for the book and a perfect complement to Tom Eckerle's magnificent photographs, throughout the book and on the jacket, and to Laura Hartman Maestro's concise illustrations. Cecilia Gallini's beautiful props enhanced the food in all the pictures. We wish to thank both Lamalle Kitchenware and the Pottery Barn for their generosity in lending props. Special thanks are due to Andrea Tutunjian, who prepared most of the food in the photographs—her organization, dedication, and plain hard work made an enormous job easy for me. Richard Simpson and Jeff Yoskowitz also prepared some of the food at the cooking school.

Many friends and colleagues shared favorite recipes, and they are: Marian Burros, Julia Child, Kyra Effren, Christopher Gargone, Daphne Giles, Lynne Giles, Prudence Hilburn, Yocheved Hirsch, Ann Nurse, Sandy Leonard, Peggy Pinckley, Sheri Portwood, Hermann Reiner, Betty Shaw, Jeff Steingarten, Bonnie Stern, and Michelle Tampakis.

Recipe testing took place over several years of developing recipes, and the following people helped: Anna Barros, Jolene Handy, Carole Harlam, Hilary Fishman Huaman, Helene Kurland, Michelle Tampakis, and Christina Wright.

My friend Richard Sax was always there to answer a question or make a suggestion about a fine point in a recipe. Thanks, Richard.

Finally, my thanks to Mott's, Fleischmann's, and White Lily for technical support.

CONTENTS

INTRODUCTION

I have taught baking and written about it for more than fifteen years and I am continually struck by how many people enjoy spending their free time baking. A home baker may specialize in something easy—a simple focaccia, a baking powder–risen quick bread, or a batch of cookies—and only occasionally try a more intricate recipe, for a celebratory cake or decorated gingerbread house. But what unifies all of us, from the home baker to the professional, is love of baking.

People who love to bake not only enjoy the finished products—great breads, cakes, and pastries that result from their efforts—they also derive pleasure from the process of preparing them. People who spend most of their work time under pressure come home and knead bread dough—or bake cookies or make a cake—to relax and work off stress.

Baking can be more than a hobby, it can be a way of life. Become involved with baking and you'll realize that a certain recipe takes on a personality of its own and you'll no longer be able to think of celebrating a particular holiday or occasion without that recipe. Baking can invest any occasion with that personal something extra that is so often lacking in our pressured lives.

Peter Fresulone, who was one of my partners in the Total Heaven Baking Company in the early 1980s, always said, "Bake something, you'll feel better." And I think his advice is especially good today. Baking is to enjoy—that's what it's all about.

How to Use This Book

Every recipe that follows is complete in itself. When a recipe refers to another one as part of the preparation, it only does so once. For example: A recipe for a pie or tart will refer to a dough recipe at the beginning of the chapter, so you'll need to prepare the dough as a separate recipe, then shape, fill, bake, and serve it according to the instructions in the particular recipe. In some cases it is also necessary to check an illustration of the identical technique in another recipe. No recipe has more than one cross-reference, which avoids the annoyance of flipping back and forth for several different preparations. Occasionally, recipe variations, listed at the end of most recipes, may suggest substituting a filling or finish from another recipe without repeating all the necessary ingredients, but again, these are suggestions, not formal recipes.

The chapters are arranged in order of ease of preparation, as they would be in a lesson. Therefore, the easiest recipes are in the earlier chapters, with more elaborate ones later on. This does not mean that the higher the chapter number, the more difficult the recipe. It means that the techniques and processes in the recipes build on each other so that you can master simple ones that require few steps before others that require slightly more effort.

About the Recipes

Each recipe contains the following information:

1. TITLE: I believe in descriptive recipe names and my recipe titles are usually self-explanatory.

"Lemon Cornmeal Scones with Dried Cherries," for instance, have dried cherries embedded in a cornmeal dough. Occasionally, a recipe title indicates its geographical origin, as in "Portuguese Rice Tart." I have given foreign recipe names in the original language when possible. When a recipe is named for a particular person, it is usually because the recipe is adapted from that person's recipe, as in "Mary Margaret McBride's Potato Biscuits."

2. HEADNOTE: This contains a little interesting background information about the recipe, or a caution, or a hint about how to divide a long recipe into stages. If the recipe has been adapted or reprinted by permission from another source, this is stated here.

3. YIELD: You can see at a glance how much the recipe makes—how many separate pieces (rolls, cookies, tartlets), or how large a single unit (loaf, pie, tart, cake) the recipe will make. If the yield varies, this is stated. The suggested number of slices or servings that constitute a single unit is also stated.

4. INGREDIENTS: All ingredients are stated in all recipes, with the exception of dough, cake batter, and certain filling recipes, which would be very repetitious.

5. BAKING PAN: When a specific pan is needed, its dimensions (9-inch springform, $9 \times 5 \times 3$-inch loaf pan, $10\frac{1}{2} \times 15\frac{1}{2}$-inch jelly-roll pan) or capacity ($1\frac{1}{2}$-quart charlotte mold) is stated. When a jelly-roll pan or cookie sheet is a surface for baking small items, such as biscuits or cookies, and the pan's dimensions are not important, they are not stated. If the pan needs to be prepared in a certain way, the preparation (oiled, buttered, and floured, lined with parchment or foil) is stated.

6. INSTRUCTIONS: When a recipe proceeds from start to baking in a short time, the first instruction in the recipe is to preheat the oven and set the oven rack at the proper level for baking. The oven will be heating during the 15 or 20 minutes it takes to prepare the pan, assemble the ingredients, and mix the dough or batter. In recipes that have multiple steps and take longer, I suggest preheating the oven at the point when the different elements of the recipe (dough, filling, topping, for a pie) are assembled. For a yeast-risen item, I suggest preheating the oven after the loaf or pastry is put aside for its final rising. Because it is impossible to predict just how long a particular dough will take to rise until it is ready to bake, it is also impossible to state the exact time to begin preheating the oven. I usually suggest to do this "when the loaf is almost completely risen."

7. ILLUSTRATIONS: Other instructions for mixing, shaping, and assembling the elements of the recipe are as specific as possible, detailing dimensions for pieces of dough and exact descriptions of the consistency of cooked fillings. When a process for shaping or forming an item is difficult to describe with words, it is accompanied by an illustration.

8. DONENESS: Baking times are given usually to within a 10-minute span. But characteristics of the fully baked item are described, so that it is not necessary to depend solely on timing to determine doneness.

9. SERVING: When appropriate, serving suggestions are at the end of the recipe. Suggested accompaniments to some recipes also appear under "Serving."

10. STORAGE: This section indicates how to keep an item until it is served and what to do with it afterwards. Instructions for refrigerator and freezer storage are also detailed here.

11. HINTS: Any extra suggestions for handling the processes in the recipe are here. Hints that apply more generally (breads, cakes, cookies) are grouped at the beginning of the appropriate chapter.

12. VARIATIONS: Ways to change the recipe by substituting other ingredients are suggested here. If the substituted quantity is the same, it is not repeated: substitute brown sugar for the sugar, for example.

A NOTE ABOUT MEASURING

It is critical that ingredients, especially dry ingredients, be measured exactly. Though I have given weights for some dry ingredients, so you can measure them by weight rather than volume, most home bakers prefer using measuring cups to scales for dry ingredients.

For dry measure, I use stainless-steel measuring cups and spoons made by Foley. To measure liquid, I use Pyrex measuring cups. This should not be construed as brand endorsement, though I recommend you use the same measuring devices I do to get the same results. Such national brands are calibrated to strict standards of accuracy—cheap generic measuring cups may not be.

MEASURING DRY INGREDIENTS

Dry ingredients may become compacted during storage, so stir them to aerate slightly before you measure. Then spoon the ingredient into a dry measure cup and level it off with the straight edge of a metal spatula. Do not sift dry ingredients before measuring.

To measure spoonfuls of dry ingredients, use the required size spoon and scoop it to overflowing with the ingredient, then level it with the edge of a spatula or knife as for cup, above. For small fractions of spoons (⅛ teaspoon, 1⁄16 teaspoon), fill the next larger size spoon and scrape out the appropriate amount with the point of a knife or the side of a rubber spatula.

The one dry ingredient measured differently is brown sugar: press and pack it into the cup to avoid air spaces in the sugar, then level it off with a metal spatula.

Recipes that call for nuts always specify a quantity of whole nuts (for almonds, hazelnuts, macadamias, or pistachios) or nut pieces (for walnuts or pecans). When nuts are to be ground, the volume specified is for the whole nuts or nut pieces, not for a ground amount.

MEASURING LIQUIDS

Use a glass measuring cup for liquids. Place the cup on a level surface, pour in the liquid, then bend to check that the surface of the liquid against the side of the cup is exactly at the line on the side of the cup indicating the amount to be measured. One word of warning: even the best measuring cups tend to be most accurate when you measure amounts that are close to their ca-

pacity. Measure quantities of less than a cup only in a 1-cup measure. If you have a 4-cup measure, by all means measure 2½ cups in it—but do not attempt to use it to measure ½ cup.

To measure spoonfuls of liquid, do so over an empty bowl in case the liquid spills. *Never* measure directly over the mixing bowl for the same reason.

ESSENTIAL INGREDIENTS

Though this is by no means a complete list of the ingredients called for in this book, it is a list of essentials to keep on hand; with them you can prepare most of the recipes without an emergency trip to the store.

FLOURS AND STARCHES

I keep several types of flour on hand at all times: unbleached all-purpose flour for breads and some other doughs; bleached all-purpose for many pastry doughs, batters for quick breads, and some cakes; cake flour, for cakes and some recipes that combine different flours. I use self-rising cake flour or self-rising all-purpose flour occasionally for baking powder biscuits. Keep flours stored at a cool room temperature in tightly sealed canisters, tins, or plastic containers.

It is best to buy specialty and whole-grain flours from a health food store that has a brisk turnover of freshly milled flours, because flours are best when they are as fresh as possible. Whole-grain flours are best stored in the freezer. If you use a great deal of a particular type, it can be stored at room temperature without risk of becoming rancid.

Cornmeal, whether yellow or white, should be stone-ground and whole meal. Store it in the freezer as you would whole-grain flours.

Cornstarch, sometimes used in combination with flour for a cake batter, should be stored at room temperature in a tightly sealed container.

SUGARS AND SWEETENERS

I use plain granulated sugar in all recipes calling for white sugar. Though other bakers like to use superfine sugar because it dissolves easily, I prefer the slight coarseness of granulated sugar, especially for those batters where butter and sugar are aerated together. Coarser sugar helps the butter to absorb air more efficiently. In preparing meringues, coarser sugar remains in suspension better and does not dissolve on contact with the egg white, which would render the meringue liquid.

Store sugar in a tightly sealed container to keep out humidity, which will cause it to cake.

Confectioners' sugar, very finely ground granulated sugar, is often used as a decoration on cakes and pastries or as an ingredient in a frosting. Once a box has been opened, empty the sugar into a tin or canister to prevent it from caking.

Brown sugar is light or dark, depending on the amount of molasses added to the white sugar to flavor and color it. I always specify light or dark, although one may be substituted for the other without disastrous results. I like granulated light brown sugar because it's easier to measure since it does not have to be packed into the cups. Store moist brown sugar airtight so it doesn't dry and cake; store opened packages, tightly resealed, in the refrigerator. If brown sugar does become dry and hard, sprinkle it with a few drops of water,

wrap it in aluminum foil, and heat it in the oven for 5 minutes to soften. Cool before using.

Light and dark corn syrup contribute flavor and sweetness to recipes as well as a suave, smooth texture.

Unsulfured molasses has a mild, delicate flavor that I prefer, so I use it in all recipes that call for molasses.

Honey comes in many different depths of color and flavor. I like to buy organic honey at a farmers' market, but when that isn't possible, I buy a dark, rather than a light-colored honey for its fuller flavor.

DAIRY PRODUCTS

In all the recipes that call for butter I mean unsalted butter. If the recipe calls for cold butter, leave it in the refrigerator until you are ready to use it. If the recipe calls for soft butter, unwrap it while it is cold and place it in the mixing bowl you'll use for the recipe so the soft butter doesn't stick to the wrapper. (If it does, scrape the wrapper with the side of a rubber spatula.) Then leave the butter at room temperature until it has a soft, flexible consistency.

In all recipes that call for milk I mean whole milk. Buttermilk, always low-fat, may be 1½% or 2% fat—I use them interchangeably. Cream called for is always heavy whipping cream—I don't differentiate between pasteurized and ultrapasteurized cream. Sour cream is full-fat sour cream, never a sour cream substitute. Low-fat and fat-free yogurt are each indicated when used in various recipes. They are not, however, used interchangeably.

Cream cheese is plain cream cheese, though you may also use the variety without gums if you wish. Do not use the whipped kind.

Cottage cheese is regular-curd cottage cheese, not small-curd.

Ricotta is whole-milk ricotta, though part-skim milk ricotta may be substituted without adjusting other ingredients. Do not substitute fat-free ricotta.

Freshly made mozzarella is best, though if you cannot find fresh mozzarella, the packaged variety is an adequate, though not perfect, substitute.

Parmesan cheese is Parmigiano-Reggiano, imported from Italy. Purchase Parmesan in a wedge and grate it as needed—it will remain fresher and more flavorful.

Pecorino Romano is another Italian grating cheese called for in several recipes. The brand most widely available in the United States is Locatelli. It is not difficult to find, but if you can't, Parmesan cheese may always be substituted.

Caciocavallo is a Sicilian cheese. Pecorino or Parmesan may be substituted.

Mascarpone, an Italian cream cheese, is extremely rich and quite expensive. Several domestic brands are lower in price than the imported original and are just as good.

I always use extra-sharp New York or Vermont cheddar. I prefer white cheddar, not the artificially colored orange variety.

All the recipes are based on eggs graded U.S. large: 24 ounces a dozen. Remember that within the dozen there might be slight variations and that individual eggs may differ slightly from each other in size. When an exact amount of egg (or white or yolk) is crucial to a recipe, the amount is given in terms of volume, as in "1 cup whole eggs (about 5 large eggs)" or "⅔ cup egg whites (about 5 large egg whites)."

LEAVENERS

I use active dry yeast for all recipes that call for yeast. If you wish to substitute compressed (fresh) yeast, see the conversion table on page 39. The quantities of dry yeast are expressed in teaspoons and tablespoons as a convenience for those who buy active dry yeast in bulk, and the number, or fraction, of envelopes is also stated. Do not use instant or rapid-rise yeast in any of the recipes.

All baking powder is the double-acting variety. Baking soda is plain bicarbonate of soda.

COCOA AND CHOCOLATE

I always use non-alkalized unsweetened cocoa powder. I like its strong chocolate flavor. Alkalized or Dutch process cocoa (processed with an alkali to make it less bitter and darker in color) will work just as well in any of the recipes that call for cocoa.

When chocolate, whether unsweetened or semisweet, is to be used in a batter or filling that will be baked, use any of the brands available in the supermarket in packages of 1-ounce blocks. If the chocolate is for an unbaked filling, such as ganache, it is better to use a fine eating chocolate because there are so few other ingredients to support the taste. There are several good domestic brands of fine chocolate as well as imported Belgian, French, and Swiss chocolates that are available in retail stores or by mail.

NUTS AND NUT PRODUCTS

Purchase nuts at a busy store that sells them in bulk. They are more likely to be fresh and reasonably priced. If you can, taste nuts before purchasing them. Nuts stored at room temperature will oxidize and become rancid after several months, just from contact between the abundant oil in the nuts and the air. But they won't look any different. Always store nuts airtight and in the freezer—refrigeration may cause mold.

Almonds called for may be whole kernels with the skin on (natural, unblanched) or without skin (blanched). To remove the skin yourself, place almonds in a saucepan and cover with cold water. Bring to a boil and drain immediately. Place hot almonds on a towel, fold the towel over to cover the almonds, and rub to loosen the skins. Go over the almonds one by one to separate the kernels from the skins.

A recipe may require slivered almonds (cut into matchsticks) or sliced (cut into thin, flat flakes). Sliced almonds may be natural (unblanched) or blanched—which I prefer. Both sliced and slivered almonds are available in the supermarket.

Almond paste is a mixture of approximately equal amounts of blanched almonds and sugar crushed together to make a firm paste. The canned domestic type, sometimes available in supermarkets, tastes and performs much better than the imported variety, which is a cylinder wrapped in cellophane. This type is often desiccated, whereas canned almond paste remains soft and malleable.

Hazelnuts may be bought blanched or unblanched. To blanch hazelnuts, place them in a single layer on a jelly-roll pan and bake at 350 degrees for about 10 minutes, until the skins crack and begin to loosen. Rub the hazelnuts in a towel to loosen the skins, then one by one separate the hazelnuts from the skins. Occasionally un-

blanched sliced hazelnuts are available in retail stores, though I don't recall seeing any for several years.

Macadamia nuts, native to Hawaii, are extremely high in fat and as expensive as they are delicious. They add a sweet crunch to cookies and occasionally to cakes. If you can only find the salted variety, rinse them well, place in a single layer on a jelly-roll pan, and bake at 325 degrees for up to 5 minutes to dry. Don't allow them to color.

Pecans are available as halves, pieces, or a mixture of the two. This distinctively American form of the hickory nut has recently been widely cultivated in Australia.

Pignoli, or pine nuts, are sometimes used to finish macaroons, or as an enrichment to a filling.

If possible, purchase pistachios in a Middle Eastern store. Pistachios from Afghanistan and Turkey have much more flavor and color than the California variety. Blanch pistachios as you would almonds. If the only pistachios you can find are salted, treat them as salted macadamias, above.

Walnuts are available in the same forms as pecans.

DRIED AND CANDIED FRUIT

When possible, I buy organic raisins, though they are not always easy to find. Dark raisins, golden raisins, and currants may be plumped by placing them in a pan, covering them with cold water, and bringing them to a boil. Drain and cool before using. If you would like to have rum-soaked raisins or currants on hand, pack the plumped fruit tightly into a container, then add enough dark rum to cover. The flavor will permeate the fruit without overpowering it or giving it a strong alcohol flavor because the fruit has already absorbed moisture from plumping and will only absorb a little rum.

Dates, figs, prunes, and apricots may be treated the same way as raisins, though I usually wait until I'm preparing a particular recipe to plump them. Always check that pitted dates and other fruit really are—mechanical pitters often miss one or two in every package. If you are using dried figs, always remove the stem, which becomes hard and sharp when it is dried.

TOOLS AND EQUIPMENT

The following is a list of the most important equipment used in this book's recipes. Though quality bakeware and hand tools may be expensive, remember that they are a lifetime investment and will not need to be replaced.

MEASURING TOOLS

See "A Note About Measuring," above. Make sure to have several sets of both liquid- and dry-measure cups and measuring spoons, saving time and effort when you do a lot of baking at once.

ELECTRIC MIXER

I use a heavy-duty KitchenAid mixer for many recipes. A heavy-duty mixer comes with a paddle attachment for general mixing, a wire whip for aerating (whipping cream or egg whites), and a dough hook to use on heavy doughs, such as some bread doughs.

A hand mixer or lightweight table model mixer has rotary blades, and while they do a good job of mixing batters and whipping cream and egg whites, they get stuck on thicker mixtures and should never be used on bread doughs or other heavy mixtures.

Some newer hand mixers can manage heavier doughs—it is best to check the instruction booklet accompanying the mixer to be sure of this before purchasing.

FOOD PROCESSOR

I consider this an essential piece of equipment. Aside from pureeing, grinding, grating, and chopping, a food processor can perform almost all the functions of a heavy-duty mixer.

KNIVES

A stainless-steel bread (serrated edge) knife, a chef's or chopping knife, and a stainless-steel paring knife are essential.

SPATULAS

Metal: Small (4-inch blade) and medium (7-inch blade) offset metal icing spatulas are easily available and are useful for a variety of purposes, including scraping the food processor bowl, icing cakes and pastries, and lifting cookies from baking pans. See the illustration of the offset spatula here.

Plastic or rubber: Six- and nine-inch rubber spatulas will accomplish most mixing and folding purposes. I prefer the traditional flat ones to the newer concave, spoonlike ones.

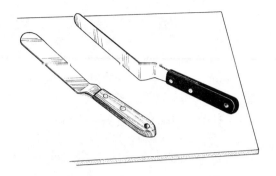

An offset metal icing spatula is useful for scraping the food processor bowl, icing cakes and pastries, and lifting cookies from baking pans.

SPOONS

Both wooden and metal kitchen spoons (both slotted and unpierced) are useful. Keep wooden spoons for baking separate from those used for cooking to avoid transferring strong flavors, which are easily absorbed by the wood.

MISCELLANEOUS TOOLS

A stainless-steel box grater is essential for grating citrus zests and small amounts of cheese, chocolate, or such spices as nutmeg.

Strainers should have stainless-steel or sturdy nylon mesh. Fine-meshed strainers are good for straining the seeds from purees, such as raspberry, or sifting lumpy mixtures, such as cocoa powder. Coarser mesh is good for straining out large particles from a syrup or other liquid and for sifting dry ingredients into a batter. Though I

never use a sifter for dry ingredients, use one if you wish.

Scrapers come in both plastic and metal. A flexible plastic bowl scraper is useful in emptying the contents of bowls or pans; a metal one is used for scraping dough from the work surface or for dividing dough into pieces.

A stainless-steel swivel-bladed peeler works best for peeling most fruit. I prefer the traditional shape to newer ones which are larger or designed to be held more comfortably—the blades on these peelers always seem to take away a large quantity of fruit along with the peel.

A set each of both plain and fluted round cutters are important for cutting baking powder biscuits and cookies. Novelty shapes may also be used for cookies.

Natural-bristle pastry brushes are softer and less likely to damage delicate doughs than are plastic brushes. Wash brushes, bristles up, in the flatware section of the dishwasher and allow to air-dry after each use, to keep them clean and free of odors.

Pastry bags are available in opaque, flexible plastic—wash them in hot, soapy water, rinse, and air-dry after each use. Tubes may be metal or plastic and are available in hardware and department stores as well as in specialty cookware stores.

BOWLS

I use both stainless-steel and Pyrex bowls for mixing. Though I use plastic containers for storage, I don't like plastic bowls for mixing—no matter how carefully they are washed they may retain fat and odors.

Most of the pots and pans I use for cooking are enameled iron—they hold heat well and are completely nonreactive, so I need never worry that an acidic preparation such as lemon curd will pick up a metallic taste from the pan in which it is cooked. Tin- or stainless-lined copper, or stainless-lined aluminum are also good choices. Stainless pans with a copper bottom or core are also excellent, but avoid all-stainless pans for anything but poaching fruit or boiling water—they heat unevenly and would scorch any custard or starch preparation cooked in them.

BAKING PANS

I regularly use the following sizes:

+ 8-inch square pan, 2 inches deep
+ 9 × 13-inch pan, 2 inches deep
+ 9- or 10-inch loose-bottomed tart pan
+ 8- or 9-inch round layer pans, 1½ inches deep

+ 9- or 10-inch springform pan, 2½ to 3 inches deep
+ 12-inch round layer pan, 2 inches deep (same volume as a 9 × 13 × 2-inch pan, which may be substituted)
+ 8½ × 4½ × 2¾-inch (small) loaf pan
+ 9 × 5 × 3-inch (large) loaf pan
+ 12 ×15-inch cookie sheets (if your oven gives strong bottom heat, invest in the insulated variety, or in several extras to stack together)
+ 10½ × 15½-inch and 11 × 17-inch jelly-roll pans (commercial aluminum half-sheet pans, 12 × 18 inches, may be substituted)

All pies are baked in a 9-inch Pyrex pie pan.

1

QUICK
BREADS,
SCONES &
MUFFINS

◆

The first project many novice bakers undertake is a quick bread, or one of its many variations, the muffin, scone, or biscuit. All are easy to prepare and even fairly fast in baking time. The "quick" refers, however, to the fact that these yeastless breads require no waiting time for the dough to rise.

Quick breads originated in the mid-nineteenth century both as an alternative to and a substitute for breads made with yeast. With the invention of baking powder—chemicals that have some of the properties of yeast in that they form carbon dioxide gas in the dough or batter that causes leavening or rising to take place during baking—many thought unreliable and often allergy-causing yeast would be replaced. Occasionally, a quick bread is leavened by baking soda or a combination of baking powder and baking soda. When baking soda is used, there is always an acid ingredient—cocoa, chocolate, sour cream, yogurt, honey, brown sugar, or molasses—present. The baking soda foams in the presence of the acid and causes a supplementary leavening that counteracts the heaviness of the acid ingredient or provides all the leavening for the dough or batter.

Fortunately for us, an intelligent public did not give up its fondness for real bread made with yeast. Even more fortunately, the discovery of baking powder contributed to many wonderful new baked foods such as muffins and biscuits as well as new cakes and contributed a lighter and better texture to many existing foods.

The recipes in this chapter fall into several categories:

SODA BREADS: Variations on the classic Irish quick bread, a soda-leavened bread usually made with buttermilk.

LOAVES: Classic not-too-sweet quick breads studded with dried fruit, nuts, or both.

CORN BREADS: Quick breads containing cornmeal and little or no sugar.

BAKING POWDER BISCUITS: Individual, usually unsweetened quick breads, most often served with meals.

SCONES: A sweet, rich cross between a baking powder biscuit and a muffin. Scones tend to be richer than biscuits, but not so sweet or rich as muffins.

MUFFINS: Individual quick breads with berries and grains; can be made low-fat, too.

QUICK BREADS

What distinguishes a quick bread from a loaf cake? They look the same, and if you made a random arrangement of loaf-shaped quick breads, pound cakes, and fruitcakes, it would be difficult to tell them apart on the basis of appearance. There are, however, fundamental differences:

1. Quick breads are not as sweet as loaf cakes. They do contain sugar, but never in as high a proportion as a cake.

2. Quick breads are lower in fat than cakes. Although they may contain eggs, butter, or oil, the proportion of fat is much less than in a cake batter.

3. Quick breads use dried fruits and nuts not only for flavor, but also for moisture, and to help make up for the low proportions of sugar and fat.

4. A quick bread has a somewhat drier texture than a cake. This is why many are served with a spread of some kind—date nut bread with cream cheese, for instance, is a classic.

5. When mixing quick breads, be careful not to overmix or the bread will be tough and heavy. In fact, I like to use bleached all-purpose flour for quick breads because it has a slightly lower protein content than unbleached all-purpose flour, making it less likely that a strong, breadlike gluten will form during mixing.

6. Finally, quick breads can be served as breakfast, brunch, and late-supper breads. They are perfect when something slightly sweet will be welcome, but a full-scale cake would be too rich.

IRISH SODA BREAD

3 cups bleached all-purpose flour
1 tablespoon sugar
1 teaspoon salt
1 teaspoon baking soda
1½ cups buttermilk

One cookie sheet or jelly-roll pan covered with parchment or buttered foil

ONE 7- TO 8-INCH LOAF, ABOUT 8 SERVINGS

Most American versions of soda bread are slightly sweet and contain raisins and/or caraway seeds—a variation of the classic called Seedy Bread (see below). This plain soda bread and its whole wheat variation are adapted from *Full and Plenty: Breads & Cakes* (Anvil Books, 1985) by Maura Laverty, a classic Irish cookbook (see an adaptation of Laverty's barm brack, a yeast-risen tea cake on page 401).

1. Combine the dry ingredients in a mixing bowl. Stir well to mix.

2. Add the buttermilk and stir gently with a rubber spatula—it will form a slightly sticky dough. Cover the bowl and allow the dough to rest for about 5 minutes.

3. Set a rack at the middle level of the oven and preheat to 450 degrees.

4. Remove the dough from the bowl to a lightly floured work surface and knead it until it is smooth, about 1 minute. Form into a round loaf and place on the prepared pan. Use a sharp knife to cut a cross about 5 inches long and 1 inch deep into the top of the loaf. Let the loaf rest, loosely covered, for about 15 minutes, while the oven is heating.

5. Bake the soda bread for about 45 minutes, until it is well risen, a deep brown color, and a skewer or toothpick inserted in the center emerges clean. Slide the loaf onto a rack to cool.

SERVING: Serve the soda bread for breakfast, brunch, or tea with butter and marmalade or jam.

STORAGE: Keep the soda bread in a plastic bag at room temperature—it is good for a day or two. Unfortunately this type of soda bread when toasted only becomes hard and crumbly, so it must be used fresh.

VARIATIONS

PART WHOLE WHEAT SODA BREAD: Substitute 2½ cups all-purpose flour and ½ cup whole wheat flour for the flour, above. Substitute an equal amount of honey for the sugar, if you wish.

SEEDY BREAD: This sweet and rich version of soda bread is probably familiar to the American palate. Although the caraway seeds are a typical part of this preparation, you may of course leave them out, if you wish. If you like raisins, add up to 1 cup dark raisins to the dough, right before adding the buttermilk.

Increase the flour to 3½ cups and sugar to 3 tablespoons; after adding salt and soda, rub in 3 or 4 tablespoons unsalted butter and add 1 tablespoon caraway seeds; mix in the buttermilk and proceed as in step 2.

QUICK BREAD WITH DRIED FRUIT

One 11- or 12-ounce package mixed dried fruit,
    coarsely chopped by hand or in the food
    processor
2 cups bleached all-purpose flour
2 teaspoons baking powder
½ teaspoon salt
6 tablespoons unsalted butter, softened
¾ cup sugar
2 eggs
¾ cup milk

One 9 × 5 × 3-inch loaf pan, buttered and floured

ONE 9 × 5 × 3-INCH LOAF, ABOUT 10 SERVINGS

Once every winter I make a compote from a supermarket box of mixed dried fruit, and this quick bread also uses the mixture to make an interesting, not-too-sweet breakfast bread.

1. Set a rack at the middle level of the oven and preheat to 375 degrees.

2. Place the chopped dried fruit in a saucepan. Cover with water and bring to a simmer. Drain and spread out on paper towels to soak up the excess moisture.

3. Combine the flour, baking powder, and salt in a mixing bowl; stir well to mix.

4. In a separate bowl, beat the butter, then beat in the sugar, just until mixed. Beat in the eggs and milk, then the flour mixture and dried fruit.

5. Scrape the batter into the prepared pan. Bake the loaf for 45 to 55 minutes, until it is well risen and a skewer or thin knife inserted in the thickest part of the bread emerges clean.

6. Cool the loaf on a rack for 5 minutes, then unmold and finish cooling.

SERVING: Serve thin slices with butter or cream cheese.

STORAGE: Keep well wrapped at room temperature for a day or two. For longer storage, refrigerate, tightly wrapped in plastic. This freezes well, wrapped tightly, for up to several months. Defrost and bring to room temperature before serving.

VARIATIONS

PRUNE AND APRICOT BREAD: Substitute 1 cup each pitted prunes and dried apricots, both coarsely chopped, as above, for the mixed dried fruit.

RAISIN PECAN BREAD: Substitute 1 teaspoon ground cinnamon, 1 cup dark raisins, and ¾ cup coarsely chopped pecan pieces for the dried fruit, above. (It is not necessary to bring these ingredients to a boil, as with the dried fruit, above.)

Substitute golden raisins or currants or a combination for the raisins. Walnuts or almonds may be substituted for the pecans. Omit cinnamon and replace it with 1 teaspoon finely grated lemon zest and 1 teaspoon vanilla extract, if you wish. For an all-nut bread, omit the raisins and double the quantity of nuts.

DATE AND WALNUT BREAD: Substitute 1 cup coarsely chopped pitted dates and 1 cup coarsely chopped walnut pieces for the dried fruit, above (no need to simmer). Substitute ½ cup dark brown sugar for the sugar, increase the baking powder to 1 tablespoon, and decrease the butter to 4 tablespoons.

FIG AND ALMOND BREAD: Substitute chopped mission figs (be sure to remove the hard, sharp stems) and coarsely chopped toasted whole blanched almonds for the dates and walnuts in the variation above.

COCOA QUICK BREAD

1¾ cups bleached all-purpose flour

¼ cup non-alkalized cocoa powder

½ teaspoon baking powder

½ teaspoon baking soda

½ teaspoon salt

½ teaspoon ground cinnamon

¼ teaspoon ground cloves

2 large eggs

¾ cup light brown sugar

4 tablespoons unsalted butter, melted, or mild
    vegetable oil

¾ cup sour cream

One 9 × 5 × 3-inch loaf pan, buttered and floured

ONE 9 × 5 × 3-INCH LOAF, ABOUT 10 SERVINGS

This rich, chocolate-flavored quick bread is a good tea or afternoon bread with a spread of tart raspberry jam, butter, or cream cheese.

1. Set a rack at the middle level of the oven and preheat to 375 degrees.

2. Sift flour, cocoa, baking powder and soda, salt, and spices together into a mixing bowl; stir well to combine.

3. In a separate bowl, whisk the eggs and whisk in the sugar. Continue whisking until light, a minute or two. Whisk in the butter or oil and the sour cream. Stir the liquid mixture into the dry ingredients, being careful not to overmix.

4. Scrape the batter into the prepared pan. Bake the loaf for 45 to 55 minutes, until it is well risen and a skewer or thin knife inserted in the thickest part of the bread emerges clean.

5. Cool on a rack for 5 minutes, then unmold and finish cooling.

SERVING: Serve the cocoa bread with cream cheese and/or jam or preserves.

STORAGE: Keep well wrapped at room temperature for a day or two. For longer storage, refrigerate, tightly wrapped in plastic. This quick bread freezes well, wrapped tightly, for up to several months. Defrost and bring to room temperature before serving.

SANDY LEONARD'S BANANA RAISIN BREAD

1 cup dark raisins
1¾ cups bleached all-purpose flour
2 teaspoons baking powder
½ teaspoon baking soda
½ teaspoon salt
½ teaspoon ground cinnamon
6 tablespoons unsalted butter, softened
⅔ cup sugar
2 eggs
1 teaspoon vanilla extract
1 cup finely mashed very ripe bananas (about
    2 bananas)

One 8½ × 4½ × 2¾-inch loaf pan, buttered and floured

One 8½ × 4½ × 2¾-inch loaf, about 8 servings

My friend Sandy Leonard, an expert home baker, recently devised this recipe to use up some bananas that were rapidly growing too brown to eat.

1. Set a rack at the middle level of the oven and preheat to 375 degrees.

2. Place the raisins in a bowl. Remove a tablespoon of flour from the measured amount and toss with the raisins to coat them.

3. Combine the remaining flour, the baking powder and soda, salt, and cinnamon in a mixing bowl and stir to mix.

4. By hand or with an electric mixer, beat the butter with the sugar until soft and light, 2 or 3 minutes. Beat in the eggs, one at a time, then the vanilla.

5. By hand, being careful not to overmix, fold in the bananas, flour mixture, then raisins.

6. Scrape the batter into the prepared pan. Bake the loaf for 45 to 55 minutes, until it is well risen and a skewer or thin knife inserted in the thickest part of the bread emerges clean.

7. Cool on a rack for 5 minutes, then unmold and finish cooling.

SERVING: Serve thin slices with butter or cream cheese.

STORAGE: Keep well wrapped at room temperature for a day or two. For longer storage, refrigerate, tightly wrapped in plastic. This freezes well, wrapped tightly, for up to several months. Defrost and bring to room temperature before serving.

HINTS FOR SUCCESS: Make sure the bananas are really ripe—the skin can even be dark brown—or the bread will have little flavor.

LOW-FAT BANANA BREAD

2½ cups bleached all-purpose flour
2 teaspoons baking powder
1 teaspoon baking soda
½ teaspoon ground allspice
1 cup sugar
3 egg whites
½ cup unsweetened applesauce
2 tablespoons vegetable oil
1 teaspoon vanilla extract
2 cups mashed very ripe bananas (about
    4 bananas)

One 8½ × 4½ × 2¾-inch loaf pan, oiled and floured

ONE 8½ × 4½ × 2¾-INCH LOAF, ABOUT 8 SERVINGS

Yet another banana bread—this time a low-fat version that works particularly well. Bananas provide the sweetness, moisture, and tenderness often lacking in baked goods that are low in fat. This is so good, the absence of fat isn't even apparent.

1. Set a rack at the middle level of the oven and preheat to 375 degrees.

2. In a mixing bowl, combine the flour, baking powder and soda, and allspice and stir well to mix.

3. In a separate bowl, whisk together the sugar, egg whites, applesauce, oil, vanilla, and bananas.

4. Being careful not to overmix, fold in the flour mixture.

5. Scrape the batter into the prepared pan. Bake the loaf for 45 to 55 minutes, until it is well risen and a skewer or thin knife inserted in the thickest part of the bread emerges clean.

6. Cool on a rack for 5 minutes, then unmold and finish cooling.

SERVING: Serve thin slices with a low-fat spread such as light cream cheese.

STORAGE: Keep well wrapped at room temperature for a day or two. For longer storage, refrigerate, tightly wrapped in plastic. This freezes well, wrapped tightly, for up to several months. Defrost and bring to room temperature before serving.

QUICK BREADS (*top to bottom*):
Dried Fruit, page 6; Cocoa, page 8;
Date and Walnut, page 7;
Sandy Leonard's Banana Raisin,
page 9.

ASSORTED SCONES,
BISCUITS, AND MUFFINS:
pages 13–31.

ASSORTED SOFT
AND HARD ROLLS:
pages 84–89.

ASSORTED BREADS: Parmesan Cheese, page 80; Cinnamon Raisin, page 43; White Pan, page 41; Honey Whole Wheat Pan, page 43; Old-Fashioned Oatmeal, page 46.

FOCACCIA: Onion, page 126;
Rosemary, page 127.

**Pizza Margherita,
page 135.**

Old-Fashioned Chicken Pie, page 103.

Pizza Rustica alla Napoletana, page 111.

TOP TO BOTTOM:
**Blueberry Lemon Crisp,
page 184;
Peach Cobbler with
Buttermilk Biscuit Crust,
page 182;
Deep Dish Apple Pie,
page 181.**

Lemon Cream Meringue Pie, page 169. *TOP:* with piped meringue topping. *BOTTOM (l to r):* with swirled meringue topping; with piped whipped cream topping; with swirled whipped cream topping.

APPLE PIES. *Top:* Double-Crust, page 156. *Bottom (l to r):* with diagonal lattice crust, page 158; Easiest Apple Pie, page 154; with woven lattice crust, page 158.

Opposite: INDIVIDUAL FRUIT TARTS
AND BARQUETTES.
Top: Almond Cream Fruit Tarts filled
with grapes, strawberries, and mangoes,
page 222.
Middle: Tartelette Gianduia, page 223;
Lemon Curd Tartlets, page 220;
Chestnut Barquette, page 224.
Bottom: Almond Cream Fruit Tart filled
with strawberries, page 222;
Pine Nut Tartlets, page 221;
Chocolate Hazelnut Barquette, page 224.

Above: TARTS. *Left:* Cuban-style Cream
Cheese and Guava, page 199.
Right: Portuguese Rice, page 200.

Right: Easiest Chocolate Raspberry,
page 191.

COOKIES (*l to r*): Scottish Shortbread, page 242; Basler Brunsli, page 244; Rugelach, page 261; Churer Zimtsterne, page 243; Checkerboard Cookies, page 251; Swiss Butter Mailaenderli, page 245.

FILLED COOKIES (*clockwise from bottom*): Double Chocolate Pecan Sandwich, page 257; Fig Bar, page 259; Linzer Augen, page 258.

BAR COOKIES (*l to r*):
Betty Shaw's Hermits, page 240;
Caramel Hazelnut Diamonds, page 236;
Fudgy Brownies, page 237.

CORN BREAD

Corn bread is a staple throughout the world because cornmeal and other processed corn products, such as hominy, have been the basic dietary starch of many cultures.

The following corn breads, perhaps the most popular of all quick breads, make good brunch dishes. They are all rich, so I serve them as the principal dish for a simple breakfast or brunch, preceded by fruit and accompanied by coffee and tea—nothing else is necessary.

A NOTE ABOUT CORNMEAL

Although cornmeal is easy to find in the supermarket, I seek a stone-ground yellow brand for these recipes. Industrially ground cornmeal has had the germ removed. This helps it retain freshness longer, but unfortunately it also removes some of the cornmeal's flavor and character.

BUTTERMILK CORN BREAD

1 cup stone-ground yellow cornmeal
1 cup bleached all-purpose flour
2 tablespoons sugar
1 tablespoon baking powder
1 teaspoon salt
½ teaspoon baking soda
¾ cup buttermilk
3 large eggs
4 tablespoons unsalted butter, melted

One 8 × 8 × 2-inch pan, buttered and lined with parchment or wax paper

ONE 8-INCH SQUARE OF CORN BREAD, ABOUT
6 SERVINGS

This is easy enough to put together in the morning, but if you wish, measure the dry ingredients and combine them the night before; then, in the morning, it is only necessary to melt the butter and whisk the eggs, butter, and buttermilk together, stir them into the dry ingredients, and bake.

1. Set a rack at the middle level of the oven and preheat to 450 degrees.

2. Combine all the dry ingredients in a mixing bowl and stir well to mix.

3. In a separate bowl, whisk the buttermilk and eggs together. Quickly whisk in the melted butter.

(continued)

4. Stir the liquids into the dry ingredients; avoid overmixing.

5. Scrape the batter into the prepared pan and smooth the top.

6. Bake the corn bread for about 20 minutes, until it is well risen and firm in the center. Cool on a rack in the pan for 5 minutes, then turn out onto the rack and remove the paper. Cover the corn bread with a platter, turn them over together and serve immediately.

SERVING: Serve with butter and jam—though it is rich enough and really needs no butter.

STORAGE: Store tightly wrapped and refrigerated or frozen. Bring to room temperature or reheat at 350 degrees for 10 minutes before serving.

VARIATIONS

To substitute milk for the buttermilk, omit the baking soda.

KERNEL CORN BREAD: Add 1 to 2 cups cooked corn kernels to the batter—a good way to use up a leftover ear or two of corn.

JALAPEÑO CORN BREAD WITH JACK CHEESE: Halve, seed, and mince 2 pickled jalapeños and add to the batter along with 1 cup coarsely grated Monterey Jack cheese. Serve the corn bread with sour cream and salsa—or even guacamole.

CORN STICKS: Preheat the oven to 400 degrees, generously brush a corn-stick pan with oil, and place in the oven to heat. Eliminate the sugar from the basic recipe, reduce the baking powder to 2 teaspoons, use 1 egg, and increase the buttermilk or milk to 1 cup. Remove the hot pan from the oven and fill each cavity to within ¼ inch of the top. Return to the oven and bake for 10 to 12 minutes, or until the corn sticks are firm and golden. Unmold the corn sticks to a rack, re-oil the pan, and return to the oven to reheat for 5 minutes. Refill the pan with the remaining batter and bake. Yields 12 to 15 corn sticks.

BACON AND SCALLION SKILLET CORN BREAD: This corn bread is so good, it's an excuse to invite guests for breakfast or brunch. Traditional skillet corn breads have often been made in heavy iron skillets that have been seasoned by years of careful use. I use a 10-inch-diameter non-stick coated pan with excellent results. Finely dice and cook ¼ pound bacon in a sauté pan over low heat. When the fat begins to render, add ½ cup thinly sliced white part of scallions and cook until the bacon is crisp and the scallions are limp. Add to the batter at the end. Bake as for corn bread, above.

CHEDDAR, BACON, AND SCALLION CORN BREAD: Add 1 cup (about 4 ounces) coarsely grated sharp cheddar cheese to the batter along with the bacon and scallions in the variation above.

BAKING POWDER BISCUITS

Baking powder biscuits, obligatory for breakfast and just about any other meal or gathering of importance in the American South, are made in many different traditional forms.

I was fortunate to have a short apprenticeship in biscuit making at the side of one of the greatest living southern bakers, Prudence Hilburn, author of the definitive *Treasury of Southern Baking* (HarperPerennial, 1993), and a veritable encyclopedia on the subject. I've also had the privilege of visiting the Hilburns several times at their home in rural Alabama, and it was during my first visit that I got to watch Prudence make her light-as-air biscuits.

Most southern cooks use a special southern brand of self-rising all-purpose flour for biscuits. This flour (White Lily is a popular brand) not only has the baking powder and salt already added, but is also lower in gluten-forming proteins than nationally available brands of all-purpose flour and therefore makes a less elastic dough, which leads to more tender biscuits. It isn't impossible to make good biscuits with the flour in your cupboard, it just requires a little adjustment in the recipe. Each of the following biscuit recipes uses a different flour or blend of flours and even provides variations at the end of each recipe for different flours so that you can produce perfect biscuits no matter what type of flour you choose to use.

In the South, the traditional way to prepare biscuits is to put flour into a large bowl, make a well in the flour, and rub in shortening, then add liquid to make a soft dough. Only about 10 percent of the flour in the bowl is used and the rest is rewrapped and put away until the next batch of biscuits is made. This is how I watched Prudence do it early on a Sunday morning in 1986. I poked, pinched, squeezed, and pressed the dough so that I would remember its consistency and be able to duplicate it. Then I came home and experimented. You'll see that the recipe calls for 2 cups of flour rather than the bowlful Prudence uses—more practical if you are not going to make biscuits every day.

CLASSIC SOUTHERN BISCUITS

2 cups White Lily, another self-rising southern
    flour, or self-rising cake flour (see Note)
4 tablespoons butter, lard, or vegetable
    shortening
⅔ to ¾ cup milk

*One cookie sheet or jelly-roll pan covered with
parchment or foil*

ABOUT TWELVE 2-INCH BISCUITS

For this recipe I have used a typical southern brand of self-rising all-purpose flour, such as White Lily, to reproduce the most common biscuits on the southern table. Though such flour isn't a staple item in supermarkets across the country, it is possible to send for it straight from the mill (see Sources of Supply).

1. Set a rack at the middle level of the oven and preheat to 500 degrees.

2. Place the flour in a mixing bowl and, using your fingertips or a pastry blender, rub the fat in quickly, leaving the mixture cool and powdery.

3. Add a minimum amount of milk and stir in briskly with a fork. If dry particles of flour remain visible in the dough, gradually stir in the remaining milk.

4. Turn the dough out onto a lightly floured work surface and fold the dough over on itself several times to distribute the moisture evenly and make the dough slightly less sticky.

5. Pat or gently roll the dough to a ½-inch thickness. Cut with a floured cutter. Avoid twisting the cutter, which distorts the sides of the biscuits. Place the biscuits on the prepared pan.

6. Press any scraps together and pat to ½-inch thickness again, then cut the remaining biscuits. Discard any scraps left after the second rolling.

7. Bake the biscuits for 10 or 12 minutes, until well risen and light golden brown.

SERVING: Serve the biscuits as soon as they are baked with butter and jam.

STORAGE: Biscuits are a little like soufflés—they are made to be eaten immediately. If you wish to make biscuits in advance and keep them, slightly underbake them, leaving them very light, then cool, wrap, and freeze them. Place frozen biscuits on a parchment- or foil-lined pan, cover loosely until thawed, then reheat at 500 degrees for about 2 minutes.

HINT FOR SUCCESS: Don't be afraid of working with such a soft dough—if the dough were dry and firm, the baked biscuits would also be dry and firm. Work with biscuit dough slowly and carefully and use a spatula to transfer cut biscuits from the work surface to the pan.

Note: Substitute 1 cup all-purpose bleached flour, 1 cup cake flour, 1 tablespoon baking powder, and ½ teaspoon salt for the White Lily flour, above.

DROP BISCUITS: These easy biscuits require no rolling or forming—they are dropped from a spoon onto the pan. They're a perfect quickly made early-morning treat for guests. Use the following ingredients:

2 cups bleached all-purpose flour
2 teaspoons baking powder
1 teaspoon salt
6 tablespoons cold unsalted butter
¾ cup milk

Make the dough as in Classic Southern Biscuits, above—the dough will be soft. To form the biscuits, drop onto the cookie sheet in 3-tablespoon mounds. Bake as above.

BUTTERMILK BISCUITS

2½ cups bleached all-purpose flour
2½ teaspoons baking powder
½ teaspoon baking soda
½ teaspoon salt
6 tablespoons cold unsalted butter
¾ to 1 cup buttermilk

One cookie sheet or jelly-roll pan covered with parchment or foil

ABOUT 12 BISCUITS

Though these are similar to Classic Southern Biscuits (page 14), I like to make them with slightly different proportions. You may also use the food processor to prepare this dough.

1. Set a rack at the middle level of the oven and preheat to 500 degrees.

2. Combine the dry ingredients in a mixing bowl or bowl of a food processor fitted with a metal blade. Stir or pulse several times to mix.

3. If you are working by hand, rub in the butter until completely blended using your fingertips or a pastry blender. If you are using a processor, add the butter and pulse about 20 times until the mixture resembles a fine meal.

4. By hand, add the buttermilk and stir in with a fork. In the processor, add the buttermilk and pulse 3 or 4 times—do not allow the dough to become a ball.

5. Turn the dough out on a lightly floured work surface and fold the dough over on itself several times to distribute the moisture evenly and to make the dough slightly less sticky.

(continued)

6. Pat or gently roll the dough ½ inch thick. Cut with a floured cutter. Avoid twisting the cutter, which distorts the sides of the biscuits. Place the biscuits on the prepared pan.

7. Press any scraps together and pat to ½-inch thickness again; cut the remaining biscuits. Discard any scraps left after the second rolling.

8. Bake the biscuits for 10 to 12 minutes, until well risen and light golden brown.

SERVING: Serve biscuits as soon as they are baked with butter and jam.

STORAGE: Biscuits are a little like soufflés—they are made to be eaten immediately. If you wish to make biscuits in advance and keep them, slightly underbake them, leaving them very light, then cool, wrap, and freeze them. Place frozen biscuits on a parchment- or foil-lined pan, cover loosely until thawed, then reheat at 500 degrees for about 2 minutes.

VARIATIONS

CHEDDAR CHEESE BISCUITS: These biscuits, which may be varied by changing the cheese to Gruyère or even Parmesan, go perfectly with baked ham. Or try adding a few fresh herbs or a pinch of hot paprika or cayenne to enliven them. Please note that these biscuits are baked at a lower temperature than the preceding ones. This is to avoid burning any cheese that may be on the surface. Add ½ teaspoon paprika, sweet or hot according to taste; ½ teaspoon dry mustard; and ¾ cup (about 3 ounces) coarsely grated sharp cheddar cheese to Buttermilk Biscuits, above. Bake the biscuits at 400 degrees for about 15 minutes.

CREAM CHEESE BISCUITS: These ultra-rich biscuits were made to be served with a slightly bitter marmalade or a sharp berry jam. Use 3 ounces (1 small package) cream cheese, chilled, and only 4 tablespoons cold unsalted butter. Use just ¾ cup buttermilk or milk to moisten the dough.

MARY MARGARET McBRIDE'S POTATO BISCUITS

1 large (8 to 10 ounces) Idaho potato
1 cup bleached all-purpose flour
1 tablespoon baking powder
1 teaspoon salt
6 tablespoons cold unsalted butter
½ cup milk

One cookie sheet or jelly-roll pan covered with parchment or foil

ABOUT TWELVE 2-INCH BISCUITS

Mary Margaret McBride, one of America's original food personalities, started out as a radio journalist in the 1930s. Though she may not have invented the interview format, she became famous for it, and all the most newsworthy personalities of the day were guests on her show. She was so well-known by the 1950s that on an early *I Love Lucy* episode Ethel Mertz (Vivian Vance) went on a local television show pretending to be "Mary Margaret McMertz" to endorse bottled salad dressing she and Lucy (Lucille Ball) had prepared.

This recipe is adapted from the *Mary Margaret McBride Encyclopedia of Cooking* produced by the Homemakers Research Institute in 1959.

1. Peel the potato and slice it into ½-inch-thick rounds. Place it in a pan and cover with cold water. Bring to a simmer over medium heat, lower the heat, and cook until the potato is tender, about 10 minutes.

2. While the potato is cooking, set a rack at the middle level of the oven and preheat to 400 degrees.

3. Measure the remaining ingredients and have them ready.

4. Drain the potato and rice or sieve it while hot. Measure 1 lightly packed cup of potato puree.

5. Place the puree in a bowl and cool to room temperature. Gently incorporate the dry ingredients into the potato puree, cutting through the puree with a rubber spatula, as though you were folding egg whites into a batter. Try to avoid stirring the potato mixture or it may become elastic.

6. Gently rub the butter into the potato and flour mixture, using your fingertips or a pastry blender. Leave the mixture a consistency of slightly wet meal.

7. Add the milk and incorporate it by cutting through the dough with a fork.

8. Turn the dough out on a lightly floured work surface and fold the dough over on itself several times to distribute the moisture evenly and to make it slightly less sticky.

9. Pat or gently roll the dough to a ½-inch thickness. Cut with a floured cutter. Avoid twisting the cutter, which distorts the sides of the biscuits. Place the biscuits on the prepared pan.

(continued)

10. Press any scraps together, pat out to ½-inch thickness again, and cut the remaining biscuits. Discard any scraps left after the second rolling.

11. Bake the biscuits for 10 to 12 minutes, until well risen and light golden brown.

SERVING: Serve the biscuits as soon as they are baked with butter and jam.

STORAGE: Biscuits are a little like soufflés—they are made to be eaten immediately. If you wish to make biscuits in advance and keep them, slightly underbake them, leaving them very light, then cool, wrap, and freeze them. Place frozen biscuits on a parchment- or foil-lined pan, cover loosely until thawed, then reheat at 500 degrees for about 2 minutes.

HINT FOR SUCCESS: Be sure to use a baking potato. A boiling potato will be starchy and elastic when pureed and make the dough gummy.

SCONES

Scones, native to Scotland, have become a favorite American quick bread. They were originally baked on a griddle—and there are still many old recipes for griddle scones, which are like thick pancakes, though I have never been served one.

Richer and sweeter than a baking powder biscuit, plain scones are served for tea in the British Isles. They are often spread with clotted cream or whipped cream and jam.

All the following recipes are easy to prepare. Take the same precautions in making scones as you would in mixing a pastry dough. Rub in the butter thoroughly, but don't let it get pasty, and be careful not to mix the dough too much after adding liquid—only enough to moisten and no more.

SHAPING SCONES

Though a dough for scones may be patted out and cut like a baking powder biscuit, there is a traditional way to form them. Divide the dough into equal parts (each recipe specifies this) and pat each into a disk. Cut each disk into quarters, to make four wedges.

PLAIN SCONES

3 cups bleached all-purpose flour
¼ cup sugar
1 tablespoon baking powder
½ teaspoon salt
5 tablespoons unsalted butter
¾ cup raisins or currants (optional)
2 eggs
¾ cup milk
Egg wash: 1 egg well beaten with a pinch of salt

One cookie sheet or jelly-roll pan covered with parchment or foil

12 LARGE SCONES

These plain scones are shaped in the classic manner. The dough is formed into round cakes, then cut into quarters, so that the baked scones have a triangular shape.

1. Set a rack at the middle level of the oven and preheat to 450 degrees.

2. Combine the dry ingredients in a bowl.

3. Cut the butter into 12 pieces and rub it evenly into the dry ingredients, until the mixture has the appearance of fine cornmeal. Add the raisins, if you are using them.

(continued)

4. Whisk the eggs and milk together and stir into the flour and butter mixture with a fork to form a smooth dough.

5. Divide the dough into 3 pieces and form each into a 5-inch disk. Using a sharp, floured knife, quarter each disk into 4 wedges. Place the wedges wide apart on the prepared pan. Apply the egg wash evenly, allow the wash to dry several minutes, then wash again.

6. Bake the scones for 10 to 15 minutes, or until they are firm but not dry. Be careful that they do not color too deeply.

SERVING: Serve scones for breakfast, brunch, or tea with jam.

STORAGE: Keep scones loosely covered at room temperature the day they are baked. For longer storage, wrap or bag in plastic and freeze. Defrost the scones, loosely covered at room temperature, in a single layer for about an hour. Reheat at 350 degrees for about 5 minutes.

VARIATIONS

WHOLE WHEAT SCONES: Replace 1 cup of the bleached all-purpose flour in the basic recipe with 1 cup whole wheat flour. Reduce the milk to ½ cup.

TOLL HOUSE SCONES: Use light brown sugar instead of white sugar, buttermilk instead of the milk, and add ½ teaspoon baking soda to the dry ingredients. Add 4 ounces of chopped semisweet chocolate or ¾ cup chocolate chips to the dough instead of the raisins after the butter has been incorporated.

CREAM SCONES OR SOUR CREAM SCONES: Substitute ¼ cup light brown sugar for the sugar and ¾ cup heavy cream or sour cream for the milk. If you use sour cream, add ½ teaspoon baking soda to the dry ingredients in addition to the baking powder. Eliminate the raisins or currants. Before baking, brush the scones with additional cream (instead of egg wash) and sprinkle with cinnamon sugar.

ROCK SCONES: Increase the sugar to ½ cup and the butter to 6 tablespoons, and use only 1 egg. Substitute ⅓ cup currants, ⅓ cup golden raisins, and ⅓ cup diced candied orange peel for the raisins. Form the scones by shaping the dough into an 18-inch cylinder. Cut into twelve 1½-inch pieces and roll each piece into a ball. Bake the scones at least 3 inches apart on a paper-lined pan. Do not use egg wash.

CURRANT TEA SCONES

3 cups bleached all-purpose flour
⅓ cup sugar
1 tablespoon baking powder
½ teaspoon salt
6 tablespoons unsalted butter
¾ cup currants
1¼ cups milk, cream, or buttermilk
Egg wash: 1 egg well beaten with a pinch of salt

One cookie sheet or jelly-roll pan covered with parchment or foil

ABOUT TWENTY-FOUR 2-INCH SCONES

This typical tea pastry has a rich, delicate, cakelike texture. The dough is so tender that you may easily press the scraps back together and recut the scones twice with no risk of toughening it. The technique for making these slightly flaky scones is a little like making puff pastry—the dough is pressed out and rolled up to create layers throughout it.

1. Set a rack at the middle level of the oven and preheat to 450 degrees.

2. Combine the dry ingredients in a bowl.

3. Cut the butter into 12 pieces and rub evenly into the dry ingredients, until the mixture has the appearance of meal. Add the currants.

4. Stir the milk, cream, or buttermilk into the flour and butter mixture to form a smooth dough. Knead lightly once or twice to complete mixing.

5. Press and roll the dough on a lightly floured surface to a 10 × 15-inch rectangle ¼ inch thick. Roll the dough up from one long side, as for a jelly roll, then flatten the dough and fold in half. Roll the dough ½ inch thick. Cut the scones with a floured, plain, or fluted 2-inch-round cutter.

6. Transfer the cut scones to the prepared pan and brush the tops carefully with the egg wash. Allow the wash to dry for 10 minutes, then apply a second coat.

7. Bake the scones for about 15 minutes, or until they are firm but not dry. Be careful that they do not color too deeply.

SERVING: Serve scones for breakfast, brunch, or tea with jam.

STORAGE: Keep scones loosely covered at room temperature the day they are baked. For longer storage, wrap or bag in plastic and freeze. Defrost scones, loosely covered at room temperature, in a single layer for about an hour. Reheat at 350 degrees for about 5 minutes.

OATMEAL RAISIN SCONES

1½ cups bleached all-purpose flour
1½ cups rolled oats (regular oatmeal)
⅓ cup granulated or light brown sugar
1 tablespoon baking powder
1 teaspoon salt
8 tablespoons (1 stick) cold unsalted butter
1½ cups (about 8 ounces) raisins
1 cup milk, plus milk or buttermilk for brushing
    tops of scones (see Note)
1 tablespoon sugar mixed with ¼ teaspoon
    ground cinnamon

One jelly-roll pan or cookie sheet lined with parchment or foil

12 LARGE SCONES

This is like a giant, tender oatmeal raisin cookie! Delicious.

1. Set a rack at the middle level of the oven and preheat to 450 degrees.

2. Combine the dry ingredients in the bowl of a food processor fitted with a metal blade. Pulse 5 times at 1-second intervals.

3. Cut the butter into 12 pieces, add to the work bowl, and pulse 12 times, until the mixture resembles fine meal.

4. Add the raisins and cup of milk and pulse 3 or 4 times to form a very soft dough.

5. Generously flour the work surface, turn the dough out onto it, and fold it over on itself 3 or 4 times, until it is less sticky.

6. Divide the dough into 3 equal parts and press each into a 5-inch disk. Using a floured knife or bench scraper, quarter each disk into wedges.

7. Arrange the scones with 2 inches distance on all sides on the prepared pan. Brush tops with milk and sprinkle with cinnamon sugar. Bake the scones for 12 to 15 minutes, until they are golden and firm. Do not overbake or they will be dry.

SERVING: Serve the scones for breakfast, brunch, or tea—they need no further embellishment.

STORAGE: Keep the scones loosely covered at room temperature on the day they are baked. For longer storage, wrap tightly and freeze. Defrost frozen scones, loosely covered at room temperature, for an hour, then warm at 350 degrees for several minutes before serving.

Note: If you want to use buttermilk, add ½ teaspoon baking soda to the dry ingredients along with the baking powder.

LEMON CORNMEAL SCONES WITH DRIED CHERRIES

2 cups bleached all-purpose flour
1 cup stone-ground yellow cornmeal
⅓ cup sugar
1 tablespoon baking powder
1 teaspoon salt
5 tablespoons unsalted butter
1 cup (about 5 ounces) dried sour cherries
1 egg
½ cup milk
1 teaspoon finely grated lemon zest
2 teaspoons vanilla extract

One cookie sheet or jelly-roll pan covered with parchment or foil

12 LARGE SCONES

These scones are particular favorites of mine. The tart flavor of the dried cherries, like raisins, really complements the slight sweetness of the cornmeal.

1. Set a rack at the middle level of the oven and preheat to 450 degrees.

2. Combine the dry ingredients in a bowl.

3. Cut the butter into 12 pieces and rub evenly into the dry ingredients, until the mixture has the appearance of fine cornmeal. Add the cherries.

4. Whisk the egg, milk, zest, and vanilla together in a bowl and stir into the flour and butter mixture with a fork to form a smooth dough.

5. Divide the dough into 3 pieces and form each into a 5-inch disk. Using a sharp, floured knife, quarter each disk into 4 wedges. Place 2 inches apart on all sides on the prepared pan.

6. Bake the scones for 10 to 15 minutes, or until they are firm but not dry. Be careful that they do not color too deeply.

SERVING: Serve scones for breakfast, brunch, or tea with jam.

STORAGE: Keep scones loosely covered at room temperature the day they are baked. For longer storage, wrap or bag in plastic and freeze. Defrost scones, loosely covered at room temperature, in a single layer for about an hour. Reheat at 350 degrees for about 5 minutes.

VARIATION

Use raisins or currants instead of the dried cherries, if you wish.

After trying many different recipes for muffins and scones, I came to realize that many muffins were exactly like scones but with more liquid in the dough. One of these recipes (Corn and Golden Raisin Muffins, page 27), in fact, came about exactly in that way—I mistakenly added too much milk to the dough.

Muffin recipes from the 1920s and '30s were fairly lean—they did not have the large amounts of butter and sugar that many contemporary muffin recipes do. In fact, I remember that when I was a child, an aunt regularly baked muffins as an afternoon coffee treat and that the muffins were only consumed hot out of the oven. After they cooled they became too dense and heavy.

The following muffins are good freshly baked or cooled—and the low-fat recipes are perfect breakfast treats for those who are weight-watching.

JORDAN MARSH BLUEBERRY MUFFINS

8 tablespoons (1 stick) soft unsalted butter

1¼ cups sugar, plus more for sprinkling tops of muffins

½ teaspoon salt

2 large eggs

2 cups bleached all-purpose flour

2 teaspoons baking powder

½ cup buttermilk or milk

1 pint blueberries, rinsed, drained, and dried

One 12-cavity muffin pan with paper liners

12 MUFFINS

These are adapted from Marion Burros's recipe that appeared in the *New York Times* several years ago. The muffins are sweet and cakelike, perfect with the melting texture of the berries. You must use paper muffin cups and be sure to butter the top surface of the pan—the tops of the muffins like to stick there. Though this recipe calls for buttermilk, it is not necessary to add baking soda.

1. Set a rack at the middle level of the oven and preheat to 375 degrees.

2. Cream the butter with the sugar and salt by hand or with an electric mixer until light. Beat in the eggs, one at a time, until smooth. Mix the

flour and baking powder together well and stir into the batter alternating with the buttermilk.

3. Crush a quarter of the berries and stir into the batter; fold in the remaining berries whole.

4. Spoon the batter into the muffin pan. Sprinkle the tops of the muffins with some sugar.

5. Bake the muffins for about 30 minutes, until well risen and deep golden. Cool the muffins in the pan.

SERVING: Serve the muffins for breakfast, brunch, or tea—they need no further embellishment.

STORAGE: Keep the muffins loosely covered at room temperature on the day they are baked. For longer storage, wrap tightly and freeze. Defrost frozen muffins, loosely covered at room temperature, for an hour, then warm at 350 degrees for several minutes before serving.

BLUEBERRY CRUMBLE MUFFINS: Do not sprinkle the surface of the muffins with sugar. Before baking the muffins, sprinkle the surface with the following crumb mixture:

8 tablespoons unsalted butter
½ cup sugar
½ teaspoon ground cinnamon
1¼ cups bleached all-purpose flour

1. Melt the butter; combine the remaining ingredients and stir in the butter.

2. Let set for a minute. Break into large crumbs by hand and sprinkle over the muffin batter in the pan.

LEMON RASPBERRY MUFFINS: Add 1 teaspoon finely grated lemon zest to the batter along with the buttermilk. Carefully fold in 2 cups firm, dry fresh raspberries after the batter is mixed, instead of the blueberries. Try not to crush the raspberries.

CHEDDAR MUFFINS

2½ cups bleached all-purpose flour

1 tablespoon sugar

2 teaspoons baking powder

1½ teaspoons salt

8 tablespoons (1 stick) cold unsalted butter

1 cup coarsely grated sharp cheddar cheese
    (about 4 ounces)

2 large eggs

¾ cup milk

One 12-cavity muffin pan with paper liners

12 MUFFINS

For a perfect lunch, serve these rich muffins with a mixed vegetable salad followed by fresh fruit for dessert.

1. Set a rack at the middle level of the oven and preheat to 450 degrees.

2. Combine the dry ingredients in a mixing bowl.

3. Cut the butter into 12 pieces, add to the dry ingredients, and rub in until the mixture resembles fine meal. Stir in the cheese.

4. Whisk the eggs into the milk and stir into the dry ingredients to form a very soft batter. Do not overmix or the muffins will be tough.

5. Spoon the batter evenly into the lined pan.

6. Bake the muffins for 20 to 25 minutes, until they are golden and firm. Do not overbake or they will be dry.

SERVING: Serve the muffins for breakfast, brunch, lunch, or tea—they need no further embellishment.

STORAGE: Keep the muffins loosely covered at room temperature on the day they are baked. For longer storage, wrap tightly and freeze. Defrost frozen muffins, loosely covered at room temperature, for an hour, then warm at 350 degrees for several minutes before serving.

CORN AND GOLDEN RAISIN MUFFINS

1½ cups bleached all-purpose flour

1½ cups stone-ground yellow cornmeal

⅓ cup sugar

1 tablespoon baking powder

1 teaspoon salt

8 tablespoons (1 stick) cold unsalted butter

1½ cups (about 8 ounces) golden raisins

1 cup milk

1 teaspoon finely grated lemon zest

1 teaspoon vanilla extract

One 12-cavity muffin pan with paper liners

MAKES 12 MUFFINS

One of my favorite cookies is from Venice, a cornmeal butter cookie studded with raisins, called *zaleti* (little yellow cookies). The flavor of these muffins recalls them quite strongly.

1. Set a rack at the middle level of the oven and preheat to 450 degrees.

2. Combine the dry ingredients in a mixing bowl.

3. Cut the butter into 12 pieces, add to the dry ingredients, and rub in until the mixture resembles fine meal.

4. Add the raisins, milk, zest, and vanilla and stir to form a very soft dough. Do not overmix or the muffins will be tough.

5. Spoon the batter evenly into the lined pans.

6. Bake the muffins for 20 to 25 minutes, until they are golden and firm. Do not overbake or they will be dry.

SERVING: Serve the muffins for breakfast, brunch, or tea—they need no further embellishment.

STORAGE: Keep the muffins loosely covered at room temperature on the day they are baked. For longer storage, wrap tightly and freeze. Defrost frozen muffins, loosely covered at room temperature, for an hour, then warm at 350 degrees for several minutes before serving.

LOW-FAT MUFFINS

Though I think the best way to ensure a healthy diet is to eat in moderation, I know that some people must follow special diets and still hate to be deprived of fine baked goods. The muffin recipes that follow are all low in fat. In addition to being a healthy breakfast choice, they make good snacks for children.

LEMON BLUEBERRY MUFFINS

2¼ cups cake flour
½ cup sugar
1 teaspoon baking powder
1 teaspoon baking soda
½ teaspoon salt
¾ cup low-fat buttermilk
½ cup unsweetened applesauce
1 egg
2 tablespoons vegetable oil
1 teaspoon grated lemon zest
1½ cups blueberries
Cinnamon sugar made with 1 tablespoon sugar
    and ¼ teaspoon ground cinnamon

One 12-cavity muffin pan with paper liners

12 MUFFINS

These moist muffins have only a small amount of fat from the low-fat buttermilk, oil, and whole egg.

1. Set a rack at the middle level of the oven and preheat to 375 degrees.

2. Combine the dry ingredients in a bowl and stir well to mix.

3. In a separate bowl, whisk together the buttermilk, applesauce, egg, oil, and lemon zest until smooth.

4. Gently fold the applesauce mixture into the flour mixture. Add the blueberries when the liquid is about half absorbed.

5. Divide among the prepared muffin cups and sprinkle each muffin with the cinnamon sugar. Bake for about 20 minutes, or until the muffins are deep golden and baked through.

6. Cool slightly and serve immediately.

SERVING: Serve the muffins for breakfast, brunch, or tea—they need no further embellishment.

STORAGE: Keep the muffins loosely covered at room temperature on the day they are baked. For longer storage, wrap tightly and freeze. Defrost frozen muffins, loosely covered at room temperature, for an hour, then warm at 350 degrees for several minutes before serving.

PUMPKIN MUFFINS

2 cups cake flour
½ cup sugar
½ teaspoon baking soda
½ teaspoon baking powder
½ teaspoon salt
½ teaspoon ground cinnamon
½ teaspoon freshly grated nutmeg
½ teaspoon ground cloves
1 cup pumpkin puree
½ cup low-fat buttermilk
1 egg
2 tablespoons vegetable oil

One 12-cavity muffin pan with paper liners

12 MUFFINS

Here the pumpkin provides moisture as applesauce does in other low-fat recipes.

1. Set a rack at the middle level of the oven and preheat to 375 degrees.

2. Combine the dry ingredients in a bowl and stir well to mix.

3. In a separate bowl, whisk the pumpkin, buttermilk, egg, and oil together until smooth.

4. Gently fold the pumpkin mixture into the flour mixture, being careful not to overmix.

5. Divide the batter among the prepared cups. Bake for about 20 minutes, or until the muffins are deep golden and baked through.

6. Cool slightly and serve immediately.

SERVING: Serve the muffins for breakfast, brunch, or tea—they need no further embellishment.

STORAGE: Keep the muffins loosely covered at room temperature on the day they are baked. For longer storage, wrap tightly and freeze. Defrost frozen muffins, loosely covered at room temperature, for an hour, then warm at 350 degrees for several minutes before serving.

APPLESAUCE CORN MUFFINS

1 cup golden raisins
1 tablespoon bleached all-purpose flour
2 cups cake flour
⅓ cup stone-ground yellow cornmeal
⅓ cup sugar
1 teaspoon baking powder
½ teaspoon baking soda
½ teaspoon salt
1 cup low-fat buttermilk
¼ cup unsweetened applesauce
1 egg
2 tablespoons corn oil

One 12-cavity muffin pan with paper liners

12 MUFFINS

Vary these muffins by adding a teaspoon of cinnamon to the batter.

1. Set a rack at the middle level of the oven and preheat to 375 degrees.

2. Combine the raisins and the tablespoon of flour in a bowl and set aside.

3. Combine the remaining dry ingredients in a separate bowl and stir well to mix.

4. In a small bowl, whisk the buttermilk, applesauce, egg, and oil together until smooth.

5. Gently fold the applesauce mixture into the flour mixture. Add the floured raisins when the liquid is about half absorbed.

6. Divide the batter among the prepared cups. Bake for about 20 minutes, or until the muffins are deep golden and baked through.

7. Cool slightly and serve immediately.

SERVING: Serve the muffins for breakfast, brunch, or tea—they need no further embellishment.

STORAGE: Keep the muffins loosely covered at room temperature on the day they are baked. For longer storage, wrap tightly and freeze. Defrost frozen muffins, loosely covered at room temperature, for an hour, then warm at 350 degrees for several minutes before serving.

BRAN CEREAL MUFFINS

½ cup skim milk

1 cup all-bran cereal

1¼ cups bleached all-purpose flour, plus 1 tablespoon for raisins

2½ teaspoons baking powder

½ teaspoon salt

½ teaspoon ground cinnamon

2 tablespoons vegetable oil, such as canola or corn

½ cup apple juice

½ cup unsweetened applesauce

⅓ cup molasses

⅓ cup sugar

1 egg, plus 1 egg white

½ cup raisins

One 12-cavity muffin pan with paper liners

12 MUFFINS

Be sure to use 100 percent bran cereal and not "raisin bran" cereal in these muffins.

1. Set a rack at the middle level of the oven and preheat to 375 degrees.

2. In a small bowl, add the skim milk to the bran. Let stand for 5 minutes.

3. In a large bowl, mix the 1¼ cups flour, baking powder, salt, and cinnamon.

4. In yet another bowl, blend the oil, apple juice, applesauce, molasses, and sugar; stir in the bran mixture. Mix well. Add the egg and egg white. Mix well.

5. Add the applesauce mixture to the flour mixture. Mix until moistened. Mix the raisins and 1 tablespoon flour in a bowl. Fold in the flour-dusted raisins.

6. Fill the muffin cups three quarters full. Bake for 20 to 25 minutes until well risen and firm.

7. Remove from the oven and cool for 20 minutes.

SERVING: Serve the muffins for breakfast, brunch, or tea—they need no further embellishment.

STORAGE: Keep the muffins loosely covered at room temperature on the day they are baked. For longer storage, wrap tightly and freeze. Defrost frozen muffins, loosely covered at room temperature, for an hour, then warm at 350 degrees for several minutes before serving.

2
BREADS
& ROLLS

When I was a child in the early 1950s, good bread was taken for granted in our community. Newark's Fourteenth Avenue, which was almost 100 percent Italian, had nearly a dozen bread bakeries within a 5-minute walk of the intersection where we lived. Some were Neapolitan, others Sicilian, but they all produced simple, sometimes rough, crisp-crusted, flavorful bread.

Though we never were so effete as to match breads to foods, there were occasions that demanded a particular bread. On holidays we always had Sicilian bread—fine-textured part-semolina bread, either braided or constructed from a series of thin ovals pressed together into a long loaf, then covered with sesame seeds—its very appearance was festive. In our home, we usually had a long, thick, baguette-type bread with seeds. My grandparents, next door, usually had a *panella,* a round loaf my grandfather ceremoniously sliced by holding the loaf against his chest, while he sliced horizontally toward himself—with a very thin, very dull knife!

Some of the bread bakeries also sold cookies, but fancy desserts and pastries were only available in pastry shops, of which there were also many.

Although we used industrially made sliced white bread ("American bread") for morning toast and for sandwiches (though my father never did), it never appeared at a meal as an accompaniment to cooked food.

Some people made bread at home, but we never did. My maternal grandmother, who lived with us, was an expert baker, but she concentrated on pastries, desserts, and pizza. Occasionally my step-great-grandmother (my father's maternal grandfather's third wife), who also lived next door, would bake small round loaves, like large rolls, which she would tear open hot and douse with olive oil, salt, and pepper. Not exactly what most American kids would think of as an afternoon snack, but delicious.

Though good bread has always been part of my life, baking bread is a relatively new pursuit for me. I spent the last twenty-odd years concentrating on pastries, desserts, chocolate, and sweet baking. But like so many other Americans, I have recently been bitten by the bread bug.

Before I began baking bread, I considered the process somewhat mysterious. How could so few ingredients combine to produce something with such a complex taste and texture? Surely there was a formula that would yield foolproof results, like a good puff pastry recipe. Reading recipes only confused me more: why would I need a baking stone or a brick or a coffee can full of ashes? Surely good bread could be made without all these affectations.

Lionel Poilâne, the great Parisian bread baker, said that bread baking is more like cooking than pastry making. Bread bakers have a "feel" for what they are doing, the same way that a sauce cook will add just the right amount of cream to a sauce to enrich it, and know to stop when the sauce looks right, or a chef will look at a roast and give it a poke with a fingertip and know to remove it from the oven.

Now, after several years of experimenting, I am happy to say that making good bread is easy. Experience does give you a feel for the dough's consistency and the amount of rising and baking it should have. But clear instructions, followed exactly, can help you to achieve the same results. I deliberately sought out people who had no experience baking bread at home to try the recipes in this section and they were all thrilled with the results of their first attempts.

Good bread needs the following ingredients and conditions:

1. GOOD FLOUR: I use an unbleached all-purpose flour for most of the breads I make.

I have used all the following brands with excellent results: Ceresota, Gold Medal Unbleached, Heckers, King Arthur, Montana Sapphire, Pillsbury Unbleached. Unbleached flour normally contains about 12 to 13 grams of protein per cup—it is the protein that enables the flour to develop the strong gluten necessary for a good, elastic bread dough.

2. GOOD WATER: If your water is highly chlorinated or very hard, try using an inexpensive bottled water, such as spring water. Your bread should have the sweet flavor of wheat rather than that of purifying chemicals or minerals.

3. COOL TEMPERATURES: If your kitchen is very hot, find a cooler place for dough to rise, or refrigerate the dough after it has begun to rise. Long, cool risings develop the best flavor in bread.

4. KNOW YOUR OVEN: If your oven has hot spots and tends to burn things on the bottom or the sides, be aware where the spots are when you are placing pans of bread to bake. A charred edge here and there will give a rustic quality to your bread—too many burned spots and the bread will be bitter.

5. GET A THERMOMETER: If you are unsure of the temperature of the water you are using, or of the interior of the baked loaf, use an "instant read" thermometer, available for less than $20 in most hardware stores.

6. KEEP IT SIMPLE: If you want a baking stone, peel (flat wooden shovel for loading a loaf onto a stone), a Cloche (an earthenware pan and cover that imitate the moist interior of a brick oven), or other devices, by all means treat yourself to them. But they are not essential. A heavy-duty electric mixer or a food processor makes most dough mixing effortless, but even they are not essential. Good bread existed long before household appliances.

7. ABOVE ALL, TAKE YOUR TIME: Nothing can replace the flavor that comes from a long, slow rise with a minimum amount of yeast (or starter). There are, of course, bread doughs that can be mixed then put into the oven quickly. But many others, especially those that have crisp crusts and a flavorful, open crumb, require starters, sponges, and doughs that ferment slowly for hours. Those doughs often are baked 24 hours after they were started. The good news is that the dough only needs minimal attention during all this time, and the long risings actually divide the work of making the bread into no-more-than-5-minute periods.

8. LAST OF ALL, PRACTICE: Think of this relaxing and rewarding pursuit as a new skill you will have throughout your life. And best of all, once the bread bug has bitten you, you will never again have to settle for mediocre bread!

BASIC BREAD VOCABULARY AND PROCESSES

What follows are the basic steps of breadmaking, along with definitions and explanations of the procedures.

1. MEASURING: Accurately measuring all ingredients.

2. MIXING: Forming a dough from the ingredients, either by hand or by machine. In the straight dough or one-step dough method, all the ingredients are combined and mixed on low speed for approximately 10 minutes or until the dough is smooth and elastic. In the sponge or two-step dough method, part of the flour, all or part of the liquid, and all or part of the yeast are combined to make a sponge that is allowed to ferment before the remaining ingredients are added.

3. FERMENTATION: Allowing the mixed dough to rise. Usually doughs are allowed to double in bulk (100 percent increase in volume at this stage). Fermentation usually occurs at room temperature. (See also page 40.)

4. DEFLATION: Punching the dough down and knocking the accumulated gases from it before beginning the shaping process. For some doughs, fermentation and deflation are repeated several times to develop flavor and texture before the dough is ready to be shaped.

5. RETARDING: Refrigerating a dough or sponge so that it ferments very slowly, or the fermentation process is interrupted.

6. DIVIDING: Cutting the dough into the required number of pieces for the breads to be made from it.

7. ROUNDING: Shaping the pieces of dough into balls so that each piece of dough presents a smooth outer skin, which will become the crust.

8. BENCH PROOFING: Allowing the rounded pieces of dough to rest or recover briefly after rounding. *Note:* In the case of small goods, such as rolls, the large, rounded, and bench-proofed pieces of dough are further divided and rounded into smaller pieces.

9. SHAPING: Forming the bench-proofed dough into the correct shape for the loaf.

10. WASHING: Brushing or spraying the shaped goods with egg wash, raw or cooked starch wash, or another liquid. This process may be performed several times or only before or after baking.

11. PANNING: Placing the shaped goods on sheets or in pans. Sufficient room must be left between items on the same sheet, or in a loaf pan, to allow each to expand up to three times larger than the shaped size.

12. FINAL RISING: The final fermentation before baking. This often takes place in a proofer or proof box, in which both temperature and humidity are high to provide a beneficial environment for the fermentation. If you are letting loaves rise at room temperature, it is best to cover them with plastic wrap that has been buttered or oiled to prevent sticking.

13. BAKING: During the initial stage of baking, air bubbles formed during fermentation expand, causing the goods to increase dramatically in volume. Before the internal temperature of the dough reaches 150 degrees, fermentation continues in a greatly accelerated manner, also causing the volume to increase. The combination of these two increases is known as oven spring.

14. DETERMINING DONENESS: Most yeast-risen goods test done when the bottom is tapped and the interior sounds hollow. An instant-read thermometer should read about 210 degrees.

15. COOLING: All yeast-risen goods must be thoroughly cooled at room temperature, usually on a rack so air can circulate around all sides.

16. STORING: Store crusty breads, uncovered, at room temperature, the day they are baked; the crust will keep them fresh for a short time. Otherwise, wrap in plastic and freeze. Delicate goods, such as croissants or brioches, may be kept uncovered at room temperature for a short time, or wrapped in plastic and frozen for longer storage. To reheat frozen bread, remove plastic and place the bread in a 350 degree oven for 10 minutes, or until the bread is thoroughly heated through. Serve warm, or cool it before serving.

USING YEAST

There are two principal forms of yeast: active dry yeast and compressed (also called fresh or cake) yeast.

Active dry yeast is available in the following varieties: standard, really just cake yeast that has been dehydrated; rapid rising, which rises dough fully in about half the time of standard yeast; and instant blending, which may be mixed directly into flour without first being mixed with liquid, as standard yeast is. Active dry yeast is packaged in retail packages of three ¼-ounce envelopes and in bulk. Store dry yeast in a cool, dark, dry place.

Compressed yeast is packaged in ⅔-ounce cakes, 2-ounce cakes, 1-pound blocks, and in bulk—usually 36-pound blocks. Store compressed yeast, tightly wrapped, in the refrigerator. If the surface of compressed yeast becomes moldy, scrape the mold off the surface, before using.

To dissolve active dry yeast, whisk it into a warm liquid and allow it to stand several minutes to dissolve; whisk again to disperse the dissolved yeast evenly in the liquid. Though yeast dissolves more easily in water, many formulas call for adding yeast to milk. If you are dissolving yeast in milk, be careful that it does not lump when it is whisked in.

To dissolve compressed yeast, crumble and whisk it into a warm liquid; compressed yeast dissolves immediately in liquid.

YEAST MATH

The following conversions make it possible to substitute one form of yeast for another.

1 envelope dry yeast = 2½ teaspoons by volume
1 envelope dry yeast = ¼ ounce by weight
1 envelope dry yeast = ⅔ ounce compressed yeast in rising power

Therefore, 2½ teaspoons or ¼ ounce dry yeast is equal to ⅔ ounce compressed yeast.

1½ envelopes dry yeast = about 1 tablespoon plus 1 teaspoon by volume
1½ envelopes dry yeast = ⅜ ounce by weight
1½ envelopes dry yeast = 1 ounce compressed yeast in rising power

Therefore, 1 tablespoon plus 1 teaspoon or ⅜ ounce dry yeast is equal to 1 ounce compressed yeast.

1. Multiply envelopes of dry yeast by ⅔ to determine ounces of compressed yeast.

2. Multiply ounces of dry yeast by ⅔ to determine ounces of compressed yeast.

3. Multiply ounces of compressed yeast by ⅜ to determine ounces of dry yeast.

4. Multiply ounces of compressed yeast by ½ to determine number of envelopes of dry yeast.

FERMENTATION WITH AND WITHOUT YEAST

Though bread making is usually associated with the use of yeast, there are other ways to make dough rise. What follows are definitions of the main leavening systems used in bread doughs and related fermented goods.

FERMENTATION: Process in which microorganisms digest carbohydrates and give off carbon dioxide (which causes dough to expand); alcohol (which contributes the "yeast-risen" flavor); and acids, produced by the alcohol (which add flavor and help retain freshness).

YEAST: A microorganism related to molds and fungi, usually made from a by-product of beer brewing. Although there are many species of yeast, the type most usually encountered is *Saccharomyces cerevisiae*, or "sugar-eating beer yeast."

STARTER OR SPONGE: A fermented mixture of flour and water caused to ferment by the addition of any one of the following: yeast; an easily fermenting food, such as grapes, hops, or potatoes; or a sourdough (see below) added instead of yeast to cause the starter or sponge to rise.

SOURDOUGH: System of fermentation which uses a "sour" to cause the fermentation. Though "sours" may be started merely with flour and water, some are started by mixing flour and water with a natural yeast-rich ingredient (such as hops, grape skins, or raisins) or a natural ingredient that ferments easily (such as mashed potato or the water in which potatoes were cooked). The resulting fermentation is due to action of plant-borne yeasts known as *Saccharomyces exiguus*, with the addition of another microorganism known as a *Lactobacillus*, which produces, among other things, lactic acid. This gives the dough and resulting bread a sour flavor, greatly appreciated in some parts of the world. A portion of the sour may be removed and "fed" with additional flour and water, then set aside for the next day's dough; the remainder of the sour is used to leaven the day's batch of dough. Or all the sour may be used in the dough, and a portion of the finished dough saved and fed to leaven the next day's dough.

PAN BREADS

Among the simplest breads to prepare, these pan breads are a good starting point. After baking and slicing (they are all great for sandwiches) they may resemble supermarket sliced bread, but all similarities end right there. These breads have a rich flavor and texture due to the small amounts of yeast used in mixing them and the good, fresh ingredients with which they are made.

Though many of the breads in this chapter are mixed using a two-step method, where some of the flour and liquid are combined with yeast to form a sponge that will ferment in advance of the actual dough, these breads are all one-step or "straight dough" formulas, where the yeast is mixed in with all the other ingredients to form a dough.

WHITE PAN BREAD

2½ teaspoons (1 envelope) active dry yeast
2 cups warm tap water (about 110 degrees)
5 to 5½ cups unbleached all-purpose flour
1 tablespoon salt
1 tablespoon sugar
5 tablespoons unsalted butter, melted, or
    vegetable oil

Two 8½ × 4½ × 2¾-inch loaf pans, oiled

TWO 8½ × 4½ × 2¾-INCH LOAVES

This simple, old-fashioned pan bread perfectly demonstrates the difference between commercially made and homemade bread.

1. Whisk the yeast into the warm water and set aside while preparing the other ingredients.

2. To mix the dough by hand, place 5 cups of flour, the salt, and the sugar in a mixing bowl and stir in the yeast mixture and melted butter. Continue to stir until the mixture forms a rough dough. Turn the dough out onto a lightly floured work surface and knead until the dough is smooth and elastic, about 5 minutes. If the dough is excessively soft and sticky, add the remaining flour, a tablespoon at a time.

To mix the dough in a heavy-duty mixer, place 5 cups of flour, the salt, and sugar in mixer bowl, add the yeast mixture and melted butter, and mix on low speed with a dough hook for about 5 minutes, or until the dough is smooth and elastic. If the dough is excessively soft and sticky, add remaining flour, a tablespoon at a time.

(continued)

To mix the dough in a food processor, place the 5 cups of flour, salt, and sugar in the work bowl of a food processor fitted with a metal blade. Pulse several times to mix. Add the yeast mixture and butter and pulse 8 or 10 times, until the dough forms a ball. If the dough is excessively soft and sticky, add the remaining flour, a tablespoon at a time, and pulse, until the dough forms a coherent ball. Let the dough rest for 5 minutes, then run the machine continuously for 30 seconds.

3. Place the dough in an oiled bowl and turn to oil all surfaces. Cover the bowl with plastic wrap and allow the dough to rise until doubled in bulk, about 1 hour.

4. Turn the risen dough out onto a lightly floured work surface (you may need the help of a scraper). Deflate the dough and divide it into two equal pieces. To form a loaf, make sure the surface is free of any excess flour, then stretch the dough into a rough rectangle. Fold in the short ends of the dough until it is approximately the length of the pan, then fold the far long edge over to the middle. Fold over the other long side and compress to form a tight cylinder, as in the illustration. Place the loaf in the pan, seam side down. Cover the pan with plastic wrap. Repeat with the second piece of dough. Allow to rise until doubled, about an hour or so.

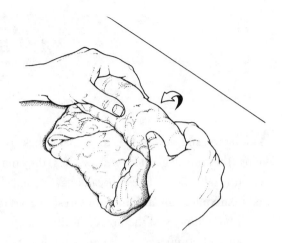

Fold in the short ends of the dough until it is approximately the length of the pan, then fold the far, long edge over to the middle. Fold over the other long side and compress to form a tight cylinder.

5. When the loaves are almost doubled, set a rack at the middle level of the oven and preheat to 400 degrees.

6. When the loaves are completely risen, place in the oven and bake for about 30 minutes, or until they are golden brown and firm and the internal temperature is about 210 degrees. Unmold the loaves to a rack to cool on their sides.

SERVING: Serve the bread for breakfast or brunch with butter and jam. This bread also makes great French toast.

STORAGE: On the day it is baked, keep the bread loosely covered at room temperature. For longer storage, wrap in plastic and freeze for up to 1 month.

VARIATIONS

HONEY WHOLE WHEAT PAN BREAD: Substitute 3 to 3½ cups unbleached flour and 2 cups whole wheat flour for the white flour above. Substitute 2 tablespoons honey for the sugar above, adding the honey with the liquid, not mixing it in with the flour as for the sugar.

CINNAMON RAISIN BREAD: The attractive—and delicious—swirl of cinnamon throughout this loaf is easy to achieve: first spread the dough with a cinnamon, butter, and sugar mixture and roll it up, jelly-roll style. Note that the recipe makes two loaves—use one right away and freeze the other.

CINNAMON SWIRL

3 teaspoons ground cinnamon
1½ teaspoons sugar
1 teaspoon unsalted butter, melted

1. To make the cinnamon swirl, combine the ingredients in a small bowl. Mix to form a smooth paste and set aside.

2. Transfer the risen dough onto a lightly floured work surface (you may need the help of a scraper). Deflate the dough and divide it into two equal pieces. To form a loaf, make sure the surface is free of any excess flour, then stretch the dough into a rough rectangle. Use a metal spatula to spread half of the cinnamon swirl mixture over the surface of the dough. Fold in the short ends of the dough until it is approximately the length of the pan, then fold the far long side down to the middle. Fold the remaining long side in and compress to form a tight cylinder, as in the illustration on page 42. Place the loaf in the pan, seam side down. Cover the pan with plastic wrap. Repeat with the second piece of dough and remaining cinnamon mixture. Allow to rise until doubled and bake as above.

CHOCOLATE ORANGE BREAD

½ cup warm tap water (about 110 degrees)

2½ teaspoons (1 envelope) active dry yeast

2¾ cups unbleached all-purpose flour

¼ cup unsweetened cocoa

3 tablespoons sugar

1 teaspoon salt

1 teaspoon finely grated orange zest

½ teaspoon ground cinnamon

2 tablespoons unsalted butter

¼ cup milk

1 egg

One 8½ × 4½ × 2¾-inch loaf pan, buttered

ONE 8½ × 4½ × 2¾-INCH-LOAF, ABOUT 6 TO 8 SERVINGS

Though this sounds more like cake than bread, it is not too sweet and makes a perfect breakfast or brunch bread.

1. Place the warm water in a small bowl and whisk in the yeast.

2. To mix the dough by hand, combine the flour, cocoa, sugar, salt, orange zest, and cinnamon in a mixing bowl and stir well to combine. Rub in the butter, until no pieces of butter remain visible. Add the milk, egg, and yeast mixture and stir to form a rough dough. Transfer the dough to a lightly floured work surface (you may need the help of a scraper) and knead until the dough is smooth and elastic, about 5 minutes.

To mix the dough in a heavy-duty mixer, combine the flour, cocoa, sugar, salt, orange zest, and cinnamon in a mixer bowl. Add the butter, cut into 12 pieces, then add the milk, egg, and yeast mixture. Mix on low speed with a dough hook until the dough is smooth and elastic, about 5 minutes.

To mix the dough in a food processor, combine the flour, cocoa, sugar, salt, orange zest, and cinnamon in a work bowl fitted with a metal blade and pulse several times to mix. Add the butter and continue to pulse until the mixture is a fine powder with no visible pieces of butter. Add the milk, egg, and yeast mixture and pulse until the mixture forms a ball. Allow the machine to run continuously for 15 seconds.

3. Place the dough in a buttered bowl and turn to coat all sides. Cover the bowl with plastic wrap and allow the dough to rise until doubled in bulk, about 1 hour.

4. Turn the risen dough from the bowl out onto a floured work surface. Press the dough with the palms of your hands to deflate. To form a loaf, stretch the dough into a rough rectangle, then fold in the short ends until the dough is approximately the length of the pan. Then fold the far long edge down to the middle. Fold over the remaining long edge and compress to form a tight cylinder, as in the illustration on page 42. Place the loaf in the pan, seam side down. Cover the pan with plastic wrap and allow the dough to rise until doubled, about 1 hour.

5. While the loaf is rising, set a rack at the middle level of the oven and preheat to 375 degrees.

6. When the loaf is completely risen, place in the oven and immediately lower the temperature to 350 degrees. Bake for 30 to 40 minutes, until the loaf is well risen and firm to the touch. The internal temperature of the bread will be about 210 degrees when it is done. Unmold the loaf to a rack to cool.

SERVING: Serve the bread for breakfast or brunch with butter and honey.

STORAGE: On the day it is baked, keep the bread loosely covered at room temperature. For longer storage, wrap in plastic and freeze for up to 1 month.

VARIATIONS

Use the dough to make 12 rolls, as in Soft Rolls (page 84), instead of a loaf. Drizzle the rolls with sugar icing (page 354), or chocolate icing (page 313), after they cool.

OLD-FASHIONED OATMEAL BREAD

OATMEAL

1 cup rolled oats (regular oatmeal)
1 cup boiling water

DOUGH

½ cup warm tap water (about 110 degrees)
2½ teaspoons (1 envelope) active dry yeast
2½ cups unbleached all-purpose flour
2 tablespoons light brown sugar
1 teaspoon salt
2 tablespoons butter

One 8½ × 4½ × 2¼-inch loaf pan, buttered

ONE 8½ × 4½ × 2¼-INCH LOAF

The nutty flavor of this oatmeal bread improves when it is toasted.

1. Place the oatmeal in a heatproof bowl and pour the boiling water over it. Stir once to mix, then set aside until cooled to room temperature.

2. To make the dough, place the warm water in a small bowl and whisk in the yeast. Combine the flour, brown sugar, and salt in the work bowl of a food processor fitted with a metal blade. Pulse until mixed. Add the butter and continue to pulse until the mixture is a fine powder with no visible pieces of butter. Remove the metal blade and fit a plastic blade. Add the cooled oatmeal mixture

and yeast mixture and pulse until the mixture forms a ball. Allow the machine to run continuously for 15 seconds.

To mix the dough in a heavy-duty mixer, combine the flour, brown sugar, and salt in mixer bowl and stir to combine. Cut the butter into 12 pieces, and add to the flour along with the oatmeal and yeast mixtures; mix on low speed with a dough hook until the dough is smooth and elastic, about 5 minutes.

To mix the dough by hand, stir together the flour, brown sugar, and salt in a mixing bowl. Rub the butter in by hand, then add the oatmeal mixture and yeast mixture. Stir to form a rough dough, then turn out onto a lightly floured work surface and knead until smooth and elastic, about 5 minutes.

3. Place the dough in a buttered bowl and turn to coat all sides. Cover the bowl with plastic wrap and allow the dough to rise until doubled in bulk, about 1 hour.

4. Turn the risen dough out onto a floured work surface (you may need the help of a scraper). Press the dough with the palms of your hands to deflate. To form a loaf, stretch the dough into a rough rectangle, then fold in the short ends until the dough is approximately the length of the pan. Then fold the far long edge down to the middle. Fold the remaining long edge over and compress to form a tight cylinder, as in the illustration on page 42. Place the loaf in the pan, seam side down. Cover the pan with plastic wrap and allow the dough to rise until doubled, about 1 hour.

5. While the loaf is rising, set a rack at the middle level of the oven and preheat to 375 degrees.

6. When the loaf is completely risen, place in the oven and immediately lower the temperature to 350 degrees. Bake for 30 to 40 minutes, until the loaf is well risen and firm to the touch. The internal temperature of the bread will be about 210 degrees when it is done. Unmold the loaf to a rack to cool.

SERVING: Slice the oatmeal bread ½-inch thick and toast. Serve with butter and bitter orange marmalade.

STORAGE: Keep the oatmeal bread at room temperature, in a paper or plastic bag, for a day or two. For longer storage, wrap tightly and freeze.

HINT FOR SUCCESS: Make sure the oatmeal mixture is cool—if it is hot it may kill the yeast.

VARIATIONS

OATMEAL RAISIN BREAD: Knead in 1 cup raisins by hand after mixing the dough.

OATMEAL CINNAMON RAISIN BREAD: After kneading in raisins, as above, and letting the dough rise, spread with cinnamon swirl mixture on page 43, as in Cinnamon Raisin Bread.

STARTER AND SOURDOUGH BREADS

The following recipes all use a starter or sourdough to leaven them, whether or not they have more yeast added when the final dough is mixed. Using the starter or sourdough to provide the bulk of the leavening in the loaf gives the resulting bread a delicate flavor impossible to achieve without the slow hours of rising that using a starter or sourdough represents. Though these long-rising doughs require some advance planning, they are well worth the time.

✦ STARTER MADE WITH YEAST

1 cup warm tap water (about 110 degrees)
¼ teaspoon active dry yeast
1 cup unbleached all-purpose flour

ABOUT 1½ CUPS STARTER, ENOUGH TO USE 1 CUP FOR A RECIPE AND RETAIN ½ CUP TO PERPETUATE THE STARTER

Though many starters are made from such naturally yeast-rich sources as grapes or raisins, this one uses a tiny amount of active dry yeast to begin the fermentation.

Called a *biga* in Italian, such a starter gives a delicate flavor to the dough it leavens.

1. Place the water in a mixing bowl and whisk in the yeast. Allow the mixture to stand for about 3 minutes so the yeast granules can melt into the water. Whisk again and add the flour. Stir in the flour with a spatula to form a soft, sticky dough.

2. Cover the bowl and leave it at room temperature until the starter is well risen, between 4 and 8 hours.

3. Use the starter in any of the bread recipes in this chapter. Before you use the starter, remove ½ cup, mix in 1 cup warm water and 1 cup flour, and proceed as above. To keep it going indefinitely, renew it in this way about once a week.

STORAGE: If you do not use the starter immediately, refrigerate it and use it within 48 hours.

VARIATIONS

PURIST STARTER: Use low- or no-sodium mineral water and organic flour for the starter to create the purest environment for the yeast.

WHOLE WHEAT STARTER: Use whole wheat flour for the starter, even if you are making white bread. This adds a subtle wheat flavor.

BEST AND EASIEST HOME-BAKED BREAD

STARTER

1 cup warm tap water (about 110 degrees)
¼ teaspoon active dry yeast
1 cup unbleached all-purpose or whole wheat flour

SPONGE

¾ cup warm tap water (about 110 degrees)
½ teaspoon active dry yeast
1 cup risen starter, above
2 cups unbleached all-purpose flour

DOUGH

All the sponge, above
1½ to 1¾ cups unbleached all-purpose flour
2 teaspoons salt

Cornmeal for bottom of loaf

ONE LARGE ROUND LOAF

Using a starter for this bread minimizes the amount of yeast in the dough and gives the bread a slow-risen, nutty flavor characteristic of the finest breads. The whole process takes about 24 hours from start to finish—but there's very little work during that time.

1. For the starter, place the warm water in a glass or stainless-steel bowl and whisk in the yeast. Stir in the flour and cover with plastic wrap. Set aside to rise at room temperature until doubled and bubbly—from 2 to 8 hours, depending on the room temperature.

2. For the sponge, place the warm water in a glass or stainless-steel bowl and whisk in the yeast. Whisk in the starter, stir in the flour smoothly, and cover with plastic wrap. Allow to rise until about triple in volume, about 4 to 8 hours (I like to do this late at night and allow it to rise all night).

3. For the dough, stir the sponge to deflate and stir in 1½ cups of the flour and the salt. Knead by hand to form a smooth, elastic, and slightly sticky dough, about 5 minutes, incorporating the remaining flour, a tablespoon at a time, if the dough is too soft.

To mix the dough in the food processor, place the sponge, 1½ cups of flour, and salt in a work bowl fitted with a metal blade. Pulse repeatedly until the dough forms a ball (if the dough will not form a ball, add the remaining flour, a tablespoon at a time, and pulse until the dough forms a ball). Let the dough rest for 5 minutes, then let the machine run continuously for 20 seconds.

To mix the dough in a heavy-duty mixer, place the sponge, 1½ cups of flour, and salt in the bowl of a mixer fitted with a dough hook. Mix on low speed to form a smooth, elastic, and slightly sticky dough, about 5 minutes, incorporating the remaining flour, a tablespoon at a time, if the dough is too soft.

4. Oil a bowl and turn the dough into it. Turn the dough over so that the top is oiled, and cover the bowl tightly with plastic wrap. Allow the dough to rise until doubled, about 1 hour or so.

5. Line a round basket or 2-quart bowl with a napkin or tea towel and flour the cloth generously. Remove the dough from the bowl, press the dough to deflate, and shape it into a sphere by tucking the bottom under and in toward the center all the way around, as in the illustration. Invert the dough into the cloth-lined basket or bowl so the tucked-under edges are on top. Cover with plastic wrap and allow to rise until doubled, about an hour.

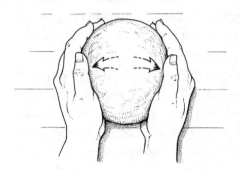

Remove the dough from the bowl, press it to deflate, and shape it into a sphere by tucking the bottom under and in toward the center, all the way around.

6. When the loaf is almost risen, set a rack at the middle level of the oven and preheat to 500 degrees. Place a heavy cookie sheet or jelly-roll pan or a baking stone on the rack. Sprinkle the top of the loaf with cornmeal and invert it onto a piece of cardboard or a peel. Holding a razor

blade at a 30 degree angle to the loaf, quickly slash a cross in the top. Slide the loaf off the peel onto the pan and lower the oven temperature to 450 degrees. Bake the loaf for about 45 minutes, or until it is well risen and a dark golden color. It should reach an internal temperature of 210 degrees.

7. Cool the loaf on a rack and do not cut it until it is completely cooled.

SERVING: Slice the bread about ½-inch thick with a sharp serrated knife.

STORAGE: On the day it is baked, keep the bread loosely covered at room temperature. For longer storage, wrap in plastic and freeze for up to 1 month.

VARIATION

PART WHOLE WHEAT BREAD: Make the starter with whole wheat flour and the sponge and dough with white flour. Or, if you make the starter with white flour, substitute ½ cup whole wheat flour and 1½ cups white flour in the sponge; and ½ cup whole wheat flour and 1 to 1¼ cups white flour in the dough.

BAGUETTES

SPONGE

1 cup warm tap water (about 110 degrees)
½ teaspoon active dry yeast
1½ cups unbleached all-purpose flour

DOUGH

All the sponge, above
1 to 1¼ cups unbleached all-purpose flour
1½ teaspoons salt

One heavy cookie sheet or jelly-roll pan,
dusted with cornmeal, or a baking stone

THREE 7-OUNCE BAGUETTES, EACH ABOUT 12 TO 15 INCHES LONG

This popular bread is what most people think of as "French bread." These long, crisp, and crusty loaves are beloved and remembered by everyone who has ever visited France.

A good baguette is not particularly difficult to prepare, but requires time. Long, slow fermentation develops both the flavor and texture of this relatively plain bread, and that part of the process cannot be rushed. Plan on starting the process the morning of the day before you intend to bake the baguettes—the dough only requires about 10 minutes of attention on the first day, then an equal amount of time for shaping the following day.

1. To make the sponge, in a 3-quart mixing bowl place the water and sprinkle the yeast on the surface. Add the flour and stir with a rubber spatula until it forms a heavy paste. Cover the bowl with plastic wrap and let the sponge rise at room temperature for about 1 hour, until the sponge has doubled, then refrigerate for at least 8 hours, or overnight.

2. For the dough, remove the sponge from the refrigerator and stir in the 1 cup of flour and the salt. Knead by hand to form a smooth, elastic, and slightly sticky dough, about 5 minutes. Incorporate the remaining flour, a tablespoon at a time, if the dough is too soft.

To mix the dough in the food processor, place the sponge, 1 cup of flour, and salt in a work bowl fitted with a metal blade. Pulse repeatedly until the dough forms a ball (if the dough will not form a ball, add the remaining flour, a tablespoon at a time, and pulse until the ball forms). Let the dough rest for 5 minutes, then let the machine run continuously for 20 seconds.

To mix the dough in a heavy-duty mixer, place the sponge, 1 cup of flour, and salt in the bowl of a mixer fitted with a dough hook. Mix on low speed to form a smooth, elastic, and slightly sticky dough, about 5 minutes. Incorporate the remaining flour, a tablespoon at a time, if the dough is too soft.

3. Scrape the dough into an oiled bowl and turn the dough over so the top is oiled. Cover the bowl with plastic wrap and allow the dough to rise at room temperature until the dough has doubled, about 1 hour or so.

4. Scrape the dough from the bowl onto a lightly floured work surface and deflate the dough by folding it over on itself 5 or 6 times. Return the dough to the oiled bowl, cover again with plastic wrap, and refrigerate for 8 hours or overnight.

5. Remove the dough from the refrigerator and deflate the dough as in step 4, above. Divide the dough into three equal pieces (about 7 ounces each). Cover two pieces loosely with plastic wrap so they don't dry out. Working with one piece at a time, shape the dough into a sphere by tucking the bottom under and in toward the center all around. Press and stretch the ball of dough into a 12 × 6-inch rectangle. Working with the long edge, fold the dough in thirds. Pinch to seal the seam. Use the side of your hand to press a depression lengthwise down the center of the dough. Pinch the sides of the depression together so the dough forms a tight cylinder, then roll the cylinder back and forth under your palms to lengthen it. Extend the ends slightly so they form points. Arrange the loaves seam side down on the prepared pan. Dust the loaves very lightly with flour and cover them with a piece of oiled plastic wrap or a lightly floured towel, then allow to rise until the loaves have doubled in volume, about 1 hour or so.

6. About 30 minutes before you intend to bake the loaves, set the racks at the middle and lowest levels of the oven and preheat to 500 degrees. Set a pan on the lowest rack. You will pour water into it to make steam during the initial part of the baking.

7. Open the oven, then averting your face, quickly pour a cup of hot water into the hot pan. Close the oven for a minute. Use a razor blade or the point of a very sharp knife to make 3 to 4 diagonal slashes across each loaf. Avert your face again and immediately place the pan with the slashed loaves in the oven. Lower the oven temperature to 450 degrees. In 10 minutes, pour another ½ cup water into the pan.

8. About 20 minutes after the loaves have gone into the oven, remove the water pan and lower the temperature again to 350 degrees. Continue baking for 20 to 30 minutes longer, or until the bread is well risen and a dark golden color. It should reach an internal temperature of about 210 degrees.

9. Remove the loaves from the oven and cool on a rack.

SERVING: Slice the bread about ½ inch thick with a sharp serrated knife.

STORAGE: On the day it is baked, keep the bread loosely covered at room temperature. For longer storage, wrap in plastic and freeze for up to 1 month.

RUSTIC WHITE BREAD

SPONGE

2 cups warm tap water (about 110 degrees)
2½ teaspoons (1 envelope) active dry yeast
3 cups unbleached all-purpose flour

DOUGH

All the risen sponge, above
2¼ to 2½ cups unbleached all-purpose flour, plus about ⅓ cup for dusting loaves
4 teaspoons salt

Two small cookie sheets or a large (at least 11 × 17-inch) jelly-roll pan dusted with cornmeal

TWO 12- TO 15-INCH LOAVES

This bread reminds me of the rough country bread found throughout France and Italy. I like to shape it into a thick baguette (long loaf) to get the most crust. I also sprinkle the loaves heavily with flour after they are formed—this keeps them from crusting during the rising and also gives the baked loaves an appetizing appearance.

The sponge, or first part of the dough, needs to rise overnight (or throughout the day) before the dough is made. If you need more time after the dough is mixed, refrigerate it instead of letting it rise.

1. To make the sponge, place the water in a 3-quart mixing bowl and sprinkle the yeast over the surface. Add the flour and stir with a rubber spatula to make a heavy paste. Cover the bowl and let the sponge rise at room temperature until the sponge has doubled, about 1 hour, then refrigerate for at least 8 hours, or overnight.

2. For the dough, remove the sponge from the refrigerator and stir in 2¼ cups of flour and the salt. Knead by hand to form a smooth, elastic, and slightly sticky dough, about 5 minutes. Incorporate the remaining ¼ cup of flour, a tablespoon at a time, if the dough is too soft.

To mix the dough in the food processor, place the sponge, 2¼ cups of flour, and the salt in a work bowl fitted with a metal blade. Pulse repeatedly until the dough forms a ball (if the dough will not form a ball, add the remaining ¼ cup of flour, a tablespoon at a time, and pulse until the dough forms a ball). Let the dough rest for 5 minutes, then let the machine run continuously for 20 seconds.

To mix the dough in a heavy-duty mixer, place the sponge, 2¼ cups of flour, and the salt in the bowl of a mixer fitted with a dough hook. Mix on low speed to form a smooth, elastic, and slightly sticky dough, about 5 minutes. Incorporate the remaining ¼ cup of flour, a tablespoon at a time, if the dough is too soft.

3. Put the dough into an oiled bowl (you may need to use a scraper) and turn the dough over so the top is oiled. Cover the bowl with plastic wrap and allow the dough to rise at room temperature until doubled, about 1 hour. If you wish to interrupt the process, let the dough begin to rise, then punch it down, cover it tightly, and refrigerate. When you are ready to proceed, bring the dough back to room temperature until the dough begins rising again.

4. To shape the loaves, scrape the risen dough onto a lightly floured surface and press the dough to deflate it. Divide the dough in half and shape one piece at a time. Press the dough into a square, then roll it up tightly. Rotate the cylinder of dough 90 degrees and roll up again from a short end. Arrange the dough seam side down, cover with plastic or a towel, and let it rest for 5 minutes. Repeat with the remaining piece of dough.

5. Roll each piece of dough under the palms of your hands to elongate it. Work from the middle of the loaf outward, pointing the ends slightly. Place the loaves, seam side down, on the prepared pans and dust each loaf heavily with flour, using about ⅓ cup in all. Cover with plastic or a towel and allow the loaves to rise until doubled, about 1 hour.

6. About 30 minutes before you intend to bake the loaves, set the racks at the middle and lowest levels of the oven and preheat to 500 degrees. Set a pan on the lowest rack to absorb some of the excess bottom heat and keep the bottom of the loaves from burning.

7. Holding a razor blade or the point of a very sharp knife at a 30 degree angle to the top of each loaf, make 3 to 4 diagonal slashes in each loaf. Immediately place the loaves in the oven and lower the temperature to 450 degrees.

8. After the loaves have baked for 20 minutes and are completely risen, lower the temperature to 350 degrees and continue baking for 20 to 30 minutes longer, until the bread is well risen and a dark golden color. It should reach an internal temperature of about 210 degrees.

9. Remove the loaves from the oven and cool on a rack.

SERVING: Slice the bread about ½ inch thick with a sharp serrated knife.

STORAGE: On the day it is baked, keep the bread loosely covered at room temperature. For longer storage, wrap in plastic and freeze for up to 1 month.

VARIATION

RUSTIC PART WHOLE WHEAT BREAD: Substitute 1 cup whole wheat flour for 1 cup of the white flour in the sponge. Make the dough with 1 cup whole wheat flour and 1¼ to 1½ cups white flour. When you form the loaves, do not elongate them, but only point the ends. Make a single slash down the middle of each loaf from one pointed end to the other. Bake as above.

ITALIAN BREAD RING

SPONGE

2 cups tepid tap water (about 85 degrees)
2½ teaspoons (1 envelope) active dry yeast
4 cups unbleached all-purpose flour

DOUGH

All the risen sponge, above
1 to 1¼ cups unbleached all-purpose flour, plus
   extra for dusting loaf
1 tablespoon salt

One cookie sheet, pizza pan, or jelly-roll pan dusted
with cornmeal

ONE LARGE DOUGHNUT-SHAPED LOAF, ABOUT 12
INCHES IN DIAMETER

This is the flavorful, round Italian loaf, with a hole in the middle, that I remember from my childhood in Newark's old Fourteenth Avenue Italian community. We had at least four great bread bakeries and one of them made this coarse, peasant ring.

There are several important points to remember about this preparation. First, it must be mixed by machine. Most of the gluten develops during the initial mixing of the sponge, so it is easiest and most efficient to mix it vigorously in a food processor or heavy-duty mixer. Second, give the dough enough time to rise. It is best to make the sponge and allow it to rise first at room temperature until doubled, then to refrigerate it at least

overnight. Finally, make sure the bread is baked through (see the temperature check for doneness in the recipe) before removing it from the oven—this will ensure a crisp crust and a crumb that is firm and resilient.

1. For the sponge, combine the ingredients in the bowl of an electric mixer fitted with the paddle. Mix on low to medium speed for about 5 minutes, until the sponge is smooth and elastic.

To mix in a food processor, combine the ingredients and pulse repeatedly until smooth. Let rest for 5 minutes, then run continuously for 30 seconds. Repeat rest and running once again.

2. Scrape the sponge into a bowl and cover tightly with plastic wrap. Allow to rise at room temperature until doubled, about 1 hour. Deflate the sponge and refrigerate for at least 8 hours or overnight.

3. To make the dough, stir the flour and salt into the sponge with a rubber spatula. Return the dough to the mixer and mix with a dough hook for about 5 minutes on low speed, until the dough is smooth and elastic.

To mix the dough in a processor, place the dough in a work bowl fitted with a metal blade. Pulse until smooth, then allow to run continuously for 30 seconds. Allow to rest for 5 minutes, then repeat the 30-second mixing.

4. Transfer the dough to an oiled bowl (you may need the help of a scraper) and cover with plastic wrap. Allow the dough to rise until doubled, about 1 hour.

(continued)

5. To shape the loaf, flour the work surface and turn the dough out onto it. Deflate the dough by pressing hard with the palms of your hands, trying to keep the dough in as even a disk shape as possible. Round the piece of dough by tucking the sides underneath all around to form a rough half-sphere. Cover with a towel or plastic wrap and allow to rest for 5 minutes.

6. Place the dough on the prepared cookie sheet or pan. Press the dough into a disk shape again. Flour the fingertips of one hand and use them, pointed together, to make a hole in the center of the dough. Spread your fingers to open out the hole until it is about 6 inches in diameter. Shape into an even doughnut.

7. Slide the loaf onto the cornmeal-dusted pan. Dust the top of the loaf lightly with flour. Cover with a towel or plastic wrap and allow to rise until doubled, about 1 hour.

8. About 30 minutes before you intend to bake the loaf, set racks at the middle and lowest levels of the oven and preheat to 500 degrees. On the lowest rack place a pan to hold water to make steam during the initial part of the baking.

9. Open the oven and, averting your face, quickly pour a cup of hot water into the hot pan. Close the oven for a minute.

10. Use a razor blade or the point of a very sharp knife to make 5 slashes on top of the loaf. Averting your face again, place the pan with the slashed loaf on the middle rack of the oven.

Lower the oven temperature to 450 degrees. In 10 minutes, add another ½ cup of water to the pan.

11. After 30 minutes, remove the water pan and lower the oven temperature to 350 degrees. Continue baking for 30 minutes longer, or until the bread is well risen and a dark golden color. It should reach an internal temperature of about 210 degrees.

12. Remove the loaf from the oven and cool on a rack.

SERVING: Slice the bread about ½ inch thick with a sharp serrated knife.

STORAGE: Keep the bread at room temperature, or in a paper bag at room temperature. To store longer, freeze the bread in a plastic bag. To reheat frozen bread, remove the plastic bag and place the bread in a 350 degree oven for about 10 minutes before serving.

VARIATIONS

HERB RING: Mix in 3 tablespoons chopped fresh rosemary leaves to the dough during step 3.

SMALL RING LOAVES: These are easier to handle. Divide the dough in half and shape each piece into a smaller ring. The procedure is the same, but the bread will be baked sooner—after about 40 minutes, usually.

OLIVE BREAD

SPONGE

1 cup warm tap water (about 110 degrees)
2 teaspoons active dry yeast
1½ cups unbleached all-purpose flour

DOUGH

2 tablespoons olive oil
1¼ to 1½ cups unbleached all-purpose flour
2 teaspoons salt
All the sponge, above
½ pound olives (1¼ to 1½ cups, to make 1 cup pitted)

Cornmeal for bottom of loaf

ONE 8- TO 9-INCH ROUND LOAF

I have memories of a bakery in the old town in Nice—le vieux Nice—and an olive bread I bought there, a large, crusty round loaf, with a deliciously strong scent of olives. Unfortunately, the olives had not been pitted and eating the bread was a challenge.

For my own version, I have added kalamata, Niçoise, Gaeta, and jarred Italian oil-cured olives for this coarse white bread. Gaeta olives are my favorite, though they might not be easy to find. All the other olives are good, too, and each contributes a unique flavor to the bread.

1. For the sponge, pour the water into a mixing bowl and sprinkle the yeast on the surface. Stir in the flour with a rubber spatula to form a heavy paste. Cover the bowl with plastic wrap and let the sponge rise at room temperature until doubled, about 1 hour.

2. For the dough, stir the oil, 1¼ cups of flour, and the salt into the sponge. Knead by hand for about 5 minutes to form a smooth, elastic, and slightly sticky dough. If the dough is too soft, incorporate the remaining flour, a tablespoon at a time.

To mix the dough in the food processor, place the sponge, oil, 1¼ cups of flour, and salt in the work bowl fitted with a metal blade. Pulse repeatedly until the dough forms a ball (if the dough will not form a ball, add the remaining flour, a tablespoon at a time, and pulse until the dough forms a ball). Let the dough rest for 5 minutes, then let the machine run continuously for 20 seconds.

To mix the dough in a heavy-duty mixer, place the sponge, oil, 1¼ cups of flour, and salt in the bowl of a mixer fitted with a dough hook. Mix on low speed to form a smooth, elastic, and slightly sticky dough, about 5 minutes. Incorporate the remaining flour, a tablespoon at a time, if the dough is too soft.

3. Place the dough in an oiled bowl (you may need the help of a scraper) and turn the dough over so the top is oiled. Cover the bowl with plastic wrap and allow the dough to rise at room temperature until doubled, about 1 hour. If you wish to interrupt the process, let the dough begin to rise, then punch it down, cover it tightly, and refrigerate. To continue, bring the dough back to room temperature until it begins rising again.

(continued)

4. Turn the risen dough out onto a floured work surface. Press the dough with the palms of your hands to deflate. Knead in the olives until they are evenly distributed throughout. Shape the dough into a sphere by tucking the dough under and in toward the center all around the bottom. Invert the dough into a round basket lined with a generously floured napkin or tea towel so the tucked ends are on top. Cover the basket with plastic wrap and allow the dough to rise until doubled, about 1 hour.

5. When the loaf is almost doubled, set a rack at the middle level of the oven and preheat to 500 degrees. Place a heavy cookie sheet, jelly-roll pan, or baking stone on the rack.

6. Sprinkle the top of the loaf with the cornmeal and invert it onto a cardboard round or peel. Slide the risen loaf from the cardboard or peel onto the baking pan or stone.

7. Bake for 35 to 45 minutes, or until the loaf is well risen and a dark golden color. It should reach an internal temperature of about 210 degrees.

8. Cool the loaf on a rack and do not cut it until it is completely cooled.

SERVING: Serve the olive bread with hors d'oeuvres and first courses; it may be too strong to accompany more delicate foods.

STORAGE: On the day it is baked, keep the bread loosely covered at room temperature. For longer storage, wrap in plastic and freeze for up to 1 month.

HINT FOR SUCCESS: While you are kneading in the olives, the dough may become elastic. Let it rest for a few minutes before continuing. You may let it rest several times if necessary.

VARIATION

OLIVE AND ROSEMARY BREAD: Add 2 tablespoons of finely chopped fresh rosemary or 1 tablespoon dried to the dough along with the olives.

SOURDOUGH STARTER

1½ to 1¾ cups distilled sodium- and chlorine-free water

3 to 3½ cups organic whole wheat or white flour

ABOUT 1 POUND STARTER, ENOUGH TO BAKE SEVERAL
LOAVES OF BREAD AND HAVE ENOUGH STARTER LEFT
TO CONTINUE GROWING THE STARTER

The easiest way to make a sourdough starter is to begin with some existing starter and add flour and water to it to increase its volume. Dehydrating the starter (see instructions, below) makes it easy to share a starter over long distances—a small plastic bag of dehydrated starter should survive mailing within the United States.

When I began making starters from scratch, I was lucky to be able to avail myself of all the knowledge and experience of my friend, Jeffrey Steingarten, *Vogue* food critic. He was a constant source of information about the technical side of sourdough production and baking, both in person and in his brilliant 1990 *Vogue* article, "Primal Bread."

The following method is based on Jeffrey's method for preparing a sour and also on the Swiss method, described in *La Boulangerie Suisse* (Swiss Breadmaking) published by the Richemont baking school in Lucerne.

The equipment for making a starter is minimal. Because my kitchen must have billions of yeast spores clinging to every surface, I boil all the equipment I will be using for the starter to sterilize it and prevent unwanted contamination from those yeast spores. If your environment is not so yeast-rich, you don't need to bother with the sterilizing. As for the ingredients, you need organically grown whole wheat or white flour and distilled sodium-free water. (See Sources of Supply for the flour.) The equipment you need is a set of dry-measure cups, a 1-cup liquid measure, a metal spoon, 2 stainless-steel or glass mixing bowls, and a pot that will hold all of it.

DAY 1

1. To prepare the equipment, scrub all the pieces with hot water and dishwashing liquid. Rinse with the hottest water possible and dry with paper towels. If you need to sterilize, bring water to a boil in the pan and add all the equipment except a larger bowl, which will not be used for several days. Boil the equipment for 5 minutes. Cover the work surface with paper towels and carefully lift the sterilized equipment from the boiling water with tongs. Allow to drain on towels.

2. To begin the starter, early in the morning, measure ¼ cup of distilled water into a sterilized bowl, using a sterilized measuring cup. Add ½ cup of the organic flour. Stir in the flour with the sterilized spoon. Cover the bowl with plastic wrap and leave for 12 hours at a room temperature of between 60 and 75 degrees.

3. After 12 hours, add ¼ cup of distilled water and ½ cup of the organic flour to the starter. Cover and leave again at room temperature.

DAY 2

4. Wash, sterilize, if necessary, and dry the measuring cups and spoon again. Add ¼ cup of distilled water and ½ cup of the organic flour to the starter. Stir well with the spoon. Cover the bowl with plastic wrap and leave for 24 hours at room temperature.

DAY 3

5. Repeat step 4. If the starter has not begun to bubble, wait one more day before discarding it and starting over.

DAY 4

6. If the starter is bubbling, repeat step 4 again, but transfer the starter to a larger bowl (sterilized if necessary) before adding water and flour. If the starter has not begun to bubble by Day 4, start over.

DAY 5

7. Discard half the starter and add ½ cup of distilled water and 1 cup of organic flour. Cover tightly with plastic wrap and leave at room temperature until bubbly. Refrigerate the starter after it begins to bubble.

MAINTAINING THE STARTER: Feed the starter by removing it from the refrigerator, discarding half of it, and repeating step 6, once a week. If any water separates out of the starter in between feedings, stir the water back in.

FREEZING THE STARTER: A practical solution if you are going away for more than a week is to combine 1 cup of starter and 1 cup of distilled water and stir well to mix. Place in a 2½- to 3-cup plastic container with a tight-fitting cover and freeze. To reactivate the starter, unmold it into a bowl, cover the bowl with plastic wrap, and defrost at room temperature. When the starter has thawed, add 1 cup of organic flour and allow the starter to bubble before refrigerating. Continue to maintain the starter as above.

DEHYDRATING THE STARTER: Remove 1 cup of starter from the refrigerator and place in a bowl with ½ cup of distilled water and 1 cup of organic flour. Cover with plastic wrap and allow to remain at room temperature until bubbly. Cut four pieces of parchment paper, each 12 × 18 inches. Spread half the starter on each of two of the papers. Cover with the remaining two pieces of paper and run a rolling pin over the top paper to spread the starter thinly between the two sheets. Pull the papers apart and leave them starter side up at room temperature until the starter is completely dry and flakes easily away from the paper. Crinkle the papers to loosen the dehydrated starter and place the flakes of starter on a large sheet pan lined with foil. Leave overnight in a cool, dry place, loosely covered, until all the starter is completely dry. Next day, pack ¼ cup of starter in individual plastic bags, seal the bags, and store in a cool, dry, dark place.

To use dehydrated starter, combine ¼ cup of dehydrated starter with ½ cup distilled water in a blender. Run the blender to dissolve the starter into the water. Pour into a bowl and add ¾ cup of organic flour. Cover tightly with plastic wrap and leave at room temperature until the starter bubbles. Refrigerate the starter and feed it after sev-

eral days to ensure that it is healthy. Continue to maintain the starter as in step 7.

After the starter is several weeks old, remove 1 cup and try feeding it with ½ cup of ordinary tap water and 1 cup of unbleached all-purpose flour. If the starter begins to bubble easily, it is strong enough to withstand the chemicals in both flour and water, and you can continue feeding it with ordinary flour and water if you wish.

SOURDOUGH BREAD

SPONGE

1 cup warm tap water (about 110 degrees)
1 cup sourdough starter (page 59)
2 cups unbleached all-purpose flour

DOUGH

All the sponge, above
1½ to 1¾ cups unbleached all-purpose flour
2 teaspoons salt

One cookie sheet or a baking stone

ONE LARGE 9- TO 10-INCH ROUND LOAF

Whether you have a real San Francisco sourdough or one that you have started yourself you may use it for this characteristically chewy, nutty-tasting, slightly sour bread.

Though a great deal of tradition surrounds the idea of using a real starter from San Francisco, in

reality, most starters, no matter what their origin, will produce good bread.

1. To make the sponge, in a large mixing bowl place the water and whisk in the starter. Stir in the flour, then slide the bowl into a large plastic bag and allow the sponge to rise at room temperature for at least 8 hours, or overnight.

2. For the dough, stir the sponge to deflate and stir in 1½ cups of flour and the salt. Knead by hand to form a smooth, elastic, and slightly sticky dough, about 5 minutes. Incorporate the remaining flour, a tablespoon at a time, if the dough is too soft.

To mix the dough in a food processor, place the sponge, 1½ cups of flour, and the salt in a work bowl fitted with a metal blade. Pulse repeatedly until the dough forms a ball (if the dough will not form a ball, add the remaining flour, a tablespoon at a time, and pulse until the dough forms a ball). Let the dough rest for 5 minutes, then let the machine run continuously for 20 seconds.

To mix the dough in a heavy-duty mixer, place the sponge, 1½ cups of flour, and the salt in the bowl of a mixer fitted with a dough hook. Mix on low speed to form a smooth, elastic, and slightly sticky dough, about 5 minutes. Incorporate the remaining flour, a tablespoon at a time, if the dough is too soft.

3. Place the dough in an oiled bowl (you may need a scraper to help you do this) and turn the dough over so the top is oiled. Cover the bowl with plastic wrap and allow the dough to rise at room temperature until doubled, about 1 hour.

4. Scrape the dough out onto a floured work surface and press to deflate. Form into an even sphere, by tucking the sides under at the bottom of the loaf all around, as in the illustration on page 50. Invert the loaf into a round basket lined with a heavily floured towel or napkin so the tucked-under part is on top. Cover the basket with plastic and allow the dough to rise until doubled, about 1 hour.

5. About 30 minutes before you intend to bake the loaves, set racks at the middle and lowest levels of the oven and preheat to 500 degrees. Place a baking stone or cookie sheet on the middle rack. Set a pan on the lowest rack to absorb some of the excess bottom heat. This will keep the loaf from burning on the bottom.

6. Invert the risen loaf onto a cardboard, a peel, or a cookie sheet covered with cornmeal. Hold a razor blade at a 90 degree angle to the top of the loaf, and use it to slash a diagonal lattice pattern on the loaf. Slide the loaf onto the stone or heated sheet pan and quickly close the oven. Lower the temperature to 450 degrees. If you wish, throw a cup of hot water onto the pan in the bottom of the oven to create steam, which will help the loaf to rise and to crisp its crust.

7. After the loaf has baked for 20 minutes and is completely risen, lower the temperature to 350 degrees and continue baking for 20 to 30 minutes longer, until the bread is well risen and a dark golden color. It should reach an internal temperature of about 210 degrees.

8. Remove the loaf from the oven and cool on a rack.

SERVING: Serve the bread on the day it is baked for best flavor and moisture.

STORAGE: On the day it is baked, keep the bread loosely covered at room temperature. For longer storage, wrap in plastic and freeze for up to 1 month.

VARIATION

PART WHOLE WHEAT SOURDOUGH BREAD: Substitute ½ cup whole wheat flour and 1½ cups unbleached all-purpose flour for the 2 cups flour in the sponge.

Though many bakers like to think that whole-grain breads are "healthier" or less caloric than breads made from white flour, I like the interesting flavors and textures these grains provide.

Such flours as whole wheat, semolina, and rye are best purchased at a health food store that has a good turnover in these items. Store unused flour in the freezer, and remember to measure flour and allow it to come to room temperature before baking with it.

SEMOLINA BREAD

SPONGE

1 cup warm tap water (about 110 degrees)
1 teaspoon active dry yeast
1½ cups unbleached all-purpose flour

DOUGH

All the sponge, above
½ cup unbleached all-purpose flour
¾ cup semolina flour
2 teaspoons salt
2 tablespoons olive oil

One heavy cookie sheet or jelly-roll pan dusted with cornmeal

ONE OVAL LOAF

The delicate, sweet taste of semolina permeates this loaf with a slight richness. Semolina, the flour made from durum wheat, is mainly used in the manufacture of dried pasta. It has limited use in baking, but adding it to a bread dough imparts a golden hue to the bread's crumb and an extra nutlike flavor to its crust.

1. To make the sponge, place the warm water in a mixing bowl and whisk in the yeast. Stir in the flour and cover the bowl with plastic wrap. Set the sponge aside to rise at room temperature until the sponge doubles, about 1 hour.

2. For the dough, stir the sponge to deflate and add the flour, semolina, salt, and oil. Turn the dough out onto a lightly floured work surface (you may need the help of a scraper). Knead by hand to form a smooth, elastic, and slightly sticky dough, about 5 minutes. Incorporate an extra tablespoon or two of flour if the dough is too soft.

To mix the dough in a food processor, place the sponge, flour, semolina, salt, and oil in the work bowl fitted with a metal blade. Pulse repeatedly until the dough forms a ball (if the dough will not form a ball, add more flour, a tablespoon at a time, and pulse until the dough forms a ball). Let the dough rest for 5 minutes, then let the machine run continuously for 20 seconds.

To mix the dough in a heavy-duty mixer, place the sponge, flour, semolina, salt, and oil in the bowl of a mixer fitted with a dough hook. Mix on low speed to form a smooth, elastic, and slightly sticky dough, about 5 minutes. If the dough is too soft, incorporate an extra tablespoon or two of flour.

3. Transfer the dough to an oiled bowl. Turn the dough so all the sides are oiled. Cover the bowl with plastic wrap and let the dough rise until doubled, about 1 hour.

4. Turn the risen dough out of the bowl to a floured work surface (you may need the help of a scraper). Press the dough with the palms of your hands to deflate. Shape the dough into an oval loaf, tucking the long sides under. Place tucked side down on the prepared pan and cover with oiled plastic wrap. Allow to rise until doubled in volume, about 1 hour.

5. When the loaf is almost doubled, preheat the oven to 400 degrees. Hold a razor blade at a 30-degree angle to the loaf, and use the blade to slash lines on each side of the loaf. Start at the middle of the top and slash down from top to bottom.

6. Bake the loaf for about 35 minutes, or until it is well risen and a dark golden color. It should reach an internal temperature of 210 degrees.

7. Cool on a rack and do not cut until completely cooled.

SERVING: Serve the bread on the day it is baked for best flavor and moisture.

STORAGE: On the day it is baked, keep the bread at room temperature, loosely covered with plastic. For longer storage, wrap in plastic and freeze for up to 1 month.

FRENCH MIXED-GRAIN BREAD

SPONGE

¼ **cup warm tap water (about 110 degrees)**

½ **teaspoon active dry yeast**

½ **cup unbleached all-purpose flour**

DOUGH

1½ **cups warm tap water (110 degrees)**

1 **teaspoon active dry yeast**

3½ **cups unbleached all-purpose flour, plus extra for dusting**

⅓ **cup medium or whole-grain rye flour**

⅓ **cup whole wheat flour**

2 **teaspoons salt**

All the sponge, above

Two small cookie sheets or a large jelly-roll pan dusted with cornmeal

THREE HEFTY BAGUETTES OR TWO LARGE ROUND OR RING-SHAPED LOAVES

This is an adaptation of a bread called *pain à l'ancienne* (old-fashioned bread) from the book *Pains Spéciaux et Décorés* (Special and Decorated Breads) (Éditions St.-Honoré) by Alain Couet and Erich Kayser.

1. To make the sponge, place the water in a mixing bowl and whisk in the yeast. Stir in the flour smoothly. Cover the bowl with plastic wrap and allow the sponge to rise at room temperature for about 8 hours, or overnight, until tripled in volume. If the temperature is warm, allow the sponge to rise until tripled, then refrigerate for the remainder of the 8 hours.

2. To mix the dough, combine the remaining ingredients in a mixing bowl and stir in the sponge. Knead by hand to form a smooth, elastic, and slightly sticky dough, about 5 minutes.

To mix the dough in a food processor, place the remaining ingredients and sponge in a work bowl fitted with a metal blade. Pulse repeatedly until the dough forms a ball. Let the dough rest for 5 minutes, then let the machine run continuously for 20 seconds.

To mix the dough in a heavy-duty mixer, place the remaining ingredients and sponge in the bowl of a mixer fitted with a dough hook. Mix on low speed to form a smooth, elastic, and slightly sticky dough, about 5 minutes.

3. Transfer the dough to an oiled bowl (you may need the help of a scraper) and turn the dough over so the top is oiled. Cover the bowl with plastic wrap and allow the dough to rise at room temperature until the dough is doubled, about 1 hour.

4. To shape the loaves, turn the risen dough out onto a lightly floured surface and press the dough to deflate. Divide it into 3 pieces and shape one at a time. Press a piece of dough into a square, then roll it up tightly. Rotate the cylinder of dough 90 degrees and roll up again from a short end. Arrange the dough, seam side down, and cover with plastic or a towel to rest for 5 minutes. Repeat with the remaining pieces of dough.

(continued)

5. Elongate each piece of dough by rolling the middle of the loaf outward under the palms of your hands. Point the ends slightly. Place the loaves on pans (two on one pan and one loaf on the other), seam side down, and dust each loaf lightly with flour. Use a tablespoon at the most per loaf. Cover with plastic or a towel and allow to rise until doubled.

6. About 30 minutes before you intend to bake the loaves, set racks at the middle and lowest levels of the oven and preheat to 500 degrees. Set a pan on the lowest rack to absorb some of the excess bottom heat and keep the bottoms of the loaves from burning.

7. Use a razor blade or the point of a very sharp knife to make 3 to 4 diagonal slashes across each loaf. Immediately place the loaves in the oven and lower the temperature to 450 degrees.

8. After the loaves have baked for 20 minutes and are completely risen, lower the temperature to 350 degrees and continue baking for 20 to 30 minutes longer, until the bread is well risen and a dark golden color. It should reach an internal temperature of about 210 degrees.

9. Remove the loaves from the oven and cool on a rack.

SERVING: Slice the bread about ½ inch thick with a sharp serrated knife.

STORAGE: On the day it is baked, keep the bread loosely covered at room temperature. For longer storage, wrap in plastic and freeze for up to 1 month.

WHOLE WHEAT WALNUT BREAD

SPONGE

1 cup warm tap water (about 110 degrees)
2½ teaspoons (1 envelope) active dry yeast
1½ cups unbleached all-purpose flour

DOUGH

2 tablespoons walnut oil (optional)
1 cup whole wheat flour
½ to ¾ cup unbleached all-purpose flour
2 teaspoons salt
All the sponge, above
2 cups walnut pieces, coarsely chopped

Cornmeal for bottom of loaf
One cookie sheet or a baking stone

ONE 9- TO 10-INCH ROUND LOAF

A whole wheat walnut bread is a perfect brunch and lunch bread. It is excellent with both mild and strong cheeses, and also makes a great base for simple sandwiches with cream cheese fillings to serve for tea.

The walnut oil in the dough emphasizes the delicate walnut flavor, but if you can't find the oil you will have a fine-tasting loaf without it.

1. To make the sponge, pour the water in a mixing bowl and sprinkle the yeast over the surface. Stir in the flour with a rubber spatula to form a heavy paste. Cover the bowl with plastic wrap and let the sponge rise at room temperature until the sponge has doubled, about 1 hour.

2. For the dough, stir the oil, whole wheat flour, ½ cup of all-purpose flour, and the salt into the sponge. Knead by hand to form a smooth, elastic, and slightly sticky dough, about 5 minutes. If the dough is too soft, incorporate the remaining flour, a tablespoon at a time.

To mix the dough in a food processor, place the sponge, oil, whole wheat flour, ½ cup of all-purpose flour, and the salt in a work bowl fitted with a metal blade. Pulse repeatedly until the dough forms a ball (if the dough will not form a ball, add the remaining flour, a tablespoon at a time, and pulse until the dough forms a ball). Let the dough rest for 5 minutes, then let the machine run continuously for 20 seconds.

To mix the dough in a heavy-duty mixer, place the sponge, oil, whole wheat flour, ½ cup of all-purpose flour, and the salt in the bowl of a mixer fitted with a dough hook. Mix on low speed to form a smooth, elastic, and slightly sticky dough, about 5 minutes. If the dough is too soft, incorporate the remaining flour, a tablespoon at a time.

3. Transfer the dough to an oiled bowl (you may need the help of a scraper) and turn the dough over so the top is oiled. Cover the bowl with plastic wrap and allow the dough to rise at room temperature until doubled, about 1 hour. If you wish to interrupt the process, let the dough begin to rise, then punch it down, cover tightly, and refrigerate. To proceed, bring the dough back to room temperature until it begins rising again.

4. Turn the risen dough out onto a floured work surface. Press the dough with the palms of your hands to deflate it. Knead in the chopped walnuts until they're evenly distributed throughout. Shape the dough into a sphere by tucking it under and in toward the center all around the bottom. Invert the dough into a round basket lined with a generously floured napkin or tea towel so the tucked dough is on top. Cover the basket with plastic wrap and allow the dough to rise until doubled, about 1 hour.

5. When the loaf is almost doubled, set a rack at the middle level of the oven and preheat to 500 degrees. Place a heavy cookie sheet, jelly-roll pan, or baking stone on the rack.

6. Sprinkle the top of the loaf with cornmeal and invert onto a cardboard round or peel. Use a razor blade held at a 90 degree angle to the loaf and slash a cross on the top. Slide the risen loaf from the cardboard or peel onto the baking pan or stone.

7. Bake the loaf for 35 to 45 minutes, or until it is well risen and a dark golden color. It should reach an internal temperature of about 210 degrees.

8. Cool the loaf on a rack and do not cut it until it is completely cooled.

SERVING: This bread is particularly good with mild or medium-strong cheeses.

STORAGE: On the day it is baked, keep the bread loosely covered at room temperature. For longer storage, wrap in plastic and freeze for up to 1 month.

HINT FOR SUCCESS: When you are kneading in the walnuts, the dough may become elastic. If so, let it rest for a few minutes before continuing. This may be repeated several times if necessary.

VARIATION

WHOLE WHEAT RAISIN WALNUT BREAD: Reduce the walnuts to 1¼ cups; knead in 1 cup dark raisins at the same time.

SWEDISH RYE BREAD

2¼ teaspoons (1 envelope) active dry yeast

¾ cup warm tap water (about 110 degrees)

2 cups unbleached all-purpose flour

1½ cups rye flour

2 teaspoons salt

½ cup beer

2 tablespoons unsulfured molasses

One heavy cookie sheet or jelly-roll pan dusted with cornmeal

ONE LARGE OVAL LOAF

A dark, rich-tasting rye bread with nuances of molasses and beer, this complements a simple meal of dried sausages and other charcuterie and strong cheeses. The recipe is adapted from one created by Jenny Akerstrom, who ran a cooking school in Stockholm during the 1920s and '30s that was attended by all the daughters of the Scandinavian royal houses, as chronicled in her *Prinsesornas Kokbok* (Princesses Cook Book).

1. Whisk the yeast into the warm water and set aside.

2. Combine the remaining ingredients in a mixing bowl, add the water and yeast mixture, and stir with a rubber spatula until the dough begins to hold together. Turn the dough out onto a floured surface and knead for about 5 minutes, until it is smooth and elastic.

To mix the dough in a heavy-duty mixer, combine the remaining ingredients with the water and yeast in a mixing bowl. Mix with a dough hook on low speed until the dough is smooth and elastic.

To mix the dough in a food processor, combine the remaining ingredients with the water and yeast in the work bowl of a food processor fitted with a metal blade. Pulse 8 or 10 times, until the dough forms a ball. Let rest for 5 minutes, then run the machine continuously for 30 seconds.

3. Turn the dough out onto a floured work surface. Gently knead, rounding the dough. Invert into an oiled stainless-steel or glass bowl and turn the dough to oil all the sides. Cover the bowl with plastic wrap and let the dough rise until doubled, about 1 to 1½ hours.

4. Turn the risen dough out onto a floured work surface again. Press the dough with the palms of your hands to deflate. Shape the dough into an oval loaf, tucking the long sides under. Place tucked side down on the prepared pan, cover with oiled plastic wrap, and allow the dough to rise again until doubled, about 1 hour.

5. When the loaf is almost doubled, set a rack at the middle level of the oven and preheat to 500 degrees.

6. Use a razor blade held at a 30 degree angle to the loaf to make 5 parallel slashes along the top of the loaf. Then make 5 more slashes perpendicular to the first ones.

7. Bake for about 30 minutes, or until it is well risen and a dark golden color. It should reach an internal temperature of 210 degrees.

(continued)

8. Cool the loaf on a rack and do not cut until it is completely cooled.

SERVING: Slice the bread about ½ inch thick with a sharp serrated knife.

STORAGE: On the day it is baked, keep the bread loosely covered at room temperature. For longer storage, wrap in plastic and freeze for up to 1 month.

SWISS RYE BREAD

SPONGE

¾ **cup warm water (110 degrees)**
1 **teaspoon active dry yeast**
1 **cup unbleached all-purpose flour**
½ **cup whole wheat flour**

DOUGH

2 **cups unbleached all-purpose flour**
1½ **cups whole-grain rye flour, plus extra for**
   outside of loaves
1¼ **cups warm water**
2 **teaspoons active dry yeast**
1 **tablespoon salt**
All the sponge, above

Two small cookie sheets or a large jelly-roll pan dusted with cornmeal

TWO 6-INCH ROUND LOAVES

This is one of my favorite rye breads. It has a rich, nutty flavor, emphasized by the little bit of whole wheat flour in the sponge.

Loosely adapted from *La Boulangerie Suisse*, a publication of the Richemont Baking School in Lucerne, this bread is typical of peasant breads made in the western, French-speaking part of Switzerland.

Please note that the sponge has a long rising time. Try to arrange to mix, form, and bake the bread soon after the sponge is ready so that the dough does not become overrisen and lose its good chewy texture and delicate flavor.

1. To make the sponge, place the water in a mixing bowl and whisk in the yeast. Stir in the flours until smooth. Cover the bowl with plastic wrap and allow the sponge to rise at room temperature for about 8 hours, or until the sponge has tripled in volume. If the temperature is warm, allow the sponge to rise until tripled, then refrigerate for the rest of the 8 hours.

2. To mix the dough, combine the remaining ingredients in a mixing bowl and add the sponge. Stir to mix all the ingredients. Knead by hand to form a smooth, elastic, and slightly sticky dough, about 5 minutes.

To mix the dough in a food processor, place the remaining ingredients and sponge in a work bowl fitted with a metal blade. Pulse repeatedly until the dough forms a ball. Let the dough rest for 5 minutes, then let the machine run continuously for 20 seconds.

To mix the dough in a heavy-duty mixer, place the remaining ingredients and the sponge in the bowl of a mixer fitted with a dough hook. Mix on low speed to form a smooth, elastic, and slightly sticky dough, about 5 minutes.

3. Transfer the dough to an oiled bowl (you may need the help of a scraper) and turn the dough over so the top is oiled. Cover the dough with plastic wrap and allow to rise at room temperature until doubled, about 1 hour.

4. To form the loaves, turn the dough out onto a lightly floured work surface. Press the dough with the palms of your hands to deflate it and divide the dough into two pieces. Round each piece of dough into a small, round loaf, tucking the edges in around the outside of the bottom as in the illustration on page 50. Place the loaves on the pans and brush each loaf with water. Immediately dust the wet surface generously with rye flour—during the rising and baking, this will become an attractive crackled pattern typical of this bread.

5. Cover the loaves with plastic wrap and allow them to rise until doubled, about 1 hour.

6. About 30 minutes before you intend to bake the loaves, set the racks at the middle and lowest levels of the oven and preheat to 500 degrees. Set a pan on the lowest rack to absorb some of the excess bottom heat and keep the bottoms of the loaves from burning.

7. Place the loaves in the oven and lower the temperature to 450 degrees. After the loaves have baked for 20 minutes and are completely risen, lower the temperature to 350 degrees and continue baking for 20 to 30 minutes longer, until the bread is well risen and a dark golden color. It should reach an internal temperature of about 210 degrees.

8. Remove the loaves from the oven and cool on a rack.

SERVING: Slice the bread about ½ inch thick with a sharp serrated knife.

STORAGE: On the day it is baked, keep the bread loosely covered at room temperature. For longer storage, wrap in plastic and freeze for up to 1 month.

VARIATION

SWISS RYE RING: Shape one or both of the loaves as for the Italian Bread Ring (page 55).

DARK CARAWAY RYE BREAD

SPONGE

1 cup warm tap water (about 110 degrees)
2½ teaspoons (1 envelope) active dry yeast
1½ cups unbleached all-purpose flour

DOUGH

½ to ¾ cup unbleached all-purpose flour
1 cup medium or whole-grain rye flour
2 teaspoons salt
1 tablespoon ground caraway seeds
1 tablespoon whole caraway seeds
1 tablespoon unsulfured molasses
1 tablespoon vegetable or olive oil
All the sponge, above

One cookie sheet or jelly-roll pan dusted with cornmeal

ONE LARGE OVAL LOAF

The secret of the rich rye flavor of this bread is the addition to the dough of ground, as well as whole, caraway seeds.

Ground caraway is sometimes available in health food stores. If you can't find it already ground, grind the seeds with a mortar and pestle, spice grinder, or clean coffee grinder.

1. To make the sponge, place the water in a mixing bowl and whisk in the yeast. Stir in the flour smoothly, then cover with plastic wrap and let the sponge rise until tripled in volume and very bubbly, about 3 hours.

2. To mix the dough by machine, place the ½ cup of flour, remaining ingredients, and the sponge in the bowl of a heavy-duty mixer. Mix with a dough hook on low speed for about 5 minutes, until the dough is smooth and somewhat elastic. If the dough is very soft, add the remaining flour, a tablespoon at a time, continuing to mix until the dough is smooth and elastic.

To mix the dough in a food processor, place the sponge, ½ cup of flour, and remaining ingredients in a work bowl fitted with a metal blade. Pulse repeatedly until the dough forms a ball (if the dough will not form a ball, add the remaining flour, a tablespoon at a time, and pulse until the dough forms a ball). Let the dough rest for 5 minutes, then let the machine run continuously for 20 seconds.

3. Transfer the dough to an oiled bowl (you may need the help of a scraper) and turn the dough over so the top is oiled. Cover the bowl with plastic wrap and allow the dough to rise at room temperature until the dough has doubled, about 1 hour. If you wish to interrupt the process, let the dough begin to rise, then punch down, cover tightly, and refrigerate. To proceed, bring the dough back to room temperature until the dough begins rising again.

4. After the dough has risen, punch it down, form it into a ball, and return it to the bowl; cover and let rise until doubled again, about 1 hour.

5. To form a loaf, turn the dough out onto a work surface and deflate the dough. Form the dough into an even ball by pushing and tucking toward the center all around the bottom. Cover with plastic wrap or a towel and allow to rest for 5 minutes. Flour your hands and roll the loaf, pressing on the center with your palms, and rolling it back and forth to elongate it slightly. Place the oval on the prepared pan and cover with oiled plastic wrap or a towel. Allow to rise until doubled, about 1 hour.

6. About 30 minutes before you intend to bake the loaf, set the racks at the middle and lowest levels of the oven and preheat to 500 degrees. Set a pan on the lowest rack to absorb some of the excess bottom heat and keep the bottom of the loaf from burning.

7. Place the loaf in the oven and lower the temperature to 450 degrees. After the loaf has baked for 20 minutes and is completely risen, lower the temperature to 350 degrees and continue baking for 20 to 30 minutes longer, until the bread is well risen and a dark golden color. It should reach an internal temperature of about 210 degrees.

8. Remove the loaf from the oven and cool on a rack.

SERVING: Slice the bread about ½ inch thick, or a little thinner for sandwiches, with a sharp serrated knife.

STORAGE: On the day it is baked, keep the bread loosely covered at room temperature. For longer storage, wrap in plastic and freeze for up to 1 month.

VARIATION

LIGHT RYE BREAD: For a milder flavor, omit the ground caraway and molasses.

PUMPERNICKEL BREAD

SPONGE

1 cup warm tap water (about 110 degrees)
2½ teaspoons (1 envelope) active dry yeast
1½ cups unbleached all-purpose flour

DOUGH

All the sponge, above
½ cup unbleached all-purpose flour, plus extra
   for dough if needed
½ cup whole wheat flour
½ cup whole-grain rye flour
1 tablespoon non-alkalized cocoa powder
2 teaspoons salt
1 tablespoon unsulfured molasses

Cornmeal for bottom of loaf
One cookie sheet or a baking stone

ONE 8- OR 9-INCH ROUND LOAF

This dark, flavorful loaf is perfect with strong cheeses or as a sandwich bread with an assertive-flavored filling such as corned beef or pastrami. I think it and the raisin-studded variation that follows make good breakfast breads. Though I like them for breakfast, I don't toast them, which distorts the breads' flavor and texture.

1. To make the sponge, place the water in a mixing bowl and sprinkle the yeast on the surface. Add the flour and stir with a rubber spatula to a heavy paste. Cover the bowl and let the sponge rise at room temperature until the sponge has doubled, about 1 hour.

2. Deflate the sponge by stirring with a wooden spoon and stir in the remaining ingredients. Knead by hand to form a smooth, elastic, and slightly sticky dough, about 5 minutes. If the dough is excessively sticky, add more flour, a tablespoon at a time.

To mix the dough in a food processor, place the sponge and remaining ingredients in a work bowl fitted with a metal blade. Pulse repeatedly until the dough forms a ball. If the dough refuses to form a ball, add more white flour, a tablespoon at a time, until the dough forms a ball. Let the dough rest for 5 minutes, then let the machine run continuously for 20 seconds.

To mix the dough in a heavy-duty mixer, place the sponge and remaining ingredients in the bowl of a mixer fitted with a dough hook. Mix on low speed to form a smooth, elastic, and slightly sticky dough, about 5 minutes. If the dough is too soft, incorporate more flour, a tablespoon at a time.

3. Transfer the dough to an oiled bowl and turn the dough over so the top is oiled. Cover the bowl with plastic wrap and allow the dough to rise at room temperature until the dough has doubled, about 1 hour. If you wish to interrupt the process, let the dough begin to rise, then punch down, cover tightly, and refrigerate. To proceed, bring the dough back to room temperature until the dough begins rising again.

4. To shape the loaf, turn the risen dough out onto a floured work surface (you may need the help of a scraper). Press the dough with the palms of your hands to deflate. Gently knead, then shape the dough into a sphere by tucking the edges under and in toward the center all around the bottom. Invert the dough into a round basket lined with a heavily floured napkin or tea towel so the tucked ends are on top. Cover with plastic wrap and allow the dough to rise until doubled, about 1 hour.

5. When the loaf is almost doubled, set a rack at the middle level of the oven and preheat to 500 degrees. Place a heavy cookie sheet, jelly-roll pan, or baking stone on the rack.

6. Sprinkle cornmeal on top of the loaf and invert it onto a cardboard round or peel. Use a razor blade held at a 30 degree angle to the loaf to slash a cross in the top of the loaf. Slide the risen loaf from the cardboard or peel onto the pan. Immediately lower the oven temperature to 450 degrees.

7. Bake the loaf for about 40 minutes, or until it is well risen and a dark golden color. It should reach an internal temperature of 210 degrees.

8. Cool the loaf on a rack and do not cut until it is completely cooled.

SERVING: Slice the bread about ½ inch thick with a sharp serrated knife.

STORAGE: On the day it is baked, keep the bread loosely covered at room temperature. For longer storage, wrap in plastic and freeze for up to 1 month.

VARIATION

RAISIN PUMPERNICKEL BREAD: Knead in 1 cup dark raisins by hand after the dough has risen the first time, before shaping the loaf.

SPECIALTY BREADS

These few special breads really don't fit into another category. Challah, the braided Jewish bread, is somewhat like a brioche dough, but it is made with oil instead of butter so that it will be *parve* or neutral, and allowable with both milk and meat meals for those who observe kosher laws.

The round challah is traditional for Rosh Hashanah, the Jewish new year, and is sweeter than an everyday challah because all foods for Rosh Hashanah are sweetened to promote the spirit of a sweet new year.

The Parmesan cheese bread and Viennese milk bread that follow are excellent brunch breads—each freezes well and goes with a variety of breakfast and brunch foods.

CHALLAH

5 cups unbleached all-purpose flour
⅓ cup sugar
2 teaspoons salt
1 cup warm tap water (about 110 degrees)
2½ teaspoons (1 envelope) active dry yeast
¼ cup vegetable oil
2 large eggs, plus 1 egg yolk
Egg wash: 1 egg well beaten with a pinch of salt

One heavy cookie sheet or jelly-roll pan lined with parchment

ONE 12- TO 15-INCH BRAID

The braided shape of this loaf, used as the Jewish Sabbath and holiday bread, symbolizes the inseparable union of God and man. It is tradi-

tionally baked by the mother of the family and served at the Friday evening or holiday meal.

1. Place the flour, sugar, and salt in the work bowl of a food processor fitted with a metal blade. Pulse until mixed.

2. Place the water in a mixing bowl and whisk in the yeast. Whisk in the oil, eggs, and yolk.

3. Add the liquid to the work bowl and pulse 8 or 10 times until the dough forms a ball. Let rest for 5 minutes, then run the machine continuously for 30 seconds.

4. Turn the dough out onto a floured work surface (you may need the help of a scraper). Knead the dough lightly to form a ball. Invert into an oiled bowl and turn the dough to coat all sides with oil. Cover the bowl with plastic wrap and allow the dough to rise at room temperature until the dough has doubled, about 1 hour.

5. Turn the risen dough out onto a floured work surface and press the dough with the palms of your hands to deflate. Divide the dough into three equal pieces. Roll each piece into a cylinder, 12 to 15 inches long. Arrange the strands side by side on the prepared pan. Begin to braid in the middle of the strands and braid to one end. Turn the pan around and braid from the middle to the other end, as in the illustration. (Braiding from the middle outward helps keep the loaf a consistent width.) Pinch each end to seal the strands together and turn the pinched parts under the loaf. Cover with oiled plastic wrap and allow to rise at room temperature until the dough has doubled, about 1 hour.

Begin to braid in the middle, braiding to one end. Turn the pan around and braid from the middle to the other end. (Braiding from the middle to the ends helps keep the loaf a consistent width.)

6. When the loaf is almost doubled, set a rack at the middle level of the oven and preheat to 400 degrees.

7. Brush the top and sides of the risen loaf with the egg wash. Bake for 20 to 25 minutes, or until the top is golden brown and the internal temperature of the loaf reaches about 210 degrees.

8. Transfer to a rack to cool.

SERVING: Serve challah sliced. Toasted, it has a wonderful nutty flavor. It also makes excellent French toast.

STORAGE: On the day it is baked, keep the bread loosely covered at room temperature. For longer storage, wrap in plastic and freeze for up to 1 month.

HINT FOR SUCCESS: For a darker, shinier finish, remove the braid from the oven after it has risen and is firm (make sure that the loaf is firm or it may deflate) and beginning to color; gently repeat the egg wash and return the loaf to the oven immediately.

YOCHEVED HIRSCH'S ROUND CHALLAH

SPONGE

⅓ **cup warm tap water (about 110 degrees)**

2½ **teaspoons (1 envelope) active dry yeast**

½ **cup unbleached all-purpose flour**

DOUGH

5 cups unbleached all-purpose flour

¼ **cup sugar**

2 teaspoons salt

All the sponge, above

1 cup warm tap water (about 110 degrees)

½ **cup oil**

2 large eggs, plus 2 egg yolks

2 cups raisins

**Egg wash: 1 egg well beaten with a pinch
   of salt**

*Two heavy cookie sheets or jelly-roll pans, lined with
parchment*

TWO 9- TO 10-INCH ROUND LOAVES

This round challah, which is traditionally made for Rosh Hashanah, the Jewish new year celebration, symbolizes the spiral of the passing seasons and years. The new year's challah is sweeter than braided challah, because sweet foods are traditional for Rosh Hashanah to encourage the new year to be sweet.

This recipe comes from my friend Yocheved Hirsch, a well-known teacher of kosher cooking, who recently left the New York area to reside in Israel.

1. To make the sponge, place the warm water in a stainless-steel or glass bowl and whisk in the yeast. Stir in the flour and cover with plastic wrap. Set aside to rise at room temperature until bubbly, about 10 minutes.

2. To make the dough, combine the flour, sugar, and salt in the work bowl of a food processor fitted with a metal blade. Pulse until mixed. Add the sponge, warm water, oil, eggs, and yolks to the work bowl and pulse 8 or 10 times, until the dough forms a ball. Let rest for 3 minutes, then run the machine continuously for 30 seconds.

To mix the dough by hand, stir the water, oil, eggs, and yolks into the sponge. Stir in the sugar, salt, and flour, continuing to stir with a rubber spatula or wooden spoon to form a soft dough. Knead on a floured surface until smooth, about 5 minutes.

To mix the dough by machine, scrape the sponge into the bowl of a mixer. Stir in the water, oil, eggs, and yolks; then the sugar, salt, and flour. Beat with a paddle on low speed about 2 to 3 minutes until smooth and elastic.

3. Turn the dough out onto a floured work surface. Knead lightly several times to be sure the dough is evenly mixed, then form the dough into a ball. Invert into a lightly oiled mixing bowl and turn so that the dough is coated with oil. Cover the bowl with plastic wrap and allow the dough to rise at room temperature until the dough has doubled, about 1 hour.

4. Turn the risen dough out onto a floured work surface. Press the dough with the palms of your hands to deflate it. Knead in the raisins, making sure they are well distributed. If kneading becomes difficult, cover the dough with a clean towel and let the dough rest for a few minutes before continuing. This may be repeated several times if necessary.

5. Divide the dough into two equal pieces, cover each with a towel, and let them rest for 5 minutes.

6. Working with one piece at a time, roll the dough under your palms into a 28-inch rope. Place on a prepared pan and, starting at the inside, coil the rope into a spiral. Seal the end by turning under. Repeat with the second dough piece. Cover with oiled plastic wrap and allow to rise at room temperature until the dough has doubled, about 1 hour.

7. When the loaves are almost doubled, preheat the oven to 375 degrees. Brush the top and sides of the risen loaves with the egg wash.

8. Bake for 30 to 40 minutes, or until they are golden brown and their internal temperature reaches about 210 degrees.

9. Cool on the pans for 5 minutes, then remove to racks to cool.

SERVING: Slice the challah about ½ inch thick with a sharp serrated knife. Raisin challah makes excellent French toast.

STORAGE: On the day it is baked, keep the bread loosely covered at room temperature. For longer storage, wrap in plastic and freeze for up to 1 month.

PARMESAN CHEESE BREAD

½ cup milk

2½ teaspoons (1 envelope) active dry yeast

2¼ cups unbleached all-purpose flour, divided

6 tablespoons unsalted butter

½ cup grated Parmigiano-Reggiano

2 tablespoons sugar

1 teaspoon salt

2 large eggs

One 2-quart charlotte or brioche mold, or a 9-inch springform or cake pan (2 inches deep), buttered

ONE 8- TO 9-INCH LOAF, ABOUT 8 GENEROUS SERVINGS

This bread, really a rich, yeast-risen cake, is very much like an Umbrian specialty called *cresca* or *crescia al formaggio,* a well-known specialty of a beautiful pastry shop in Perugia called Sandri. In Umbria, it is possible to find the glazed earthenware molds, similar in shape to flowerpots. My substitute is a 2-quart charlotte or fluted brioche mold. A 9-inch diameter by 2-inch-deep cake pan or a 9-inch springform pan also makes a good substitute.

1. In a small saucepan over low heat, warm the milk until it just feels warm, about 110 degrees. Remove from the heat and pour into a small bowl. Whisk in the yeast, then stir 1 cup of the flour into the yeast and milk mixture. Cover the bowl with plastic wrap and set aside at room temperature while preparing the other ingredients. The yeast mixture will rise slightly before you add it to the other ingredients.

2. Cut the butter into 6 or 8 pieces and combine it with the cheese, sugar, and salt in the work bowl of a food processor fitted with a metal blade. Pulse at 1-second intervals until the mixture is soft and smooth, scraping the inside of the bowl several times to ensure even mixing. Add the eggs, one at a time, and process until smooth. If the mixture appears curdled, continue to process for about 1 minute longer, until it smooths out. Do not be concerned if it remains somewhat curdled in appearance. Add the remaining 1¼ cups of flour, then use a rubber spatula to scrape in the milk, yeast, and flour mixture from the bowl. Pulse at 1-second intervals until the ingredients form a soft, smooth dough. Then process continuously for 15 seconds.

To mix the dough with a heavy-duty mixer, combine the butter, cheese, sugar, and salt in the mixer bowl. Beat with a paddle on medium speed until the mixture is soft and smooth, scraping the bowl and beater several times to ensure even mixing. Add the eggs, one at a time, and continue beating until smooth between each addition. If the mixture appears curdled, continue to beat on medium speed for about 1 minute longer, until it looks smoother. It may still look somewhat curdled. That's okay. Add the remaining 1¼ cups of flour, then, with a rubber spatula, scrape in the milk, yeast, and flour mixture from the bowl. Continue beating on medium speed until the ingredients form a soft, smooth dough.

3. Turn dough out onto a generously floured work surface and fold the dough over on itself several times to make it more elastic. Press it into a rough square, then fold in the corners of the square to make a roughly round piece of dough. Invert the dough into the prepared mold or pan so the turned-under parts are on the bottom.

4. Cover the pan with a piece of buttered plastic wrap or a towel and allow to rise at room temperature until the dough has doubled in bulk, about 1 hour.

5. While the loaf is rising, set a rack at the lower third of the oven and preheat to 350 degrees. When the loaf is sufficiently risen, place the pan on a jelly-roll pan or heavy cookie sheet to insulate the bottom.

6. Bake the loaf for about 40 minutes, until it is well risen and a deep golden color. It should reach an internal temperature of about 210 degrees.

7. Unmold and cool on a rack.

SERVING: Serve the cheese bread in thin slices for brunch or lunch or with drinks.

STORAGE: On the day it is baked, keep the bread loosely covered at room temperature. For longer storage, wrap in plastic and freeze for up to 1 month.

HINT FOR SUCCESS: If the top of the loaf begins to color too deeply too early during baking, cover it loosely with aluminum foil to keep it from burning.

VIENNESE MILK BREAD
(WIENER MILCHBROT)

1 cup milk

2 teaspoons active dry yeast

4 cups unbleached all-purpose flour

1 teaspoon salt

¼ cup sugar

6 tablespoons unsalted butter, melted

1 cup dark raisins, brought to a boil in water,
   drained, and cooled

Egg wash: 1 egg well beaten with a pinch of salt

Two cookie sheets or jelly-roll pans lined with parchment paper

TWO LARGE LOAVES, ABOUT 12 INCHES LONG

In the United States and the British Isles the name "Vienna Bread" usually indicates a commercially or industrially made milk-based bread. The following recipe is an authentic Viennese one, adapted from Eduard Mayer's *Wiener Süssspeisen* (Viennese Sweets) (Trauner Verlag, 1982). The close-textured loaf studded with raisins makes an excellent breakfast or brunch bread.

1. Heat the milk until it just feels lukewarm (110 degrees). Whisk in the yeast and allow to stand while assembling the remaining ingredients.

2. Combine the flour, salt, and sugar in the work bowl of a food processor fitted with the metal blade. Pulse to mix. Whisk the melted butter into the yeast mixture and add to the work bowl. Pulse at 1-second intervals until the dough forms a ball. If the dough remains extremely slack and refuses to form a ball, add up to 2 tablespoons more flour, one tablespoon at a time. After the dough forms a ball, process the dough continuously for 15 seconds. Remove to a lightly floured work surface and knead in the raisins.

To mix the dough in a heavy-duty mixer, combine the flour, salt, and sugar in the mixer bowl. Whisk the melted butter into the yeast mixture and add to the work bowl. Mix on low speed with a dough hook until the dough forms a ball. If the dough remains extremely slack and refuses to form a ball, add up to 2 tablespoons more flour, one tablespoon at a time. After the dough forms a ball, add the raisins and mix them in.

3. Place the dough in a buttered bowl, turn it over so that the top is buttered, and cover the bowl with plastic wrap. Allow the dough to rise at room temperature until doubled, about 1 hour.

4. Deflate the dough, return it to the bowl, cover again, and allow it to rise a second time until doubled, about 1 hour.

5. Deflate the dough and divide it into two pieces. Round each piece, cover with a towel, and allow to rest for 5 minutes. Run a rolling pin over the center of each piece to elongate it into an oval. Then roll over the ends to point them

slightly. Arrange each loaf on a prepared pan. Cover and allow the loaves to rise at room temperature until they're doubled, about 1 hour.

6. While the loaves are rising, set a rack at the middle level of the oven and preheat to 350 degrees.

7. Paint the loaves with the egg wash. Slash the length of each loaf to within an inch of the ends using a razor or the point of a sharp knife.

8. Bake the loaves for about 40 minutes, until well colored and baked through. They should have an internal temperature of 210 degrees.

9. Cool on racks.

SERVING: Serve the *Milchbrot* for breakfast or brunch. It is rich and does not need to be buttered.

STORAGE: On the day it is baked, keep the bread loosely covered at room temperature. For longer storage, wrap in plastic and freeze for up to 1 month.

ROLLS AND OTHER INDIVIDUAL BREADS

More elegant than a slice cut from a loaf, individual rolls have long been a sign of refined dining. I remember as a child buying small, slightly sweet, knotted rolls from a neighborhood bakery—the crumb was bright yellow and we called them "egg rolls" though I doubt they had a name beyond "rolls" at the bakery where they were made. This type of soft roll is particularly good for breakfast or with a light meal—it is a little too rich to accompany a substantial meal, I think. All sorts of other individual breads are covered here, from elaborate, small rolls, through English muffins and bagels. Rolls and individual breads are a practical choice if you don't have a lot of time for bread baking—they are relatively quick to prepare and may be frozen soon after baking.

SOFT ROLLS

4½ cups unbleached all-purpose flour
1 tablespoon sugar
1 tablespoon salt
1 cup warm tap water (about 110 degrees)
2 teaspoons active dry yeast
2 large eggs
4 tablespoons butter, melted, or mild olive oil
Egg wash: 1 egg well beaten with a pinch of salt

Two cookie sheets or jelly-roll pans covered with parchment paper

ABOUT 16 FINISHED ROLLS

Often called "dinner rolls" and even "egg rolls," these tender, slightly sweet rolls are a perfect accompaniment to a light meal.

Though individual rolls such as these were a common feature of home baking in the past, they are not much used anymore, which is a pity. They only require a few minutes' more work than making a whole loaf of bread, and they always appear festive and appetizing.

Though it is fun to make them in many different shapes, they may be left rounded and merely sprinkled with a little flour.

1. To mix the dough in a food processor, combine the dry ingredients in a work bowl with a metal blade and pulse several times to mix. Place the water in a bowl and whisk in the yeast, eggs, and butter or oil. Add to the work bowl, then pulse 6 or 8 times to form a ball of dough. Let the machine run continuously for 30 seconds.

To mix in a heavy-duty mixer, combine the dry ingredients in the bowl of a mixer fitted with a dough hook. Allow the mixer to run on the lowest speed for 1 minute. Add the water, yeast, eggs, and butter and continue mixing for 1 minute. Stop and scrape the bowl to incorporate all the ingredients, then continue mixing for about 5 minutes on low speed, until the dough is smooth and elastic.

To mix the dough by hand, combine the dry ingredients in a large mixing bowl. Stir in the water, yeast, eggs, and butter with a rubber spatula, continuing to stir until the dry ingredients are evenly moistened and the dough is ropy and uneven in appearance. Cover the bowl tightly with plastic wrap and allow the dough to rest for 5 minutes. After the rest, beat the dough vigorously with a rubber spatula or heavy wooden spoon, until the mixture is smooth and elastic.

2. Butter or oil a mixing bowl and transfer the dough to the bowl (you may need the help of a scraper). Turn the dough to coat on all sides with butter or oil. Cover the bowl and let the dough rise at room temperature until the dough has doubled in bulk, about 1 hour.

3. Turn the risen dough out onto a lightly floured work surface. Press the dough with the palms of your hands to deflate it. Divide the dough in half. Roll each half into a thick cylinder; slice each cylinder into 8 pieces.

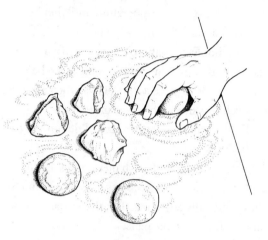

Round each piece of dough by gently pressing and rotating your hand over the dough to form a sphere. This will stretch a smooth, even skin around the outside of the sphere.

4. Shape the rolls as in the illustration. Round each of the 16 pieces of dough by gently pressing and rotating your hand over the piece of dough to form it into a sphere and to stretch a smooth, even skin around the outside of the sphere. The smooth skin will become the crust of the roll, and any blemishes or uneven areas will mar the crust's appearance. Cover the rolls with a towel and allow them to rest. The rest lets the elastic gluten strands in the dough relax so the dough will be easy to handle and won't spring back when shaped. Keeping the dough covered prevents a thick, uneven crust from forming.

5. For the simplest rolls, arrange the rounded pieces of dough on the prepared pans, cover with a towel or a piece of oiled plastic wrap, and allow them to rise at room temperature until they're doubled, about 1 hour.

The simplest variation in shape is to roll over each rounded piece under the palm of the hand once or twice to make it a small oval, then arrange the ovals top side up on the pans to rise.

To form sticks, roll the rounded dough out to a 6-inch stick.

To make twists, roll each piece into a 12-inch stick, fold in half so it becomes a doubled 6-inch stick, pinch the edges together, then twist several times. Arrange on the pans.

To make Parker House rolls, wrap a small heavy pan in a non-terry-cloth towel and flour the towel covering the bottom of the pan. Place a rounded piece of dough on a floured surface and flour the top of the dough. Slam the pan bottom hard against the dough several times to flatten, making a disk about 3 inches in diameter and ½ inch thick. Press the handle of a wooden spoon across the diameter of the disk, then brush the surface of the dough with melted butter. Fold the dough over at the diameter line and arrange them on the pans to rise.

To form knots and braids, roll each rounded piece of dough into a cylinder and cover the cylinders of dough with a towel. Shape the rolls one at a time. Single knots, double knots, and rosettes are formed in this way, as in the illustrations.

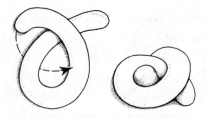

SINGLE KNOT: Tie the length of dough into a loose knot, leaving one end under the roll.

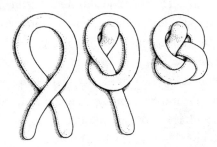

DOUBLE KNOT: Tie the length of dough into a loose knot, pulling one end through twice. Leave the other end under the roll.

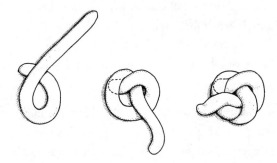

ROSETTE: Tie the length of dough into a loose knot, pulling one end through three times. Finish with both ends under the roll.

To make butterflies, roll a half batch of dough into a 10-inch square. Paint the dough with 2 teaspoons of melted butter or mild olive oil, then roll the dough up, jelly-roll style. Position the seam on the bottom, then slice the roll into 8 pieces. Leave each slice standing as it was cut and press the handle of a wooden spoon hard into the center of the roll, parallel to the cut edges. Arrange on the pans.

To make crescents, roll a half batch of dough into a 12-inch disk. Cut the disk into 8 wedges and paint with melted butter or mild olive oil. Roll up from the wide base of the wedge to make crescents. Arrange on the pans to rise.

6. When the rolls are almost doubled, set racks at the upper and lower thirds of the oven and preheat to 400 degrees. Carefully brush the rolls with the egg wash.

7. Bake for about 20 minutes, until the rolls are well colored and firm, or until they have reached an internal temperature of about 210 degrees.

8. Cool rolls on racks.

SERVING: Serve the rolls for breakfast or with another meal. To warm the rolls before serving, place them on a cookie sheet in a 350 degree oven for about 5 minutes, until just heated through.

STORAGE: Rolls will keep well for 24 hours, loosely covered at room temperature. For longer storage, place in a plastic bag and freeze. Defrost the rolls for a few minutes at room temperature, then place on a cookie sheet and reheat at 350 degrees for about 5 minutes.

HINT FOR SUCCESS: For rounding, a light dusting of flour on the palm of the hand is all that is necessary. If you are having trouble rounding the pieces of dough, make sure the work surface is not covered with flour.

VARIATION

HONEY WHOLE WHEAT WALNUT ROLLS: Substitute 1 cup whole wheat flour for 1 cup of the white flour, above. Substitute honey for the sugar, adding the honey with the eggs, not directly to the flour. Add 1 cup finely chopped walnuts to the dough if you are making plain round rolls. If you are making fancy shapes, omit the walnuts, because the walnut pieces will mar the surface of the rolls.

HARD ROLLS

SPONGE

1 cup warm tap water (about 110 degrees)
½ teaspoon active dry yeast
1½ cups unbleached all-purpose flour

DOUGH

All the sponge, above
1¼ to 1½ cups unbleached all-purpose flour
1½ teaspoons salt
1 teaspoon sugar
1 egg white, lightly beaten

One heavy cookie sheet or jelly-roll pan dusted with cornmeal

SIXTEEN 1½-OUNCE ROLLS

Crisp hard rolls mixed in with an assortment of Soft Rolls (page 84) have always been a popular bread-basket offering. To get a sufficiently crisp crust in a home oven, closely follow the instructions for steaming as the rolls are baking. Make certain the rolls are quite done before you remove them from the oven by checking that the internal temperature has reached at least 210 degrees—if the rolls are not completely baked through, the excess moisture trapped in them will soften the crusts as they are cooling.

1. To make the sponge, place the water in a mixing bowl and sprinkle the yeast on the surface. Add the flour and stir with a rubber spatula to produce a heavy paste. Cover the bowl and let the sponge rise at room temperature until the sponge has doubled, about 1 hour, then refrigerate overnight or for at least 8 hours.

2. Remove the sponge from the refrigerator and stir in 1¼ cups of flour, salt, sugar, and egg white. Knead by hand to form a smooth, elastic, and slightly sticky dough, about 5 minutes, incorporating more flour, a tablespoon at a time, if the dough is too soft.

To mix the dough in a food processor, place the sponge, 1¼ cups of flour, salt, sugar, and egg white in a work bowl fitted with a metal blade. Pulse until the dough forms a ball (if the dough will not form a ball, add the remaining flour, a tablespoon at a time, and pulse). Let the dough rest for 5 minutes, then let the machine run continuously for 20 seconds.

To mix the dough in a heavy-duty mixer, place the sponge, 1¼ cups of flour, and the salt in the bowl of a mixer fitted with a dough hook. Mix on low speed to form a smooth, elastic, and slightly sticky dough, about 5 minutes. If the dough is too soft, incorporate the remaining flour, a tablespoon at a time.

3. Transfer the dough to an oiled bowl and turn the dough over so the top is oiled. Cover the bowl with plastic wrap and allow the dough to rise at room temperature until the dough has doubled, about 1 hour. If you wish to interrupt the process, let the dough begin to rise, then punch it down, re-cover the bowl tightly, and refrigerate. To proceed, bring the dough back to room temperature until the dough begins rising again.

4. To form rolls, turn the dough out onto a lightly floured work surface (you may need the help of a scraper). Press the dough with the palms of your hands to deflate it. Divide the dough into 16 pieces (about 1½ ounces each). Cover loosely with plastic wrap and form one piece at a time. Round each piece by pressing it under the palm of your hand as you rotate your hand around the dough, as in the illustration on page 85. Cover the rounded pieces of dough with a towel and allow to rest for 5 minutes.

5. Working with one piece of dough at a time, stretch the dough into a rough rectangle. Fold in the short ends to meet at the center, then roll up the long edge to form a tight cylinder. Place on the prepared pan, leaving enough room between rolls to allow for rising. Cover with oiled plastic wrap and allow the rolls to rise at room temperature until they've doubled, about 1 hour.

6. When the rolls are almost doubled, set racks at the middle and lowest levels of the oven and preheat to 500 degrees. On the lowest rack, set a pan to hold water to make steam.

7. When the rolls are completely risen, use a razor blade held at a 30 degree angle to make a deep slash along the length of each roll.

8. Open the oven, avert your face, and quickly pour a cup of hot water onto the hot pan. Close the oven for a minute, then, averting your face again, place the pan of rolls in the oven. Lower the oven temperature to 450 degrees. In 10 minutes, add ½ cup water to the water pan.

9. After 20 minutes, remove the water pan and lower the temperature to 350 degrees. Continue baking for 10 to 15 minutes longer, until the rolls are well colored and firm, and have reached an internal temperature of about 210 degrees.

10. Remove from the oven and cool on a rack.

SERVING: Serve the rolls with a meal. To reheat them before serving, place rolls on a cookie sheet in a 350 degree oven for about 5 minutes, or until heated through.

STORAGE: On the day they are baked, keep the rolls loosely covered. For longer storage, wrap in plastic and freeze for up to a month.

VARIATIONS

POPPY-SEED ROLLS: After rounding the rolls, prepare a bowl of egg wash (1 egg beaten with a pinch of salt) and a bowl of poppy seeds. Dip the rounded rolls into the egg wash, being careful to note where the top is, then place them, top down, in the bowl of poppy seeds and coat completely. Place the rolls right side up on the pan, cover loosely with plastic wrap, and after the rolls are about half risen, snip a deep X in the top of each roll with a pair of scissors. Bake as above.

CHAMPIGNONS: These mushroom-shaped rolls are popular in France. After rounding 12 rolls, wrap the remaining dough in plastic wrap and refrigerate it. Arrange the rolls on the pan, cover, and let rise. When the rolls are almost completely risen, remove the reserved dough from the refrigerator and roll it on a floured surface to about ¼-inch thickness, then cut it into twelve 3-inch circles. Carefully brush the top of each roll with water and gently glue on a circle of dough. Allow the rolls to finish rising and bake as above. For this variation use steam.

ENGLISH MUFFINS

2 teaspoons active dry yeast

1 cup warm tap water (about 110 degrees)

2¾ cups unbleached all-purpose flour, plus
2 tablespoons if necessary

2 teaspoons salt

4 tablespoons butter, melted

1 tablespoon honey

Cornmeal for pan and muffins

Two heavy cookie sheets or jelly-roll pans dusted with cornmeal

ABOUT 10 MUFFINS

English muffins have a coarse, open crumb. They are unusual in that they are baked on a griddle rather than in the oven and are always split and toasted before they are served.

Better than the industrially made variety, these muffins are delicate and tender.

1. Whisk the yeast into the warm water and set aside while preparing the other ingredients.

2. Place the flour and the salt in the work bowl of a food processor fitted with a metal blade, and pulse several times at 1-second intervals to mix. Add the butter, honey, and the yeast mixture and continue to pulse until the dough forms a ball. If the dough remains extremely soft, add up to 2 tablespoons more flour, one at a time, pulsing again after each addition. After the dough forms a ball, pulse 5 times at 1-second intervals.

To mix the dough in a heavy-duty mixer, place the flour and salt in a mixer bowl, then add the butter, honey, and the yeast mixture, and mix on low speed with a dough hook until the dough is smooth and elastic, about 5 minutes. If the dough remains extremely soft, add up to 2 tablespoons more flour, one at a time, then continue to mix for 3 to 4 minutes longer.

To mix the dough by hand, place the flour and salt in a mixing bowl and stir to combine. Add the butter, honey, and the yeast mixture, and continue stirring to form a rough dough. Turn the dough out on a lightly floured work surface and knead the dough until smooth and elastic, about 5 minutes. If the dough remains extremely soft, add up to 2 tablespoons more flour, one at a time, and continue to knead until the dough no longer sticks.

3. Use a scraper to transfer the dough from the bowl to a floured cookie sheet or jelly-roll pan. Flour the top of the dough and use your hands to press the dough out approximately ½ inch thick. Cover loosely with plastic wrap and refrigerate the dough for 15 minutes.

4. Remove the dough from the refrigerator and slide it onto a floured work surface. Flour the dough and, with a rolling pin, gently roll it to ¼-inch thickness. With a floured 4-inch cutter, cut the dough into circles. Arrange the muffins well apart on the prepared pan. Dust the tops of the muffins with more cornmeal. Cover the muffins with a cloth and allow to rise at room temperature for up to 1 hour, or until almost doubled in bulk.

5. After cutting the first muffins, knead the scraps together and press the dough out ½ inch thick on a floured pan. Cover and refrigerate for 15 minutes. Roll and cut as before, but keep this second batch on a separate cornmeal-dusted pan. Cover and let rise, as in step 4. Cook the second muffins after the first batch. Reknead the remaining scraps and cut into 3- to 4-inch squares to use later to test the temperature of the griddle before beginning to cook the muffins. Cover the squares, too, and let rise as above.

6. Heat a well-seasoned aluminum or cast-iron griddle or shallow cast-iron pan over low heat. Test the temperature of the griddle with the scraps about 15 minutes before the first batch of muffins is completely risen. If the scraps are the same thickness as the muffins, they should bake through after about 8 minutes per side.

7. When the griddle heat is right, place 4 muffins at a time on it, depending on its size. The muffins should begin to rise immediately. Bake for about 8 minutes, then turn the muffins with a wide spatula after the first side is done. After baking the first batch, allow the griddle to recover heat for 5 minutes before baking more muffins.

8. Cool the muffins on a rack.

SERVING: Split and toast the muffins before serving them with butter and jam or preserves. For the best texture, use a fork to split the muffins horizontally, rather than cutting through them with a knife.

STORAGE: Keep the muffins uncovered or in a paper bag at room temperature. For longer storage, freeze the muffins in a plastic bag. Thaw them before attempting to split and toast them.

VARIATION

PART WHOLE WHEAT ENGLISH MUFFINS: Substitute ¾ cup whole wheat flour for ¾ cup of the flour, above.

CRUMPETS

2½ teaspoons (1 envelope) active dry yeast
1½ cups warm tap water (about 110 degrees)
2 cups unbleached all-purpose flour
2 teaspoons salt
2 tablespoons unsalted butter, melted
1 tablespoon honey

Four 4 × 1-inch muffin rings, buttered

ABOUT SIX 4-INCH CRUMPETS

Typically British, crumpets have become popular in the Pacific Northwest, especially Seattle—could it be the similarity in annual rainfall? Though crumpets are easy to make, you will need a set of four 4-inch rings and a griddle for cooking them. The rings are inexpensive and available at kitchenware stores. Or you can save some 4-inch cans—tuna cans, for instance. Remove both the top and bottom of the cans to use them as crumpet rings.

1. In a bowl, whisk the yeast into the warm water and set aside while preparing the other ingredients.

2. To mix by hand, place the flour and salt in a mixing bowl and add the yeast mixture, butter, and honey. Beat vigorously with a wooden spoon for 5 minutes.

To mix the dough in a heavy-duty mixer, place the flour and salt in a mixer bowl and add the yeast mixture, butter, and honey. Beat with a paddle on low speed for 5 minutes.

To mix in the food processor, place the flour and salt in a work bowl fitted with a metal blade. Pulse to mix. Add the yeast mixture, butter, and honey to the work bowl, and run the machine continuously for 30 seconds.

3. Pour the batter into a stainless-steel or glass bowl. Cover with plastic wrap and allow the batter to rise at room temperature until the batter has almost tripled, about 1 hour.

4. While the batter is rising, begin to heat the griddle. Grease the surface of the griddle and the inside of the rings, then set the rings on the griddle.

5. Beat the crumpet batter vigorously with a wooden spoon to deflate it. Pour ½ cup of the batter into each ring.

6. Bake the crumpets on the griddle for about 20 minutes, until the top surface is dull and riddled with holes. Remove the crumpets from the griddle (it is not necessary to cook the other side) with a wide spatula to a rack to cool. Carefully lift off rings. Replace 2 of the rings on the griddle and bake the remaining batter. The second batch may take longer if the griddle has not sufficiently reheated—be sure the top surface of the crumpets is dull before removing them from the griddle.

SERVING: Toast crumpets, split or not, and spread with butter. Serve jam or preserves separately. Good for breakfast; excellent for tea.

STORAGE: On the day they are baked, keep the crumpets loosely covered at room temperature. For longer storage, freeze for up to 1 month.

HINT FOR SUCCESS: Though I have several cast-iron griddles and skillets, for crumpets I have had the best results using an aluminum griddle. Whatever griddle you use, place it over low heat for 10 to 15 minutes before you begin to bake the crumpets. Test the heat of the griddle with a teaspoonful of the batter—if it sets and becomes dull on top within a minute, the griddle temperature is perfect.

BAGELS

2½ teaspoons (1 envelope) active dry yeast
1½ cups warm tap water (about 110 degrees)
5 to 6 cups unbleached all-purpose flour
3 tablespoons sugar
2 teaspoons salt
Egg wash: 1 egg white well beaten with 1
    tablespoon water
Sesame seeds, poppy seeds, or coarse salt for the
    outside of the bagels (optional)

Two cookie sheets or jelly-roll pans lined with oiled foil

ABOUT 10 TO 12 MEDIUM BAGELS

Bagels stem from an Eastern European-Jewish baking tradition, and are a staple food for many New Yorkers.

They are easy to prepare. The formed bagels are poached before baking, which adds a little time after the dough has risen but it does not rise a second time. Poached breads are rare, though bagels are not the only ones—pretzels and a crisp Italian version of pretzels, *taralli,* are also poached before baking. Poaching imparts stability and sheen to the crust.

1. In a bowl, whisk the yeast into the warm water and set aside while preparing the other ingredients.

2. Combine the smaller amount of flour, sugar, and salt in the work bowl of a food processor fitted with a metal blade. Pulse to mix. Add the yeast mixture to the work bowl and pulse until the dough forms a ball. Let rest for 5 minutes, then run the machine continuously for 30 seconds. The dough will be very firm. Knead in remaining flour by hand, a little at a time.

To mix the dough by machine, combine all the ingredients except the egg wash and seeds in the bowl of a heavy-duty mixer. Mix on low speed with a dough hook for about 10 minutes, until the dough is smooth and elastic.

3. Turn the dough out onto a lightly floured work surface. Shape the dough into a ball and place it in an oiled stainless-steel or glass bowl. Turn the dough to coat all sides with oil. Cover the bowl with plastic wrap and allow the dough to rise at room temperature until the dough has doubled, about 1 hour.

(continued)

4. Bring a 5- or 6-quart saucepan or casserole of water to a simmer.

5. Turn the risen dough out onto a lightly floured work surface. Divide the dough into ten or twelve equal pieces and roll each piece into a 10-inch cylinder. Keep the dough covered as you work to prevent it from drying. Moisten the ends of each cylinder with water and press them together to form a closed circle.

6. Set a rack at the middle level of the oven and preheat to 450 degrees.

7. Lower 2 bagels at a time into the simmering water and cook for about a minute, turning them once using a large mesh slotted spoon or a skimmer. Remove with the skimmer and drain on a rack. Repeat with the remaining bagels. When the bagels are dry, arrange them on the prepared pans. Brush the bagels with the egg white wash and sprinkle with desired toppings, or leave plain.

8. Bake for about 30 minutes, or until golden brown and shiny.

9. Transfer to a rack to cool.

SERVING: Bagels are usually split horizontally and spread with butter or cream cheese—the traditional "schmeer." They may also be toasted after they have been split. For a typically rich New York Sunday breakfast, serve bagels with cream cheese, sliced red onions, sliced tomatoes, and smoked Nova Scotia salmon.

STORAGE: Keep unused bagels in a plastic bag at room temperature for a day, or in the freezer for up to a month.

HINT FOR SUCCESS: Be sure that the water is only simmering gently. The bagels may break apart in rapidly boiling water.

3
SAVORY
PASTRIES

Since the use of sugar did not become prevalent in western Europe until the late Middle Ages, we may safely assume that many of the first pastries made were of the savory—and not sweet—type. A fancy, old-fashioned *pâté en croûte* is probably the quintessential savory pastry—delicately seasoned meat surrounded by a dough to both contain and insulate it as it bakes. But savory pastries may also be much more simple—a quiche, other savory pie or tart, a little hors d'oeuvre tart or cheese cookie, and even a day-after-Thanksgiving turkey pie all qualify as savory pastries and always please.

Most savory pies probably originated as foods wrapped in bread dough, and as culinary skill increased, the bread doughs gave way to more delicate and refined pastry doughs. Perhaps this is why it is logical to include pizza, focaccia, and the related calzone in this chapter.

Pizza specialties, made from a yeast-risen dough not unlike a simple bread dough, are among the most popular savory pastries, and though the quiche may have crested in popularity in the seventies, I'm sure it never really was a threat to pizza, one of the world's most popular foods. Aside from typical pizza and focaccia recipes, there are also French and Ligurian versions of these specialties to round out the assortment.

One note about using savory pastries: They are a favorite of mine for entertaining. Easy to prepare in advance, they are festive and fun to serve, and by eliminating last-minute preparations, they make entertaining easier. Whether you choose to use them as first courses or as main courses of lighter meals, most only need a salad and a dessert to round out a casual meal. And if you have spent all your baking time on the savory pastry or pie, then fruit will make a perfect dessert.

DOUGHS FOR SAVORY TARTS

The following doughs are used in the recipes for savory tarts in this chapter. Though they shouldn't necessarily be used interchangeably, each can be baked raw with a raw filling in it, a practical and time-saving alternative to the more familiar method of weighing down the formed crust with paper and beans and partially baking it before the filling is added.

FLAKY DOUGH FOR SAVORY PASTRIES

1½ cups bleached all-purpose flour
½ teaspoon salt
⅛ teaspoon baking powder
10 tablespoons (1¼ sticks) unsalted butter
4 to 5 tablespoons cold water

ABOUT 12 OUNCES DOUGH, ENOUGH FOR ABOUT 24 SMALL (1½- TO 2-INCH) PASTRIES, OR ABOUT 8 LARGE (3- TO 4-INCH) TARTS

Use this dough for any small empty baked shells, whether they are to be filled with sweet or savory mixtures. It is my favorite to use for small hors d'oeuvre pastries, because it has a delicate texture and a flavor that does not interfere with the flavor of the filling.

Because this dough has a little less butter in it than a standard flaky dough, it may be rolled thinner without worrying about its melting or disintegrating.

1. To mix the dough by hand, combine the flour, salt, and baking powder in a medium mixing bowl and stir well to mix. Cut the butter into 1-tablespoon pieces and add to the dry ingredients. Toss once or twice to coat the pieces of butter. Using your hands or a pastry blender, break the butter into tiny pieces and pinch and squeeze it into the dry ingredients. Occasionally reach down to the bottom of the bowl and mix all the ingredients evenly together. Continue rubbing the butter into the dry ingredients until the mixture resembles coarsely ground cornmeal and no large pieces of butter remain visible. Scatter the minimum amount of water over the butter and flour mixture and stir gently with a fork. The dough should begin holding together.

If it still appears dry and crumbly, add the remaining water, a teaspoon at a time, until the dough holds together easily.

To mix the dough in a food processor, combine the flour, salt, and baking powder in the work bowl fitted with a metal blade. Pulse 3 times at 1-second intervals to mix. Cut the butter into 1-tablespoon pieces and add to the work bowl. Process, pulsing repeatedly at 1-second intervals, until the mixture is fine and powdery and resembles coarsely ground cornmeal with no large pieces of butter remaining visible, about 15 pulses in all. Scatter the minimum amount of water over the butter and flour mixture and pulse 5 or 6 times—the dough should begin holding together. If the mixture still appears dry and crumbly, add the remaining water, a teaspoon at a time, until the dough holds together easily.

2. Scrape the dough out onto a lightly floured surface and form into a rectangle. Wrap in plastic and refrigerate until firm, or until you are ready to use it, but for at least 1 hour.

STORAGE: Keep the dough in the refrigerator for up to 2 days, or double-wrap in plastic and freeze for up to several weeks.

HINT FOR SUCCESS: For best results, have all ingredients cold and work quickly so the butter doesn't melt, which would make the crust tough.

VARIATION

ANOTHER FLAKY DOUGH FOR SAVORY PASTRIES: For a rustic-tasting dough, substitute lard for half the butter in the above recipe. To moisten the dough, use 1 egg, adding a tablespoon of water afterwards, if necessary.

QUICHE DOUGH

1¼ cups bleached all-purpose flour
¼ teaspoon salt
¼ teaspoon baking powder
6 tablespoons cold unsalted butter
1 large egg
1 tablespoon cold water

ABOUT 10 OUNCES DOUGH, ENOUGH FOR A 10- TO 11-INCH TART

This dough, which is used for the traditional custard and bacon tart called Quiche Lorraine, may also be used for other savory tarts. The cheese variation that follows is great with any type of vegetable or cheese pie or tart.

1. To mix the dough by hand, combine the flour, salt, and baking powder in a medium mixing bowl and stir well to mix. Cut the butter into 1-tablespoon pieces and add to the dry ingredients. Toss once or twice to coat the pieces of butter. Using your hands or a pastry blender, break the butter into tiny pieces and pinch and squeeze it into the dry ingredients. Occasionally reach down to the bottom of the bowl and mix all the ingredients evenly together. Continue rubbing the butter into the dry ingredients until the mixture resembles coarsely ground cornmeal and no large pieces of butter remain visible. Beat the egg and water together in a small bowl and stir into the flour and butter mixture with a fork. Continue to stir until the dough begins to hold together.

To mix the dough in the food processor, combine the flour, salt, and baking powder in the work bowl fitted with a metal blade. Pulse 3 times at 1-second intervals to mix. Cut the butter into 1-tablespoon pieces and add to the work bowl. Process, pulsing repeatedly at 1-second intervals, until the mixture is fine and powdery and resembles coarsely ground cornmeal with no large pieces of butter remaining visible, about 15 pulses in all. Beat the egg and water together in a small bowl and add to the work bowl; pulse 10 times or so, until the dough forms a ball.

2. Scatter a teaspoon of flour on the work surface and scrape the dough onto it. Press and knead the dough quickly 3 or 4 times, until it is smooth and uniform.

3. Press the dough into a rough circle. Sandwich the dough between two pieces of plastic wrap and press it into a 6-inch circle. Refrigerate the dough until firm, or until you are ready to use it, at least 1 hour.

STORAGE: Keep the dough in the refrigerator up to 2 days, or double-wrap in plastic to freeze it. Because the dough is thin, it will defrost quickly at room temperature.

VARIATION

CHEESE DOUGH FOR SAVORY TARTS: Add 3 tablespoons finely grated hard cheese, such as Parmesan or Romano, to the flour before you begin to mix the dough. If you prefer other grating cheeses, such as sharp aged cheddar, Swiss Gruyère, or even a smoked Gouda, use ¼ cup grated cheese.

CORNMEAL DOUGH
FOR SAVORY TARTS

¾ cup bleached all-purpose flour
¾ cup yellow cornmeal
1 teaspoon salt
½ teaspoon baking powder
6 tablespoons cold unsalted butter
1 egg

ABOUT 12 OUNCES DOUGH, ENOUGH FOR A 10- OR 11-INCH TART

The combination of flour and cornmeal makes this dough easier to roll and form than one made entirely with cornmeal. Yet the cornmeal contributes its distinctive flavor and color to the dough. I like to use this with the Pepper and Onion Frittata Tart (page 108) and with any filling variations that include sweet-tasting elements, such as peppers or tomatoes. It is also good with any of the quiches (page 109).

You may find the cornmeal dough a little difficult to roll, since the cornmeal makes the dough less elastic and coherent than an all-flour dough. If it starts to break apart, just patch it into place in the tart or pie pan—it will be fine.

1. To mix the dough by hand, combine the dry ingredients in a medium mixing bowl and stir well to mix. Cut the butter into 1-tablespoon pieces and add to the dry ingredients. Toss once or twice to coat the pieces of butter. Rub the butter into the dry ingredients with your hands or a pastry blender, continuously pinching and squeezing it. Occasionally reach down to the bottom of the bowl and mix all the ingredients evenly together. Continue rubbing the butter into the dry ingredients until the mixture resembles coarsely ground cornmeal and no large pieces of butter remain visible. Beat the egg in a small bowl and pour over the flour and butter. Stir in with a fork and continue to stir until the dough begins to hold together.

To mix the dough in a food processor, combine the dry ingredients in a work bowl fitted with a metal blade. Pulse 3 times at 1-second intervals to mix. Cut the butter into 1-tablespoon pieces and add to the work bowl. Process, pulsing repeatedly at 1-second intervals, until the mixture is fine and powdery and resembles coarsely ground cornmeal with no large pieces of butter remaining visible, about 15 pulses in all. Add the egg to the work bowl; pulse 10 times or so, until the dough forms a ball.

2. Scatter a teaspoon of flour over the work surface and scrape the dough out onto it. Press and knead the dough quickly 3 or 4 times, until it is smooth and uniform.

3. Press the dough into a circle. Sandwich it between two pieces of plastic wrap and press it into a 6-inch circle. Refrigerate the dough until firm, or until you are ready to use it, at least 1 hour.

STORAGE: Keep the dough in the refrigerator up to 2 days, or double-wrap in plastic to freeze it. Because the dough is thin, it will defrost quickly at room temperature when you intend to use it.

OLIVE OIL DOUGH
FOR SAVORY TARTS

1¼ **cups bleached all-purpose flour**
½ **teaspoon salt**
½ **teaspoon sugar**
½ **teaspoon baking powder**
2 **large eggs**
¼ **cup olive oil**

ABOUT 12 OUNCES DOUGH, ENOUGH FOR A 10- OR 11-INCH TART SHELL

This is a variation on the dough I was taught to make during my first season as a *commis* (chef's assistant) at the Sporting Club in Monte Carlo in the early seventies. The recipe is one I learned in Monaco from Alexandre Frolla, who is of Monegasque descent.

The dough was used for a Swiss Chard Tart (page 114), popular in the Nice-Monaco region. We often cut it into squares and served it as an hors d'oeuvre.

1. To mix the dough by hand, combine the dry ingredients in a mixing bowl and stir well to mix. In a small bowl, beat the eggs and oil together. Make a well in the dry ingredients, add the eggs and oil, and stir with a fork until the mixture begins to form a dough.

To mix the dough in a food processor, combine the dry ingredients in a work bowl fitted with a steel blade and pulse 3 or 4 times to mix. Add the eggs and oil and pulse 10 to 15 times, until the dough forms a ball.

2. Scatter a teaspoon of flour over the work surface and scrape the dough from the bowl to the surface. Knead the dough lightly, 3 or 4 times, until it is smooth, being careful not to overwork it.

3. Press the dough into a circle. Sandwich between two pieces of plastic wrap and press it into a 6-inch circle. Refrigerate the dough until firm, or until you are ready to use it, at least 1 hour.

STORAGE: Keep the dough in the refrigerator up to 2 days, or double-wrap in plastic to freeze it. Because the dough is thin, it will defrost quickly at room temperature when you intend to use it.

OLD-FASHIONED CHICKEN PIE

POACHED CHICKEN

One 3½-pound frying or roasting chicken
1 leek, split and thoroughly rinsed
1 large rib celery
1 large carrot, peeled
4 sprigs fresh flat-leaf parsley
3 sprigs fresh thyme, or ½ teaspoon dried
1 imported bay leaf
1 medium (about 6 ounces) onion, peeled and
　　stuck with a clove
1½ teaspoons salt

1 recipe Flaky Dough for Savory Pastries
　　(page 98)

SAUCE

Chicken poaching liquid
1 cup heavy cream
Salt and freshly ground white pepper to taste

VEGETABLE GARNISH

1 teaspoon salt
8 pearl onions, about 1 inch in diameter, peeled
3 medium carrots, peeled, split, and cut into
　　1½-inch lengths
1 cup green beans, tipped and cut diagonally
　　about 1-inch long

1 cup shelled fresh or frozen peas

Egg wash: 1 egg well beaten with a pinch of salt

One 2-quart baking dish

ONE PIE, ABOUT 4 SERVINGS AS A MAIN COURSE

Although I don't prepare chicken pie often, there are some occasions that absolutely demand it, such as an informal late supper in early spring or a fall lunch or a holiday brunch. And it is perfect for entertaining—you can assemble the pie completely the night before, then bake it the following day, or even poach the chicken and make the dough on the first day, prepare the vegetables and assemble the pie on the second, and bake and serve it on the third.

I have strong opinions about chicken pie: the chicken must be off the bone; the sauce must be well flavored, creamy, and not too plentiful; vegetables must support, not drown out the chicken; the crust must be crisp and tender; and finally, the pie must be served as soon as it is ready or the crust may become soggy. If you have the pie all assembled, it is easy to figure the 30 minutes or so it takes to bake it in relation to the meal you have planned, so that you and your guests can enjoy a perfect pie fresh from the oven.

(continued)

1. To poach the chicken, rinse it thoroughly, then place in a large casserole or soup pot. Cover with cold water and place on low heat. With a large kitchen spoon or ladle, carefully skim the foam that accumulates on the surface of the liquid.

2. Meanwhile, tie the vegetables and herbs, except the onion, in a bunch with kitchen twine (if you are using dried thyme, tie in a cheesecloth bag). Add the bouquet and the onion to the pot. Regulate the heat so the liquid just simmers and continue to skim as necessary. Add the salt and cook for about 1 hour. Turn off the heat and allow the chicken to cool in the liquid. If you are preparing the chicken in advance, refrigerate it, uncovered, after it has cooled for 30 minutes.

3. When the chicken has cooled completely, remove and discard the bouquet. Strain the poaching liquid and reserve. Remove the chicken skin and discard. Pull the meat from the bones in large pieces and reserve the bones and carcass.

4. While the chicken is cooking, prepare and chill the dough. It can remain refrigerated for a day.

5. To make the sauce, combine the carcass and poaching liquid in a large pan and continue to cook until the poaching liquid is reduced to about 3 cups. Pass through a fine strainer into another pan, add the cream, and reduce to about 2½ cups (if you like more sauce, reduce only to 3½ cups). Season well with salt and pepper.

6. To prepare the vegetables, bring a 3- to 4-quart pan of water to a boil and add the salt. Add the onions and return to a boil. Cook at a low boil for about 5 minutes, then add the vegetables, and cook for about 5 minutes longer. (Do not bother to blanch frozen peas.) Drain and cool the vegetables. This may be done the day before; cover and refrigerate until needed.

7. To assemble the pie, pour the cooled sauce into a bowl and add the chicken and vegetables. Fold the ingredients gently together and taste for seasoning. Pour the filling into the baking dish.

8. Set a rack at the middle level of the oven and preheat to 375 degrees.

9. Lightly flour the work surface and dough and roll the dough out to the size and shape of the baking dish. Slide the dough onto the filling and press it against the rim of the dish. Flute the dough at the edge (page 150), cut several vent holes in it, and carefully paint with the egg wash. With any extra dough, cut out crescents or other shapes to decorate the crust. Adhere and paint the pastry cutouts with egg wash.

10. Bake for about 30 minutes, or until the dough is a deep golden brown and the filling is gently bubbling. Serve immediately.

SERVING: To serve the pie, cut away a portion of the crust with a large serving spoon and place the crust on a heated plate. Spoon out the filling and place on the plate alongside the portion of crust.

This pie followed by a green salad and a fruit dessert makes a memorable meal. Serve with a light red wine or a chilled rosé.

STORAGE: Serve the pie immediately and refrigerate leftovers.

HINT FOR SUCCESS: When you are timing the pie to serve to guests, remember, everyone would rather wait a few minutes for the pie to be baked than have it wait and become cold and soggy.

VARIATIONS

CHICKEN AND MUSHROOM PIE: Replace the vegetables in the pie above with 1 pound mushrooms. To cook the mushrooms, leave the stems attached and rinse, dry, and slice about ¼ inch thick. Heat 2 tablespoons butter or oil in a sauté pan and add the mushrooms, then ½ teaspoon salt, ½ teaspoon freshly ground pepper, and a squeeze of lemon juice. Cover and allow the juices to exude, 2 or 3 minutes. Uncover, lower the heat, and continue cooking until the juices have become syrupy. Add to the chicken in the baking dish.

CHICKEN PIE AFTER JUNE PLATT: Early Cordon Bleu graduate and friend of James Beard, June Platt wrote several interesting cookbooks in the 1930s and '40s. In *June Platt's Party Cook Book* (Houghton Mifflin Company, 1936) she gives a recipe for a rich chicken custard, made from poached chicken baked with eggs and cream. To make a chicken pie in the style of this rich dish, reduce and cool the sauce, above, and overseason it somewhat. Whisk in 5 large eggs. Assemble the pie as above.

DAY AFTER THANKSGIVING TURKEY PIE: For lunch on the day after Thanksgiving, I always make a big turkey pie. It is like my chicken pie, but all the ingredients are leftovers. Usually the only thing I have to make is the dough— although there is often dough left over from Thanksgiving pie baking. Dice turkey meat and place in the baking dish. Add any vegetables you wish—I always serve some green beans and mushrooms with the turkey, so I add those. Taste the turkey gravy for seasoning, add a little cream if you wish, and pour it over the meat and vegetables in the baking dish. Cover with dough and bake as in the master recipe above.

SICILIAN SWORDFISH PIE

(IMPANATA DI PESCE SPADA ALLA MESSINESE/'MPANATA DI PISCI SPATA)

RICH PASTRY DOUGH FOR SAVORY PIES

2½ cups bleached all-purpose flour

1 teaspoon salt

½ teaspoon baking powder

4 tablespoons chilled lard

4 tablespoons cold unsalted butter

3 large eggs

FILLING

6 tablespoons olive oil

1 pound boneless swordfish, each piece about
    ½-inch thick

Flour for dredging the fish

¼ teaspoon salt, plus extra to taste

Black pepper to taste

1 medium onion, chopped (about 6 ounces)

1 small rib celery, chopped

1½ cups well-drained and chopped canned
    tomatoes, or peeled, seeded, and chopped
    fresh vine-ripened tomatoes

¼ cup chopped fresh flat-leaf parsley

2 tablespoons shredded fresh basil

2 tablespoons drained capers

¼ cup raisins

½ cup whole oil-cured black olives, pitted and
    sliced

2 tablespoons pine nuts

1 cup (about 5 ounces) coarsely grated
    Caciocavallo cheese, or ½ cup finely grated
    Pecorino Romano

Egg wash: 1 egg well beaten with a pinch of salt

One 9-inch Pyrex pie pan

ONE 9-INCH PIE, ABOUT 8 SERVINGS

This great specialty of Messina, the port town on the east coast of Sicily closest to the Italian mainland, combines many typical Sicilian flavors in a single dish. The meaty texture of swordfish, the fish most widely served in Sicily, blends well with the highly seasoned sauce.

Though this is usually presented in a straight-sided pan, I think a standard pie pan is more practical—it makes the pie easier to assemble and to serve.

As with many Sicilian recipes, there are many interpretations of the dish. Some call for a yeast dough similar to the dough for focaccia. The dough I use has a combination of lard, butter, and eggs and produces a rich, yet flaky, crust.

1. To make the dough, combine the flour, salt, and baking powder in the work bowl of a food processor fitted with a metal blade. Pulse 3 or 4 times to mix. Cut the lard and butter into 1-tablespoon pieces and add to the bowl. Pulse first until the mixture resembles cornmeal—do not overprocess and allow the mixture to become pasty. Whisk the eggs in a bowl and add the eggs to the work bowl; pulse until the dough forms a ball.

To mix the dough by hand, combine the flour, salt, and baking powder in a mixing bowl. Add the lard and butter and rub in finely by hand or with a pastry blender. Stir in the eggs with a fork and continue stirring until the dough holds together.

Divide the dough in half and press each half into a large circle. Wrap each piece in plastic wrap and refrigerate while you prepare the filling.

2. To make the filling, heat 3 tablespoons of the oil in a skillet over medium heat. While the oil is heating, dredge the pieces of fish in the flour and shake off the excess. Cook the fish for about 2 minutes on each side, to stiffen it. Remove the fish to a nonreactive pan and sprinkle with some salt and pepper. Pour off the oil in which the fish was cooked and add the remaining oil. Add the onion and celery and cook until they are limp. Add the tomatoes, parsley, and basil; bring to a simmer, lower the heat, and cook for about 20 minutes, stirring often, until the sauce has thickened. Add the capers, raisins, and olives and cook for 5 minutes longer.

3. Set a rack at the lowest level of the oven and preheat to 375 degrees.

4. To make the bottom crust, lightly flour a work surface and one of the pieces of dough and roll it into a 12-inch circle. Fold the dough in half and place it in the pan, then unfold it and fit it into the pan. Trim any excess dough even with the edge of the pan.

5. Spoon half the filling over the dough and top with half the pine nuts and half the grated cheese. Arrange the fish on this and top with the remaining filling, pine nuts, and cheese.

6. To make the top crust, lightly flour the work surface and the remaining piece of dough and roll it into a 10-inch circle. Fold the dough in half and place over the filling. Unfold the dough to cover the pie and trim away all but ½ inch of the excess dough around the rim. Fold the edge of the top crust under the edge of the bottom crust and press well to seal, but do not flute the edge. Cut several vent holes in the top crust and brush it with the egg wash.

7. Bake the pie for about 40 minutes, or until the crust is a deep golden brown. Cool the pie on a rack.

SERVING: Serve the pie as an appetizer, as part of a buffet, or as a main course. If the pie is a main course in summer, serve fresh figs and prosciutto as an appetizer and follow the pie with a green salad. Serve a well-chilled white Sicilian wine, such as Regaleali Nozze d'Oro or Corvo, with the pie. For dessert, serve fresh fruit and cookies (see Chapter 6).

STORAGE: Serve the pie when it has cooled; wrap and refrigerate leftovers.

VARIATION

If you wish, cut the fish into 1-inch dice after it has cooked and gently mix with the cooled sauce, pine nuts, and cheese. Scrape the mixture into the bottom crust and proceed as above.

PEPPER AND ONION FRITTATA TART

1 recipe Cornmeal Dough for Savory Tarts
   (page 101)

FILLING

3 medium red, green, or yellow bell peppers
   (about 1 pound total)
1 medium red onion (about 4 ounces)
3 tablespoons olive oil
½ teaspoon each salt and pepper
1 tablespoon chopped fresh marjoram, or
   1 teaspoon dried
1 cup whole-milk or part-skim ricotta
4 eggs
¼ cup grated Parmesan

One 9- to 10-inch tart pan

ONE 9- TO 10-INCH TART, 8 TO 10 SERVINGS

The cornmeal crust on this tart gives it a vaguely southwestern flavor. If you choose to use a variety of peppers in this tart, use only red and yellow, for they are sweeter than green.

1. Prepare and chill the dough.

2. To make the filling, slice the peppers and onion thin. Heat the olive oil in a wide, shallow pan and add the vegetables. Season with the salt and pepper and cook over medium heat, stirring or tossing frequently, until the vegetables are wilted, about 10 minutes. Stir in the marjoram, pour into a mixing bowl, and cool. Place the remaining filling ingredients in a food processor and process for about 1 minute until smooth.

3. Set a rack at the lower third of the oven and preheat to 350 degrees.

4. To make the crust, place the dough on a lightly floured work surface and scatter flour over it. Roll the dough out into a 13- to 14-inch circle. Fit the dough into the pan and trim away all but ½ inch of the excess around the edge of the pan. Fold the excess back into the pan. Press the dough firmly against the bottom and side of the pan, then using the thumb and index finger of one hand, press against the side of the crust and down on the top edge to make the rim smooth and even, as in the illustration on page 194.

5. Combine the ricotta and pepper mixtures, correct the seasoning if necessary, and pour into the crust. Bake for 30 to 40 minutes, until the filling is set and the crust is baked through. Cool on a rack.

6. To unmold the tart, stand the tart pan on a large can or canister and allow the pan to fall away. Slide the tart from the pan bottom onto a large, flat-bottomed platter.

SERVING: Serve the tart warm or at room temperature. It gains flavor as it cools a bit.

STORAGE: Keep the tart at room temperature until served. Refrigerate, covered with plastic wrap, for longer storage.

HINT FOR SUCCESS: Cook the peppers and onions slowly to avoid burned patches of skin and consequent bitterness.

BACON AND CUSTARD QUICHE

1 recipe Quiche Dough (page 100)

FILLING

¼ **pound thick-sliced bacon, cut into ½-inch**
   pieces
½ **cup milk**
½ **cup heavy cream**
3 large eggs
¼ **teaspoon salt**
¼ **teaspoon freshly ground white pepper**
Pinch of freshly grated nutmeg
2 tablespoons unsalted butter

One 9- or 10-inch tart pan

ONE 9- OR 10-INCH TART, ABOUT 8 SERVINGS

In its simplest form, the quiche is an excellent brunch or lunch dish—you get your eggs, bacon, and pastry all in one neat package. With more elaborate additions (cooked vegetables; cheese; other meats, such as prosciutto or boiled ham), it becomes more substantial and appropriate to serve as a first course or hors d'oeuvre at a larger meal.

Fortunately, many of the ills that befell the quiche (and caused it to fall from grace) are easy to remedy. One thing the quiche is not is a recycling container for little bits of various leftovers, or an excuse to be "creative" with every jar and package in the refrigerator and cupboard. The best quiches are the simplest ones.

1. Roll out the dough and fit it into the tart pan. Chill the crust while you prepare the filling.

2. Set a rack at the lowest level of the oven and preheat to 375 degrees.

3. For the filling, place the bacon in a 1½-quart saucepan and cover with cold water. Bring to a boil over low heat and drain immediately. Return the bacon to the pan and cook over low heat until the bacon renders some of its fat and begins to sizzle, about 5 minutes. Do not cook the bacon until it's crisp, or it will be hard in the quiche. Remove the bacon pieces from the pan and place on a plate lined with a paper towel to drain. Combine the remaining filling ingredients, except the butter, in a bowl and whisk to blend. Arrange the bacon evenly over the chilled crust and strain the filling over it. Dot with the butter.

4. Bake the quiche for about 40 minutes, or until the pastry is baked through and the filling is set and puffed.

5. Place the pan on a rack to cool for a few minutes. To unmold the quiche, stand the pan on a large can or canister and allow the side to fall away. Slide the quiche from the pan bottom onto a large, flat-bottomed platter.

SERVING: Serve the quiche cut into wedges with a green salad if it is the main course of a light meal, or unaccompanied, if it is a first course.

STORAGE: Serve immediately. Refrigerate leftovers well covered with plastic wrap. Serve leftovers cold or reheat briefly.

(continued)

HINT FOR SUCCESS: Roll the dough thin and even to ensure that it will bake completely on the bottom of the quiche.

VARIATIONS

CHEESE QUICHE: Sprinkle 1 cup coarsely grated Gruyère, Emmenthal, or cheddar over the crust when you put in the bacon and before pouring on the filling. Omit the bacon if you wish.

HAM AND CHEESE QUICHE: Replace the bacon in the Cheese Quiche, above, with 1 cup finely diced boiled ham or prosciutto. Do not boil or sauté the ham.

ALSATIAN ONION TART: Peel, slice, and sauté 3 medium onions (about 1 pound total) in 3 tablespoons butter very slowly, until well cooked through. Cool the onions, then spread them on the tart shell before adding the bacon and filling.

NEAPOLITAN RICOTTA, MOZZARELLA, AND PROSCIUTTO PIE
(PIZZA RUSTICA ALLA NAPOLETANA)

PASTA FROLLA

3 cups bleached all-purpose flour

½ cup sugar

1 teaspoon salt

1 teaspoon baking powder

12 tablespoons (1½ sticks) cold unsalted butter

3 large eggs

FILLING

2 pounds whole-milk or part-skim-milk ricotta

6 large eggs

1 teaspoon freshly ground black pepper

¼ cup grated Pecorino Romano cheese

1 pound mozzarella, coarsely grated

½ pound sweet dried sausage, peeled and diced

½ pound prosciutto, shredded

½ cup chopped fresh flat-leaf parsley

Egg wash: 1 egg well beaten with a pinch of salt

One 12-inch-diameter × 2-inch-deep cake pan, or an 11 × 17-inch jelly-roll pan, buttered

ONE LARGE PIE, ABOUT 20 SERVINGS

In Italy, this typical savory pie is served at Carnevale (the day before Ash Wednesday) and then again at Easter. Though many recipes for *pizza rustica* specify that the dried sausage, mozzarella, and other filling ingredients be layered, in this Neapolitan version they are diced and added to the ricotta filling, which makes the pizza easier to cut into wedges.

The dough used here is a *pasta frolla,* a sweet, tender, and typical Italian pastry dough. The combination of a sweet dough and a savory filling may seem bizarre, but it yields a good contrast— the sweetness of the dough tempers the rather salty filling. If the combination does not appeal to you, leave out the sugar; add a tablespoon or two of water to make the dough form a ball.

1. To make the dough, combine the dry ingredients in the bowl of a food processor fitted with a metal blade and pulse several times to mix. Cut the butter into 1-tablespoon pieces and distribute evenly over the dry ingredients in the work bowl. Pulse until very finely powdered. Add the eggs and continue to pulse until the dough forms a ball on the blade.

To mix the dough by hand, combine the dry ingredients in a mixing bowl. Add the butter and rub in finely by hand or with a pastry blender. Stir in the eggs with a fork and continue stirring until the dough holds together.

(continued)

Remove the dough and divide into 2 pieces, one of which is two thirds of the dough and the other one third. Press the larger piece into a circle and wrap in plastic. Press the smaller piece into a square and wrap it too. Refrigerate both while preparing the filling.

2. To make the filling, place the ricotta in the work bowl of the food processor and pulse to puree smoothly. Transfer the ricotta to a mixing bowl and stir in the eggs, one at a time; stir in the remaining filling ingredients in the order listed.

3. Set a rack at the lower third of the oven and preheat to 350 degrees.

Arrange five strips over the filling. Arrange the remaining strips across the first ones at a 45 degree angle.

4. Lightly flour a work surface and the larger piece of dough and roll the dough out into a 17-inch circle. Fold the dough into quarters and place in the prepared pan. Unfold the dough and press into the pan, allowing any excess dough to hang over the sides. Pour in the filling (it will come to about ¾ inch below the top of the pan) and smooth the top.

5. Roll the remaining dough into a 10-inch square and cut into 1-inch strips. Paint the dough strips with the egg wash. Arrange 5 strips over the filling. Arrange the remaining strips at a 45 degree angle across the first ones, as in the illustration (left). Press the strips against the rim of the pan to make them stick and trim away excess dough—only from the strips—around the top of the pan. Use a small knife to loosen the bottom crust dough around the rim of the pan and fold it over to form an edge for the top crust, as in the illustration (opposite).

6. Bake the pizza for about 45 minutes, until the filling is set and the dough is baked through. Cool in the pan on a rack.

7. To unmold, place a platter over the pizza and invert it, then remove the pan. Replace the pan with another platter and invert the pizza again. Remove the top platter.

Press the strips against the rim of the pan to make them stick and trim away any excess dough — only from the strips — around the top of the pan. Using a small knife, loosen the bottom crust around the rim of the pan and fold it over to form an edge for the top crust.

SERVING: Serve in wedges as an appetizer (see variation, below), or as part of a buffet. *Pizza rustica* is a perfect brunch dish.

STORAGE: Keep the *pizza rustica* at room temperature on the day it is baked. For longer storage, wrap in plastic and refrigerate for up to several days. Bring to room temperature before serving.

HINT FOR SUCCESS: Don't overbake the *pizza rustica* or the filling will become watery and soak through the bottom crust.

To make a rectangular *pizza rustica,* roll the larger amount of dough into a 14 × 20-inch rectangle. Fit into a buttered 11 × 17-inch jelly-roll pan. Spread the filling on the dough. Roll the remaining dough into a 12-inch square and cut into 12 strips. Paint the strips of dough with the egg wash and arrange 6 strips across the width of the pan. Arrange the 6 remaining strips at a 45 degree angle to them. Press the ends of the strips in place and trim away excess dough even with the rim of the pan. Bake for about 35 minutes (the filling is in a thinner layer and therefore will bake through more quickly). Cool and cut into 1½- to 2-inch squares.

SWISS CHARD TART FROM NICE
(TOURTE DE BLETTES À LA NIÇOISE)

2 recipes Olive Oil Dough for Savory Tarts
    (page 102)

FILLING

2½ pounds Swiss chard

1 quart water

2 teaspoons salt

½ cup long-grain rice

1 large (about 8 ounces) mild onion

3 tablespoons olive oil

2 cloves garlic, finely minced

4 large eggs

½ cup grated Gouda or Swiss Gruyère

½ teaspoon each salt and pepper

¼ cup toasted pine nuts

¼ cup yellow raisins

¼ cup fresh basil, rinsed, dried, and finely
    shredded

One 9- to 10-inch tart pan

ONE 9- TO 10-INCH TART, ABOUT 8 TO 10 SERVINGS

If you visit le vieux Nice, Nice's old town, you will find this chard tart offered for sale in the same establishments that sell *Socca* (page 130) and Pissaladière (page 136). Although this tart is associated with the French and Italian Rivieras, there are versions made as far east as Genoa.

1. Prepare and chill the dough.

2. To make the filling, rinse, drain, and separate the leaves from the stems of chard. Save the stems and sauté in olive oil and garlic as a side dish to meat or fish. Bring several quarts of water to a boil over medium heat and add 1 teaspoon salt. Add the chard leaves and cook until the water returns to a boil. Cook for 2 minutes. Drain and cool the chard. Chop the chard finely and in several batches wring out in the corner of a towel. There should be about 1½ cups of chopped chard. Set aside.

3. Bring the quart of water to a boil over medium heat, add the remaining salt, then the rice. Cook the rice for about 12 minutes, until just tender. Drain, rinse, and cool the rice.

4. Peel and slice the onion. Heat the oil in a shallow pan and cook the onion gently until it has wilted and is becoming transparent, about 5 minutes. Add the chard, and cook for about 5 minutes, to heat it through and evaporate excess moisture. Add the garlic and cook for only 1 or 2 minutes longer so the garlic doesn't burn. Pour into a bowl and add the cooled rice. Stir in the remaining ingredients in the order listed.

5. Set a rack at the lower third of the oven and preheat to 400 degrees.

6. To make the crust, place half the dough on a lightly floured work surface and scatter flour over it. Roll the dough out into a 11- to 12-inch circle. Fit the dough into the pan and trim away all but ½ inch of the excess dough out over the rim of the pan.

7. Spread the filling in the pan and moisten the overhanging dough with water. Roll the remaining dough into a 10- or 11-inch circle and place over the filling. Press the crusts together at the rim of the pan, then press again around the outer edge of the pan to remove excess dough. Cut several rough slashes in the top crust for vent holes.

8. Bake the tart for 30 to 40 minutes, until the dough is well colored and the filling is set. Cool on a rack.

9. To unmold the tart, stand the tart pan on a large can or canister and allow the side to fall away. Slide the tart from the pan bottom onto a large, flat-bottomed platter.

SERVING: Serve the tart warm or at room temperature.

STORAGE: Keep the tart at room temperature until you are ready to serve it. For longer storage, wrap in plastic and refrigerate for several days. Reheat the tart at 350 degrees for about 20 minutes, and cool slightly before serving.

HINTS FOR SUCCESS: When you are making the dough, mix it only enough to make it smooth, or it will be too elastic and possibly tough.

Be sure to wring out the chard leaves well or the filling will be watery.

VARIATIONS

Substitute spinach for the chard.

Substitute 2 pounds zucchini, grated, salted, drained, rinsed, and sautéed in 2 tablespoons olive oil until limp, for the chard.

LIGURIAN EASTER PIE
(TORTA PASQUALINA)

DOUGH

6 cups unbleached all-purpose flour
2 teaspoons salt
½ cup olive oil
2 cups warm water (110 degrees)

FILLING

12 medium artichokes
¾ cup olive oil
½ cup thinly sliced onion
½ teaspoon salt, plus extra to taste
1 lemon, halved
2 cups fresh breadcrumbs
¾ cup milk
2 pounds ricotta
13 eggs
½ cup plus 2 tablespoons grated Parmesan
Black pepper to taste
2 tablespoons butter

One 12-inch cake pan, 2 inches deep, oiled

ONE 12-INCH-DIAMETER PIE, ABOUT 12 GENEROUS
SERVINGS

This is one of the most unusual of all Italian pastries. A pan is lined with layers of a thinly pulled dough, like strudel dough. Then a rich filling of eggs, ricotta, and artichokes (or chard) is placed over the dough and it is topped with more layers of dough. Traditionally, 33 layers of dough

are used, though many modern versions use only 18 or 24 layers. You may substitute packaged phyllo dough.

1. To make the dough, combine the flour and salt in a mixing bowl. Combine the oil and water and stir in to form a soft dough. Knead until smooth, about 10 minutes. Divide the dough into 12 to 33 pieces and oil each and wrap it separately in plastic wrap. Allow to rest at room temperature for 1 hour.

2. To make the filling, trim the artichokes: with a stainless-steel knife trim the bottoms flat, cutting away any stem. Bend back and pull off all the green outer leaves. When you reach the thin yellow leaves at the center of the artichokes, slice off the tops, leaving about 1 inch of the base and leaves. Cook in boiling salted water until almost tender. Scrape away the chokes and slice the hearts thinly. Heat ¼ cup of the oil in a large pan and cook the onion briefly. Add the artichokes and season with the salt and lemon juice. Allow to cook gently for about 20 minutes. Cool. Soak the breadcrumbs in the milk, then combine with the ricotta, 5 of the eggs, and ½ cup grated Parmesan. Season with salt and pepper and stir in the artichokes.

3. Set a rack at the middle level of the oven and preheat to 350 degrees.

4. Unwrap one of the dough pieces and roll it out as thinly as you can. Pull and stretch the dough into a large circle and line the prepared pan with it. Allow the excess dough to extend up over the edge of the pan. Paint with some of the remaining ½ cup of oil and repeat with half the remaining dough pieces. Pour the filling over the dough in the pan. Make 8 openings in the filling and place a piece of butter and break a whole egg into each. Sprinkle each egg with some of the remaining grated cheese. Cover the filling with the remaining layers of dough. Evenly trim any excess overhanging dough an inch away from the edge of the pan. The excess dough will shrink back while the *torta* is baking.

5. Bake for about 1¼ hours until the pastry is golden and the filling is set (a knife will emerge clean from the center).

SERVING: Serve the *torta* warm or at room temperature, as the main course of a light meal. In Genoa, it is common to find this and other vegetable *torte* served as part of an assortment of *antipasti*. With a salad and a simple dessert it is a perfectly satisfying lunch or supper.

STORAGE: Refrigerate leftovers tightly covered with plastic wrap. Before serving, remove the plastic and reheat briefly, loosely covered with foil, at 350 degrees for about 20 minutes, until just warmed through.

ANN NURSE'S SCALLION TARTS

1 recipe Flaky Dough for Savory Pastries
  (page 98)

FILLING

4 tablespoons olive oil

6 bunches scallions, rinsed and sliced, white part
  only

One 2-ounce can anchovy fillets, drained and
  chopped

½ cup pitted green Italian or Greek olives

Pinch of hot pepper flakes

Egg wash: 1 egg well beaten with a pinch of salt

*Eight to ten 3½- to 4-inch tart pans (see Sources of
Supply), buttered*

ABOUT EIGHT 3- TO 4-INCH TARTS

Cooking teacher and dearest friend Ann Amendolara Nurse serves these wonderful tarts as an appetizer for a light meal. They are absolutely addictive—try them in a smaller size, too, as an hors d'oeuvre.

1. Prepare and chill the dough.

2. To make the filling, heat the olive oil in a heavy sauté pan over a medium flame. Add the scallions and cook slowly until they are limp, about 10 minutes. Drain the scallions in a strainer or colander for 5 minutes. Transfer the scallions to a bowl and gently stir in the remaining filling ingredients.

3. Set a rack at the lowest level of the oven and preheat to 400 degrees.

4. To make the crusts, divide the dough in half, then divide one half into 8 or 10 pieces and on a floured surface roll each out into a thin circle. Use the dough to line the prepared pans. Press the dough well into the pans and roll a rolling pin over the top of each pan to trim away any excess dough. As it is lined, arrange each pan on a jelly-roll pan.

5. Divide the cooled filling among the dough-lined pans and smooth the top of the filling flat. Cut the remaining dough into as many pieces as there are tarts. Roll out and place on the filling in each tart. Sever the excess dough at the rim of each pan and cut a small vent hole in each top crust. Brush the top crusts with the egg wash.

6. Bake the tarts for about 30 minutes, until the crust is baked through and browned. Place the tarts on a rack to cool.

7. Unmold the tarts and arrange them on a platter or pan.

SERVING: Serve the tarts at room temperature or reheat them at 300 degrees for about 5 minutes before you serve them.

STORAGE: Keep the tarts loosely covered, at room temperature, until you serve them. For longer storage, refrigerate the tarts covered with plastic wrap on a pan. Reheat them before serving.

HINT FOR SUCCESS: Be careful not to overcook the scallions or the filling will be dry.

VARIATION

LEEK AND MUSHROOM TARTS: To make the filling, rinse and slice the white part of 1½ pounds leeks. Cook as above, in olive oil over medium heat. Add ¾ pound rinsed and sliced mushrooms, then season with salt and pepper.

Continue cooking for about 10 minutes longer, until the mushroom juices have evaporated substantially. Cool the filling, adjust the seasoning with salt and pepper, and divide among the lined shells. Top the filling in each tart crust with 1 tablespoon coarsely grated Swiss Gruyère. Place the top crusts on and bake as above.

SICILIAN EGGPLANT TARTS

**1 recipe Flaky Dough for Savory Pastries
   (page 98)**

FILLING

1 large (about 2 pounds) eggplant
Salt
4 tablespoons olive oil
1 large (about 8 ounces) onion, chopped
1 clove garlic, minced
**1 cup tomato puree or peeled, seeded, and
   chopped fresh tomatoes**
½ teaspoon sugar
**¼ cup oil-cured olives, pitted and coarsely
   chopped**
2 tablespoons currants
2 tablespoons toasted pine nuts

Egg wash: 1 egg well beaten with a pinch of salt

*Eight to ten 3½- to 4-inch tart pans (see Sources of
Supply), buttered*

ABOUT EIGHT 3- TO 4-INCH TARTS

The filling for these tarts, like the *Sfinciuni*
(page 128), evokes all the flavors of Sicily. Grilled
eggplant is diced and combined with a sharp
sauce of tomatoes, onions, and olives rounded out
with the very Sicilian currants and toasted pine
nuts. These tarts are perfect for a spring lunch.

1. Prepare and chill the dough.

2. To make the filling, peel the eggplant and slice
it about ½ inch thick. Salt the slices and place
them in a colander. Cover with a small plate and a
weight, such as a heavy can of tomatoes, and
allow to drain.

3. Preheat the broiler and place the broiler pan
about 2 inches from the heating element. Lightly
brush the eggplant slices with half the oil and grill
them for about 2 minutes on each side. Cool and
dice the eggplant.

4. Heat the remaining oil in a heavy sauté pan
over a medium flame. Add the onion and cook
slowly until it's limp, about 10 minutes. Add the
garlic, tomatoes, and sugar and continue cooking
for about 10 minutes, until the sauce is somewhat
reduced. Add the cooled, diced eggplant, the
olives, currants, and pine nuts and remove from
the heat. Adjust the seasoning with salt and
pepper. Cool the filling.

5. Set a rack at the lowest level of the oven and
preheat to 400 degrees.

6. To make the crusts, divide the dough in half
and divide one half into 8 or 10 pieces and on a
floured surface roll each out into a thin circle.
Use the dough to line the prepared pans,
pressing it well into the pans and rolling a rolling
pin over the tops of the pans to trim off the excess
dough. As it is lined, arrange each pan on a jelly-
roll pan.

7. Divide the cooled filling among the
dough-lined pans and smooth the top of the

filling flat. Cut the remaining dough into as many pieces as there are tarts. Roll out and place on the filling in each tart. Sever the excess dough at the rim of each pan and cut a small vent hole in each top crust. Brush the top crusts with the egg wash.

8. Bake the tarts for about 30 minutes, until the crust is baked through and browned. Place the tarts on a rack to cool.

9. Unmold the tarts and arrange them on a platter or pan.

SERVING: Serve the tarts at room temperature or reheat them at 300 degrees for about 5 minutes before serving.

STORAGE: Keep the tarts loosely covered at room temperature until you serve them. For longer storage, refrigerate the tarts covered with plastic wrap on a pan. Reheat them before serving.

HINT FOR SUCCESS: Make sure the eggplant is well drained or it will make the filling too pungent.

SCOTTISH MINCE PIES

**1 recipe Flaky Dough for Savory Pastries
(page 98)**

FILLING

1 pound lean ground lamb
1 teaspoon salt
½ teaspoon freshly ground black pepper
⅛ teaspoon freshly grated nutmeg
4 tablespoons water

Egg wash: 1 egg well beaten with a pinch of salt

*Eight to ten 3½- to 4-inch tart pans (see Sources of
Supply), buttered*

ABOUT EIGHT 3- TO 4-INCH TARTS

Variously called "Scotch pies" or "mutton pies," these are made from lean ground lamb simply seasoned with salt, pepper, and a dash of nutmeg. I remember tasting these for the first time in my teens, at the home of my late childhood friend, Noel Giles. The Gileses always made special pilgrimages to Kearny, New Jersey, where several butchers supplied specialties such as these pies to a thriving Scottish community there. The Gileses always served the pies with a bit of a bottled British condiment called HP Sauce, a little like American steak sauce, poured on the plate next to the pie.

These are great for a quick, informal meal—followed by a salad and fresh fruit.

1. Prepare and chill the dough.

2. To make the filling, combine all the ingredients in a mixing bowl.

3. To make the crusts, divide the dough in half, then divide one half into 8 or 10 pieces, and on a floured surface roll each to a thin circle. Use the dough to line the prepared pans, pressing it into the pans and rolling the top of each pan with a rolling pin to trim the excess dough. As each is lined, arrange the pans on a jelly-roll pan.

4. Divide the filling among the dough-lined pans and smooth the top of the filling flat. Cut the remaining dough into as many pieces as there are tarts. Roll out and place on the filling in each tart. Sever the excess dough at the rim of each pan and cut a small vent hole in each top crust. Brush the top crusts with the egg wash. Refrigerate the pies until 1 hour before baking.

5. About 20 minutes before baking, set a rack at the lowest level of the oven and preheat to 400 degrees.

6. Bake the tarts for about 30 minutes, until the crust is baked through and browned. Place the tarts on a rack to cool.

7. Unmold the tarts and arrange them on a platter or pan.

SERVING: Serve the tarts at room temperature or reheat them at 300 degrees for about 5 minutes before serving.

STORAGE: Keep the tarts loosely covered at room temperature until you serve. For longer storage, refrigerate on a pan, covered with plastic wrap. Reheat before you serve.

CHEDDAR SHORTBREADS

8 tablespoons (1 stick) unsalted butter
4 ounces sharp cheddar cheese (about 1 cup
    coarsely grated)
½ teaspoon salt
½ teaspoon dry mustard
½ teaspoon Hungarian paprika
1 cup unbleached all-purpose flour

Two jelly-roll pans, or cookie sheets, lined with
parchment paper

ABOUT 36 COOKIES

These delightful savory cookies make a good accompaniment to a glass of wine and are easy to prepare. The cheese can be varied, so long as you don't substitute too soft or hard a cheese.

1. Cut the butter into 10 or 12 pieces and place in a food processor. Grate the cheese coarsely and add to the processor. Pulse until well mixed but be careful not to overmix and soften the butter too much. Add the salt, mustard, and paprika and pulse to mix them in.

2. Add the flour to the processor and pulse until the butter and cheese have absorbed all the flour. Remove the dough from the bowl to a lightly floured work surface and press it together.

3. Roll into a cylinder about 2 inches in diameter. Wrap in plastic wrap and refrigerate until firm.

4. Preheat the oven to 350 degrees about 20 minutes before baking.

5. Cut the cylinders of dough into ¼-inch slices and arrange them about 1 inch apart on the prepared pans.

6. Bake for about 15 minutes, until pale golden. Remove and cool on a rack.

SERVING: Serve the shortbreads with drinks.

STORAGE: The shortbreads keep well at room temperature in an airtight container, such as a tin. Or arrange them between layers of wax paper and freeze for storage longer than a few days.

HINT FOR SUCCESS: Do not overprocess the dough, or it will be too soft to work with.

VARIATIONS

Substitute Gruyère, Gouda, or any firm—but not dry—cheese for the cheddar. Blue-veined cheeses turn the dough an unappetizing color and are not recommended.

For a shape variation, roll the chilled dough on a lightly floured surface and cut into shapes with a 2-inch cutter.

FOCACCIA, PIZZA, AND CALZONE

Focaccia, pizza, and calzone are among the most popular preparations made from yeast-risen dough.

Focaccia, Italian flatbread, is nothing more than flour, water, yeast, salt, and a little oil—added both for flavor and to make handling easy. Most *focacce* (the plural) are usually no more than an inch thick, and round or rectangular in shape. They are served as an accompaniment to a meal, or, especially the rectangle, split to make sandwiches.

Typically, a focaccia is baked with a topping, often just a drizzling of olive oil and a sprinkling of coarse salt. More elaborate toppings include fresh and/or dried herbs, sautéed onions, slivers of garlic, anchovies, cooked mushrooms, and even chopped tomatoes. Toppings are to flavor and enhance the focaccia and are never applied as generously as the toppings for a pizza. That is the principal difference between the two breads. Although a focaccia is usually thicker than a pizza, there are thick-crusted focaccia-like pizzas.

Pizza, of course, needs very little explanation. According to *Pizza Today* magazine, Americans purchased approximately 30 billion pizzas in 1991! Having been raised in an Italian-American home, I developed very definite tastes in pizza and believe many American pizzas have too much topping (especially mozzarella, which makes the pizza gooey and too rich). Pizzas would be immeasurably improved if the bakers were invited on a short trip to Naples, where pizzerias originated in the second quarter of the nineteenth century. In fact, the famous pizzeria of Port'Alba, opened in 1830, is still in business.

A typical Neapolitan pizza (*pizza alla Napoletana*) is about 12 inches in diameter and is served as an individual portion. The crust is thin and crisp, and the toppings are as simple or as elaborate as the imagination of the maker, though they never overpower nor overburden the dough.

In Italy, pizzas are usually baked in a wood-burning oven, and the high temperature and scent of the wood ash give the pizza a quickly baked, crisp texture and a special smoky flavor. Diners gather at pizzerias or restaurant/pizzerias for an evening meal of either thin-crusted pizza, or the thick-crusted variety, typical of Rome, which is similar to a focaccia but has more topping. These thick-crusted pizzas are baked in large rectangular pans and sold by the piece in many Roman pizzerias. This type of pizza also is often prepared at home, because the bread dough can be purchased at the local bakery or made easily from scratch.

What Americans call "Sicilian pizza," thick-crusted and generously covered with cheese, tomato sauce, et cetera, is a creation of the American pizza industry and does not exist in Sicily. But its ancestor is probably a kind of focaccia called *sfinciuni,* with a typically Sicilian topping of breadcrumbs, onions, anchovies, and just a bit of tomato.

The same dough that makes thin-crusted Neapolitan pizza is also used for calzone or a large turnover, originally a specialty of Naples. Though *calzoni* (the plural) may be filled with a great variety of foods, alone or in combination, they most often contain ricotta or other soft cheese.

In this section you will find recipes for different focacce and pizzas as well as for regional dough specialties, such as calzone and *sfinciuni* from Italy, and *pissaladière* and *socca* from the south of France.

EASY ITALIAN FOCACCIA

1⅓ cups warm tap water (about 110 degrees)
2½ teaspoons (1 envelope) active dry yeast
6 tablespoons olive oil
3¼ cups unbleached all-purpose flour
2 teaspoons salt
1 teaspoon kosher or coarse salt

One 10½ × 15½-inch jelly-roll pan, or a 14-inch round pan, plus a second pan of the same size or larger to insulate the first pan if the bottom of the focaccia begins to brown too quickly

ONE 10½ × 15½-INCH RECTANGULAR OR 14-INCH ROUND FOCACCIA, ENOUGH FOR 4 TO 6 SERVINGS

If you're pressed for time but still would like to serve a homemade bread, try this focaccia. Though you can't skimp on the rising time, the mixing and shaping require so little work that the focaccia practically makes itself.

Mix the focaccia in the morning, then let it rise in the refrigerator all day. At the end of the day (or whenever you need to bake it) press the dough onto the oiled pan and let it rise before baking it.

A plain focaccia such as this one makes a great accompaniment to first courses or to an entire meal; one with a topping is an excellent hors d'oeuvre to serve with drinks.

1. Measure the water into a bowl and whisk in the yeast and 3 tablespoons of the oil. Measure the flour and 2 teaspoons salt into a mixing bowl and stir well to combine. With a rubber spatula

or wooden spoon, stir the yeast mixture into the flour mixture until all the flour is evenly moistened, then beat vigorously for a minute. Cover the bowl with plastic wrap and allow the dough to rise at room temperature until doubled in bulk, about 1 hour.

2. Spread 1½ tablespoons of the remaining oil on the baking pan. Turn the dough out of the bowl onto the pan and pat and press until the dough fills the pan completely. If the dough resists, let it rest for a few minutes before continuing. Cover the dough with a piece of oiled plastic wrap (oiled side down) and allow it to rise again until doubled, up to 1 hour.

3. Set a rack in the lower third of the oven and preheat to 450 degrees.

4. Dimple the surface of the risen focaccia by using your fingertip to poke cavities in the dough at 2-inch intervals. Drizzle with the remaining 1½ tablespoons of oil and sprinkle with the kosher or coarse salt.

5. Bake the focaccia for about 25 minutes, or until deep golden. Lift the side of the focaccia with a spatula or pancake turner and check the bottom about halfway through baking time. If it is getting too dark, slide the pan onto another pan to insulate the bottom.

6. To serve immediately, slide the focaccia from the pan to a cutting board. If it will be served later, slide it off the pan onto a rack to cool.

SERVING: Cut narrow slices or squares to split horizontally for sandwiches.

STORAGE: Keep the focaccia loosely covered at room temperature, if it will be served on the day it is made. For longer storage, wrap in plastic and freeze. Unwrap and reheat the focaccia for about 7 minutes at 375 degrees.

HINT FOR SUCCESS: When pressing the dough into the pan, keep the thickness even.

VARIATIONS

HERB FOCACCIA: Sprinkle the top of the focaccia with 2 or 3 tablespoons of such coarsely chopped fresh herbs as rosemary, thyme, or sage, immediately before baking.

SAGE OR ROSEMARY FOCACCIA: Insert a leaf of fresh sage or sprig of rosemary into each cavity when you press the dimples into the dough.

ONION FOCACCIA: Peel and thinly slice 2 medium yellow onions, about 4 or 5 ounces each, and cook them in 3 tablespoons olive oil in a sauté pan, covered, for about 20 minutes, until they just begin to color slightly. Season the onions with salt and pepper and cool. Spread the onions on the risen focaccia and sprinkle with ½ teaspoon dried oregano.

ONION AND GARLIC FOCACCIA: Add 2 peeled and thinly sliced cloves garlic to the onions before cooking them.

TOMATO AND OLIVE FOCACCIA: Scatter 1 cup seeded, chopped, and drained canned plum tomatoes on the risen focaccia. Sprinkle with salt; pepper; oregano; 2 or 3 tablespoons of halved and pitted oil-cured olives; and 1 clove garlic, sliced into paper-thin shreds.

ROSEMARY FOCACCIA

1 cup warm tap water (about 110 degrees)

2½ teaspoons (1 envelope) active dry yeast

6 tablespoons olive oil

5 cups unbleached all-purpose flour

2 teaspoons salt

**2 tablespoons chopped fresh rosemary, or
1 tablespoon dried, plus rosemary sprigs
(optional)**

1 cup milk

1 teaspoon kosher or coarse salt

*One 11 × 17-inch jelly-roll pan, plus a second pan
of the same size or larger to insulate the first pan if
the bottom of the focaccia begins to brown too quickly*

ONE 11 × 17-INCH FOCACCIA, 4 TO 6 SERVINGS

This differs in two ways from the preceding recipe: it makes a slightly larger focaccia and it uses milk as part of the liquid, which makes for a moister dough. Adding the herbs directly to the dough gives the focaccia more flavor.

1. Measure the water into a bowl and whisk in the yeast, then 3 tablespoons of the oil. Measure the flour, 2 teaspoons salt, and chopped or dried rosemary into a mixing bowl and stir well to combine. With a spatula or wooden spoon, stir the yeast mixture and the milk into the flour mixture until all the flour is evenly moistened, then beat vigorously for a minute. Cover the bowl with plastic wrap and allow the dough to rise until it has doubled in bulk, about 1 hour.

2. Spread 1½ teaspoons of the oil on the baking pan. Turn the dough out of the bowl onto the pan and pat and press it to fill the pan completely. If the dough resists, let it rest for a few minutes before continuing. Dimple the surface of the focaccia by using a fingertip to poke cavities in the dough at 2-inch intervals. Drizzle with the remaining 1½ tablespoons of oil and sprinkle with the kosher or coarse salt and the rosemary sprigs. Allow the dough to rise again until doubled in bulk, about an hour.

3. About 20 minutes before baking, set a rack at the lower third of the oven and preheat to 450 degrees.

4. Bake the focaccia for about 25 minutes, until deep golden. Lift the side of the focaccia with a spatula or pancake turner to check the bottom about halfway through the baking time. If it is coloring too quickly, slide the pan onto another pan to insulate the bottom.

5. If you are serving immediately, slide the focaccia from the pan onto a cutting board. If you will be serving later, slide the focaccia off the pan to a rack to cool.

SERVING: Cut narrow slices, or squares to split horizontally for sandwiches.

STORAGE: Keep the focaccia loosely covered at room temperature if it will be served on the day it is made. For longer storage, wrap in plastic and freeze. Unwrap and reheat the focaccia on the pan used to bake it for about 7 minutes at 375 degrees.

SFINCIUNI

DOUGH

3¼ cups unbleached all-purpose flour
2 teaspoons salt
1⅓ cups warm tap water (about 110 degrees)
2½ teaspoons (1 envelope) active dry yeast
3 tablespoons olive oil

TOPPINGS

4 tablespoons olive oil
1 medium (about 6 ounces) onion, thinly sliced
One 2-ounce can anchovies packed in olive oil,
  drained and cut into ½-inch pieces
½ cup tomato puree
1 cup finely grated Caciocavallo cheese, or ½ cup
  finely grated Pecorino Romano
¾ cup fine dry breadcrumbs

One 10½ × 15½-inch jelly-roll pan, plus a second pan of the same size or larger to insulate the bottom of the pan, if necessary

ONE 10½ × 15½-INCH SFINCIUNI, ABOUT 6 SERVINGS
AS AN HORS D'OEUVRE OR SNACK

This Sicilian hybrid of focaccia and pizza is a popular street food in Palermo's famous Vucciria market. Though many variations exist, this recipe contains all the essentials: anchovies, onions, tomato, breadcrumbs, and Caciocavallo cheese.

1. To make the dough, place the flour and salt in a 2-quart mixing bowl and stir well to mix; make a well in the center. Measure the water and pour it into a small bowl. Whisk in the yeast, then 2 tablespoons of the olive oil. Pour the liquid mixture into the well in the flour and stir with a rubber spatula until it forms a soft, sticky dough. Beat the dough for a minute, until it looks smoother. Cover the bowl tightly with plastic wrap and allow the dough to rise until it is doubled in bulk, about 1 hour.

2. Grease the baking pan with the remaining tablespoon of oil. Without stirring or folding the dough, use a rubber spatula to scrape it from the bowl onto the oiled pan. Oil your hands and press, pull, and pat the dough into the pan. If it resists, let it rest for 5 minutes, then continue. Cover the dough with a sheet of oiled plastic wrap. Let the dough rise for about 30 minutes, or until it puffs slightly.

3. Set a rack at the lowest level of the oven and preheat to 450 degrees.

4. For the toppings, heat 2 tablespoons of the olive oil in a sauté pan. Add the onion slices and cook over a low heat until they are limp, about 10 minutes. Add the anchovies and cook for 2 more minutes. Add the tomato puree and cook until the sauce is somewhat thickened, about 5 minutes longer. Allow to cool.

5. When the dough is risen, spread with the sauce. Sprinkle on the remaining ingredients in the order listed, ending with the breadcrumbs. Drizzle the remaining 2 tablespoons of oil over the toppings.

6. Bake the *sfinciuni* for about 30 minutes, until it is well risen and the top surface is fairly dry.

7. Cool to room temperature in the pan on a rack.

SERVING: Serve the *sfinciuni* as an hors d'oeuvre with drinks or as a lunch dish.

STORAGE: Keep the *sfinciuni* loosely covered at room temperature until it is served. Refrigerate or freeze leftovers wrapped in plastic or foil. Unwrap and bring to room temperature before serving.

HINT FOR SUCCESS: Make sure that the surface of the *sfinciuni* is fairly dry before removing it from the oven. If the *sfinciuni* seems baked through but the top is still wet, move it to the top rack of the oven for 5 minutes.

❖

GRILLED PIZZA

Grilled pizza is one of the most popular items at Al Forno, Johanne Killeen and George Germon's charming restaurant in Providence, Rhode Island. In their book *Cucina Simpatica* (HarperCollins, 1991), they give detailed instructions for preparing pizza their way. My method is simplified using a partially baked pizza crust on a covered charcoal or gas grill.

To grill any of the thick- or thin-crusted pizzas in this chapter, allow the dough to rise in the pan and bake it on the middle rack of a preheated 450 degree oven, without the toppings, for about 10 minutes, until the dough is set and no longer sticky. Brush oil on the surface of the dough and immediately turn the dough out of the pan onto a preheated grill. Cook for 2 to 3 minutes, or until well colored. Turn the dough back over on the grill and quickly place the toppings on the already grilled side. Cover with a tent of foil or the lid of the grill and cook for 5 minutes longer. Serve immediately.

SOCCA

1 cup chick-pea flour
1 teaspoon salt
1½ cups warm water (110 degrees)
4 tablespoons olive oil

One 10½ × 15½-inch jelly-roll pan

ONE 10½ × 15½-INCH PAN OF SOCCA, ENOUGH FOR
ABOUT 6 SERVINGS

This primitive focaccia, rather like a pancake made with chick-pea flour, is a common dish in Nice and Monaco. When it appears in parts of Tuscany and on the Ligurian coast near Genoa, it is known as *la farinata*. My favorite place in Nice for *socca* is Chez René (see Pissaladière Niçoise, page 136); in Monaco, I always enjoy it in the covered market in Monte Carlo where it is made by two aged men known to everyone simply as *les frères socca*. This recipe is loosely adapted from one published in *From Julia Child's Kitchen* (Alfred A. Knopf, 1975).

Chick-pea flour is available in both Italian and Indian grocery stores and in some health food stores. Or see Sources of Supply at the end of this book.

1. Set a rack at both the highest and lowest levels of the oven and preheat it to 450 degrees.

2. Combine the chick-pea flour and salt in a mixing bowl and stir to mix well. Add the water all at once and whisk in smoothly. Check the batter for lumps; if necessary, strain through a medium-fine strainer. Cover the bowl loosely and allow the batter to rest at room temperature for at least 1 hour to soften the granules of chick-pea flour. Whisk in 2 tablespoons of the oil.

3. Use the remaining 2 tablespoons of oil to grease the pan, then place the pan in the oven for about 2 minutes, until the oil is hot, but not smoking. Remove the hot pan from the oven and place it on the stove top. Bring the bowl close to the top of the pan and pour the batter onto the pan. Spread the batter to even it with a metal spatula. Quickly return the pan to the lower rack.

4. Bake the *socca* for about 10 minutes, until it appears dry and set. Move the *socca* to the higher rack and bake for about 5 minutes longer, until it colors lightly.

SERVING: Cut the *socca* immediately into 1 × 2-inch shreds, and serve as finger food to be eaten from a small plate or napkin. Have plenty of paper napkins available for greasy fingers. Because it tends to be a bit sloppy to eat, *socca* is best served with drinks for a very informal occasion.

HINT FOR SUCCESS: Don't skimp on the time for resting the batter, or the *socca* will have a grainy texture.

HOME-STYLE PIZZA

DOUGH

2½ cups unbleached all-purpose flour

1 teaspoon salt

1 cup warm tap water (about 110 degrees)

2½ teaspoons (1 envelope) active dry yeast

3 tablespoons olive oil

TOPPING

One 28-ounce can plum tomatoes

¼ cup coarsely grated mozzarella

¼ cup finely grated Parmesan or Romano cheese

1 clove garlic, cut into thin slices

1 teaspoon dried oregano

3 tablespoons olive oil

One 10½ × 15½-inch jelly-roll pan, plus a second pan of the same size or larger to insulate the bottom of the pan if the bottom of the pizza begins to brown too quickly

ONE 10½ × 15½-INCH PIZZA, ABOUT 4 GENEROUS SERVINGS

This is the quick and easy way to prepare pizza that I remember my grandmother using for birthdays and other special family occasions. Both the thickness of the crust and the toppings are typically southern Italian. It will not be easily recognizable to those used to designer pizza, American pizzeria pizza, or so-called Sicilian pizza. The topping is simple: crushed tomatoes (not a cooked sauce), grated Parmesan or Romano cheese, a little mozzarella, olive oil, a few slivers of garlic, and a dash of oregano.

1. For the dough, stir the flour and salt in a 2-quart mixing bowl to combine; make a well in the center. Measure the water and pour it into a small bowl; whisk in the yeast, then 2 tablespoons of the olive oil. Pour the liquid mixture into the well in the flour and stir with a rubber spatula until a soft, sticky dough forms. Beat the dough for a minute, until it looks smoother. Cover the bowl tightly with plastic wrap and allow the dough to rise until it is doubled in bulk, about 1 hour.

2. Grease the jelly-roll pan with the remaining tablespoon of oil. Without stirring or folding the dough, use a rubber spatula to scrape it from the bowl into the oiled pan. Oil your hands and press, pull, and pat the dough into the pan. If it resists, let it rest for 5 minutes, then continue. Let the dough rise for about 30 minutes, or until it puffs slightly, while you prepare the topping.

3. Set a rack at the lowest and highest levels of the oven and preheat to 450 degrees.

4. For the topping, drain the plum tomatoes and reserve the juice for soup or a pasta sauce. Squeeze the tomatoes to extract the seeds and excess liquid, then chop them coarsely. Place the chopped tomatoes in a strainer or colander to drain while you gather the remaining ingredients. Scatter the tomatoes evenly over the surface of the dough. Then, one at a time, evenly scatter on the remaining ingredients, ending with the oil.

5. Bake the pizza on the bottom rack of the oven for about 25 to 30 minutes. After about 10

minutes, lift an end with a metal spatula to check that the bottom is not burning. If the bottom is coloring too quickly, slide another pan under the first one. If the color is a light golden, check the bottom again after another 10 minutes. When the pizza is done, the top should be sizzling gently, the cheese melted and a deep golden color, and the bottom a dark brown. If the top has not colored sufficiently when the bottom is done, place the pizza on the top rack of the oven for an additional 5 minutes.

SERVING: Cut the pizza into large slabs with a pizza wheel or serrated knife.

STORAGE: Serve immediately. Wrap leftovers in plastic and refrigerate; this type of pizza reheats very well in a toaster oven.

HINT FOR SUCCESS: Be sure that the oven has preheated sufficiently before you bake the pizza. There is nothing worse than a pizza with an underdone crust.

❖

PIZZA STONES

Pizza stones, which are now widely available in kitchenware and department stores, simulate the effect of a real pizza oven. There the bottom of the crust rests directly on the hearth, which eliminates any possibility of an underdone bottom and ensures even crispness. The pizza stone, which is really a large unglazed ceramic tile, should be placed on the bottom rack of the oven and allowed to heat at 450 degrees for 30 to 60 minutes before you bake the pizza. In some ovens the bottom rack will make the stone too hot—experiment with a couple of crusts before deciding which rack you want to place the stone on.

If you are using a pizza stone, sprinkle a piece of stiff cardboard or a wooden peel (a flat, thin wooden shovel made especially for loading the oven with pizzas) with cornmeal or semolina. Instead of placing the dough in a pan, place the formed crust on the cardboard or peel and allow to rise or not, according to the particular recipe. Add toppings and poise the cardboard or peel over the stone. Then, with a sharp, deft backward pull, slide the pizza onto the stone. The cornmeal or semolina will provide the traction to make this easy. The heat retained by the stone accelerates the baking process, so begin checking the pizza for doneness after about 15 minutes.

NEAPOLITAN PIZZA

(PIZZA NAPOLETANA)

3 cups unbleached all-purpose flour
2 teaspoons salt
1¼ cups warm tap water (about 110 degrees)
2½ teaspoons (1 envelope) active dry yeast
4 tablespoons olive oil

TOPPINGS

2 cups chopped, well-drained canned tomatoes
4 tablespoons finely grated Parmesan or
    Pecorino Romano
1 teaspoon dried oregano
4 tablespoons olive oil

Two 12-inch or 14-inch round pizza pans

TWO ROUND PIZZAS, EACH ABOUT 12 INCHES IN DIAMETER

I always linger at pizzerias to watch the pizza maker stretching the dough. The more theatrical toss the dough above their heads or twirl it on a fingertip and generally make the process look a lot more difficult than it is. All that is necessary is to pull and stretch the dough into an evenly thin disk with a slightly thicker half-inch border. The process described below may sound long, but it only takes a minute or two to accomplish.

Use this dough for a thin-crusted pizzeria-style pizza. If you double this recipe to make 2 pizzas, do not double the quantity of yeast.

1. Place the flour and salt in a 2-quart mixing bowl and stir well to combine; make a well in the center.

2. Measure the water and pour it into a small bowl. Sprinkle the yeast on the surface of the water and leave it to soften for 3 or 4 minutes. Whisk the yeast and water together, then whisk in 1 tablespoon of the oil.

3. Pour the liquid mixture into the well in the flour and stir with a rubber spatula to form a soft, sticky dough.

4. Turn the dough out on a floured work surface. Knead the dough gently, folding it over on itself, and scraping it off the surface with a spatula or plastic scraper if it is very sticky. Avoid adding more flour to the dough—that will produce a tough pizza. Knead for about 5 minutes, until the dough is smooth and no longer so sticky.

5. Rinse and dry the bowl. Spread 1 tablespoon of oil all around the inside of the bowl. Form the dough into a ball and place in the bowl. Turn the ball upside down, so that the top surface of the dough is oiled, and cover the bowl with plastic wrap. Allow the dough to rise at room temperature for about 1 hour, or until the dough has doubled in bulk. For advance preparation, cover and refrigerate the dough for several hours or even overnight.

6. To form the pizza crusts, generously flour the work surface. Flour your hands and scrape the dough from the bowl in one piece, without stretching or folding it. Place the dough on the floured work surface so that what was on top in the bowl is now underneath. Divide the dough in half using a knife or scraper. Scatter a tablespoon or so of flour over the dough and press down on each piece of dough with the palm of your hand. Be careful to keep the dough an even disk shape. If the dough is freshly made, it may resist slightly. Should that happen, cover it with plastic wrap and allow it to rest for about 5 minutes, then resume the process. If the dough has been rested for a long time either in the refrigerator or at room temperature, it will respond easily.

7. Form your right hand into a fist and begin to press the dough in a circle, about ½ inch in from the edge of the dough, with the middle joints of your fingers (as though knocking on a door). Pull gently with your other hand on the edge of the dough, opposite where the dough is being pressed. Continue around the crust 2 or 3 times in this manner to flatten and widen it.

8. Pour the remaining 2 tablespoons of olive oil onto the pizza pan and spread it with the palm of one hand. Fold the crust in half and transfer it to the oiled pan. Unfold the dough and press it into place in the pan with the palms of both hands, gently stretching the dough from the center outward. If the dough resists, cover with plastic wrap and allow it to rest for about 5 minutes, then resume the process. Repeat with the other piece of dough.

9. When the dough is properly stretched, it should be about ⅛ inch thick and have a ½-inch-wide border which is slightly thicker.

10. Set racks at the lowest and highest levels of the oven and preheat to 450 degrees.

11. Place toppings on the pizza in the order given. Bake the pizza on the bottom rack of the oven for about 30 minutes. After about 10 minutes, lift an end of the pizza with a metal spatula to check that the bottom is not burning. If the bottom is coloring too quickly, slide another pan under the first one. If the bottom is light golden, check again after another 10 minutes. When the pizza is done, the top should be sizzling gently, and the bottom a dark brown. If the top has not colored sufficiently when the bottom is done, place the pizza on the top rack of the oven for an additional 5 minutes.

SERVING: Cut the pizza into wedges with a pizza wheel or serrated knife.

STORAGE: Serve immediately. If the pizza has to wait, the crust may become soggy and reheating may make it hard rather than crisp.

HINT FOR SUCCESS: Be sure that the oven has preheated sufficiently before putting in the pizza. A pizza with an underdone crust is very unappetizing.

VARIATIONS

PIZZA MARGHERITA: This pizza was invented in 1889 by Neapolitan *pizzaiolo* Raffaele Esposito and named for Queen Margherita of Italy. The pizza echoes the colors of the flag of the newly united Italy: red (tomatoes), white (mozzarella), and green (basil). It is perfect in summer when fresh, perfectly ripe tomatoes and basil are in season. If you use fresh tomatoes, you will need about 2 pounds, perfectly ripe, either round or plum, for 2 pizzas. Plunge them into boiling water for half a minute, remove, and peel them. Halve the tomatoes and squeeze out the seeds, then chop and drain the pulp.

Sprinkle 4 tablespoons coarsely chopped fresh basil on the pizzas before adding the tomatoes and 2 tablespoons olive oil. Sprinkle the pizzas with 1 cup shredded mozzarella.

PIZZA NUDA: This is really a focaccia, but it is made with the crust for *pizza Napoletana.* Bake the pizza crust with a drizzle of oil and a sprinkling of coarse salt. The result will be thin and delicate, somewhat like a thick flour tortilla in flavor and texture.

ALTERNATIVE TOPPINGS FOR PIZZAS

Though I am partial to a typically Italian tomato and mozzarella pizza topping, there are many alternatives. The following should inspire you on to create your own favorite pizzas, either the thick- or thin-crusted variety. Remember, though: too much of any topping makes for a wet and soggy pizza, no matter how long it is baked.

Each is for 2 round pizzas:

1. Two cups coarsely grated assorted cheeses, such as Gruyère, Fontina, Gorgonzola, or Roquefort (crumbled), and Parmesan, plus a drizzle of 2 tablespoons olive oil.

2. Two cups roasted peppers cut into thin strips, plus a drizzle of 2 tablespoons olive oil, a thinly sliced clove of garlic, and a sprinkling of 1 or 2 tablespoons grated Parmesan.

3. Substitute 1 cup crumbled mild goat cheese for the Parmesan with the roasted peppers, above.

PISSALADIÈRE NIÇOISE

DOUGH

2 cups unbleached all-purpose flour

1 teaspoon salt

¾ cup plus 2 tablespoons warm tap water (about 110 degrees)

2½ teaspoons (1 envelope) active dry yeast

3 tablespoons olive oil

FILLING

6 medium onions (about 1½ pounds total)

3 tablespoons olive oil

Salt and pepper

One 2-ounce can anchovies packed in olive oil

⅔ cup pitted oil-cured black olives or Niçoise olives

One 10½ × 15½-inch jelly-roll pan

ONE 10½ × 15½-INCH PISSALADIÈRE, ENOUGH FOR 4 TO 6 SERVINGS

Pissaladière, a Provençal tart, is a classic of Niçoise cooking. Pissaladière is available throughout the historic le vieux Nice. Old Nice, with narrow, winding streets that haven't changed much in the last hundred years, still retains the scents and appearance of a crowded nineteenth-century working-class neighborhood where the residents gather daily in the various stores to buy the day's provisions. I usually buy my pissaladière, as well as *socca*, the chick-pea flour focaccia (page 130), at Chez René, an open-air restaurant on the Rue Peyrolière.

This version is adapted from the somewhat sketchy instructions in *La Véritable Cuisine Provençale et Niçoise* (The Real Cooking of Provence and Nice), Jean-Noël Escudier's Bible of southern French food. (Published in English by Harper & Row, 1988, as *The Wonderful Food of Provence,* by Escudier and Peta J. Fuller and now out of print, it is worth searching for in secondhand bookstores and old book catalogues.)

1. For the dough, in a 2-quart mixing bowl stir the flour and salt well to combine; make a well in the center. Measure the water and pour it into a small bowl; whisk in the yeast, then 2 tablespoons of the olive oil. Pour the liquid mixture into the well in the flour and stir with a rubber spatula to form a soft, sticky dough. Beat the dough for a minute, until it becomes smoother. Cover the bowl tightly with plastic wrap and allow the dough to rise until it doubles in bulk, up to 1 hour.

2. For the filling, peel, halve, and slice the onions about ⅛ inch thick. Heat the oil in a sauté pan or skillet over a medium flame and add the onions. Salt and pepper the onions lightly and cook until the onions begin to sizzle. Lower the heat, cover the pan, and cook, checking and stirring often, for about 30 minutes. The onions should be reduced almost to a puree. Uncover the pan and continue to cook for about 5 minutes longer, until the onions are fairly dry. Pour the onions from the pan to a plate to cool.

3. Set a rack at the lowest level of the oven and preheat to 450 degrees.

4. To assemble the pissaladière, grease the pan with the remaining tablespoon of oil from the dough. In one piece, without folding the dough, turn it onto a generously floured work surface. Flour the dough and pat it into a rough rectangle with the palms of your hands. Then use a rolling pin to roll it into a rectangle about 12 × 16 inches. If the dough resists, cover it with plastic wrap and allow it to rest for 5 minutes before continuing. Fold the dough in half and transfer it to the pan. Unfold the dough and press it firmly into the bottom and against the sides of the pan. Pierce the dough with a fork at 2-inch intervals.

5. Spread the onion puree evenly over the dough. Drain and halve the anchovies and scatter them and the olives evenly over the onion puree.

6. Bake the pissaladière for about 30 minutes, until the dough is golden and the filling still appears moist.

7. Cool in the pan on a rack.

SERVING: Serve the pissaladière on the day it is baked, at a picnic, as a first course, or as an hors d'oeuvre. A chilled rosé de Provence is a perfect wine to accompany this dish.

STORAGE: Keep the pissaladière loosely covered, in the baking pan, at room temperature, until it is served. Wrap leftovers in plastic or foil and refrigerate. Bring to room temperature before serving again.

HINT FOR SUCCESS: Be patient about both cooking the onions and rolling the dough as thinly as necessary. Neither process benefits from being rushed.

VARIATION

Chop the anchovies and stir them into the cooked onions. If you've bought salted anchovies, soak and rinse them before using.

SANDY LEONARD'S POTATO PIZZA

DOUGH

2½ cups unbleached all-purpose flour
1 teaspoon salt
1 cup warm tap water (110 degrees)
2½ teaspoons (1 envelope) active dry yeast
3 tablespoons olive oil

TOPPING

1½ pounds waxy boiling potatoes
3 tablespoons olive oil
Salt and pepper
2 teaspoons chopped fresh rosemary, or
    1 teaspoon dried
3 tablespoons grated Parmesan cheese

One 10½ × 15½-inch jelly-roll pan, plus a second pan of the same size or larger to insulate the bottom of the first pan if the pizza begins to brown too quickly

ONE 10½ × 15½-INCH PIZZA, ABOUT 4 GENEROUS SERVINGS

My friend Sandy Leonard, the most dedicated consumer and maker of potato pizza I know, first became enamored of this variety at Pizzeria Da Pasquale on Via de' Prefetti in Rome. He then went to great lengths to reproduce the pizza at his home in Cambridge, Massachusetts. He once went so far as to smuggle in an entire potato pizza as well as several kilos of Italian potatoes.

This pizza makes a perfect main course and needs only a green salad and some fresh fruit for dessert to complete the menu.

1. For the dough, in a 2-quart mixing bowl stir the flour and salt well to combine; make a well in the center. Measure the water and pour it into a small bowl, whisk in the yeast, then 2 tablespoons of the olive oil. Pour the liquid mixture into the well in the flour and stir with a rubber spatula until it forms a soft, sticky dough. Beat the dough for a minute, until it looks smoother. Cover the bowl tightly with plastic wrap and allow the dough to rise until it is doubled in bulk, up to 1 hour.

2. For the topping, rinse the potatoes and place in a shallow pan that has a tight-fitting cover. Cover the potatoes with water and bring to a rolling boil over medium heat. Cover and turn off the heat. Allow the potatoes to cool in the water—about 2 hours. Drain, peel, and slice the potatoes about ¼ inch thick.

3. Use the remaining tablespoon of oil for the dough to grease the jelly-roll pan. Scrape the dough from the bowl to the oiled pan with a rubber spatula, being careful not to stir or fold it. Oil your hands and press, pull, and pat the dough into the pan. If it resists, let it stand for 5 minutes, then continue. Cover the dough loosely with plastic wrap and set aside for about 30 minutes, or until it puffs slightly.

4. Set a rack at the highest and lowest levels of the oven and preheat to 450 degrees.

5. When the dough has puffed, sprinkle it with 1 tablespoon of oil. Arrange the potato slices so

they overlap slightly. Around the edges leave a ½-inch border uncovered. Salt and pepper generously and sprinkle evenly with the rosemary and cheese. Finally, drizzle on the remaining 2 tablespoons of oil.

6. Bake the pizza on the bottom rack of the oven for about 30 minutes. After about 10 minutes, lift an end of the pizza with a metal spatula to check that the bottom is not burning. If the bottom is coloring too quickly, slide another pan under the first one. If the bottom is a light golden color, check it again after another 10 minutes. When the pizza is done, the top should sizzle gently, be a deep golden color, and the bottom should be a dark brown. If the bottom is done but the top has not colored sufficiently, move the pizza to the top rack of the oven for an additional 5 minutes.

SERVING: Cut the pizza into large rectangles with a pizza wheel or serrated knife.

STORAGE: Wrap leftovers in plastic and refrigerate; bring leftovers to room temperature or reheat at 350 degrees for 7 or 8 minutes before serving again.

HINTS FOR SUCCESS: Be sure that the oven has preheated sufficiently before putting the pizza in. A soggy crust under the potatoes would be awful.

Do not use mealy baking potatoes for this or they will break into tiny pieces and be impossible to arrange over the dough.

MIXING PIZZA AND FOCACCIA DOUGHS

The doughs from which pizza and focaccia are made tend to be soft and easy to mix by hand. If you wish to use a heavy-duty electric mixer or food processor for mixing, follow these instructions:

In a heavy-duty mixer, use the paddle attachment and mix the dry ingredients on low speed for a few seconds; add liquid while the mixer is running and mix for about 1 minute. Scrape the bowl and the paddle with a rubber spatula and mix again for about 30 seconds. You may leave the dough in the mixer bowl to rise: remove the paddle and cover the bowl with plastic wrap.

In a food processor, pulse the dry ingredients 2 or 3 times, stop the machine, and add liquid. Pulse to moisten the dough evenly, then allow the machine to run continuously for 15 or 20 seconds. Carefully remove the blade and scrape the dough from the work bowl into an oiled bowl to rise.

PROSCIUTTO AND RICOTTA CALZONE

DOUGH

1½ cups unbleached all-purpose flour
1 teaspoon salt
⅔ cup warm tap water (110 degrees)
2½ teaspoons (1 envelope) active dry yeast
2 tablespoons olive oil

FILLING

1 cup whole-milk or part-skim ricotta
Freshly ground pepper
2 tablespoons chopped fresh parsley or basil
1 tablespoon finely grated Parmesan
¾ cup coarsely grated mozzarella
4 ounces thinly sliced and shredded prosciutto,
   or skinned and diced dried sausage, or a
   combination

*One 12-inch round pizza pan, cookie sheet, or
jelly-roll pan, oiled*

ONE 12-INCH CALZONE, ENOUGH FOR 2 SERVINGS

A calzone (literally "trouser leg") is a turnover made from pizza dough, usually filled with cured meats, cheeses, and often herbs. So that the flavors and textures of the dough and the filling may be appreciated, the calzone should not be overstuffed. A calzone is delicious served hot or at room temperature, which makes it a practical picnic food.

This may be made as individual calzoni—see the variation at the end of the recipe.

1. For the dough, in a 2-quart mixing bowl, stir the flour and salt well to combine; make a well in the center. Measure the water and pour it into a small bowl. Whisk in the yeast, then 1 tablespoon of the oil. Stir the liquid mixture into the well in the flour and stir with a rubber spatula to form a soft, sticky dough.

2. Turn the dough out onto a floured work surface. Knead the dough gently, folding it over on itself. If it is very sticky, scrape it off the surface with a spatula or plastic scraper. Avoid adding more flour or it will produce a tough dough. Knead for about 5 minutes, until the dough is smooth and only slightly sticky.

3. Rinse and dry the bowl and spread 1 tablespoon of the oil all around the inside. Form the dough into a ball and place in the bowl. Turn the ball of dough upside down so that the top surface is oiled, and cover the bowl with plastic wrap. Allow the dough to rise at room temperature until doubled in bulk, about 1 hour.

4. Set a rack at the middle level of the oven and preheat to 450 degrees.

5. To make the filling, place the ricotta in a mixing bowl and stir in the other ingredients in the order listed. Taste the mixture, and if it seems excessively bland, stir in a few pinches of salt; not too much—the sausage or prosciutto is salty.

6. To shape the calzone, generously flour the work surface and scrape the risen dough from the bowl, in one piece, onto the work surface. Fold the dough over on itself from the outside edge inward, all around, to form an even ball of dough, cover the dough with a towel and allow it to rest on the work surface for 5 minutes. Flour the dough and press it with the palms of your hands so it forms an even disk. With a rolling pin, roll out the dough until it is about 12 inches in diameter and about ⅛ inch thick. Add pinches of flour to the work surface and the dough as necessary to keep it from sticking to the surface or the rolling pin.

7. Fold the disk in half, transfer it to the pan, and arrange the folded piece of dough in the position in which it will bake on the pan. Unfold the dough and spread the filling over half of it, leaving about an inch of uncovered dough around the edges. Paint the dough border around the filling with water and refold the unfilled dough over it. Press the edges together very firmly to seal and slash the top of the calzone in several places to allow steam to escape during baking.

8. Bake the calzone for about 30 minutes, until the dough is baked through and has turned a deep golden color.

SERVING: Cut the calzone into two or more pieces and serve immediately. Or allow the calzone to cool and serve at room temperature.

STORAGE: Wrap any leftover calzone in plastic or foil and refrigerate. Allow to come to room temperature or rewarm in a 375 degree oven for 10 minutes before serving.

HINTS FOR SUCCESS: If the dough resists being rolled, cover it with a piece of plastic wrap and allow it to rest for 5 minutes before you continue.

Seal the open edges of the calzone carefully, by making lots of small, overlapping folds around the edge

VARIATIONS

For spinach and ricotta calzone, add ¾ cup cooked, drained, chopped spinach to the filling. Omit the sausage and/or prosciutto if you wish, though I like those rich flavors with the spinach.

Substitute boiled ham and Gruyère cheese for the prosciutto and mozzarella.

Also, you can substitute ½ pound cooked, cooled, and crumbled sweet Italian sausage for the dried sausage/prosciutto.

INDIVIDUAL SAUSAGE AND PEPPER CALZONI: A double batch of calzone dough, above (do not increase yeast)

FILLING

    3 tablespoons olive oil
    1 pound sweet Italian pork sausage, with or
        without fennel seeds
    2 small (about 4 ounces each) red or green bell
        peppers, halved, seeded, and sliced thin
    1 medium (about 6 ounces) onion, sliced thin
    1 clove garlic, sliced thin
    Salt and pepper
    1 teaspoon hot pepper flakes (optional)
    ¾ cup (about 3 ounces) coarsely grated
        mozzarella (optional)

1. To make the filling, heat 1 tablespoon of the oil in a sauté pan over a medium flame and cook the sausage until it begins to sizzle. Lower the heat and continue cooking, turning the sausage occasionally, until it has cooked through, about

15 minutes. Remove to a plate to cool. Drain all but 1 tablespoon of the accumulated fat from the pan and add the peppers, onion, and garlic. Add the salt, pepper, and optional hot pepper and cook, stirring often, for about 20 minutes, until the vegetables wilt and are just beginning to color. Cool the vegetable mixture, slice the cooled sausages, and stir them in.

2. To shape the calzoni, flour the work surface and turn the risen dough out onto it in one piece. Fold the dough over on itself from the outside edge inward, all around, to form an even ball. Cut the dough into 4 equal pieces and fold each piece of dough inward again to make 4 balls. Cover the pieces of dough with a towel and allow them to rest on the work surface for 5 minutes.

3. Flour each piece, then press them, one at a time, with the palms of your hands to form even disks. Use a rolling pin to roll the disks of dough out, one at a time, until each is about 8 or 9 inches in diameter and about ⅛ inch thick. Add pinches of flour to the work surface and the dough as necessary to keep it from sticking to the surface or the rolling pin.

4. Fold the disks in half and transfer them to the pans, arranging the folded pieces of dough in the position in which they will bake on the pans. Unfold the disks of dough and spread a quarter of the filling over half of each of the disks on the pans. Leave a 1-inch border of dough around the edges of the filling. Sprinkle the filling with the optional mozzarella. Paint the uncovered borders with water and refold the unfilled dough over it. Press the edges together very firmly to seal and slash the top of the calzoni in several places to allow steam to escape during baking.

5. Bake as above.

4
PIES

In restaurants in the United States today, pie is the dessert most frequently ordered. Although pies as we know them were perfected by American and British bakers in the nineteenth century, covered pies were served by the Greeks and Romans two thousand years ago.

Most pies consist of a layer of pastry dough or a crumb crust mixture lining a sloping-sided pan. The crust may be baked blind (without a filling) and filled later, or the filling may be baked with the crust, with or without a top crust. A pie is always served from the pan in which it was baked. A deep dish pie has a fruit filling and only a top crust and is baked in a casserole or other deep baking dish. Cobblers, buckles, grunts, and slumps, the first cousins of pies, have fruit fillings and are baked in shallow dishes with top crusts only. These crusts may be made from pastry dough, baking powder biscuit dough, or a thinner version of the biscuit dough that is poured over the filling before baking.

In the British Isles, where a pie dish is an oval bowl several inches deep, most pies are of the deep dish variety. When a British pie does have a top and bottom crust, it is usually baked in a straight-sided pan and unmolded for serving.

I like to classify pies according to their fillings:

FRUIT PIES: The filling is made from cooked or uncooked fresh or dried fruit assembled in an unbaked bottom crust, with or without a top crust made from a pastry dough or crumb mixture. Crust(s) and filling bake together.

CREAM PIES: The filling is made from a cooked custard or mousse mixture, spread in a previously baked pastry or crumb crust.

CUSTARD PIES: The filling is an uncooked custard mixture poured over an unbaked bottom crust. There is no top crust. Crust and filling bake together.

NUT PIES: The filling is a sugar-based mixture added to eggs and butter and poured over nutmeats in an unbaked bottom crust. There is no top crust. Crust and filling bake together.

DEEP DISH PIES AND COBBLERS: Fruit pies with a top crust only, made either of pastry dough or baking powder biscuit dough.

SAVORY PIES: Main course or appetizer pies with salty rather than sweet fillings.

Though I have used many different types of pie pans over the years, I still prefer a Pyrex pan to all others. Glass conducts heat more efficiently than most metals used for pie pans, so the bottom crust has a better chance of baking through than it does in a pan of another material. A Pyrex pan also allows you to see whether the bottom crust is sufficiently baked before you remove the pie from the oven.

FLAKY PIE DOUGH

FOR A ONE-CRUST PIE
(ABOUT 10 OUNCES DOUGH)

1¼ cups bleached all-purpose flour
¼ teaspoon salt
⅛ teaspoon baking powder
8 tablespoons (1 stick) cold unsalted butter
2 to 3 tablespoons cold water

FOR A TWO-CRUST PIE
(ABOUT 1¼ POUNDS DOUGH)

2½ cups bleached all-purpose flour
½ teaspoon salt
¼ teaspoon baking powder
16 tablespoons (2 sticks) cold unsalted butter
4 to 6 tablespoons cold water

Of all the pie doughs I have ever worked with, this is the best and easiest to prepare and roll out. It is the dough I use for many of the one- and two-crust pies in this chapter. Though it is not much effort to mix the dough by hand, I find that using a food processor makes it almost instant. The baking powder encourages the dough to puff slightly during baking so that it presses into the hot pan bottom and bakes through evenly. (Though the dough would normally rise away from the pan due to the action of the leavening, it is weighted when baked empty, and of course the filling weights it down when there is one.) This helps prevent an underdone bottom crust.

The amount of water added to the dough is always variable. When the flour and butter are rubbed together to create a fine mixture and they have warmed slightly, the dough will absorb less water; when the dough is dry and cool, and a little undermixed, it will absorb more. Too little water makes a flaky crust that will crack when it is rolled out; too much water makes an elastic, breadlike crust that lacks flakiness. To avoid erring in either direction, use this simple test. After you have added the minimum amount of water, pick up several tablespoons of the dough and squeeze gently; if the dough holds together easily without cracks and dry areas, it has absorbed enough water. If it does not hold together, add the remaining liquid about a teaspoon at a time, testing again after each addition.

This dough may be baked blind (without a filling) and used for one-crust pies with creamy fillings that are added after the crust is baked. It may also be used for two-crust pies with fairly dry fillings, such as apple or mincemeat.

1. To mix the dough by hand, combine the flour, salt, and baking powder in a medium-sized mixing bowl and stir well to mix. Cut the butter into 1-tablespoon pieces and add to the dry ingredients. Toss once or twice to coat the pieces of butter. Then using your hands or a pastry blender, break the butter into tiny pieces and pinch and squeeze it into the dry ingredients. Keep the mixture uniform by occasionally reaching down to the bottom of the bowl and mixing all the ingredients evenly together. Continue rubbing the butter into the dry ingredients until the mixture resembles a coarse-ground cornmeal and no large pieces of butter remain visible. Sprinkle the minimum amount of water over the butter and flour mixture and stir gently with a fork—the dough should begin holding together. If the mixture still appears dry and crumbly, add the remaining water, 1 teaspoon at a time, for the smaller quantity of dough, a tablespoon at a time for the larger quantity, until the dough holds together easily.

To mix the dough in the food processor, combine the dry ingredients in the work bowl fitted with a metal blade. Pulse 3 times at 1-second intervals to mix. Cut the butter into 1-tablespoon pieces and add to the work bowl. Process, pulsing repeatedly at 1-second intervals, until the mixture is fine and powdery, resembles a coarse-ground cornmeal, and no large pieces of butter remain visible—about 15 pulses in all. Scatter the minimum amount of water on the butter and flour mixture and pulse 5 or 6 times— the dough should begin holding together. If the mixture still appears dry and crumbly, add the

remaining water, 1 teaspoon at a time for the smaller quantity of dough, a tablespoon at a time for the larger quantity, until the dough holds together easily.

2. Turn the dough out onto a lightly floured surface and form it into a disk (two equal disks for the larger amount of dough). Sandwich the disk(s) of dough between two pieces of plastic wrap and press it into a 6-inch circle. Refrigerate the dough until firm, or until you are ready to use it, at least 1 hour.

STORAGE: Keep the dough in the refrigerator up to 2 days, or freeze it double-wrapped in plastic. Because the dough is thin, it will defrost quickly at room temperature when you intend to use it.

VARIATION

OLD-FASHIONED PIE DOUGH: Substitute lard for half the butter in the above recipes to make a very flaky, tender, and rustic-tasting crust.

For a richer dough, substitute a well-beaten egg yolk for the minimum amount of liquid in the one-crust recipe and a well-beaten whole egg for the minimum amount of liquid in the two-crust recipe.

To make a crust with whole wheat flavor, substitute ½ cup whole wheat flour for ½ cup of the flour in the one-crust recipe, and 1 cup whole wheat flour for 1 cup of the flour in the two-crust recipe.

ROLLING DOUGHS AND FORMING PIE SHELLS

Pie doughs are easy to roll—once you know a few general rules:

1. Flour the work surface and the dough before beginning to roll—the flour will keep the dough from sticking to the surface and the rolling pin. Flour sparingly and repeat the flouring often and the dough will not absorb too much flour and toughen.

2. If the dough is hard from the refrigerator, pound it gently with the rolling pin to soften it—trying to roll a hard piece of dough without softening it first will just make it break apart.

3. To roll, position the rolling pin at the edge of the dough nearest you and roll away to the opposite edge, using a gentle pressure. Do not roll over the opposite edge or the dough will become thinner and have an uneven thickness. Roll back again toward you, refraining from rolling over the near edge. Slide the dough away from the spot where you rolled it and add flour to the surface, if necessary. Rotate the dough about 30 degrees (after rotating the dough several times, it will become fairly round in shape) and roll over again. Repeat rolling, rotating, and flouring until the dough reaches the correct size.

4. To transfer the dough to the pan, fold it in half, then gently slide both hands under to support it. Line up the fold with the diameter of the pan and unfold the dough into the pan.

5. For a two-crust pie, trim the dough even with the edge of the pan. For a single-crust pie, trim away all but ½-inch of the overhanging dough, then turn it under at the rim of the pan. Flute the edge as in the instructions on page 150.

SWEET DOUGH
FOR PIES

FOR A ONE-CRUST PIE
(ABOUT 10 OUNCES DOUGH)

1 cup bleached all-purpose flour
3 tablespoons sugar
¼ teaspoon baking powder
⅛ teaspoon salt
4 tablespoons cold unsalted butter
1 large egg

FOR A TWO-CRUST PIE
(ABOUT 1¼ POUNDS DOUGH)

2½ cups bleached all-purpose flour
6 tablespoons sugar
½ teaspoon baking powder
¼ teaspoon salt
8 tablespoons (1 stick) cold unsalted butter
2 large eggs

I was raised on *pasta frolla,* the Italian sweet dough (see Pizza Rustica alla Napoletana, page 111), and I remain partial to pies with sweet crusts. And this sweet pastry dough is simplicity itself to prepare—there are no variable ingredients and, if you use the food processor, it is ready in 1 minute.

Though many people prefer a flaky dough, I like to use this cakelike dough for any single- or double-crust pie with a juicy fruit or a nut filling. Because of the sugar and egg in the recipe, the dough is always tender, never tough, and the slight foaming action of the baking powder as-

sures that the bottom crust is always well done. The dough also tolerates rerolling without becoming tough, unlike a more buttery flaky pie dough. Its easy rolling qualities make it ideal if you have never rolled out a piecrust.

1. To mix the dough by hand, combine the dry ingredients in a medium mixing bowl and stir well to combine. Cut the butter into 1-tablespoon pieces and add to the dry ingredients. Toss once or twice to coat the pieces of butter. Then using your hands or a pastry blender, break the butter into tiny pieces and pinch and squeeze it into the dry ingredients. Occasionally reach down to the bottom of the bowl and mix all the ingredients evenly together. Continue rubbing the butter into the dry ingredients until the mixture resembles a coarse-ground cornmeal and no large pieces of butter remain visible. Beat the egg(s) in a small bowl and pour over the flour and butter mixture. Stir in with a fork until the dough begins to hold together but still appears somewhat dry. Scatter a teaspoon of flour on the work surface and scrape the dough out onto it. Press and knead the dough quickly 3 or 4 times, until it is smooth and uniform.

To mix the dough in the food processor, combine the dry ingredients in the work bowl fitted with a metal blade. Pulse 3 times at 1-second intervals to mix. Cut the butter into 1-tablespoon pieces and add to the work bowl. Process, pulsing repeatedly at 1-second intervals, until the mixture is fine and powdery, resembles a coarse-ground cornmeal, and no large pieces of butter remain visible, about 15 pulses in all. Add the egg(s) to the work bowl and pulse 10 times or so, until the dough forms a ball. Scatter a teaspoon of flour on the work surface and scrape the dough out onto it. Press and knead the dough quickly 3 or 4 times, until it is smooth and uniform.

2. Press the dough into a disk (two equal disks for the larger amount of dough). Sandwich the disk(s) of dough between two pieces of plastic wrap and press it into a 6-inch circle. Refrigerate the dough until firm, or until you are ready to use it, at least 1 hour.

STORAGE: Keep the dough in the refrigerator up to 2 days, or freeze it double-wrapped in plastic. Because the dough is thin, it will defrost quickly at room temperature when you intend to use it.

VARIATIONS

SPICE CRUST: Add ½ teaspoon ground cinnamon and ¼ teaspoon each freshly grated nutmeg and ground cloves to the dry ingredients before mixing in the butter. Double the quantities for the two-crust recipe.

COCOA DOUGH: Add 2 tablespoons sifted non-alkalized cocoa powder to the dry ingredients before mixing in the butter. Double the quantities of cocoa for the two-crust recipe. If the dough seems dry after adding the egg(s), add a teaspoon or two of water, no more.

FLUTING PIE EDGES

Fluting (or crimping) the edge of a piecrust serves several purposes beyond the obviously decorative one. If the pie has a liquid filling, such as a custard or pumpkin pie, the fluting slightly extends the capacity of the pan so that when the crust is completely filled there is less risk of the filling overflowing or sloshing out on the way into the oven.

Folding over the extra dough creates a double layer which will not dry out and/or burn as easily as a single layer would during baking; a single layer usually becomes too dark and sticks long before the pie is completely baked.

Use any of the following methods for fluting the edge of a pie:

✦ Pinched Fluting: Position one hand outside the edge of the crust and pinch an inch of the edge with your thumb and index finger. At the same time, use the index finger of the other hand to push the dough into the pinch from the inside, as in the illustration. Continue all around until the entire edge is fluted.

✦ Pulled Fluting: These directions are for right-handed people. If you are left-handed, reverse them. Position your thumb and the index finger of the right hand an inch apart on the inside edge of the dough. From the outside of the shell press the index finger of your left hand between the thumb and index finger of your right hand and pull outward, making an arc, as in the illustration. Continue all around until the entire edge is fluted. Also good for one-crust pies.

♦ Rope Edge: Position the thumb of your right hand over the edge of the dough at a 45 degree angle across the rim of the pan. Press the side of your index finger from the outside of the pan against your thumb and squeeze gently to form a diagonal ridge on the rim of the crust, as in the illustration. Continue all around until the entire edge is fluted. This is particularly suited to two-crust pies.

♦ Pressed Edge: Use the back of the tines of a fork to press a series of lines around the edge of the pie. Flour the fork to prevent it from sticking to the dough. Press the fork with the tines pointing toward the center or, to vary the appearance, make the lines diagonal around the edge of the crust, or alternate directions of diagonal lines.

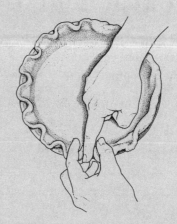

PULLED EDGE: *Position the thumb and index finger of your right hand an inch apart on the inside edge of the dough. From the outside of the shell press the index finger of your left hand between the thumb and index finger of your right hand and pull outward, making an arc. Continue around until the entire edge is fluted.*

PINCHED EDGE: *Positioning one hand outside the edge of the crust, pinch an inch of the edge with your thumb and index finger. At the same time, use the index finger of your other hand to push the dough into the pinch from the inside. Continue around until the entire edge is fluted.*

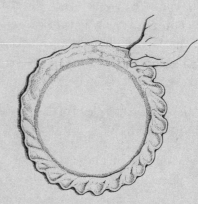

ROPE EDGE: *Position the thumb of your right hand over the edge of the dough at a 45 degree angle across the rim of the pan. Press the side of your index finger from outside the pan against your thumb and squeeze gently to form a diagonal ridge on the rim of the crust. Continue around until the entire edge is fluted.*

NUT CRUMB CRUST

½ cup (2 to 3 ounces) nutmeats (almonds,
    hazelnuts, walnuts, or pecans)
1 cup bleached all-purpose flour
⅓ cup sugar
¼ teaspoon ground cinnamon
⅛ teaspoon salt
6 tablespoons unsalted butter, melted

One 9-inch Pyrex pie pan, buttered

ONE 9-INCH PIECRUST

Crumb crusts are quick and easy to prepare and good for cream pies (beginning on page 169) in which a cooked custard or mousse filling is spread in a prebaked piecrust. Although crumb crusts are not rolled out as pastry doughs are, they must be pressed evenly and precisely into the pie pan. Watch them carefully when baking because their high sugar and fat content makes them burn easily.

1. Set a rack at the middle level of the oven and preheat to 350 degrees.

2. Place the nutmeats in the bowl of a food processor fitted with a metal blade. Pulse 10 or 12 times at 1-second intervals to grind finely without reducing them to a paste. Remove the cover and scrape the inside of the work bowl with a metal spatula.

3. Add the remaining dry ingredients, and pulse once or twice to combine.

4. Add the butter and pulse 3 or 4 times, until the mixture is evenly moistened and looks crumbly. Remove the blade and turn the mixture out into the prepared pan.

5. Using your fingertips, distribute the crumb mixture evenly over the bottom and sides of the pan, gently pressing it into place. Make sure that the crumb coating is even because thin spots will burn during baking.

6. Use the back of a spoon to smooth the surface of the crust and to make the rim of the crust straight and even.

7. Bake the crust for about 20 minutes, or until it is a deep golden brown.

8. Cool on a rack.

STORAGE: Keep the crust loosely covered at room temperature until you intend to use it, up to 48 hours.

HINT FOR SUCCESS: Watch the crust carefully as it bakes to avoid having it become overdone and bitter.

VARIATIONS

Omit the cinnamon, if you wish.
    Use light brown sugar for a stronger flavor.

THICKENERS FOR FRUIT PIES

The filling in a fruit pie should be moist and juicy, with the fruit just cooked through and not mushy. The juices should be slightly thickened so that the filling holds together when wedges of the pie are served, but it should not be so thick that it holds its shape completely. When a piece of pie is on a plate, the filling should flow slightly.

If I am making a fruit pie with an uncooked filling, I add a small amount of flour (usually 2 tablespoons) to the fruit before placing it in the crust—the juices thicken when the filling comes to a gentle simmer before the pie is removed from the oven. You may substitute instant tapioca for the flour, if you wish, though I prefer flour, used in moderation. I find that tapioca solidifies rather than thickens the juices in the pie.

When I'm making berry pies, I usually cook some of the berries with the sugar called for in the recipe, then thicken the resulting juices with cornstarch and allow the mixture to come to a full boil. I then add the rest of the fruit to the thickened liquid before filling and baking the pie. In this method, the starch cooks twice, once when it is added to the hot berry juices and again when the pie bakes, so any starchy taste in the filling is eliminated.

If you prefer the filling of a fruit pie to be very runny, halve the amount of thickening or leave it out altogether. But then remember to move fast when you are serving the pie.

EASIEST APPLE PIE

1 recipe Flaky Pie Dough for a one-crust pie
  (page 146)

CRUMB TOPPING

⅓ cup light brown sugar
1 cup bleached all-purpose flour
6 tablespoons unsalted butter, melted

FILLING

2½ pounds firm, tart apples, such as Northern
  Spy, Granny Smith, Pippin, or Golden
  Delicious
⅔ cup sugar, light brown sugar, or a combination
  of both
2 tablespoons bleached all-purpose flour
1 teaspoon ground cinnamon
1 teaspoon finely grated lemon zest
3 tablespoons cold unsalted butter

One 9-inch Pyrex pie pan

ONE 9-INCH PIE, ABOUT 8 SERVINGS

Peeling and dicing the apples is the only time-
consuming aspect of this pie—the rest is a breeze.
And you can bake the pie early in the day, or even
the night before, and warm it up before serving, to
eliminate any last-minute fuss.

1. Roll the prepared dough out and line the pan
as on page 148. Chill the crust while preparing
the topping and filling.

2. To make the topping, combine the sugar and
flour in a mixing bowl; add the butter and stir in

evenly. Set the mixture aside for 5 minutes, then
use your fingertips to break the mixture into ¼- to
½-inch crumbs. Set aside.

3. Set a rack at the lowest level of the oven and
preheat to 400 degrees.

4. To make the filling, peel, halve, and core
apples. Cut the apples into ½-inch dice. Place the
diced apples in a bowl and add the remaining
filling ingredients, except the butter, tossing well
to combine. Place the filling in the dough-lined
pan, mounding it slightly in the center. Dot the
filling with butter and sprinkle to cover with the
prepared crumb topping.

5. Place the pie in the oven and immediately
lower the temperature to 375 degrees. Bake the
pie for about 40 minutes, or until the crust and
topping are baked through and a deep golden
brown, and the filling is gently bubbling.

6. Place the pie on a rack to cool.

SERVING: Serve wedges of pie alone or with ice
cream or sharp cheddar cheese. I prefer it alone.

STORAGE: Keep the pie at room temperature on
the day it is baked. For longer storage, refrigerate
the pie, well wrapped in plastic, and reheat the
pie at 350 degrees for about 15 minutes before
serving.

HINT FOR SUCCESS: Don't neglect to chill the
dough before rolling it. Chilling makes the dough
easier to handle and helps to relax the elasticity
formed by the mixing, making for a more tender
crust. Chilling after rolling helps to relax
elasticity formed during rolling.

Omit or reduce the cinnamon from the filling, if you wish, and add ½ teaspoon ground cinnamon to the crumb topping.

Use 2 pounds apples and 1 cup cranberries for a more pungent filling.

Add ½ cup raisins or currants to the apples for a sweeter filling.

Add 1 tablespoon lemon juice to the apples (sprinkle it on the filling after it is in the crust) for a more tart filling.

Add a pinch each of freshly grated nutmeg and ground cloves to the apples along with the cinnamon.

❖
PIE APPLES

Finding an apple that combines good texture and flavor isn't always easy. Few varieties have the right, tart flavor necessary to make a good pie filling and are also firm enough so they won't fall apart or release too much water during baking.

Northern Spies make the best uncooked pie filling (when crust and filling bake together, page 154). Their flavor is slightly tart and the texture is perfect—the apples hold their shape after baking and exude just enough liquid to make the filling juicy, but not watery. Look for Northern Spies in the Northeast and the eastern parts of the Midwest (Ohio, Michigan, Illinois) from October 15 onward for a one-month season. Although many farmers now have cold storage facilities for apples and pears, the Spies really don't last much beyond the middle of December.

Rhode Island Greenings, another Northeast fall apple, have an extremely tart flavor and a fairly firm texture, which makes them ideal for an uncooked filling as well.

In the West, Pippins are a good choice for a pie—their tart flavor and firm texture make them appropriate for either a cooked or uncooked filling.

You may also make an uncooked filling with Granny Smiths or Golden Delicious, but I prefer to cook these varieties as in the recipe on page 156. The Granny Smiths need to have some of the moisture cooked out of them, or the filling will be too liquid. And Golden Delicious tend to be somewhat bland and their flavor improves greatly if they are cooked with butter and sugar.

Avoid McIntosh and all its variations, such as Macoun, Baldwin, and Cortland. Red Delicious should only be eaten uncooked because its firm, rather starchy texture only dries and hardens when cooked. Likewise, Rome Beauties make good baked apples, but are heavy and bland in a pie.

DOUBLE-CRUST APPLE PIE

1 recipe Flaky Pie Dough for a two-crust pie (page 146)

FILLING

3 pounds firm, tart apples, such as Granny Smith, Pippin, or Golden Delicious (see the box on Pie Apples, page 155)
3 tablespoons unsalted butter
1 tablespoon lemon juice
⅔ cup sugar
1 teaspoon ground cinnamon

Egg wash: 1 egg well beaten with a pinch of salt
1 teaspoon sugar for finishing top of pie (optional)

One 9-inch Pyrex pie pan

ONE 9-INCH PIE, ABOUT 8 SERVINGS

If you have ever made an apple pie with a top crust and a filling of uncooked apples, you have probably noticed what I call the "empty pie phenomenon," a space between the top of the filling and the inside of the top crust. This happens because moisture is lost during baking with a consequent decrease in volume. It is easy to avoid, however, by simply cooking the filling before placing it in the crust.

Be sure to use a firm apple for this pie, or the filling will become applesauce when it is cooked.

1. Prepare and chill the dough.

2. To make the filling, peel, halve, and core the apples. Cut each half into 5 or 6 wedges. Melt the butter in a wide, shallow, sloping-sided pan over medium heat. When the butter begins to sizzle, add the sliced apples and cook, tossing or gently stirring, until they begin to sizzle—about a minute. Add the lemon juice and sugar and continue to toss or gently stir often until the apples are tender, but still fairly firm—about 5 minutes longer. If the apples have exuded a large quantity of juice, they will reabsorb it as they cool.

3. Pour the filling out into a nonreactive pan, or a pan lined with plastic wrap, on which the apple slices will fit in a single layer. Sprinkle with the cinnamon and let cool.

4. Set a rack at the upper and lower thirds of the oven and preheat to 400 degrees.

5. Roll out the bottom crust and arrange in the pan as on page 148. Pour the cooled filling into the bottom crust. Roll out and place the top crust for a double-crust pie (page 158). Cut several slashes in the top crust and carefully brush with the egg wash. Be careful not to leave puddles of liquid on the crust. If you wish, sprinkle the top crust with sugar.

6. Place the pie in the oven on the lower rack and lower the temperature to 375 degrees. Bake the pie for about 40 minutes, until the crust is

baked through and a deep golden brown and the filling is gently bubbling. If the top crust has not colored sufficiently after 30 minutes, move the pie to the upper rack of the oven for the last 10 minutes.

7. Cool the pie on a rack.

SERVING: Serve wedges of pie alone or with ice cream or sharp cheddar cheese. I prefer it alone.

STORAGE: Keep the pie at room temperature on the day it is baked. For longer storage, refrigerate the pie, well wrapped in plastic. Remove the plastic and reheat at 350 degrees for about 15 minutes before serving.

VARIATIONS

Use the crumb topping as in Easiest Apple Pie (page 151), instead of a top crust.

Omit or reduce the cinnamon from the filling, if you wish, and add ½ teaspoon ground cinnamon to the crumb topping, if used.

Use 2 pounds apples and 1 cup cranberries for a more pungent filling.

Add ½ cup raisins or currants to the apples for a sweeter filling.

Add a pinch each of freshly grated nutmeg and ground cloves to the apples along with the cinnamon.

◆ TOP CRUSTS

A two-crust pie is judged by the appearance of its top crust. A full top crust always has a few slashes in it to allow steam to escape during baking. After the pie is baked, the slashes reveal the filling beneath, and add color and texture to the top of the pie. A lattice-top pie, whether perpendicular or diagonal, consists of a series of strips of dough placed over the filling. The filling shows in the spaces between the strips of dough, and gives the pie a homey, rustic appearance.

I suppose the ultimate top crust for a pie is a woven lattice. This crust, a bit of trouble to prepare, may be designed so that there are openings in the weave to reveal the filling, or the strips of dough may be placed next to each other and touching, so that the weave is closed and forms a full top crust. I think the latter woven lattice gives the pie a sleek, striking appearance.

To make a full top crust for a pie, lightly flour both the work surface and the dough. Roll the dough to a 10-inch disk. Lightly brush the rim of the bottom crust with egg wash or water. Fold the top crust in half and place it over the filling; unfold it to cover the filling completely. Tuck the edge of the top crust under the edge of the bottom crust and flute the rim of the pie (page 150). Cut several slashes in the top crust and carefully brush with egg wash or milk, making sure not to leave puddles of liquid on the crust. If you wish, sprinkle the top crust with a teaspoon of sugar—just enough to give the crust a homey, caramelized appearance, but not to add significant sweetness.

To make a diagonal or perpendicular lattice crust, lightly flour the work surface and dough and roll the dough out to a 9 × 12-inch rectangle. Cut the dough the short way into 12 strips, each 9 inches long and an inch wide. Egg wash the strips and arrange 5 of them, equidistant from each other, over the top of the filling, as in the illustration on page 112. Place 5 more strips diagonally or at right angles to the first ones. Trim away excess dough around the edge of the plate and apply the last 2 strips around the rim of the pie, egg wash side down. Flute the edges and carefully brush the lattice with egg wash. If you wish, sprinkle the top with sugar.

To make a woven lattice crust:

1. Lightly flour the work surface and dough and shape the dough into a square, by pressing the sides against the work surface.

2. Roll the dough to a 9 × 12-inch rectangle.

3. Cut the dough the short way into 24 strips, each ½ inch wide and 9 inches long.

4. Arrange 12 of the strips, ¼ inch apart, on a floured cookie sheet or the floured back of a jelly-roll pan. Position the pan so that the strips are facing vertically to you.

5. Beginning with the first strip of dough on your left, fold every other strip in half, back toward you.

6. Place one of the reserved 12 strips of dough horizontally across the unfolded strips, just above the fold of the other strips, as in the illustration.

7. Unfold the strips away from you, back to their original position, over the horizontal strip.

8. Now begin with the second vertical strip from your left and fold back every other strip again.

9. Insert another horizontal strip and unfold the vertical strips. Repeat steps 5 through 9 twice more until you have inserted 6 horizontal strips to the top of the pan.

10. Turn the pan 180 degrees and repeat the process, beginning with the first vertical strip, and inserting 6 more horizontal strips of dough, that is, steps 5 through 9, 3 more times.

11. Gently press the top of the lattice to make the strips stick together slightly, and refrigerate the lattice until firm, which will make it easier to slide onto the pie.

12. Moisten the rim of the bottom crust with egg wash or water. Remove the lattice from the refrigerator and slide it to the far edge of the cookie sheet away from you. Hold the cookie sheet about 1 inch above the pie, tilt it slightly, and allow about an inch of the lattice to hang off the far edge so that you can easily line it up over the far edge of the pie. Lower the far edge of the lattice onto the far edge of the pie and pull the cookie sheet toward you, allowing the lattice to

fall in place over the pie. If the lattice is still very firm, allow it to soften for a few minutes at room temperature, then press the edge of the lattice firmly against the edge of the bottom crust and trim away the excess dough around the rim of the pan. Flute the edge of the pie if you wish, though I think that fluting detracts from the symmetry of the lattice.

13. Carefully brush the lattice with egg wash and sprinkle with sugar.

To make a completely closed woven lattice, roll the dough into a 9 × 18-inch rectangle and cut the dough into twenty-four 9 × ¾-inch strips. Weave the lattice as above, positioning the strips of dough so they touch each other.

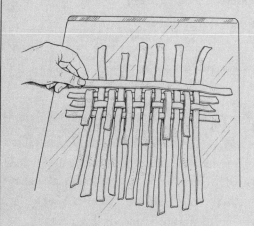

Just above the fold, place one of the twelve reserved strips of dough across the folded strips.

BLUEBERRY LATTICE PIE

1 recipe Sweet Dough for a two-crust pie
   (page 149)

FILLING

2 pints blueberries, rinsed, drained, and picked
   over
¾ cup sugar
3 tablespoons cornstarch
3 tablespoons water
1 teaspoon finely grated lemon zest
½ teaspoon ground cinnamon
¼ teaspoon freshly grated nutmeg
2 tablespoons unsalted butter

Egg wash: 1 egg well beaten with a pinch of salt
1 teaspoon sugar for finishing top of pie
   (optional)

One 9-inch Pyrex pie pan

ONE 9-INCH PIE, ABOUT 8 SERVINGS

For me, summer means blueberry pies (and tarts, cobblers, muffins, and pancakes). At the height of berry season, I tend to buy quarts and quarts, and when I get home, I wonder what to do with them all: pies are frequently the answer.

The technique for preparing this filling thickens it without sacrificing flavor or texture. Since most of the berries go into the filling raw, the filling is always juicy and just slightly thickened after baking.

I like to use a sweet dough for this pie; its melting texture matches the pie's tender sweet/pungent flavor perfectly. If you prefer a flaky dough, feel free to substitute the one on page 146.

1. Prepare and chill the dough.

2. To make the filling, combine 1 cup of the blueberries with the sugar in a nonreactive saucepan. Bring to a simmer over low heat, stirring occasionally, until the sugar is melted and the mixture is very liquid, about 5 minutes. Combine the cornstarch and water in a small bowl and whisk the blueberry and sugar mixture into it. Return everything to the pan and cook, stirring constantly, over low heat, until the mixture comes to a boil, thickens, and becomes clear. If it does not become clear, continue to cook over low heat for a few more minutes, until it does. Pour into a large bowl and stir in the remaining filling ingredients, except the blueberries, then add the remaining 3 cups of blueberries. Cool.

3. Set a rack at the upper and lower thirds of the oven and preheat to 400 degrees.

4. Roll out the bottom crust and arrange in the pan (page 148). Pour the cooled filling into the bottom crust. Prepare a lattice-top crust (page 158). Flute the edge of the pie and carefully brush it with the egg wash. If you wish, sprinkle the top of the pie with sugar.

5. Place the pie in the oven on the lower rack and reduce the temperature to 375 degrees. Bake for about 40 minutes, until the crust is baked through and a deep golden brown and the filling

is gently bubbling. If the top crust has not colored sufficiently after 30 minutes of baking, move the pie to the upper rack of the oven for the last 10 minutes.

6. Cool the pie on a rack.

SERVING: Serve wedges of pie alone or with ice cream.

STORAGE: Keep the pie at room temperature on the day it is baked. For longer storage, refrigerate the pie, well wrapped in plastic. To reheat, remove the plastic and bake the pie at 350 degrees for about 15 minutes before serving.

VARIATION

Use the crumb topping as in Easiest Apple Pie (page 154), instead of a top crust.

ONCE-A-YEAR CHERRY PIE

1 recipe Sweet Dough for a two-crust pie
(page 149)

FILLING

3 pints fresh sour cherries, stemmed, rinsed, and
picked over

¾ cup sugar

3 tablespoons cornstarch

3 tablespoons water

1 teaspoon almond extract

¼ teaspoon ground cinnamon

2 tablespoons unsalted butter

Egg wash: 1 egg well beaten with a pinch of salt
1 teaspoon sugar for finishing top of pie
(optional)

One 9-inch Pyrex pie pan

ONE 9-INCH PIE, ABOUT 8 SERVINGS

Though I would be happy to bake (and eat) a cherry pie once a week, the season for fresh sour cherries is so short that I'm lucky to get in one pie a year.

Sour cherries never appear in supermarkets, so they may be difficult to find. Begin checking farmers' markets and roadside fruit stands in late June and early July, or try to locate a source for IQF (individually quick frozen) sour cherries. Unfortunately, sweet cherries and canned sour ones do not make a good pie.

Save the cherry pits. Rinse them and dry them on a parchment-lined jelly-roll pan in the oven and store them in a jar—they are much better than beans for weighting tart and pie crusts baked blind, because the pits are not porous and will not absorb fat and become rancid after several uses the way beans do.

1. Prepare and chill the dough.

2. To make the filling, pit the cherries over a bowl. Slash the side of each one with a stainless-steel paring knife and squeeze gently to extract the pits. Put the cherries in the bowl as they are pitted.

3. When all the cherries have been pitted, drain the juices from the bowl into a nonreactive saucepan and add 1 cup of the cherries and the sugar. Bring to a simmer over low heat, stirring occasionally, until the sugar is melted and the mixture is very liquid, about 5 minutes.

4. Combine the cornstarch and water in a small bowl and whisk the cherry and sugar mixture into it. Return to the pan and cook, stirring constantly, over low heat, until it comes to a boil, thickens, and becomes clear. If it does not become clear, continue to cook over low heat for an additional few minutes until it does. Pour into a large bowl and stir in the remaining filling ingredients, except the cherries, then add the remaining cherries.

5. Set racks at the upper and lower thirds of the oven and preheat to 400 degrees.

6. Roll out the bottom crust and arrange in the pan (page 148). Pour the cooled filling into the bottom crust. Prepare a lattice-top crust (page 158). Flute the edge of the pie and carefully brush it with the egg wash. If you wish, sprinkle the top of the pie with sugar.

7. Place the pie in the oven and lower the temperature to 375 degrees. Bake for about 40 minutes, until the crust is baked through and a deep golden brown and the filling is gently bubbling. If the top crust has not colored sufficiently after 30 minutes, move the pie to the upper rack of the oven for the last 10 minutes.

8. Cool the pie on a rack.

SERVING: Serve wedges of pie alone or with ice cream.

STORAGE: Keep the pie at room temperature on the day it is baked. For longer storage, refrigerate the pie, well wrapped in plastic. To reheat, remove the plastic and bake the pie at 350 degrees for about 15 minutes before serving.

VARIATION

Use the crumb topping as in Easiest Apple Pie (page 154), instead of a top crust.

PEACH PIE WITH ALMOND CRUMBLE TOPPING

1 recipe Sweet Dough for a one-crust pie (page 149)

ALMOND CRUMBLE TOPPING

1 cup bleached all-purpose flour
3 tablespoons sugar
¼ teaspoon freshly grated nutmeg
½ cup (2 ounces) sliced almonds
6 tablespoons unsalted butter, melted

FILLING

3 pounds (8 or 9 medium) firm, ripe, yellow-fleshed freestone peaches
½ cup sugar
2 tablespoons bleached all-purpose flour
½ teaspoon almond extract
⅛ teaspoon freshly grated nutmeg
2 tablespoons cold unsalted butter

One 9-inch Pyrex pie pan

ONE 9-INCH PIE, ABOUT 8 SERVINGS

This fragrant almond crumb–topped pie is perfect summer baking—it is fast to prepare and makes use of the best seasonal fruit.

1. Prepare and chill the dough.

2. To make the topping, combine the flour, sugar, and nutmeg in a mixing bowl; stir well to combine and stir in the sliced almonds. Stir in the butter evenly. Set aside for 5 minutes, then, using your fingertips, break the mixture into ¼- to ½-inch crumbs. Set aside again while you prepare the filling.

3. Set racks at the middle and lowest levels of the oven and preheat to 400 degrees.

4. Roll out the bottom crust and arrange in the pan (page 148).

5. To make the filling, peel the peaches by cutting a cross in the blossom end of each and dropping them 3 at a time into a pan of boiling water. Remove after 20 or 30 seconds with a slotted spoon or skimmer, and drop them into a bowl of ice water. If the peaches are ripe, the skin will slip off easily. If it does not, remove the skin with a sharp stainless-steel paring knife. (If you have to peel with a knife, use an extra peach to make up for what is peeled away.)

6. Hold each peeled peach gently in your left hand over a mixing bowl (if you are left-handed, reverse). With a stainless-steel paring knife, make a cut through to the pit, from stem to blossom end. Make another cut about ¾ inch to the right of the first one along the outside of the peach. Angle the knife blade back so the cuts meet against the pit. Twist the knife blade upward slightly and a wedge of peach will fall into the bowl. Continue in the same manner around the peach, cutting it into 8 or 10 wedges. Discard the pit and repeat with the remaining peaches.

7. Add the remaining ingredients, except the butter, to the peaches and stir gently with a rubber spatula to combine. Pour the filling into the prepared pastry shell and smooth. Dot with the butter.

8. Scatter the crumb topping evenly over the filling, then place the pie on the bottom rack of the oven and bake for 15 minutes. Lower the temperature to 350 degrees and move the pie to the middle rack. Bake for another 30 minutes, or until the crust and the crumble are a deep golden and the juices are just beginning to bubble up.

9. Cool the pie on a rack and serve warm or at room temperature.

SERVING: Serve wedges of pie alone or with sweetened, vanilla-flavored whipped cream.

STORAGE: Keep the pie at room temperature on the day it is baked. For longer storage, refrigerate the pie well wrapped in plastic. To reheat, remove the plastic and bake the pie at 350 degrees for about 15 minutes before serving.

HINT FOR SUCCESS: If your peaches are not ripe, allow them to ripen for a few days at room temperature. If you use unripe peaches the filling will be tasteless and dry.

VARIATIONS

PEACH AND CHERRY OR RASPBERRY PIE: For the filling, use 2½ pounds (about 7 or 8) peaches and 1 cup pitted cherries or raspberries.

APRICOT PIE: Substitute 3 pounds (about 18) ripe apricots, rinsed, pitted, and quartered, for the peaches, above.

PEACH AND SOUR CREAM PIE: To make the filling, use 2 pounds (about 6) peaches and arrange them in the crust after they are peeled and sliced. In a mixing bowl, beat 2 eggs, mix ½ cup sugar with 2 tablespoons flour, and whisk that in. Whisk in ½ cup sour cream, ½ teaspoon almond extract, and ⅛ teaspoon freshly grated nutmeg. Pour over the sliced peaches in the pastry crust and finish as above. (If you want to include raspberries or cherries, use 1½ pounds peaches.)

APRICOT AND SOUR CREAM PIE: Substitute 2 pounds (about 12) ripe apricots, rinsed, pitted, and quartered, for the peaches, in the Peach and Sour Cream Pie variation, above. Substitute heavy cream, crème fraîche, or yogurt for the sour cream, if you wish.

LATTICE PEACH PIE: Make a lattice top (page 158). For this you will need the larger amount of the Sweet Dough recipe (page 149). (I don't use a top crust for Peach and Sour Cream Pie or its variations.)

STRAWBERRY RHUBARB PIE WITH WOVEN LATTICE TOP

**1 recipe Flaky Pie Dough for a two-crust pie
(page 146)**

FILLING

2 pints (about 4 cups) fresh, ripe strawberries
1 pound fresh rhubarb stalks, without leaves
¾ cup sugar
½ cup strained orange juice
3 tablespoons cornstarch
**1 tablespoon high-quality orange liqueur, such as
Cointreau or Grand Marnier**
2 tablespoons unsalted butter

Egg wash: 1 egg well beaten with a pinch of salt
1 teaspoon sugar (optional)

One 9-inch Pyrex pie pan

ONE 9-INCH PIE, ABOUT 8 SERVINGS

Both the flavor and look of this pie are homey and old-fashioned. The sweet-sour filling makes me imagine farmhouses and the days when country folk had pie for breakfast. And the woven lattice top, like tall layer cakes and saucer-sized cookies, represents the simple appearance of the best American specialties.

This pie has the best flavor when you can use fresh, height-of-the-season strawberries and rhubarb. If you purchase fresh rhubarb that still has some of the leaf left, though, carefully cut away the leaves and discard them; they are mildly toxic.

1. Prepare and chill the dough.

2. To make the filling, rinse, hull, and halve the strawberries; set them aside.

3. Rinse the rhubarb, then string it. Cut off the top and bottom of the stalk and pull them away, taking some of the fibrous strings that run the length of the outside of the stalk. If the stalks are more than ½ inch thick, split them lengthwise. Cut into 1½-inch lengths.

4. Combine the sugar and orange juice in a stainless-steel or other nonreactive wide, shallow pan that can hold the rhubarb in one layer and has a tight-fitting cover. Bring to a boil, uncovered, over low heat, stirring occasionally to dissolve the sugar. When the syrup is boiling, add the rhubarb pieces, and cook, stirring constantly, for 2 minutes, or until the rhubarb begins to render some of its juices and the syrup becomes thinner. Cover the pan and remove from the heat. Allow the rhubarb to steam in the hot syrup for 15 minutes.

5. Roll out half the dough and form it into a woven lattice crust (page 158). Chill on a cookie sheet.

6. To finish the filling, lift the rhubarb out of the syrup with a slotted spoon and place in a bowl. In a nonreactive saucepan, whisk the rhubarb syrup into the cornstarch. Cook, stirring

constantly, over low heat, until the mixture comes to a boil, thickens, and becomes clear. If the mixture does not become clear, continue to cook over low heat for a few more minutes. Pour into a large bowl and gently fold in the strawberries, cooked rhubarb, the liqueur, and butter. Set aside while preparing the bottom crust.

7. Set the racks at the middle and lowest levels of the oven and preheat to 400 degrees.

8. Roll out the remaining dough to form the bottom crust and arrange it in the pan (page 148). Pour the filling into the bottom crust and moisten the rim with the egg wash or some water.

9. Remove the lattice top from the refrigerator and slide it off the cookie sheet onto the pie. Flute the edge of the pie if you wish, though I think that fluting detracts from the symmetry of the lattice. Carefully brush the lattice with egg wash and sprinkle with the optional sugar.

10. Bake the pie for 15 minutes on the bottom rack of the oven. Lower the temperature to 350 degrees and move the pie to the middle rack. Bake the pie about 30 minutes longer, until the crust is a deep golden and the juices are just beginning to bubble up.

11. Cool the pie on a rack and serve warm or at room temperature.

SERVING: Serve wedges of pie alone or with sweetened whipped cream.

STORAGE: Keep the pie at room temperature on the day it is baked. For longer storage, refrigerate the pie, well wrapped in plastic. To reheat, remove the plastic and bake the pie at 350 degrees for about 15 minutes and cool briefly before serving.

VARIATIONS

Use the crumb topping as in Easiest Apple Pie (page 154), instead of a top crust.

Add ½ cup raisins or currants to the filling. This is traditional in the Midwest.

MINCE PIE

A double batch Flaky Pie Dough for a two-crust
  pie (page 146)

MINCEMEAT

2 pounds (4 to 5 medium) Granny Smith or other
  tart, firm apples
2 pounds (5 to 6 medium) McIntosh apples
2 medium oranges
2 medium lemons
2½ cups (one 15- or 16-ounce package) dark or
  golden raisins
1⅔ cups (one 12-ounce package) currants
½ cup diced candied orange peel
1¼ cups light brown sugar
⅔ cup dark rum or brandy
¼ cup distilled white vinegar
8 tablespoons (1 stick) unsalted butter cut into 1-
  tablespoon pieces
1 teaspoon freshly grated nutmeg
1 teaspoon ground cinnamon
½ teaspoon ground cloves
½ teaspoon ground ginger

Egg wash: 1 egg well beaten with a pinch of salt
2 teaspoons sugar for finishing top of pies
  (optional)

Two 9-inch Pyrex pie pans

TWO 9-INCH PIES, ABOUT 16 TO 20 SERVINGS

Mincemeat, a survivor of the medieval
British custom of cooking meat (which was probably rather strong in flavor) with fruits and spices,
is one of our major imports from British bakers. I
have never been keen on American and British
recipes that suggested using chopped boiled
tongue, beef brisket, or venison—excellent foods
in their own right—as an ingredient in a dessert
pie. When I found meatless versions in Isabella
Beeton's *Book of Household Management,* the
Bible of British cooking, I discovered they were
common as early as 1861, the year in which Mrs.
Beeton was first published.

The first of her two recipes for mincemeat includes beef and suet (beef fat) among the typical
ingredients of apples, raisins, spices, and brandy,
but strangely gives no instructions for cooking either the meat or the whole filling. The next
recipe, entitled "Excellent Mincemeat," includes
only suet, but calls for the fruit to be cooked separately and for combining all the ingredients and
aging the mixture for several weeks.

The filling in my recipe substitutes a small
amount of butter for the suet (Mrs. B. used
1 pound beef fat in a 7-pound batch) and has as
robust a flavor or texture as any version that contains meat or suet.

The recipe uses two types of apples, which
gives better texture: the Granny Smiths will hold
their shape, while the McIntoshes will disintegrate and thicken the mincemeat.

Note: Mincemeat has a better flavor and texture
when a large amount is simmered slowly for a
long time. You may bake both pies and freeze one,
or just use half the mincemeat and keep the rest in
a sterilized canning jar with a tight-fitting lid in
the refrigerator for up to 1 month, or freeze it for
several months. Of course, you may also halve the
recipe.

(continued)

1. Prepare and chill the dough.

2. To make the mincemeat, peel, halve, and core the apples. Grate them coarsely by hand or in the food processor. Place the grated apples in a large nonreactive saucepan. Grate the zest of both the oranges and lemons, then squeeze both fruits and strain the juice and add it with the zest into the pan. Stir in the remaining ingredients.

3. Bring the mincemeat to a simmer over low heat, stirring occasionally. Continue cooking for about 45 minutes longer, stirring often—this scorches easily—until the mixture is reduced to a thick, jamlike consistency. Let cool.

4. Set racks at the middle and lowest levels of the oven and preheat to 400 degrees.

5. Divide the double batch of dough into quarters. Roll one quarter out to form a bottom crust and arrange in a pan (page 148). Repeat with the second piece. Spread half the mincemeat evenly in each crust.

6. To make the top crusts, see page 158. Flute the edge of the pies and carefully brush with the egg wash. If you wish, sprinkle the top of each pie with sugar.

7. Bake the pies for 15 minutes on the bottom rack of the oven. Lower the temperature to 350 degrees and move the pies to the middle rack. Bake for 20 to 30 minutes longer, until the crust is a deep golden and the juices are just beginning to bubble up.

8. Cool the pies on racks and serve warm or at room temperature.

SERVING: Serve wedges of pie alone or with ice cream.

STORAGE: Keep the pies at room temperature on the day they are baked. For longer storage, refrigerate the pies, well wrapped in plastic. To reheat, remove the plastic and bake at 350 degrees for about 15 minutes before serving.

VARIATIONS

APPLE MINCEMEAT PIE: For a lighter mincemeat flavor, add 1½ pounds (3 large) firm, tart apples, such as Granny Smiths, peeled, halved, cored, and grated, to one quarter of the quantity of the mincemeat, above, for 1 pie.

GREEN TOMATO MINCEMEAT: If you have tomatoes in your garden, this is a good use for the last of the crop that doesn't have a chance to ripen before the first frost. Substitute green tomatoes, peeled with a sharp paring knife or a vegetable peeler and ground or finely chopped, for the apples in the above recipe—an old Pennsylvania Dutch approach to mincemeat.

LEMON CREAM MERINGUE PIE

1 recipe Flaky Pie Dough for a one-crust pie (page146)

FILLING

2 cups milk

⅔ cup sugar

3 to 4 medium lemons

¼ cup cornstarch

4 egg yolks

2 tablespoons unsalted butter, softened

MERINGUE

4 egg whites

⅔ cup sugar

Pinch of salt

One 9-inch Pyrex pie pan

ONE 9-INCH PIE, ABOUT 8 SERVINGS

I have never liked the idea of water as the main ingredient in a lemon meringue pie filling, so in this recipe milk replaces the water. It makes for a richer and more delicate flavor but is still sharp enough to please the most dedicated lemon lovers.

If you live in California or Florida (or visit either during the winter), you may find Meyer lemons for sale. A different variety from commercially grown lemons, Meyers have a strong lemon perfume and relatively low acidity. They are not widely marketed because a fungus they harbor makes it impractical to store them. Occasionally they appear in fancy produce stores here in New York at high prices, but when I can find them, I always buy a supply and make a pie or lemon curd (page 220). Robert Is Here, a fruit stand in south Florida, will ship them (see Sources of Supply). If you manage to find a quantity of Meyers, grate the zest and mix it with about half its volume in sugar, then squeeze and strain the juice. Freeze the zest in small plastic bags and the juice in ½-cup batches in small plastic containers.

The Swiss meringue I use here is probably different from meringue pie toppings you have already encountered. Heating the egg whites and sugar together before whipping the meringue makes it more stable and less likely to weep after it is baked.

1. Prepare and chill the dough.

2. To make the filling, combine the milk and sugar in a nonreactive saucepan, preferably enameled iron. Strip the zest from the lemons with a sharp vegetable peeler, making sure you remove the yellow zest but none of the white pith beneath. If you do remove some of the white pith, scrape it off the strips of zest with the point of a paring knife and discard it. Add the zest to the milk and sugar and bring to a simmer over low heat. Remove from the heat and allow to steep for 5 minutes; remove the strips of zest with a slotted spoon or skimmer and discard them.

3. Squeeze the lemons to make ½ cup strained juice. Place the juice in a mixing bowl and whisk in the cornstarch, then yolks.

(continued)

4. Return the milk and sugar mixture to a boil over low heat and whisk about a third of the boiling milk into the lemon juice mixture. Return the remaining milk and sugar mixture to a boil once more and whisk the lemon juice and yolk mixture back into it, whisking constantly until the filling comes to a boil and thickens. Allow to boil, whisking constantly, for about 30 seconds. Remove from the heat, whisk in the butter, and pour into a nonreactive bowl. Press plastic wrap against the surface of the filling and chill until it is approximately 75 degrees. (If you prepare the filling in advance, let it come to room temperature before proceeding.)

5. Set a rack at the middle level of the oven and preheat to 350 degrees.

6. Roll out the dough to make a bottom crust and arrange in the pan (page 148). Chill the crust until firm, about 20 minutes.

7. To bake the crust, pierce it all over with the tines of a fork at ½-inch intervals. Line it with a disk of parchment or wax paper and fill with cherry stones or dried beans. Bake for about 20 minutes, until lightly colored. Remove the paper and beans and continue baking until the crust is a deep golden brown. Cool the crust on a rack.

8. Spread the cooled filling evenly in the cooled crust. Increase the oven temperature to 400 degrees.

9. To make the meringue, bring a small pan of water to a boil. Lower the heat so that the water simmers. Combine the ingredients in the bowl of a mixer or, if you are using a hand whisk, in another heatproof bowl. Place the bowl over the pan of simmering water and whisk the egg white mixture gently for about 2 minutes, until the egg whites are hot (about 140 degrees) and the sugar has dissolved. Whip the meringue on medium speed until it has cooled and is able to hold a shape, but it should not be dry. Distribute spoonfuls of the meringue all over the top of the pie, then use the back of a spoon or a small offset metal spatula to spread the meringue evenly. It should cover the top of the pie and touch the edges of the crust all around. Here and there, bring up the surface of the meringue so that it is swirled. Place the pie on a cookie sheet and bake for 5 to 10 minutes, until the meringue is colored evenly.

10. Cool on a rack.

SERVING: Serve in wedges; it needs no accompaniment.

STORAGE: Keep the pie at room temperature—it tastes best if it is served after it has cooled on the day it is baked. Cover and refrigerate leftovers.

HINTS FOR SUCCESS: When you are making the filling, don't leave the lemon zest to steep in the milk for more than a few minutes or the filling may develop a bitter taste.

Don't overwhip the meringue or it will be dry and difficult to spread.

To avoid having a layer of moisture develop between the filling and the meringue, make sure the filling is not ice-cold when you pour it into the crust. In fact, if you are going to assemble the pie soon after cooking the filling, let the filling cool only to room temperature before you spread it in the cooled shell.

VARIATIONS

LEMON BLUEBERRY OR RASPBERRY MERINGUE PIE: Fold 1 cup rinsed and dried blueberries or raspberries into the filling before pouring it into the baked crust.

ORANGE MERINGUE PIE: Substitute orange zest for the lemon zest. Substitute ⅓ cup orange juice and 2 tablespoons lemon juice for the lemon juice.

LIME MERINGUE PIE: Substitute lime zest and juice for the lemon zest and juice in the above recipe. This is excellent with 1 cup raspberries folded into the filling.

LEMON, ORANGE, OR LIME CREAM PIE: Omit the meringue and top the pie with 1 cup heavy cream whipped with 2 tablespoons sugar and 1 teaspoon vanilla extract. Spread or pipe the whipped cream on the cooled filling and refrigerate the pie. Sprinkle the whipped cream with toasted, sliced almonds if you wish.

BUTTERSCOTCH CREAM PIE

1 recipe Nut Crumb Crust, made with almonds or pecans and light brown sugar (page 152)

FILLING

2½ cups milk
⅔ cup light brown sugar
Pinch of salt
⅓ cup cornstarch
3 large eggs
4 tablespoons unsalted butter, softened
2 teaspoons vanilla extract

TOPPING

1 cup heavy cream
2 tablespoons sugar
1 teaspoon vanilla extract

One 9-inch Pyrex pie pan

ONE 9-INCH PIE, ABOUT 8 SERVINGS

In the past few years, butterscotch has once again become a popular flavor. So, why not butterscotch pie?

This is an ideal recipe for a crumb crust, but if you prefer a pastry crust, follow the directions for the baked pie shell in the recipe for Lemon Cream Meringue Pie (page 169).

1. Prepare and bake the crust. Let it cool.

2. To make the filling, combine 2 cups of the milk, the sugar, and salt in a nonreactive saucepan; whisk once to mix and bring to a boil over low heat.

3. Place the remaining ½ cup of milk in a mixing bowl and whisk in the cornstarch, then the eggs. Return the milk and sugar mixture to a boil over low heat, then whisk about a third of it into the egg mixture. Return the remaining milk and sugar mixture to a boil and whisk in the egg mixture, whisking constantly until the filling thickens and comes to a boil. Allow to boil, whisking constantly, for about 30 seconds. Remove from the heat, whisk in the butter and vanilla; pour into a nonreactive bowl. Press plastic wrap against the surface of the filling and chill until it is approximately 75 degrees.

4. Spread the cooled filling evenly in the cooled crust.

5. To finish the pie, whip the cream with the sugar and vanilla until it holds a firm peak. Use a hand mixer on medium speed or a heavy-duty mixer fitted with the whisk. Spread the cream over the filling, making sure it touches the edges of the crust all around.

SERVING: A rich pie such as this needs no accompaniment.

STORAGE: Refrigerate the cream-covered pie for up to 12 hours, or until it is time to serve it. Or, prepare the crust and filling early in the day, assemble them, cover loosely, and refrigerate. Top with cream and refrigerate up to several hours again until serving time.

VARIATIONS

CHOCOLATE CREAM PIE: For the brown sugar in the filling, substitute ⅓ cup white sugar. Reduce the cornstarch to ¼ cup. Add 4 ounces semisweet or bittersweet chocolate, finely cut, to the filling with the butter and vanilla and whisk until the chocolate melts. Cover the whipped cream on the finished pie with shaved or grated chocolate.

CHOCOLATE BANANA CREAM PIE: Peel 1 pound (2 medium) bananas and slice ¼ inch thick. Fold into the chocolate filling from the Chocolate Cream Pie variation before pouring it into the shell. Finish as above.

BANANA CREAM PIE: Omit the chocolate from the Chocolate Cream Pie filling. Fold in the bananas, as in the Chocolate Banana Cream Pie variation. Finish as above.

COCONUT CREAM PIE: For the brown sugar in the filling, substitute ⅓ cup white sugar. Substitute ½ cup coconut cream, such as Coco Lopez, for the ½ cup milk with which the cornstarch is mixed. After the filling has cooled, fold in ½ cup toasted sweetened coconut. After covering the pie with the whipped cream (you may add up to ¼ cup coconut cream to the cream before whipping it to replace the sugar), sprinkle the whipped cream with ½ cup toasted sweetened coconut. (To toast coconut, place it on a jelly-roll pan on the middle rack of a preheated 325 degree oven for about 15 minutes. Stir often so that the coconut colors evenly to a light golden brown.)

If you wish, finish the top of the pie with meringue instead of whipped cream as in Lemon Cream Meringue Pie (page 169).

BANANA CUSTARD PIE WITH CINNAMON WHIPPED CREAM

1 recipe Sweet Dough for a one-crust pie (page 149)

FILLING

½ cup sugar
1 tablespoon all-purpose flour
⅛ teaspoon ground cinnamon
Large pinch of freshly grated nutmeg
4 large eggs
1½ cups milk
1 teaspoon vanilla extract
1 tablespoon white rum
3 large (about 1½ pounds) ripe bananas

CINNAMON WHIPPED CREAM

1 cup heavy cream
2 tablespoons sugar
1 teaspoon vanilla extract
¼ teaspoon ground cinnamon, plus extra for sprinkling over whipped cream

One 9-inch Pyrex pie pan

ONE 9-INCH PIE, ABOUT 8 SERVINGS

Like many others, this recipe came about when a friend called to ask advice about making a dessert. He wanted a banana cream pie in a hurry. I suggested using a sweet dough and placing the sliced bananas and custard cream in the unbaked piecrust and baking the three together. Then the only work left would be to whip the cream and spread it over the pie. Of course this technique may be used with almost all fruit; many variations follow the recipe.

1. Prepare and chill the dough.

2. Set a rack at the lowest level of the oven and preheat to 350 degrees.

3. Roll out the dough for the bottom crust and arrange in the pan (page 148).

4. To make the filling, combine the sugar, flour, and spices in a small bowl and stir well to mix. In another bowl, whisk the eggs until they are liquid, then whisk in the sugar mixture. Whisk in the milk, vanilla, and rum. Set aside.

5. Peel the bananas and slice them ¼ inch thick; arrange in the prepared piecrust. Skim the custard to remove any foam from the surface. Strain it over the bananas.

6. Bake the pie for about 45 minutes, until the crust is baked through and the filling is set. Cool the pie on a rack.

7. To finish the pie, whip the cream with the sugar, vanilla, and ¼ teaspoon cinnamon, until it holds firm peaks. Use a hand mixer on medium speed or a heavy-duty mixer fitted with the whisk. Spread the cream over the filling and make sure it touches the edge of the crust all around. Sprinkle the whipped cream with cinnamon.

(continued)

SERVING: A rich pie such as this needs no accompaniment.

STORAGE: Refrigerate the cream-covered pie for up to several hours until it is time to serve it. Or, prepare the crust and filling early in the day, assemble, cover loosely, and refrigerate. Top with cream and refrigerate again for up to several hours until serving time.

HINTS FOR SUCCESS: Don't slice the bananas until just before you are going to place them in the piecrust or they will darken unattractively.

VARIATIONS

APRICOT CUSTARD PIE: Replace the bananas with 1½ pounds (about 9) ripe apricots, rinsed, pitted, and quartered. Omit the spices from the custard. Omit the cinnamon from the whipped cream.

PEACH CUSTARD PIE: Replace the apricots in the above variation with 1½ pounds (4 or 5) peaches, peeled, pitted, and cut into wedges.

BLUEBERRY CUSTARD PIE: Replace the bananas with 3 cups blueberries, rinsed, drained, and picked over. Add 1 teaspoon finely grated lemon zest to the custard cream. Omit the cinnamon from the whipped cream.

SOUR CHERRY CUSTARD PIE: Replace the bananas with 3 cups pitted sour cherries. Replace the white rum with kirsch. Omit the nutmeg from the custard. Omit the cinnamon from the whipped cream.

Before baking the pie or any of the variations, top it with the Almond Crumble from the Peach Pie (page 163). Omit the whipped cream, or serve whipped cream with the pie.

Cover any of the fruit custard pies with meringue as in Lemon Cream Meringue Pie (page 169).

OLD-FASHIONED COCONUT CUSTARD PIE

1 recipe Sweet Dough for a one-crust pie (page 149)

FILLING

1 large (about 1½ pounds) fresh coconut
2 cups milk
¾ cup sugar
1 teaspoon vanilla extract
4 large eggs
Tiny pinch of freshly grated nutmeg

One 9-inch Pyrex pie pan

ONE 9-INCH PIE, ABOUT 8 SERVINGS

Coconut custard pie was one of my child-hood favorites and every so often I crave its rich texture and flavor. Although it is rarely served nowadays, it is a perfect ending to a light meal.

1. Prepare and chill the dough.

2. Set a rack at the middle level of the oven and preheat to 350 degrees.

3. Use a large nail or an ice pick to puncture one of the 3 eyes on the coconut (only one can be punctured so you will need to try each until you find it). Drain the coconut over a bowl. Strain the resulting liquid to remove any flecks of shell and reserve it.

4. Place the coconut on the oven rack and bake it until it cracks, 10 to 15 minutes. Remove the

coconut from the oven and let it cool slightly. Remove the shell (it will come away easily), then cut the coconut meat into 8 or 10 pieces. With a vegetable peeler, remove the brown skin. Coarsely grate 1 cup of coconut, either by hand or in the food processor, and reserve it for the filling. Process the remaining coconut until it is very fine.

5. In a large saucepan over low heat, scald the milk until there are bubbles around the edges. Add the finely processed coconut. Remove from the heat and allow the mixture to cool completely. Pour it through a fine strainer into a bowl; press the coconut to extract as much moisture as possible.

6. In 3 or 4 batches, place the coconut in the corner of a clean dish towel and wring out over the bowl to extract all the remaining liquid. (If you wish, you can toast the wrung-out coconut, though it will have very little flavor remaining after soaking in the milk.) Measure the coconut-flavored milk and add more milk, if necessary, to make 2 cups. (This may be done earlier in the day or even the day before and set aside, tightly covered, in the refrigerator.) Pour the milk into a bowl and whisk in the remaining ingredients and the reserved coconut milk. Stir in the reserved coarsely grated coconut.

7. Preheat the oven to 350 degrees. Set a rack at the lowest level of the oven.

8. Roll out the dough for the bottom crust and arrange it in the pan (page 148). Pour the filling into the piecrust.

(continued)

9. Bake the pie for about 45 minutes, until the crust is baked through and the filling is set, but not overcooked. After the pie has baked for 30 minutes, check it frequently so it does not overcook. Once the pie is wobbly-textured when the pan is gently shaken, remove it from the oven; it will continue to cook for a few minutes longer after it is removed from the oven. If the pie is overbaked, it will be heavy and watery.

10. Cool the pie on a rack.

SERVING: A rich pie such as this needs no accompaniment.

STORAGE: Refrigerate the pie until it is time to serve it—up to 12 hours.

VARIATIONS

You can use prepared coconut in this pie, but if you do, reduce the sugar in the filling to ½ cup and add ½ cup canned coconut cream, such as Coco Lopez, to the filling. Use 1 cup canned or packaged sweetened coconut for the coarsely grated coconut—it's not as flavorful, but actually closer to the bakery versions of my childhood.

OLD-FASHIONED CUSTARD PIE: Omit the coconut. Add ½ cup heavy or light cream to the milk. Mix the sugar with a teaspoon of cornstarch before adding to the milk. Bake as above.

THANKSGIVING DAY PUMPKIN PIE

1 recipe Sweet Dough for a one-crust pie (page 149)

FILLING

1 small (about 2 pounds) sugar pumpkin, or 1½ cups canned pumpkin

½ cup water

2 eggs plus 2 egg yolks

⅔ cup sugar

½ teaspoon salt

1 teaspoon ground cinnamon

¼ teaspoon ground ginger, or 1 teaspoon finely grated fresh

¼ teaspoon freshly grated nutmeg

1¼ cups light cream or half-and-half

One 9-inch Pyrex pie pan

ONE 9-INCH PIE, ABOUT 8 SERVINGS

No one is neutral about pumpkin pie—people either love or hate it. I fall into the former category and often dream of the smooth spicy filling in midsummer and wish I had frozen some cooked pumpkin the previous fall.

In truth, I use canned, cooked pumpkin as often as I do fresh. If you wish to use fresh pumpkin, make sure you get an orange-fleshed sugar pumpkin or pie pumpkin, available in the fall at farmers' markets and at roadside stands. Don't, under any circumstance, use a jack-o'-lantern–type pumpkin, which is watery and tasteless when cooked. Also, see the variations below for using sweet potatoes or acorn squash.

1. Set a rack at the middle level of the oven and preheat to 350 degrees.

2. Rinse, stem, and halve the pumpkin around its equator. Scrape away the seeds and filaments and cut the pumpkin into 2-inch chunks (toast seeds on a jelly-roll pan with a pinch of salt, if you wish, for snacks). Use a paring knife to remove the rind and place the pumpkin in a large baking dish. Add the water and cover the dish tightly with aluminum foil. Bake for about 1 hour, until it is soft. Check occasionally to make sure the water has not evaporated and add more if it has. Cool the pumpkin and puree in the food processor. (The puree may be refrigerated, tightly covered, for several days before making the pie filling.) Keep the oven on and lower the rack to the lowest level.

3. Roll out the dough to make the crust and arrange in the pan (page 148).

4. To make the filling, scrape the pumpkin into a bowl and whisk in the eggs and yolks. Whisk in the remaining ingredients in the order listed, whisking smooth after each addition. Pour the filling into the prepared crust.

5. Bake the pie for about 1 hour, until the crust is baked through and the filling is set.

6. Cool the pie on a rack.

SERVING: Serve with lightly sweetened whipped cream on the side.

(continued)

STORAGE: Refrigerate the pie, loosely covered with plastic wrap, until it is time to serve it. This pie can be baked the day before you plan to serve it.

HINT FOR SUCCESS: If there is more pumpkin than you need for the filling, salt lightly and freeze for up to several months in a tightly sealed plastic container.

VARIATIONS

Substitute the same volume of pureed baked sweet potatoes or acorn squash for the pumpkin.

To cook sweet potatoes, bake at 350 degrees for about 1 hour, or until tender. Cool, peel, and cut away any dry areas. Cut into large dice and mash or puree in a food processor. For 1½ cups puree, cook about 1 pound.

To cook acorn squash, quarter the squash and scrape away the filaments with a spoon. Do not peel; place on a pie pan with water and cover with foil as for the pumpkin, above. Bake for about 1 hour, or until tender. Cool and scrape the cooked flesh from the skin. Puree in the food processor. For 1½ cups puree, cook about 1½ pounds.

FAT-FREE PUMPKIN PIE: Generously spray the pie pan with vegetable cooking spray and press 1 cup dry breadcrumbs against the pan. Chill. Substitute 4 egg whites for the eggs and yolks; substitute evaporated skim milk for the cream. Bake as above.

SOUTHERN PECAN PIE WITH SPICE CRUST

1 recipe Sweet Dough Spice Crust variation for a one-crust pie (page 150)

FILLING

1 cup dark corn syrup
¾ cup sugar
6 tablespoons butter
3 large eggs
Pinch of salt
2 tablespoons bourbon
2 cups (about 8 ounces) pecan halves or pieces or a combination

One 9-inch Pyrex pie pan

ONE 9-INCH PIE, ABOUT 8 SERVINGS

In the early 1980s, when my Total Heaven Baking Company produced pastries and desserts for New York City restaurants, this pie was one of our biggest sellers. One Thanksgiving, when we knew we'd be swamped with orders, we made 300 pecan pies the week before and froze them. We tasted them after they had been defrosted and reheated, and there was no difference between those and the freshly baked pies.

I like to use the spiced variation of the Sweet Dough with this pie. If you prefer a less assertively flavored crust, use the basic Sweet Dough without the spices.

1. Prepare and chill the dough.

2. To make the filling, combine the corn syrup and sugar in a saucepan and stir to mix. Place over low heat and bring to a boil, without stirring. Remove from the heat, add the butter, and allow the butter to melt. In a mixing bowl, whisk the eggs until they're liquid and whisk in the salt and bourbon. Whisk in the syrup and butter mixture, being careful not to overmix. Allow to cool.

3. Set a rack at the lowest level of the oven and preheat to 350 degrees.

4. Roll out the crust and set in the pan (page 148). Arrange the pecans in the crust. Skim foam from the top of the filling (or the top will have an unattractively mottled surface) and pour over the pecans. With the back of a fork, press the pecans down into the filling so that they are covered.

5. Bake the pie for about 45 minutes, until the crust is baked through and the filling is set and well puffed in the center.

6. Cool the pie on a rack and serve warm or at room temperature.

SERVING: Serve wedges of pie alone or with sweetened, bourbon-flavored whipped cream.

STORAGE: Keep the pie at room temperature on the day it is baked. For longer storage, refrigerate or freeze the pie well wrapped in plastic. To reheat the pie, remove the plastic and bake the pie at 350 degrees for about 15 minutes before serving.

(continued)

CHOCOLATE PECAN PIE: Use the Cocoa Dough variation of Sweet Dough (page 150) instead of the Spice Crust. Add 4 ounces coarsely chopped semisweet or bittersweet chocolate to the hot syrup mixture along with the butter. Allow the chocolate to melt and whisk the filling smooth. Stir the pecans into the filling, rather than pouring it over them.

WALNUT RUM PIE: Replace the bourbon in the filling with dark rum; replace the pecans with walnut halves and pieces. Use the plain Sweet Dough (page 149) rather than the Spice Crust.

Substitute other nuts, such as hazelnuts or almonds, or a combination of several kinds of nuts.

DEEP DISH BLACKBERRY PIE

1 recipe Flaky Pie Dough for a one-crust pie (page 146)

FILLING

5 to 6 cups blackberries, rinsed, drained, and allowed to dry on paper towels

¾ cup sugar

3 tablespoons bleached all-purpose flour

¼ teaspoon ground cinnamon

¼ teaspoon freshly grated nutmeg

3 tablespoons unsalted butter

Egg wash: 1 egg well beaten with a pinch of salt

1 tablespoon sugar for finishing

One 1½-quart ovenproof baking dish or gratin dish, about 2 inches deep

ONE DEEP DISH PIE, ABOUT 8 SERVINGS

If you have a source for wild blackberries in midsummer, be sure to make this top-crust-only pie, which I think is the best possible use for the berries. If you have to buy the berries, the pie will not only be expensive, but the berries will probably not be ripe (commercially grown ones rarely are) and the pie may be very sharp tasting.

1. Prepare and chill the dough.

2. Set a rack at the middle level of the oven and preheat to 400 degrees.

3. For the filling, place the blackberries in a large mixing bowl. Combine the remaining ingredients, except the butter, pour over the berries, and fold gently with a rubber spatula to mix. Place the filling in the baking dish and dot with butter.

4. Lightly flour the work surface and the dough and roll the dough a little less than ¼ inch thick to the approximate size of the baking dish. Transfer the dough to the top of the filling (use a large, floured cookie sheet, sliding it under the dough, then easing it off onto the filling, for best results) and trim away any excess dough around the rim of the dish. Flute the outer edges of the dough. Slash 4 or 5 vent holes, each about an inch long, in the center of the dough, then paint it with the egg wash and sprinkle with sugar.

5. Bake the pie for about 30 minutes, or until the crust is deep golden brown and the filling is bubbling gently. (To avoid dirtying the oven from spills, center a large baking pan with a sheet of foil on it on the bottom rack of the oven, directly under the pie. If the juices boil out, the pan will catch them.)

6. Cool on a rack.

SERVING: Serve the pie warm or at room temperature. Use a large spoon to cut and place a portion of the top crust on a plate, then spoon some of the filling next to the crust.

STORAGE: Keep the pie at room temperature until serving time.

HINT FOR SUCCESS: Be careful not to bruise the berries when you are handling them, or the pie will be watery.

VARIATIONS

See Variations of Peach Cobbler (page 183). By the way, you may use any of the cobbler fillings on pages 183 to 184 for a deep dish pie; just substitute the dough and baking instructions above.

DEEP DISH APPLE PIE: Use filling for Easiest Apple Pie (page 154) instead of the blackberry filling above.

PEACH COBBLER WITH BUTTERMILK BISCUIT CRUST

FILLING

3 pounds (8 to 10) firm, ripe yellow-fleshed freestone peaches

⅔ cup sugar

2 tablespoons bleached all-purpose flour

2 tablespoons unsalted butter

BUTTERMILK BISCUIT CRUST

¾ cup unbleached all-purpose flour

¾ cup cake flour

½ teaspoon salt

1½ teaspoons baking powder

½ teaspoon baking soda (if the dough is made with cream or milk, omit baking soda)

4 tablespoons cold unsalted butter

⅔ cup buttermilk, cream, or milk

GLAZE

1 tablespoon buttermilk, cream, or milk

1 tablespoon sugar

One 1½-quart ovenproof baking dish

ABOUT 8 SERVINGS

Though there are many interpretations of what constitutes the top crust for a cobbler, I always use this buttermilk biscuit dough, similar to the buttermilk biscuits in Chapter 2. If you have self-rising soft wheat flour, such as White Lily, substitute it for both flours, the salt, and baking powder in the recipe for the dough.

1. To make the filling, peel the peaches by cutting a cross in the blossom end of each and lowering them a few at a time into a pan of boiling water. Leave the peaches in the water for 20 to 30 seconds, then lift them out with a slotted spoon or skimmer and put them in a bowl of ice water. If the peaches are ripe, the skin will slip off easily. If it does not, remove the skin with a sharp stainless-steel paring knife. (If you have to use a knife to peel the peaches, add an extra peach to make up for what is peeled away.)

2. These instructions are for right-handed people. If you are left-handed, reverse them. Hold a peeled peach gently in your left hand over a mixing bowl. With a stainless-steel paring knife, make a cut from stem to blossom end. The blade of the knife should touch the pit. Make another cut about ¾ inch ahead of the first one along the circumference of the peach. Angle the knife blade so it meets the first cut at the pit. Twist the blade upward slightly and a wedge will fall off the peach into the bowl. Continue around the outside of the peach, cutting it into 8 or 10 wedges. Discard the pit and repeat with the remaining peaches.

3. Combine the sugar and flour and gently fold them into the peaches. Scrape the filling into the baking dish and dot the surface of the filling with butter. Set aside while preparing the dough.

4. Set a rack at the middle level of the oven and preheat to 450 degrees.

5. For the crust, combine the dry ingredients in a mixing bowl and stir well to combine. Cut the butter into 8 or 10 pieces and rub into the dry

ingredients until the mixture resembles coarse meal (or pulse in a food processor fitted with the metal blade). Make a well in the center and add the buttermilk, cream, or milk. Stir gently with a fork to mix in the buttermilk, being careful not to overwork the dough. Let the dough stand in the bowl for a minute or two to let the flours absorb the liquid.

6. Flour the work surface and turn the dough out onto it. Fold the dough over on itself 2 or 3 times, until it is smooth and less sticky. Lightly reflour the work surface and the dough and roll the dough to a little less than ¼ inch thick and the approximate size of the baking dish.

7. Transfer the dough to the top of the filling (use a large, floured cookie sheet, sliding it under the dough, then easing it off onto the filling, for best results) and trim away any excess dough around the rim of the dish. Flute the edge of the dough at the rim of the dish. Slash 4 or 5 vent holes, each about an inch long, in the center of the dough; paint with the buttermilk and sprinkle with sugar.

8. Bake the cobbler for about 20 minutes, or until the crust is deep golden brown and the filling is bubbling gently. (To avoid dirtying the oven from spills, center a large baking pan covered with a sheet of foil on the bottom rack of the oven, directly under the cobbler. This will catch any juices that boil out of the cobbler.)

9. Cool on a rack.

SERVING: Serve the cobbler warm or at room temperature. Use a large spoon to cut and place a portion of the top crust on a plate, then spoon some of the filling next to the crust.

STORAGE: Keep the cobbler at room temperature until serving time.

HINT FOR SUCCESS: If your peaches are not ripe, allow them to ripen for a few days at room temperature. Unripe peaches in the filling will make it tasteless and dry.

VARIATIONS

PEACH CRISP: To make a crisp rather than a cobbler from the above recipe or any of the following variations, make a double batch of Almond Crumble Topping (page 163). Omit the top crust and scatter the crumb mixture over the filling in the baking dish. Bake at 375 degrees for about 30 minutes, or until the topping is well colored and the filling is bubbling.

PEACH OR APRICOT AND RASPBERRY COBBLER: Use 2½ pounds peaches or apricots (do not peel apricots), 1 cup (½-pint basket) raspberries, ½ cup sugar, 2 tablespoons flour, ½ teaspoon almond extract, and ⅛ teaspoon freshly grated nutmeg for the filling.

APRICOT AND CHERRY COBBLER: Substitute apricots for the peaches and pitted sour cherries for the raspberries in the recipe above. Do not peel the apricots.

(continued)

APPLE AND BLACKBERRY OR CRANBERRY COBBLER: Substitute 3 pounds Granny Smith or Pippin apples, peeled, cored, and sliced, for the peaches; substitute 1½ cups blackberries or cranberries for the raspberries. Add ½ teaspoon ground cinnamon to the filling.

APPLE AND CURRANT OR PRUNE COBBLER: Omit the blackberries from the Apple and Blackberry Cobbler variation above. Add 1 cup dried currants or sliced pitted prunes that have been brought to a boil and drained. Add 1 teaspoon finely grated lemon zest to the filling along with the cinnamon.

PLUM COBBLER: Use the seasonings as for the Apple and Currant Cobbler variation above. Omit the currants and use 3 pounds plums, rinsed, pitted, and sliced. This is especially good with a combination of several different varieties of plums.

BLUEBERRY LEMON COBBLER OR CRISP: Substitute 2 pints blueberries, rinsed, drained, and picked over, for the peaches. Add 1 teaspoon finely grated lemon zest, ¼ teaspoon ground cinnamon, and ¼ teaspoon freshly grated nutmeg to the sugar and flour. Top with Almond Crumble Topping (page 163).

COBBLERS, SLUMPS, BUCKLES, AND GRUNTS

Cobblers belong to the same dessert family as the grunt, buckle, slump, crisp, and pandowdy—all are made from fruit or berries in a baking dish covered with a baking powder biscuit or dumpling dough or a crumb mixture. In the South, many cooks prefer to cover their cobblers with pastry doughs. Other southern recipes for cobblers call for a batter to be poured over the fruit in the baking dish. The batter rises back to the top during baking and forms a crust. I like biscuit crust on a cobbler—it is fast and easy to prepare and bakes to a light, delicate crispness.

Grunts, buckles, and slumps usually call for the fruit to be cooked with sugar and water in a pan on top of the stove, then covered with a dumpling dough spooned over the cooked fruit. The type of fruit and whether it is then baked or steamed loosely determines the name of the dessert, though recipes often exchange, overlap, and generally confuse the terminology.

5

TARTS

❖

A tart differs from a pie in several ways: a tart is baked in a straight-sided pan which may or may not be fluted; a pie is baked in a sloping-sided pan. A tart is usually half the depth of a pie and is free standing—removed from the pan and placed on a platter for serving. A tart may have a top crust (lattice or whole), though it is not usual.

You may use many of the same fillings in tarts as in pies, but I consider tarts more refined and less rustic and homey than pies. Fruit is featured in many of these tarts; a few call for rich fillings, which are more practical in a low tart shell than in a deep pie form. A marbled filling of dark and white chocolate sounds appealing as a tart, but too rich as a pie.

These dessert tarts use doughs that are crumbly, delicate, and cookie-like; some are flavored and enhanced with ground nuts, cocoa, or spices.

Similar doughs are used for small tarts (3½ to 4 inches in diameter) or for miniature tartlets (about 2 to 2½ inches in diameter) and miniature barquettes (about 3 inches long and about 1 inch wide at the middle). I tend to use smooth, nonfluted versions of these pans for the ease of removing the baked pastries and cleaning up.

A small tart is meant to be a full individual portion of dessert and I think these do best as just that. Think of using some of the fillings in the pie chapter for small tarts—mincemeat comes immediately to mind as a perfect choice. And, of course, large tarts make great smaller versions—the chocolate raspberry tart in this chapter works well as small tarts with either plain or chocolate dough.

Tiny tartlets and barquettes are perfect for tea and for lavish entertaining. They are also a perfect pastry to serve with a creamy or custardy dessert for a special dinner. Though fruit-topped tartlets and barquettes need to be finished close to the time of service, others, such as pine nut tartlets or empty tartlets or barquettes to be filled later with chestnut cream or lemon curd, are perfect for advance preparation, making entertaining that much easier.

TART DOUGHS

Though I often suggest either Flaky Pie Dough (page 146) or Sweet Dough (page 149) for the tarts in this chapter, I've also included recipes for some fragile, buttery doughs particularly appropriate for delicate tart crusts. Most are variations of the Sweet Tart Dough, below.

SWEET TART DOUGH

8 tablespoons (1 stick) unsalted butter, softened
¼ cup sugar
1 teaspoon vanilla extract
1 egg yolk
1¼ cups bleached all-purpose flour

ABOUT 11 OUNCES DOUGH, ENOUGH FOR A 9- TO 10-INCH CRUST

Perfectly suited to the subtle fillings of most tarts, this dough may be used both for crusts baked empty (baked blind) to be filled after baking, or those in which a raw filling and the raw dough bake together. Flavored variations of the pastry (which follow the basic recipe) are best used for tarts with fillings that have an assertive flavor.

Tart dough is easy to prepare. For a smoothly mixed dough, have the butter and egg yolk at room temperature. After mixing the dough, chill it. Before you roll the dough, everything should be cold: the dough, the rolling pin, the work surface, and even the tart pan.

1. Combine the butter and sugar in a medium mixing bowl or the bowl of an electric mixer fitted with the paddle. Beat on medium speed for 5 minutes, until the mixture is soft, fluffy, and almost white in color.

2. Beat in the vanilla and the egg yolk and continue beating for another 2 minutes, until the mixture is soft and smooth and resembles buttercream. (If the mixture appears curdled, the butter, egg yolk, or both were too cold and not soft enough when combined. Continue to beat and the mixture will become smooth in a few minutes.) Scrape the bowl and beater(s) and remove the bowl from the mixer.

3. Place the flour in a strainer or sifter and sift it, all at once, over the butter mixture. Using a rubber spatula, fold the flour into the butter mixture until no traces of flour remain visible.

4. Scrape the dough onto the center of a 12-inch square of plastic wrap and shape it into a rough disk. Cover with another 12-inch square of plastic and press the dough between the two pieces of plastic until it is about ¼ inch thick. Refrigerate the dough.

STORAGE: Keep the dough refrigerated until you are ready to assemble the tart. You can refrigerate it for up to 5 days or freeze it. To freeze, double-wrap the package of dough in plastic wrap (to keep the edges from drying). The dough is thin so it will defrost quickly at room temperature. If it has softened too much in defrosting, chill it again before rolling.

HINT FOR SUCCESS: If the butter has not softened sufficiently to prepare the dough, cut it into small pieces before proceeding with the recipe. Beat the butter and sugar for about 2 to 3 minutes longer until they are soft and light before adding the egg yolk.

VARIATIONS

This dough derives flavor, richness, and sweetness from such ingredients as nuts, cornmeal, cocoa, and spices.

ALMOND TART DOUGH: Add ½ cup (about 2 ounces) finely ground blanched almonds to the butter mixture before adding the flour.

HAZELNUT TART DOUGH: Substitute ground, toasted, skinned hazelnuts for the almonds in the Almond Tart Dough variation, above.

SPICED NUT TART DOUGH: Add ½ teaspoon ground cinnamon and ¼ teaspoon ground cloves to either the Almond or Hazelnut Tart Dough variations, above, when folding in the flour.

CHOCOLATE (OR CHOCOLATE ALMOND, CHOCOLATE HAZELNUT, OR CHOCOLATE SPICED NUT) TART DOUGH: Substitute 1 cup flour and ¼ cup unsweetened cocoa powder, sifted together, for the flour in the Sweet Tart Dough, or any of the variations, above.

TART PAN SIZES

You can vary the shapes of the tarts by using the chart below to calculate how to increase the quantities of dough and filling.

✦ 7-inch round tart pan—half the ingredients (or make two tarts from one recipe)

✦ 12-inch round tart pan—1⅓ times ingredients

✦ 10½ × 15½-inch jelly-roll pan—2 times ingredients

✦ 11 × 17-inch jelly-roll pan—2 times ingredients

✦ 9-inch square tart pan—same ingredients

✦ 7 × 10-inch rectangular tart pan—same ingredients

NO-ROLL TART CRUST

1¼ cups bleached all-purpose flour
3 tablespoons sugar
Pinch of salt
¼ teaspoon baking powder
4 tablespoons cold unsalted butter
1 large egg

One 9- or 10-inch loose-bottomed tart pan, well buttered

ABOUT 11 OUNCES DOUGH, ENOUGH FOR ONE 9- TO 10-INCH TART SHELL

This no-roll crust is made from a doughlike mixture that remains in dry and crumbly pieces which are then pressed into the tart pan, thus avoiding having to roll dough out.

The most critical part of this preparation is to make sure the dough remains in separate, dry crumbs after the egg is added. This is best accomplished by mixing the dough by hand. A mixer or food processor makes it too easy to overmix the dough into a smooth mass.

You may substitute this easy-to-prepare crust for any crust called for in a dessert tart recipe in this chapter. It may be baked empty (blind) or baked with the filling.

1. Combine the dry ingredients in a mixing bowl and stir to combine.

2. Cut the butter into 6 or 8 pieces and distribute over the dry ingredients. Rub in the butter, using your fingertips or a pastry blender, until the mixture resembles a fine powder. Do not allow the mixture to become pasty.

3. Beat the egg in a small bowl and stir into the flour mixture. The dough should remain dry and crumbly.

4. Turn the dough out into the prepared pan. Distribute the crumbly mixture evenly around the bottom and sides of the pan, pressing it into place with floured fingertips. As you press the dough into place, it will adhere to and line the pan. Avoid pressing the dough too hard or it will become thin in places. Make sure that the crust is pressed evenly against the inside angle where the side meets the bottom of the pan. If the crust slopes it will form a thick area that will become hard when it's baked. After the pan is lined, inspect the dough for any excessively thick or thin spots and make them even before proceeding.

STORAGE: Use the tart crust immediately or slide the pan into a plastic bag and refrigerate or freeze. It will not be necessary to defrost it before baking.

VARIATIONS

Any of the ingredients that may be added to make variations of Sweet Tart Dough (page 189) can also be added to this dough in the same proportions.

EASIEST CHOCOLATE RASPBERRY TART

1 recipe No-Roll Tart Crust (page 190)

CHOCOLATE FILLING

1 cup heavy cream
10 ounces semisweet or bittersweet chocolate
2 tablespoons raspberry liqueur or 1 tablespoon framboise (raspberry eau-de-vie)

FINISHING

Three ½-pint baskets fresh raspberries
2 tablespoons confectioners' sugar
½ teaspoon unsweetened cocoa powder

One 9- to 10-inch loose-bottomed tart pan, buttered

ONE 9- TO 10-INCH TART, 8 TO 10 SERVINGS

Now that raspberries are available in stores just about 12 months a year, they are rapidly replacing strawberries as almost everyone's berry of choice. Also out-of-season raspberries have infinitely more flavor and color than out-of-season strawberries.

If you make and chill the filling while the tart crust is baking, you may assemble the tart as soon as the crust has cooled.

1. Set a rack at the middle level of the oven and preheat to 350 degrees.

2. Bake the tart shell for 20 to 30 minutes, or until it is dry and a deep golden color. Cool on a rack.

3. To make the chocolate filling, bring the cream to a boil in a medium saucepan over low heat. Remove from the heat and add all the chocolate at once. Shake the pan so that the chocolate is submerged, and let stand for 3 minutes to melt. Add the liqueur and whisk until smooth. Pour the filling into a mixing bowl and refrigerate it until thickened, but not hardened, about 20 minutes. Stir occasionally while it is chilling.

4. Whisk the filling slightly to make it smooth enough to spread. (If it has hardened, stand the bowl in a larger bowl filled with an inch of hot water and whisk until the right consistency is achieved.) Spread the filling evenly over the cooled tart shell.

5. Arrange the raspberries over the chocolate filling, pressing them down slightly. To unmold the tart, stand the pan on a large can or canister and allow the side to fall away. Slide the tart from the pan bottom onto a large, flat-bottomed platter.

6. Immediately before serving, dust the raspberries with the confectioners' sugar. Dust the center of the tart sparingly with cocoa, on top of the sugar.

SERVING: Serve the tart within a few hours of assembling it—do not refrigerate, or both the filling and crust will harden.

OLD-FASHIONED STRAWBERRY TART

1 recipe Sweet Tart Dough (page 188)

PASTRY CREAM

1 cup milk
¼ cup sugar
3 egg yolks
3 tablespoons flour
1 teaspoon vanilla extract

GLAZE

1 cup strawberry preserves
2 tablespoons kirsch

FINISHING

2 to 3 pints strawberries
½ cup (2 ounces) toasted sliced almonds
Confectioners' sugar for sprinkling

One 9- to 10-inch loose-bottomed tart pan, buttered

ONE 9- TO 10-INCH TART, 8 TO 10 SERVINGS

If you can get fresh, locally grown strawberries in season where you live, be sure to make this tart. Although it can be prepared at any time of the year with shipped-in berries, it is best when the strawberries are at their best.

1. Prepare and chill the dough.

2. To make the pastry cream, combine the milk and half the sugar in a saucepan over low heat. Whisk the yolks with the remaining sugar, sift the flour over the yolks, and whisk them together.

Beat one third of the boiling milk into the yolk mixture and return the remaining milk to a boil. Beat the yolk mixture back into the boiling milk and continue beating until the cream thickens and comes to a boil. Remove from the heat and stir in the vanilla. Scrape the cream onto a clean plate, press plastic wrap against the surface, and chill.

3. Set a rack at the middle level of the oven and preheat to 325 degrees. Roll out the dough and fit it into the prepared pan (page 194).

4. Cut a circle of parchment or wax paper about 2 or 3 inches larger in diameter than the pan. Gently press it down over the dough and fill with dried beans or cherry pits. Bake the tart shell for about 20 minutes, until it's set. Remove the paper and beans and continue baking for 5 minutes more to color the pastry. Do not overbake. Cool the shell in the pan.

5. Spread the cooled pastry cream over the cooled tart shell.

6. Rinse, dry, hull, and halve the berries, stem to point, then arrange them cut side down in concentric circles over the pastry cream.

7. For the glaze, bring the preserves and kirsch to a boil and strain into another pan. Return to low heat and allow to reduce for a minute or two, until it thickens slightly. Brush the glaze onto the berries.

8. Edge the tart with the almonds and sprinkle the almonds with the confectioners' sugar.

9. To unmold, stand the tart pan on a large can

or canister and allow the side to fall away. Slide the tart from the pan bottom onto a large, flat platter.

SERVING: Serve the tart alone, or with a small spoonful of whipped cream.

STORAGE: Keep the tart at room temperature if you are serving it within a few hours. Refrigerate for longer storage.

HINT FOR SUCCESS: Don't glaze the tart more than a few hours before you serve, or the strawberries will become watery.

OLD-FASHIONED RASPBERRY TART: Substitute raspberries for the strawberries, above.

ASSORTED FRUIT TART: Substitute a variety of different fruits (raspberries, peeled and sliced kiwis, orange segments, and hulled and halved strawberries) for the strawberries. Arrange the fruit in concentric circles over the pastry cream.

TART PAN CARE

The recipes in this chapter call for a 9- or 10-inch diameter tart pan with straight, fluted sides and a removable bottom. This type of pan is widely available in department and hardware stores (see Sources of Supply).

I prefer the shiny, tin-plated pans over the black steel ones. The tin-plated pans are easier to maintain and do not rust quite so easily as the steel ones.

Before using a new tart pan, wash it thoroughly with a nonabrasive cloth and mild dishwashing detergent. Make sure to remove all traces of any glue that may have attached a label to the pan. Rinse and dry the pan thoroughly with a soft cloth. The first few times you use the pan, butter it thoroughly with soft, not melted, butter. After the first few uses, it will be unnecessary to butter the pan. Always wash and dry the pan thoroughly after each use.

If anything does stick, soak the pan for no more than 10 minutes in hot, soapy water. Rub away the stuck material with a dishcloth, never an abrasive scouring pad, which would wear away the tin plating and expose the base metal that would then rust. Wash and dry the pan as described above.

Treated carefully, the delicate tin plating on a tart pan will last through years of use and hundreds of tarts.

FORMING TART SHELLS

It is easier to mold pastry dough in a shallow tart pan than a deeper pie pan, and the edge of a tart pastry shell does not need to be fluted, though it shouldn't be neglected.

Follow these simple steps to form neat, professional-looking tart shells:

1. Roll the dough out into a circle about 3 inches larger in diameter than the pan.

2. To transfer the dough to the pan, fold it in half and line up the fold along the middle of the pan, the open edges facing away from you. Grip the dough gently with both hands so it doesn't tear, and unfold it toward you.

3. Gently press—using the palm of your hand and fingertips—the dough against all the interior surfaces of the pan, bottom and side.

4. If you are using Flaky Pie Dough (page 146), fold the excess dough around the rim over the inside of the tart shell and gently press it into place. (If the excess dough is more than ½ inch long, trim it with scissors or the back of a knife before you fold it.)

5. If you are working with any dough except Flaky Pie Dough, make sure the dough is pressed firmly against the side and bottom of the pan and the excess falls to the outside. Roll the rolling pin over the top of the pan to trim away excess dough. If the dough has been stretched rather than pressed, it will shrink back into the pan after you roll over it and won't cover the side.

6. To finish the top edge of the tart shell, position your floured thumb and index finger of one hand so that the thumb is inside the pastry and the tip is against the bottom of the crust. The tip of your index finger should rest against the top edge of the crust. Press gently with both thumb and finger to make the top of the crust straight and even as in the illustration. Proceed to press all the way around the top.

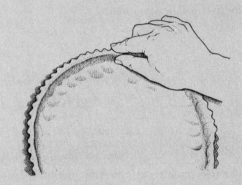

Press gently with both the thumb and index finger to make the top of the crust straight and even, proceeding to press all the way around the top.

7. If possible, before you bake the crust, chill it until it is firm. This will minimize shrinkage.

8. If the filling is to be baked in the crust, you may add it after the crust is chilled. If the tart shell is to be baked without the filling (baked blind), pierce the dough at 1-inch intervals with the tines of a fork. Line the pastry crust with a disk of parchment or wax paper and fill with dry beans. Bake according to the instructions in the individual recipes.

MILANESE PEAR AND CHOCOLATE TART
(TORTA DI PERE ALLA CIOCCOLATA)

1 recipe Chocolate Tart Dough (page 189)

CHOCOLATE CRUMB TOPPING

1 cup bleached all-purpose flour
⅓ cup sugar
¼ cup unsweetened cocoa powder
8 tablespoons (1 stick) unsalted butter, melted

PEAR FILLING

4 (1½ to 2 pounds) ripe Bartlett pears
3 tablespoons sugar
2 tablespoons unsalted butter, melted
1 tablespoon pear eau-de-vie (see Note)

One 9- to 10-inch loose-bottomed tart pan, buttered

ONE 9- TO 10-INCH TART, 8 TO 10 SERVINGS

I first saw this tailored pear and chocolate tart several years ago at Ada Parasiliti's wonderful store, l'Angolo della Gastronomia, in Milan. Though the tart is not difficult to prepare, it must be made with perfectly ripe pears, or the flavor is bland and uninteresting.

1. Prepare and chill the dough.

2. Roll the dough out and line the pan (page 194).

3. Combine the flour and sugar in a bowl, sift in the cocoa, and mix. Stir in the butter and allow to stand for a few minutes. Break up into coarse crumbs.

4. Set a rack at the lower third of the oven and preheat to 350 degrees.

5. To make the filling, peel, halve, core, and slice the pears into a bowl and toss with the remaining ingredients. Pour the filling into the dough-lined pan, smooth the top, and scatter the crumbs over the surface.

6. Bake the tart for 30 to 35 minutes, until the crust and crumbs are baked through and the filling is bubbling.

7. Cool on a rack and serve at room temperature.

8. To unmold, stand the tart pan on a large can or canister and allow the side to fall away. Slide the tart from the pan bottom onto a large, flat-bottomed platter.

SERVING: Serve the tart on the day it is baked accompanied by a little whipped cream, if you wish.

STORAGE: Keep the tart loosely covered at room temperature until you serve it.

Note: The best pear eau-de-vie comes from the canton of Valais in western Switzerland. If you cannot find the pear eau-de-vie, substitute white rum.

CHOCOLATE BANANA CREAM TART

1 recipe Chocolate Tart Dough (page 189)

CHOCOLATE FILLING

1 cup milk
¼ cup sugar
3 egg yolks
3 tablespoons all-purpose flour
1 teaspoon vanilla extract
4 ounces semisweet chocolate
¾ cup heavy cream
3 large bananas

FINISHING

1 cup heavy cream
Chocolate shavings

One 9- to 10-inch loose-bottomed tart pan, buttered

ONE 9- TO 10-INCH TART, 8 TO 10 SERVINGS

In this tart, the chocolate pastry and pastry cream give an added flavor dimension to the usual combination of custard and bananas.

1. Prepare and chill the dough.

2. Roll the dough out and line the pan (page 194).

3. To make the chocolate filling, combine the milk and 2 tablespoons of the sugar in a saucepan over low heat and bring to a boil.

4. Whisk the yolks with the remaining 2 tablespoons of sugar, sift the flour over it, and whisk together.

5. Beat a third of the boiling milk into the yolk mixture and return the remaining milk to a boil. Beat the yolk mixture back into the boiling milk and continue beating until the cream thickens and returns to a boil. Remove from the heat and stir in the vanilla and chocolate. When the chocolate has melted, scrape the cream into a bowl. Press plastic wrap against the surface and chill to set.

6. While the filling is setting, set a rack at the middle level of the oven and preheat to 325 degrees.

7. Cut a circle of parchment or wax paper about 2 or 3 inches larger in diameter than the pan. Gently press it down over the dough and fill with dried beans or cherry pits. Bake the crust for about 20 minutes, until it's set and no longer wet and shiny. Remove the paper and beans and bake for 5 to 10 minutes longer, just until the dough is set. Do not overbake the dough or it will be dry.

8. To finish the filling, whip the heavy cream and fold into the cooled chocolate mixture. Slice the bananas and fold them into the chocolate filling. Spread evenly over the cooled tart shell.

9. To finish, whip the heavy cream and spread over the filling. Cover with the chocolate shavings.

10. To unmold the tart, stand the tart pan on a large can or canister and allow the side to fall away. Slide the tart from the pan bottom onto a large, flat-bottomed platter.

SERVING: Serve small wedges of this rich tart—no accompaniment is necessary.

STORAGE: Keep the tart refrigerated until it is served, up to several hours.

HINT FOR SUCCESS: For perfect chocolate shavings, use a vegetable peeler and scrape the side of a bar of chocolate. Or use a melon ball scoop and draw it across the surface of the bar. Milk chocolate is softer and easier to shave than dark chocolate.

APRICOT AND PISTACHIO TART

1 recipe Sweet Tart Dough (page 188)

FILLING

1 cup (about 4 ounces) shelled unsalted pistachios

½ cup sugar

1 teaspoon almond extract

2 eggs

4 tablespoons unsalted butter

¼ cup all-purpose flour

12 medium (2 to 2½ pounds) apricots, washed, halved, and pitted

APRICOT GLAZE

1 cup apricot preserves or jam

2 tablespoons water or white rum

One 9- to 10-inch loose-bottomed tart pan, buttered

ONE 9- TO 10-INCH TART, 8 TO 10 SERVINGS

Unless you live in the Southwest or have an apricot tree in your garden, apricots in a state of perfect ripeness are difficult to find.

When apricots come into season, I usually buy the ones that have begun to soften slightly and close them in a paper bag at room temperature to ripen for a day or two before I use them. If the apricots remain excessively tart, I glaze them heavily with apricot preserves, below.

The best pistachios can be found in Middle Eastern grocery stores and usually come from Turkey or Afghanistan. I blanch the pistachios to remove the skins so that the filling has a tender green color characteristic of the best pistachios.

1. Prepare and chill the dough.

2. For the filling, place the pistachios in a saucepan and cover with water. Place the pan on medium heat and bring to a boil. Drain the pistachios in a strainer, then pour into a clean kitchen towel. Fold the towel over and rub the pistachios to loosen the skins. Go over the pistachios carefully, separating the kernels from the skins. Discard the skins.

3. Remove and coarsely chop ¼ cup of the pistachios to use for finishing the tart. Combine the remaining pistachios and the sugar in a food processor fitted with a metal blade. Pulse on and off repeatedly until the mixture is finely ground, about 1 minute. Add the almond extract and one of the eggs and continue to pulse until the mixture becomes a smooth paste. Divide the butter into 8 pieces and add to the work bowl.

(continued)

Pulse again repeatedly until the butter is smoothly mixed with the nut mixture. Scrape down the inside of the bowl with a metal spatula. Add the remaining egg and pulse until smooth. Allow the machine to run continuously for 30 seconds and scrape down the inside of the bowl. Add the flour and pulse until just incorporated. Set aside, covered, until the crust is ready.

4. Set a rack at the lowest level of the oven and preheat to 350 degrees.

5. Roll out the dough and line the pan (page 194).

6. Spread the pistachio filling on the dough. Arrange the apricots, cut side up, on the filling, in 2 or 3 concentric circles, depending on the size of the apricots.

7. Bake the tart for about 35 minutes, until the crust and filling are baked through and the apricots are cooked. Cool the tart on a rack.

8. To make the glaze, bring the preserves and water or rum to a boil and strain. Reduce to thicken if necessary. Brush the hot glaze over the surface of the cooled tart. Edge the tart with the reserved chopped pistachios.

9. To unmold the tart, stand the tart pan on a large can or canister and allow the side to fall away. Slide the tart from the pan bottom onto a large, flat-bottomed platter.

SERVING: Serve the tart alone, or with a small spoonful of whipped cream.

STORAGE: Keep the tart at room temperature if you are serving it within a few hours. Refrigerate the tart for longer storage.

HINT FOR SUCCESS: If the apricots are excessively tart, add 2 tablespoons sugar to the glaze.

VARIATIONS

PEACH AND PISTACHIO TART: Substitute the same weight of peeled, quartered peaches for the apricots.

RASPBERRY AND PISTACHIO TART: Substitute two ½-pint baskets of raspberries for the apricots.

CUBAN-STYLE CREAM CHEESE AND GUAVA TART
(TORTA DE QUESO Y GUAYABA)

**1 recipe Sweet Dough for a two-crust pie
(page 188)**

FILLING

1 pound cream cheese
One 18-ounce can guava shells, well drained

One 9- to 10-inch loose-bottomed tart pan, buttered

ONE 9- TO 10-INCH TART, 8 TO 10 SERVINGS

When I wanted to learn to prepare some typically Hispanic recipes, I called upon Anna Barros, a former student of Cuban descent. Together we worked out many of the Hispanic-style recipes I now use in classes, including this very sweet, subtle tart. The original, available in many of the Cuban bakeries in northern New Jersey, doesn't have a top crust—though I think that adding a bit of extra dough makes the total dessert seem much less sugary.

Usually we use the best fresh fruit for tarts like this—in this case the fresh guavas are largely unobtainable, and even when found are not as ripe or sweet as the canned variety. Canned guava shells may be found in grocery stores in Hispanic neighborhoods or mail-ordered (see Sources of Supply).

1. Prepare and chill the dough.

2. Roll out half the dough and line the pan (page 194).

3. Set a rack at the lower third of the oven and preheat to 350 degrees.

4. For the filling, cut the cream cheese into thin slices and distribute all over the bottom crust. Drain the guava shells and arrange over the cream cheese, cut sides down.

5. Roll the remaining dough into a 12-inch square and cut into ½-inch strips. Cover the filling with a diagonal lattice of the dough as in the illustration on page 112.

6. Bake the tart for about 40 minutes, until the crust is baked through and golden. Cool on a rack.

7. To unmold the tart, stand the tart pan on a large can or canister and allow the side to fall away. Slide the tart from the pan bottom onto a large, flat-bottomed platter.

SERVING: Serve the tart in small wedges—it is very sweet.

STORAGE: Keep the tart at room temperature until it is served. Refrigerate, covered with plastic wrap, for longer storage.

VARIATION

Use a 9-inch square tart pan. Place all the lattice strips diagonally on the tart in one direction only.

PORTUGUESE RICE TART
(PASTEIS DE ARROZ)

1 recipe Sweet Tart Dough (page 188)

RICE FILLING

Pinch of salt
⅓ cup long-grain rice
4 cups milk
½ cup granulated sugar
1 teaspoon finely grated lemon zest
¼ teaspoon ground cinnamon
6 egg yolks
½ cup (about 2 ounces) toasted slivered almonds

FINISHING

½ cup (about 2 ounces) raw slivered almonds
Confectioners' sugar

One 9- to 10-inch loose-bottomed tart pan, buttered

ONE 9- TO 10-INCH TART, 8 TO 10 SERVINGS

A few years ago, I was looking for an interesting recipe for a rice tart to use in a class, and I came across this version in Maria de Lourdes Modesto's monumental cookbook *Cozinha Tradicional Portuguesa* (Traditional Portuguese Cooking). It is based on a tart made in the Azores, the bleak islands which are Europe's westernmost point in the Atlantic.

1. Prepare and chill the dough.

2. To make the filling, bring a large pan of water to a boil and add the salt. Stir in the rice, return to a boil, and cook for about 10 minutes, until the rice begins to split open. Drain and rinse the rice.

3. Combine the rice with the milk and sugar in a saucepan and bring to a boil over low heat. Lower to a simmer and cook the rice, stirring occasionally, until it has absorbed all the milk and become thickened and creamy, 20 to 30 minutes. Remove from the heat and stir in the lemon zest and cinnamon. Beat the yolks to break them up and beat some of the hot rice into the yolks, then beat the yolk mixture into the remaining rice. Cool and stir in the toasted almonds.

4. Set a rack at the lower third of the oven and preheat to 350 degrees.

5. Roll out the dough and line the pan (page 194).

6. Spread the cooled filling over the dough and strew the raw slivered almonds on the surface of the filling.

7. Bake for about 30 minutes, until the crust is golden and the filling is set. Remove from the oven and cool on a rack. Before serving, dust with confectioners' sugar.

8. To unmold the tart, stand the pan on a large can or canister and allow the side to fall away. Slide the tart from the pan bottom onto a large, flat-bottomed platter.

SERVING: Serve the tart with a spoonful of whipped cream, if you wish.

STORAGE: Keep the tart at room temperature until ready to serve. Refrigerate, covered with plastic wrap, for longer storage.

HINT FOR SUCCESS: Be patient while cooking the rice—the creamy texture of the filling comes from long, slow cooking.

VARIATIONS

Add ½ cup raisins or chopped candied orange peel to the filling before spreading it in the crust.

ALMOND AND OTHER NUT FILLINGS

A delicious and practical way to assemble a fruit tart is to use a nut filling, sometimes referred to as "frangipane." The origin of the name is not clear, though it was the name of a Roman family as well as that of a highly scented tropical flower used to make *leis* in Hawaii. The name was used in nineteenth-century French cookbooks for a kind of cooked, flour-thickened pastry cream filling enriched and flavored with crushed macaroons. Nowadays, frangipane means a delicate and buttery nut-cake batter.

It is most often used in two ways. Either it is spread over a pastry crust and topped with fruit, which allows the frangipane to absorb juices from the fruit during and after baking, and keeps the crust dry and crisp; or it is used as a topping for fruit arranged directly on the crust. This is good for fruit that should not be exposed to air, such as bananas. Either way, the frangipane must be baked, because it contains raw eggs and flour.

The recipe that follows may be varied infinitely. So long as you are careful to keep the proportion of nuts to sugar the same, you may substitute any type of nut you like in the recipe.

Frangipane

- ¾ cup (about 3 ounces) whole blanched almonds
- ½ cup sugar
- 1 teaspoon almond extract
- 2 eggs
- 4 tablespoons unsalted butter
- ¼ cup bleached all-purpose flour

ABOUT 14 OUNCES, ENOUGH TO FILL A 9- TO 10-INCH TART

1. Combine the almonds and sugar in a food processor fitted with the metal blade. Pulse on and off repeatedly until the mixture is finely ground, about 1 minute.

2. Add the almond extract and one of the eggs and continue to pulse until the mixture becomes a smooth paste.

3. Divide the butter into 8 pieces and add them to the work bowl. Pulse again repeatedly

until the butter is smoothly mixed in. Scrape down the inside of the bowl with a spatula.

4. Add the remaining egg and pulse until smooth. Allow the machine to run continuously for 30 seconds and scrape down the inside of the bowl. Add the flour and pulse until just incorporated.

5. Scrape the filling from the work bowl into a small bowl. Use immediately or store according to the instructions below.

STORAGE: Keep the frangipane tightly covered in the refrigerator for a day or two. Because it contains raw eggs, this should not be frozen.

HINT FOR SUCCESS: Make sure the butter is well blended into the almond mixture and that there are no tiny lumps. They would cause the frangipane to separate as it is baking and have a heavy texture after it is baked.

VARIATIONS

To make the frangipane in a mixer, grind the almonds and sugar in a blender, or some other grinding machine. If you use a hand nut grinder, grind only the almonds, add the sugar later. Then, using a hand-held or heavy-duty mixer with the paddle attachment set at medium speed, beat the almonds and sugar with the extract and the first egg. Beat in the butter, then the remaining egg and the flour, scraping the bowl and beater(s) after each addition.

PISTACHIO OR MACADAMIA FRANGIPANE: Substitute blanched (skinned) pistachios or unsalted macadamias for the almonds; use the almond extract.

HAZELNUT FRANGIPANE: Substitute blanched (skinned) hazelnuts for the almonds; omit the almond extract.

WALNUT OR PECAN FRANGIPANE: Substitute 1 cup walnut or pecan pieces (they are lighter in weight than the nuts above) for the almonds. Use light or dark brown sugar for some or all of the sugar in the recipe. Omit the almond extract and add ½ teaspoon ground cinnamon and 2 teaspoons vanilla extract or dark rum.

Chocolate Pecan Dacquoise,
page 309.

CAKES (*clockwise from lower left*):
Rehrücken, page 313; Chocolate Mousse
Cake with Raspberry Eau-de-Vie, page 316;
Chocolate Almond, page 314;
Chocolate Mocha Walnut Roll, page 319;
Chocolate Pastry, page 311;
Swiss Chocolate Truffle, page 315.

OPPOSITE: CAKES (*clockwise from bottom*):
Strawberry Sunburst, page 303; Michelle Tampakis's
Carrot, page 305; Coconut Layer, page 306.

ABOVE (clockwise from bottom): Plum Crumb Cake,
page 293; Cherry Crumb Cake Squares, page 294;
Apricot Crumb Cake, page 292.

RIGHT: Oxford Fruitcake, page 296.

Devil's Food Cake, page 272; with vanilla buttercream, page 324.

Classic White, page 271; with Whipped Cream, page 327.

Classic White, page 271; with coffee buttercream, page 324.

Classic White, page 271; with raspberry buttercream, page 324.

Devil's Food Cake, page 272; with Whipped Cream, page 327.

Devil's Food Cake, page 272; with chocolate icing, page 313; and chocolate streaking, page 325.

Old-Fashioned Spice Cake with
Boiled Icing, page 310.

Chocolate Chestnut Bûche
de Noël, page 320.

Banana Feuilletés with
Caramel Sauce, page 359.

Top (l to r): Palmiers, page 349;
Swiss Pretzels, page 352; Shoe Soles, page 350.

Right: Coffee Rum Éclairs, page 373.

Opposite (clockwise from top left):
Boules de Neige (Snowballs), page 371;
Italian Cream Puffs, page 370; Sugar Rings,
page 369; Almond Puffs, page 369; Sugar S's,
page 369; Almond Rings, page 369.

LEFT TO RIGHT: **Parmesan and Paprika Palmiers, page 380; Caraway Salt Sticks, page 380; Mozzarella and Prosciutto Turnovers, page 382.**

TOP: Brioche Rolls, page 391;
Brioches au Sucre, page 392;
Brioches à Tête, page 392.
BOTTOM: Croissants, page 415;
Almond Croissants, page 417;
Petits Pains au Chocolat, page 417.

Orange Babas Marcella,
page 407.

Wiener Gugelhupf,
page 403.

LEFT TO RIGHT:
Selkirk Bannock,
page 402;
Bara Brith, page 402;
Barm Brack, page 401.

DANISH PASTRIES.
Top: Danish Walnut
Braid, page 421.
Bottom (l to r):
Danish Roll, page 431;
Danish Knots,
with and without crumb
topping, page 433;
Danish Cheese Pocket,
page 426.

RHUBARB AND ORANGE TART

1 recipe Sweet Dough for a one-crust pie
    (page 149)

POACHED RHUBARB

1½ pounds fresh rhubarb
1 cup sugar
2 cups water

CRUMB TOPPING

1¼ cups all-purpose flour
½ cup sugar
¼ teaspoon ground cinnamon
8 tablespoons (1 stick) unsalted butter, melted

ORANGE CUSTARD

⅔ cup heavy cream
¼ cup sugar
Grated zest of 1 medium orange, about ½ teaspoon
1 teaspoon vanilla extract
4 egg yolks

One 9- to 10-inch loose-bottomed tart pan, buttered

ONE 9- TO 10-INCH TART, 8 TO 10 SERVINGS

Though it requires a little extra effort to poach the rhubarb before using it in the tart, it makes the filling creamier and much less watery. The method used for poaching the rhubarb is an interesting one—the rhubarb cooks from the heat retained in the pan and the syrup without going on the fire itself. (If rhubarb approaches a simmer it will disintegrate.)

1. Prepare and chill the dough.

2. To prepare the rhubarb, trim away the leaves completely (they are toxic) and if the rhubarb is well developed and tough looking, string it. Cut the stalks into 2-inch lengths. Bring the sugar and water to a boil in a large, shallow pan, add the rhubarb, cover, turn off the heat, and allow the rhubarb to cool completely.

3. Roll out the dough and line the pan (page 194).

4. To make the crumbs, combine the dry ingredients in a bowl. Stir the melted butter into the dry ingredients. Allow to stand a minute, then by hand break into coarse crumbs. Set aside.

5. To make the orange custard, in a mixing bowl, whisk the ingredients together until smooth.

6. Set a rack at the lower third of the oven and preheat to 350 degrees.

7. To assemble the tart, drain the rhubarb well. Reserve the syrup in the refrigerator and use it to poach another batch of rhubarb later on. Arrange the rhubarb in the tart shell and pour on the orange custard filling. Scatter the crumbs evenly over the filling.

8. Bake the tart for about 40 minutes, until the filling is set and the crumbs have browned lightly. Cool on a rack.

9. To unmold the tart, stand the tart pan on a large can or canister and allow the side to fall

away. Slide the tart from the pan bottom onto a large, flat-bottomed platter.

SERVING: Serve the tart after a light meal: it is rich.

STORAGE: Keep the tart at room temperature until ready to serve. Refrigerate, covered with plastic wrap, for longer storage.

HINT FOR SUCCESS: Look for thin (about 1-inch-wide) rhubarb. It is more tender and will cook through more quickly.

VARIATIONS

Substitute 1 pint blueberries, rinsed and drained, or 1 quart sour cherries, stemmed and pitted, for the rhubarb. Substitute lemon zest for the orange.

FREE-FORM TART SHELL

To make a free-form tart crust, roll any of the tart doughs (pages 188 to 190) to a 12-inch disk and transfer it to a parchment- or foil-lined cookie sheet or the back of a jelly-roll pan. Using a plate or cardboard disk as a pattern, trim the dough to an even 12-inch diameter. Fold under about ½ inch of dough at the edge of the disk of dough, then flute the edge as if it were a pie, page 194, to make the edge stand up. Use the thumb and index finger of one hand on the outside of the tart shell and the index finger of the other hand on the inside, and pinch gently from the outside while pressing lightly from the inside; repeat all around the edge of the crust. Dock, but do not line and weight, to avoid crushing the delicate edge of the crust.

DOUGHS FOR INDIVIDUAL TARTS, TARTLETS, AND BARQUETTES

Though the doughs in the previous section of this chapter can be used to form tartlets and other individual and miniature pastries, the recipes that follow are for doughs especially suited to small pastries.

FLAKY DOUGH FOR TARTLETS: Especially useful because it is mixed until somewhat elastic, and it can be rolled thinner than the conventional flaky dough used for large pies and tarts.

COOKIE DOUGHS: Variations on the French *pâte sablée* (literally, sandy dough). For delicate tartlet and barquette shells baked empty.

ALMOND OR HAZELNUT DOUGH: These round out the selection of doughs to use for small pastries. Both doughs, which are soft, can also be pressed into tiny pans, which avoids having to roll them out.

FLAKY DOUGH
FOR TARTLETS

1½ cups bleached all-purpose flour
½ teaspoon salt
⅛ teaspoon baking powder (measure ¼ teaspoon,
  then place on a flat surface and divide it with
  the point of a knife)
10 tablespoons (1¼ sticks) unsalted butter
4 to 5 tablespoons cold water

ABOUT 12 OUNCES DOUGH, ENOUGH FOR ABOUT 24
SMALL (2- TO 2½-INCH) PASTRIES OR 8 TO 10 LARGER
(3½- TO 4-INCH) PASTRIES

Use this dough for any small shells baked empty, whether they will be filled with sweet or savory mixtures. It is my favorite for small hors d'oeuvre pastries.

1. To form the dough by hand, combine the flour, salt, and baking powder in a medium mixing bowl and stir well to combine. Cut the butter into 1-tablespoon pieces and add to the dry ingredients. Toss once or twice to coat the pieces of butter. Use your hands or a pastry blender to rub the butter into the dry ingredients. Break it into tiny pieces and keep pinching and squeezing it into the dry ingredients. Occasionally reach down to the bottom of the bowl and mix all the ingredients evenly together to keep it uniform. Continue rubbing the butter into the dry ingredients until it resembles a coarse-ground cornmeal and no large pieces of

butter remain visible. Sprinkle the minimum amount of water on the butter and flour mixture and stir gently with a fork—it should begin holding together. If it still appears dry and crumbly, add the remaining water, 1 teaspoon at a time, until the dough holds together easily.

To mix the dough in a food processor, combine the flour, salt, and baking powder in the work bowl fitted with a metal blade. Pulse 3 times at 1-second intervals to mix. Cut the butter into 1-tablespoon pieces and add to the work bowl. Process, pulsing repeatedly, at 1-second intervals, until the mixture is fine and powdery and resembles a coarsely ground cornmeal and no large pieces of butter remain visible, about 15 pulses in all. Sprinkle the minimum amount of water on the butter and flour mixture and pulse 5 or 6 times—the dough should begin holding together. If it still appears dry and crumbly, add the remaining water, 1 teaspoon at a time, until the dough holds together easily.

2. Whichever process you use to form the dough, at this point turn it out onto a lightly floured surface and form it into a rectangle. Wrap in plastic and refrigerate until firm, or until you are ready to use it, but for at least 1 hour.

STORAGE: Keep the dough in the refrigerator for up to 2 days, or double-wrap in plastic and freeze it for up to several weeks.

HINT FOR SUCCESS: For best results, have all ingredients cold and work quickly so the butter doesn't melt, which would toughen the dough.

COOKIE DOUGH

8 tablespoons (1 stick) unsalted butter, softened

¼ cup sugar

1 egg yolk

1 teaspoon vanilla extract

1¼ cups cake flour

ABOUT 12 OUNCES OF DOUGH, ENOUGH TO MAKE
ABOUT 24 SMALL PASTRIES

Both of these doughs make a delicate crust for individual and miniature pastries, whether they are baked empty or filled. What makes this dough so delicate is that it is made with cake flour. The low protein content of cake flour permits only very weak gluten to form during mixing, which results in a dough that has a delicate, crumbly texture after baking. One note of caution: because the dough is weak in gluten, it is very inelastic and does not hold together well after it has been rolled. But if you follow the instructions in the recipes using this dough, and only roll small pieces of dough at a time, you should have no problems handling it.

1. Beat the butter and sugar together until smooth and light with a hand mixer set at medium speed or in a heavy-duty mixer fitted with the paddle attachment. Continue beating until the mixture is light and fluffy and resembles buttercream, about 5 minutes. Beat in the egg yolk and vanilla extract and continue beating until the mixture is smooth and light, about 3 minutes longer.

2. Sift the cake flour through a strainer or sifter over the butter mixture. Fold it in with a rubber spatula.

3. Scrape the dough onto a piece of plastic wrap and shape it into a rough rectangle. Wrap and chill until you are ready to use it.

STORAGE: Keep the dough in the refrigerator for up to 2 days, or double-wrap it in plastic and freeze it for up to several weeks.

HINT FOR SUCCESS: Be sure the butter, sugar, and yolk mixture is perfectly smooth before you add the cake flour or the baked pastry, rather than having a light, delicate texture, could be heavy and hard.

VARIATION

CHOCOLATE COOKIE DOUGH: Substitute 1 cup cake flour and ¼ cup unsweetened non-alkalized cocoa powder for the 1¼ cups cake flour, above.

ALMOND OR HAZELNUT DOUGH

½ cup (about 2 ounces) whole blanched almonds
  or hazelnuts
¼ cup sugar
1¼ cups bleached all-purpose flour
⅛ teaspoon salt
¼ teaspoon baking powder
4 tablespoons cold unsalted butter
1 large egg

ABOUT 13 OUNCES DOUGH, ENOUGH FOR ABOUT
24 TARTLETS OR BARQUETTES

Delicate nut doughs such as this one are a perfect complement to the rich and delicate fillings used in tiny pastries. This dough and its variations are particularly good in the recipes for Tartelettes Gianduia (page 223) and Raspberry and Almond Tarts (page 212).

1. Combine the nuts and sugar in the bowl of a food processor and pulse repeatedly, about 20 times in all, until the mixture is finely ground. Scrape down the inside of the work bowl with a metal spatula, making sure that the end of the spatula reaches the inside edge of the bowl where a firm paste of ground nuts may accumulate.

2. Add the flour, salt, and baking powder and pulse several times to mix.

3. Cut the butter into 6 or 8 pieces, add it to the work bowl, and pulse 8 or 10 times to mix the butter finely into the dry ingredients. Add the egg and pulse repeatedly until the dough forms a ball, about 6 or 8 times.

4. Scrape the dough onto a piece of plastic wrap and wrap it tightly. Chill the dough for about 1 hour, or until it is firm.

STORAGE: Keep the dough in the refrigerator for up to 2 days, or double-wrap in plastic and freeze it for up to several weeks.

HINT FOR SUCCESS: If the nuts are cool when they are ground, they will be easier to reduce to a fine powder with less risk that they will become pasty.

VARIATION

CHOCOLATE ALMOND (OR HAZELNUT) DOUGH: Substitute 1 cup flour and 3 tablespoons unsweetened, non-alkalized cocoa powder for the flour, above.

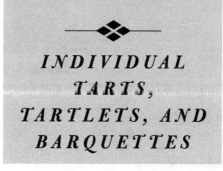

INDIVIDUAL TARTS, TARTLETS, AND BARQUETTES

Individual and miniature tarts, barquettes (little boat shapes), and other tiny pastries often contain the same fillings as larger pies and tarts, but always seem more delicate, in flavor as well as appearance.

Individual tartlets and other pastries differ from miniature ones only in size. An individual round pastry may be anywhere from 2 to 4 inches in diameter, larger if oval or rectangular. Miniatures are usually from 1 to 1½ inches across. An individual pastry is meant to be a single dessert portion, whereas a miniature pastry is usually part of an assortment served after dinner with coffee, or at teatime.

Individual and miniature pastries require more time to roll than one large one. Finishing requires only a little more time. And they save the host cutting and serving time (and effort).

Many savory pastries are formed as individuals or miniatures. Meat and vegetable turnovers can be the main course of a light meal while tiny, rich tartlets and barquettes make delicate hors d'oeuvres.

The recipes in this section fall into the following categories:

INDIVIDUAL DESSERT TARTLETS: These are small tarts, each of which is a single portion of dessert.

TARTLETS: Miniature tarts with sweet or savory fillings.

BARQUETTES: Miniature boat-shaped shells with either sweet or savory fillings.

CARAMEL APPLE TARTS

1 recipe Flaky Dough for Tartlets (page 206)

FILLING

6 (about 3 pounds) tart apples, such as Granny Smith

1¼ cups sugar

½ teaspoon lemon juice

3 tablespoons unsalted butter

2 tablespoons water

1 tablespoon Calvados, applejack, or dark rum

GLAZE

½ cup caramel from filling, above

⅔ cup apricot preserves

2 tablespoons water

Eight to ten 3½- to 4-inch tart pans (see Sources of Supply), buttered

EIGHT TO TEN 3½- TO 4-INCH TARTS

These rich tarts are perfect after a light dinner.

1. Prepare and chill the dough.

2. To make the filling, peel, halve, and core the apples. Wrap 3 of the apple halves in plastic and refrigerate them until you are ready to assemble the tarts. Dice the remaining apples into ½-inch cubes and set aside near the stove.

3. To make the caramel, combine the sugar and lemon juice in a large aluminum or enameled iron sauté pan (do not use tin-lined copper or the tin coating may melt). Mix well until the mixture resembles wet sand. Place over low heat and cook until the sugar begins to melt and caramelize, 3 to 4 minutes. Stir occasionally so that the sugar caramelizes evenly. When the caramel is a deep amber color, remove from the heat and add the butter; water; and Calvados, applejack, or rum. Swirl the pan to mix, then set aside ½ cup of the caramel in a small saucepan to use later for the glaze.

4. Add the apples to the sauté pan and place it over medium heat, swirling it to coat the apples with caramel. Cook until the apples have exuded juices and diluted the caramel, about 10 minutes. Continue cooking until the apples are fairly dry, about 10 minutes longer. Pour the filling out into a ceramic heatproof glass or stainless-steel pan and refrigerate it while rolling the crusts.

5. Set a rack at the lowest level of the oven and preheat to 400 degrees.

6. To make the crusts, divide the dough into 8 or 10 small pieces and on a floured surface roll each to a thin circle. Press the circles of dough well into the prepared pans, then roll over the top of each pan with a rolling pin to trim off the excess. Arrange the pans on a jelly-roll pan as they are lined.

7. Divide the cooled filling among the dough-lined pans and smooth the top of the filling flat. Cut the reserved apple halves into ⅛-inch slices and arrange 4 or 5 slices over the filling in each tart.

8. Bake the tarts for about 30 minutes, until the crust is baked through and the sliced apples have browned. Place the tarts on a rack to cool.

9. To make the glaze, add the apricot preserves and water to the reserved caramel in the saucepan. Bring to a simmer over low heat, stirring occasionally. Strain the glaze into another pan and return it to a low heat to reduce and thicken slightly, about 5 minutes longer.

10. Unmold the cooled tarts and arrange them on a platter or pan. Brush the tarts with the hot glaze and allow the glaze to set.

SERVING: Serve the tarts at room temperature. If you wish to serve them warm, reheat them at 300 degrees for about 5 minutes before serving.

Accompany them with some sweetened whipped cream flavored with applejack or Calvados and a pinch of cinnamon.

STORAGE: Keep the tarts loosely covered, at room temperature, until time to serve them. For longer storage, refrigerate the tarts on a pan, covered with plastic wrap. Reheat them before serving, and serve warm or cooled.

HINTS FOR SUCCESS: Watch the caramel carefully—if it colors unevenly remove from the heat and stir well. Return the pan to lower heat and continue cooking.

Apply the glaze with a soft brush to avoid putting too much on the tart.

VARIATION

CARAMEL PEAR TARTS: Substitute ripe Bartlett pears for the apples, above. To avoid discolored pears, peel, core, and dice about 2 pounds pears immediately before you cook them. Then peel, core, and slice the remaining pears only just before placing them on top of the filling.

FORMING TARTS AND TARTLETS

Tiny pastries can be awkward to form. The doughs tend to soften, and trying to fit a small, soft piece of dough into a tiny pan is enough to try the patience of even the saintliest baker. Follow these rules to make the job easier:

When you are making large tarts, divide the dough into as many pieces as there are pans, and roll the pieces of dough out one at a time. If it is warm in the room, keep both the unrolled pieces of dough and the buttered tart pans on a pan or tray in the refrigerator. As each piece of dough is rolled, lay it in one of the pans. When all the pieces of dough are rolled and in pans, remove the pans one at a time from the refrigerator, and press and fit the dough into them. Treated this way, the dough won't soften and always remains easy to handle.

When you are making small tarts, roll the dough out into a rectangle (or several rectangles) and cut out circles with a fluted cutter slightly larger in diameter than the tart pan. A fluted cutter gives the crust at the edge of the tart a pretty scalloped finish. Gently press the dough into the pan so that it is flat against the bottom and sides.

RASPBERRY AND ALMOND TARTS

1 recipe Cookie Dough for Tartlets (page 207)

ALMOND FILLING

¾ **cup (about 3 ounces) whole blanched almonds**

½ **cup sugar**

1 teaspoon almond extract

2 eggs

4 tablespoons unsalted butter

¼ **cup all-purpose flour**

⅓ **cup seedless raspberry preserves or jam**

2 baskets (8 to 12 ounces each) fresh raspberries

Confectioners' sugar for dusting

Eight to ten 3½- to 4-inch tart pans (see Sources of Supply), buttered

EIGHT TO TEN 3½- TO 4-INCH TARTS

The tart, juicy berries offer an ideal contrast to the dense, rich, and aromatic almond filling. This exquisite tart is best at teatime, when your appetite has not been sated.

1. Prepare and chill the dough.

2. To make the almond filling, combine the almonds and sugar in a food processor fitted with the metal blade. Pulse on and off repeatedly until the mixture is finely ground, about 1 minute. Use a metal spatula to scrape the inside of the bowl, dislodging any of the mixture stuck along the inside bottom edge of the bowl.

3. Add the almond extract and one of the eggs and continue to pulse until the mixture becomes a smooth paste. Divide the butter into 8 pieces and add them to the work bowl. Pulse again repeatedly until the butter is smoothly mixed with the almond paste. Scrape down the inside of the bowl with a metal spatula. Add the remaining egg and pulse until smooth. Allow the machine to run continuously for 30 seconds and scrape down the inside of the bowl. Add the flour and pulse until it's just incorporated.

4. Set a rack at the lowest level of the oven and preheat to 350 degrees.

5. To make the crusts, divide the dough into 8 or 10 small pieces and on a floured surface roll each to a thin circle. Press the circles of dough well into the prepared pans and roll a rolling pin over the top of each pan to trim off the excess. Arrange the pans on a jelly-roll pan.

6. Spread a teaspoon of the jam in each dough-lined pan. Divide the almond filling among the pans and smooth the top of the filling flat. Arrange the raspberries over the almond filling, pressing them in gently.

7. Bake the tarts for about 30 minutes, until the crust is baked through and the filling is set. Place the tart pans on a rack to cool.

8. Unmold the tarts and arrange them on a platter or pan. Immediately before serving, dust them with the confectioners' sugar.

SERVING: Serve the tarts at room temperature, with sweetened whipped cream, if you wish.

STORAGE: Keep the tarts loosely covered at room temperature until time to serve them. For longer storage, refrigerate the tarts on a pan covered with plastic wrap. Bring the tarts to room temperature before serving.

HINT FOR SUCCESS: Avoid overbaking the tarts, or the raspberries will shrivel and blacken. If the crust seems underdone after the tarts have baked for 30 minutes, cover the whole jelly-roll pan loosely with a sheet of aluminum foil to protect the berries.

VARIATIONS

Substitute pitted sour cherries, seedless red or green grapes, or blueberries for the raspberries.

❖
TARTLET PANS
———

Although tartlet pans are available in many shapes and sizes, I use several over and over again.

When I am making larger tarts, such as the Caramelized Raspberry Tarts (page 215), I use a 3¾-inch diameter, nonstick tart pan that is about ¾ inch deep. It has gently sloping sides and is available through Bridge Kitchenware in New York (see Sources of Supply). If you must, you may substitute muffin pans for this type of tart pan, but if you do you will have to make more tarts. You can only put about a 1-inch depth of the fillings intended for these large tarts into muffin pans or they will take too long to bake through and the crusts will burn.

When I make miniature tarts and barquettes, I use some 2¼-inch diameter (across the top) sloping-sided tart pans and 3-inch-long barquette pans.

Small fluted pans are available for miniature tartlets and barquettes and they usually come packed in a tin in sets of 24 or 36 tiny pans of several different shapes and patterns. These are available through kitchenware stores and often in department stores. Use these pans for the recipes in which a little ball of dough is pressed into the pans. They would be awkward to line with a sheet of dough because of their irregular shapes and fluted sides.

Whichever type of pan you choose will last a lifetime if properly cared for. Don't wash and scrub the pans after you use them—a good wipe with a slightly damp paper towel or dishcloth should be enough. Scrubbing wears away the tin plating, and once it's gone the pans can rust if they are exposed to humidity. If you live in a very humid climate, wipe the pans, place them on a jelly-roll pan, and bake the empty pans at 350 degrees for about 10 minutes. Then sift cornstarch over them as soon as you take them from the oven. As soon as they have cooled, pack the pans into an airtight tin, still covered with the starch. Wipe off the starch before you use the pans the next time.

CRANBERRY, APPLE, AND WALNUT TARTS

2 recipes Flaky Dough for Tartlets (page 206)

CRANBERRY, APPLE, AND WALNUT FILLING

4 (about 2 pounds) tart apples, such as Granny Smith
One 12-ounce bag cranberries
1 cup light brown sugar
2 tablespoons unsalted butter
½ teaspoon ground cinnamon

1 cup lightly toasted walnut pieces
Confectioners' sugar for dusting

Eight to ten 3½- to 4-inch tart pans (see Sources of Supply), buttered

EIGHT TO TEN 3½- TO 4-INCH TARTS

This filling, somewhat like a very tart version of mincemeat, appeals to those who find most desserts too sweet.

1. Prepare and chill the dough.

2. To make the filling, peel, halve, and core the apples. Combine with the remaining filling ingredients, except walnuts, in a large, nonreactive saucepan. Place over low heat and cook, stirring occasionally, until reduced to a thick, jamlike consistency, 15 to 20 minutes. Pour the filling out into a heatproof glass or stainless-steel bowl and refrigerate it while rolling the crusts.

3. Set a rack at the lowest level of the oven and preheat to 400 degrees.

4. To make the crusts, divide the dough in half. Divide one of the halves into 8 or 10 pieces and on a floured surface roll each out to a thin circle. Press the circles of dough well into the prepared pans and roll a rolling pin over the top of each pan to trim off the excess. Arrange the pans on a jelly-roll pan as they are lined.

5. Stir in the walnuts and divide the cooled filling among the dough-lined pans and smooth the top of the filling flat.

6. To make the top crusts, roll the remaining dough to a rectangle approximately 3×20 inches and cut the dough into 1×3-inch strips. Crisscross 2 strips of dough over each tart in the form of an X. Press the ends of each strip of dough against the edge of the pan to sever the excess.

7. Bake the tarts for about 30 minutes, until the bottom crust is baked through and the top crust has browned. Place the tarts on a rack to cool.

8. Unmold the tarts and arrange them on a platter or pan. Dust with confectioners' sugar immediately before serving.

SERVING: Serve the tarts at room temperature or reheat them at 300 degrees for about 5 minutes before serving.

STORAGE: Keep the tarts loosely covered at room temperature until time to serve them. For longer storage, refrigerate the tarts on a pan, covered

with plastic wrap. Reheat them and serve warm
or cooled.

HINTS FOR SUCCESS: Watch the tarts while
they are baking; lower the oven temperature
25 degrees if the filling begins to simmer before
the crust is baked through.

VARIATION

MINCEMEAT TARTS: Use half the recipe for
Mincemeat (page 107) as a filling in these tarts.

CARAMELIZED RASPBERRY TARTS

1 recipe Cookie Dough (page 207)

CUSTARD FILLING

1½ cups heavy cream
¼ cup sugar
A 2-inch length of vanilla bean
12 egg yolks

1 small (4 to 5 ounces) basket fresh raspberries
¼ cup sugar for caramelizing tarts

Eight to ten 3½- to 4-inch tart pans (see Sources of Supply), buttered

EIGHT TO TEN 3½- TO 4-INCH TARTS

These rich tarts, which resemble a crème brûlée, combine a custard cream and raspberries under a caramelized top. To finish the tops you will need a blowtorch (available for under $20 in most hardware stores). The edge of the crust would burn if these tarts were placed under the broiler to caramelize the sugar topping.

1. Prepare and chill the dough.

2. Set a rack at the middle level of the oven and preheat to 325 degrees.

3. To make the crusts, divide the dough into 8 or 10 small pieces and on a floured surface roll each into a thin circle. Press the circles of dough well into the prepared pans and roll a rolling pin over the top of each pan to trim away excess dough. Arrange the pans on a jelly-roll pan as they are lined. Place a circle of parchment or wax paper in each pan and fill to the top with dried beans or cherry pits. Bake the tart shells for about 20 minutes, checking them often, until they just begin to color. Remove the shells from the oven, allow to cool for a few minutes, then remove the paper and beans from each. If some of the beans fall into the shells, remember to remove them before filling. Return the tart shells to the oven to color, 5 to 10 minutes longer. Check them frequently at this point—they burn easily. Cool on a rack.

4. While the tart shells are cooling, prepare the custard filling. Combine the cream, sugar, and vanilla bean in a heavy nonreactive pan and place over a low heat. Set a bowl and a strainer near he pan on the stove. In another bowl, whisk the egg yolks for a few seconds until they are liquid. When the cream mixture comes to a boil, whisk about half of it into the yolks. Return the remaining cream to a boil and whisk the yolk mixture back into it. Continue to whisk slowly until the cream thickens, coats the back of a metal spoon, and reaches a temperature of 180 degrees, about 2 minutes. Be careful not to overcook the cream or it will curdle. As soon as the cream has thickened, strain it into the waiting bowl and whisk occasionally for the first few minutes the cream is off the heat.

5. To fill the tart shells, unmold them and arrange them on a platter or a jelly-roll pan. Arrange 4 or 5 raspberries in each and fill to the top with the warm custard cream. Refrigerate the tarts until the custard cream has set, at least 2 hours.

6. To caramelize the tops of the tarts, sprinkle the top of the filling evenly with about 2 teaspoons sugar. Light a blowtorch and adjust the flame to medium-low. Move it over each tart in a series of short loops so that the flame does not remain in one place too long. Move the flame more quickly once the sugar begins to melt and caramelize. If the sugar begins to flame, use a flat, nonflammable object, such as a small plate, to smother the flame. Continue caramelizing the tarts, one at a time. Refrigerate the tarts until serving time.

SERVING: These need no accompaniment.

STORAGE: Keep the tarts loosely covered with plastic wrap in the refrigerator until time to serve them, no more than 3 hours. Refrigerate leftovers—though the crust will soften after half a day.

HINT FOR SUCCESS: Make sure the custard cream is completely cooked or it will not set in the tart shells.

VARIATIONS

Substitute other berries, such as blueberries or blackberries, for the raspberries.

PUMPKIN CHEESE TARTS

1 recipe Cookie Dough (page 207) or Almond Dough (page 208)

PUMPKIN CHEESE FILLING

12 ounces cream cheese, softened
½ cup sugar
3 eggs
1 cup pumpkin pie filling (page 177)
½ teaspoon ground cinnamon
¼ teaspoon ground cloves
¼ teaspoon freshly grated nutmeg

Eight to ten 3½- to 4-inch tart pans (see Sources of Supply), buttered

EIGHT TO TEN 3½- TO 4-INCH TARTS

Although it is a little extra work to prepare these individual tarts for a holiday meal, it makes the serving easier at dessert time. If you wish, you can substitute a low-fat cheese for the cream cheese to make a less rich filling.

1. Prepare and chill the dough.

2. To make the filling, beat the cream cheese with an electric mixer on low speed until smooth. Beat in the sugar, then the rest of the ingredients, one at a time, in the order given. Stop the mixer and scrape the bowl and beaters several times as you are beating. Set the filling aside while you roll out the crusts.

3. Set a rack at the lowest level of the oven and preheat to 350 degrees.

4. To make the crusts, divide the dough into 8 or 10 small pieces and on a floured surface roll each out into a thin circle. Press the dough well into the prepared pans. Roll a rolling pin over the top of each pan to trim away the excess. Arrange the pans on a jelly-roll pan as they are lined.

5. Divide the filling among the dough-lined pans and smooth the top of the filling flat.

6. Bake the tarts for about 30 minutes, until the crust is baked through and the filling is set.

7. Unmold the tarts and arrange them on a platter or pan.

SERVING: Serve the tarts with some sweetened whipped cream flavored with a pinch of ground cinnamon.

STORAGE: Keep the tarts loosely covered in the refrigerator until time to serve.

HINT FOR SUCCESS: Watch the tarts while they are baking; lower the oven temperature 25 degrees if the edges of the crusts seem to be coloring too quickly.

VARIATIONS

Substitute cooked winter squash or sweet potatoes for the pumpkin.

BAKING "BLIND"

Tiny tartlet and barquette shells are often baked without a filling (blind) and filled just before they are served. This is to prevent the crisp, delicate pastry shells from absorbing too much moisture.

There are several easy ways to bake the empty shells so they hold their shape:

Butter the outside of another small pan of the same size and place it inside the dough-lined pan. This is the quickest and easiest way to bake blind, but of course you need many pans to accomplish this.

Fill the pans with dried beans or cherry pits, *never* rice (too small and difficult to remove) or metal or porcelain pellets (dangerous if left by mistake in one of the tarts). Remember to oil the beans before their first use and to store them in the freezer so that they do not become rancid.

Bake tartlet shells on the middle rack of a preheated 325 degree oven for about 20 minutes, until they are a deep golden color.

After removing the tiny bean-filled shells from the oven, turn the pans upside down while they are still warm so that when you lift the tiny pan and tartlet shell off the jelly-roll pan, most of the beans will have already fallen out. Slide the crusts out of their pans.

Either method for baking blind works equally well for barquettes.

MAPLE WALNUT BUTTER TARTS

1 recipe Flaky Dough for Tartlets (page 206)

FILLING

½ **cup dark corn syrup**
½ **cup maple syrup**
½ **cup sugar**
6 tablespoons unsalted butter
3 large eggs
Pinch of salt

½ **cup chopped walnuts**
½ **cup raisins**

Eight to ten 3½- to 4-inch tart pans (see Sources of Supply), buttered

EIGHT TO TEN 3½- TO 4-INCH TARTS

This recipe is based on one given to me by my Canadian friend, Bonnie Stern.

1. Prepare and chill the dough.

2. To make the filling, combine the corn syrup, maple syrup, and sugar in a saucepan and stir to mix. Bring to a boil over low heat without stirring. Remove from the heat, add the butter, and allow the butter to melt. Whisk smooth.

3. In a mixing bowl, whisk the eggs to break them up and whisk in the salt, then the syrup and butter mixture; take care not to overmix. Set aside while you roll the dough.

4. Set a rack at the lowest level of the oven and preheat to 400 degrees.

5. To make the crusts, divide the dough into 8 or 10 small pieces and on a floured surface roll each out into a thin circle. Press the dough well into the prepared pans, then roll a rolling pin over the top of each pan to trim away the excess. Arrange the pans on a jelly-roll pan as they are lined.

6. Divide the raisins and walnuts equally among the pans. Pour in the filling.

7. Bake the tarts for about 30 minutes, until the crust is baked through and the filling is set. Place the tarts on a rack to cool.

8. Unmold the tarts and arrange on a platter.

SERVING: Serve the tarts at room temperature or reheat them at 300 degrees for about 5 minutes and cool before serving.

STORAGE: Keep the tarts loosely covered, at room temperature, until time to serve them. For longer storage, refrigerate the tarts on a pan, covered with plastic wrap. Remove the plastic and reheat them before serving.

HINT FOR SUCCESS: Make sure the bottom crusts of the tarts are sufficiently baked through before you remove them from the oven. After the filling has set, and the crust seems to be baked through, turn one of the tarts out on a plate to check the crust. If it is underdone, turn it back into its pan and continue to bake for another 10 minutes. Check again for doneness before removing the tarts from the oven.

LEMON CURD TARTLETS

1 recipe Cookie Dough (page 207)

LEMON CURD

¾ cup strained lemon juice
8 tablespoons (1 stick) unsalted butter
¾ cup sugar
6 egg yolks

Crystallized violets for finishing

Twenty-four 2- to 2½-inch tartlet pans, buttered

24 TARTLETS

A mainstay of the tea table, these little tarts are easy to prepare ahead. Both the shells and the curd may be made in advance; then it takes only minutes to assemble.

If you can find Meyer lemons (see Sources of Supply) for the lemon curd, it will be sublime.

1. Prepare and chill the dough.

2. To make the lemon curd, combine the lemon juice, butter, and sugar in a heavy enamel pan. Bring to a simmer over low heat, stirring occasionally.

3. Whisk the yolks in a bowl and whisk in ½ cup of the hot lemon mixture. Return the remaining lemon mixture to a simmer and whisk the yolk mixture back into it. Continue whisking for 3 to 4 minutes, until the lemon curd has thickened and shows a slight simmer around the edge of the pan. Do not allow it to boil or it may curdle.

4. Pour the lemon curd into a heatproof glass or other nonreactive bowl and press plastic wrap against the surface. Refrigerate for at least 3 hours, or until cold and very thick.

5. Set a rack at the middle level of the oven and preheat to 325 degrees.

6. On a floured surface roll out the chilled cookie dough ⅛ inch thick. With a floured fluted cutter, cut the dough into 24 circles. Line the pans with dough and bake blind as on page 218.

7. To assemble the tartlets, spoon or pipe about 1 tablespoon of the lemon curd into each little shell. Top with a crystallized violet.

SERVING: Serve the tartlets for dessert or tea.

STORAGE: Keep the tartlets at a cool room temperature; refrigerate leftovers.

HINT FOR SUCCESS: When you are filling the tartlet shells, spoon the lemon curd gently out of the bowl without stirring or beating or it might liquefy. The lemon curd keeps almost indefinitely (the acidity acts as a preservative). Store it in a wide-mouthed jar with plastic wrap pressed against the surface of the curd.

VARIATIONS

LIME CURD: Substitute lime juice for the lemon juice in the recipe above. Top each tartlet with a raspberry.

ORANGE CURD: Substitute ½ cup orange juice and ¼ cup lemon juice for the lemon juice in the recipe above.

PINE NUT TARTLETS

1 recipe Cookie Dough (page 207)

FILLING

¾ cup (about 3 ounces) whole blanched almonds
½ cup sugar
1 teaspoon almond extract
2 eggs
4 tablespoons unsalted butter
¼ cup all-purpose flour

2 tablespoons seedless raspberry preserves or
   jam
⅓ cup pine nuts
Confectioners' sugar for dusting

Twenty-four 2- to 2½-inch tartlet pans, buttered

24 TARTLETS

The combination of almonds and pine nuts in these little tarts makes them flavorful and luxurious. If you don't have any pine nuts, you can substitute sliced or slivered almonds for them.

1. Prepare and chill the dough.

2. To make the almond filling, combine the almonds and sugar in a food processor fitted with the metal blade. Pulse on and off repeatedly until the nuts are finely ground, about 1 minute. Add the almond extract and one of the eggs and continue to pulse until the mixture becomes a smooth paste.

3. Divide the butter into 8 pieces and add to the work bowl. Pulse again repeatedly until the butter is smoothly mixed into the almond mixture. Scrape down the inside of the bowl with a metal spatula. Add the remaining egg and pulse until smooth. Allow the machine to run continuously for 30 seconds and scrape down the inside of the bowl. Add the flour and pulse until just incorporated.

4. Set a rack at the lowest level of the oven and preheat to 350 degrees.

5. On a floured surface, roll out the chilled dough ⅛ inch thick. With a floured fluted cutter about ½ inch larger in diameter than the pans, cut the dough into 24 circles. Line the pans with the dough.

6. Spread a drop or two of the preserves over the bottom of each crust—no more than ¼ teaspoon. Use about half the preserves. Carefully spoon or pipe the almond filling into the tartlets. Fill each shell about two-thirds full. Scatter the pine nuts on the almond filling.

7. Bake the tartlets for about 20 minutes, until the crusts are baked through and the filling is pale golden. Place the jelly-roll pan on a rack to cool.

8. When the tartlets are cool enough to handle, remove them from the little pans and place them on the racks to cool completely. Dust with confectioners' sugar before serving.

(continued)

SERVING: Serve the tartlets for dessert or tea.

STORAGE: Keep the tartlets loosely covered, at room temperature, until time to serve them. They will keep for a few days at room temperature in an airtight container.

HINT FOR SUCCESS: Don't overfill the tartlets, or the filling will overflow and the tops of the tartlets will not look neat and precise.

VARIATION

STRAWBERRY, OR RASPBERRY, OR OTHER FRUIT TARTLETS: Omit the pine nuts and top the baked almond-filled tartlets with fresh berries or other fruit. Dust with confectioners' sugar immediately before serving.

To use mango, cut ⅜-inch slices off the fruit parallel to the flat side of the pit. Use a cookie cutter to make mango slices the same diameter as the tartlets. If you wish, substitute barquette pans (see lining barquette pans, page 224) for the tartlet pans.

CHOCOLATE CARAMEL TARTLETS

1 recipe Chocolate Cookie Dough (page 207)

CARAMEL GANACHE

⅔ cup sugar
1 teaspoon water
⅔ cup heavy cream
2 tablespoons unsalted butter
10 ounces semisweet chocolate

CARAMEL DECORATION

⅔ cup sugar
½ teaspoon strained lemon juice

Twenty-four 2- to 2½-inch tartlet pans, buttered

One jelly-roll pan lined with parchment paper and buttered

24 TARTLETS

The easy decoration on these tartlets, a shard of caramel lace, makes them look especially impressive and professional.

1. Prepare and chill the dough.

2. To make the filling, combine the sugar and water in a saucepan and stir well to mix. Place over low heat and stir occasionally as the sugar melts and caramelizes.

3. Meanwhile, bring the cream to a boil in a small saucepan. When the caramel is a deep amber color, pour in the cream and return to the boil—it should boil up only once. Remove the pan from the heat and stir briefly to be sure all the caramel has melted. If not, return the pan to a low heat and stir to melt the caramel completely.

4. Off the heat, add the butter and chocolate and allow to stand for 5 minutes. Whisk smooth,

pour into a bowl, and cool at room temperature or in the refrigerator, until the ganache is about 80 degrees and set, but not hard.

5. Set a rack at the middle level of the oven and preheat to 325 degrees.

6. On a floured surface roll the chilled chocolate cookie dough out ⅛ inch thick. With a floured fluted cutter about ½ inch larger in diameter than the pans, cut the dough into 24 circles. Line 24 tartlet pans with the dough and bake blind, as on page 218.

7. While the tartlets are baking, prepare the caramel decoration. Combine the sugar and lemon juice and prepare the caramel as in step 2. When the caramel is cooked, cool it slightly by immersing the bottom of the pan in cold water. When the caramel has thickened, drizzle it from the end of a spoon in crisscrossing lines on the prepared jelly-roll pan. (If the caramel hardens too much, return to a very low heat to soften, stirring constantly.) Allow the caramel on the jelly-roll pan to set and harden.

8. To finish the tartlets, beat the filling with an electric mixer on medium speed until it lightens, and pipe into the cooled tartlet shells with a medium star tube. Break the caramel sheet into irregular pieces and top each tartlet with one.

SERVING: Serve the tartlets for dessert or tea.

STORAGE: Keep the tartlets at a cool room temperature until ready to serve; refrigerate leftovers.

HINT FOR SUCCESS: Prepare the caramel (both filling and decoration) over low heat in a heavy pan for most even color and flavor. Caramel cooked over high heat will burn unevenly and have a bitter, scorched flavor.

VARIATION

TARTELETTES GIANDUIA: The name originated in northern Italy where chocolate candies called Gianduiotti are a specialty of Turin. Now Gianduia is used internationally to indicate a combination of chocolate and hazelnuts. Add 1 cup toasted, skinned hazelnuts, ground to a paste in the food processor, to the filling along with the chocolate. Proceed as in the main recipe, above. Decorate with a whole toasted hazelnut or a chocolate shaving.

If you wish, substitute barquette pans (see lining barquette pans, page 224) for the tartlet pans.

BARQUETTES AUX MARRONS

1 recipe Cookie Dough or Chocolate Cookie Dough (page 207)

FILLING

½ pound (2 sticks) unsalted butter

1 cup prepared, sweetened chestnut spread (see Sources of Supply)

2 tablespoons kirsch

Chocolate shavings

Confectioners' sugar for dusting

Twenty-four 2½- to 3-inch barquette pans, buttered

24 BARQUETTES

These little chestnut boats are extremely simple to prepare and very rich to eat. The chestnut filling is a perfect contrast to either the plain or chocolate cookie dough shells.

1. Prepare and chill the dough.

2. Set a rack at the middle level of the oven and preheat to 325 degrees.

3. It is a little more complicated to line barquette pans but, once mastered, this method makes the job extremely easy. First, arrange the pans to be lined in rows. Then roll the dough into a rectangle approximately the same size and shape and the configuration of little pans and drape the dough over the pans to cover them. Use your fingertip or a spare piece of dough to press the dough gently into the pans. Flour the surface of the dough lightly, then roll a rolling pin over the tops of the pans to cut away the excess dough. Pull the excess dough away gently in case the rolling pin has not completely severed it from the dough in the pan. Line up the pans on a jelly-roll pan to bake. Bake blind as on page 218.

4. While the barquettes are baking, prepare the filling. Beat the butter by machine on medium speed until soft and light. Beat in the chestnut spread and kirsch and continue beating until the filling is very light.

5. To finish the barquettes, pipe a spiral of filling into the cooled barquettes with a medium star tube. Sprinkle the filling with chocolate shavings and dust them lightly with confectioners' sugar just before serving.

SERVING: Serve the barquettes for dessert or tea.

STORAGE: Keep the barquettes at a cool room temperature until ready to serve; refrigerate leftovers.

HINT FOR SUCCESS: If you can only find unsweetened chestnut puree, add ½ cup light corn syrup to the filling with the puree and proceed with the recipe as above.

6

COOKIES
& SMALL
PASTRIES

More than any other type of baking, making cookies always fills me with a sense of peace and well being. Perhaps it stems from the fact that many cookies give off a "holiday" scent—that buttery mixture of spices, brown sugar, and perhaps a hint of rum—while baking.

Cookies are, of course, popular also because, with few exceptions, they are among the fastest and easiest homemade baked items to prepare. Most cookie doughs or batters are quickly mixed and, if the quantity is not too large, equally quick to bake.

The selection of cookies here is a personal one—all are favorites, collected over the course of the past twenty-five years. All of them are the best of their kind.

Keep the following points in mind when baking cookies:

+ Unless specified otherwise, have all ingredients at room temperature. If it is very warm, beware of having butter become too soft, or cookies may spread too much.

+ Mix quickly, but do not beat cookie batters or doughs to aerate them unless specified in the recipe—overmixing can cause cookies to inflate, then collapse in the oven.

+ Prepare pans accurately. Follow the instructions for pan preparation, it may mean the difference between cookies that release easily from the pan and those that stick.

+ Know your oven—though good-quality cookie sheets and jelly-roll pans help cookies to bake evenly, the best guarantee of well-baked (and unburned) cookies is to be familiar with the hot areas in your oven. If the oven gives strong bottom heat—as most electric ovens do—avoid positioning a rack in the bottom of the oven. Or if you must use it, stack two pans together or use an insulated cookie sheet to protect cookies from burning on the bottom.

+ Check cookies several times while they are baking for signs of excessive heat. If your oven is unusually hot on the sides, try to avoid positioning a pan near the sides. Or if your oven can accommodate two pans, side by side, reverse and rotate them during baking so that the same edge of the pan is not always against the side of the oven.

+ Unless instructions state the contrary, do not move cookies from pans until they have cooled. To reuse the cookie sheet, slide the paper or foil from the pan to a rack to cool the cookies.

+ After the cookies have cooled, store them carefully. Place delicate cookies in a tin or a plastic container that has a tight-fitting lid, between sheets of wax paper. Sturdier cookies may be piled into a tin or container without being layered between paper.

Among the easiest cookies to prepare, drop cookies may be formed by literally dropping the batter from a spoon onto a cookie sheet. Using a small ice-cream scoop—a number 64, which has the capacity of 1 tablespoon, is perfect in all recipes except where another size is indicated—makes sure all the cookies will be uniform and, more important, all bake to the same degree of doneness at once.

You may use a pastry bag to shape drop cookies. For small cookies, fit the pastry bag with a ½-inch plain tube, such as Ateco #6. For larger cookies, use a larger tube, or use the pastry bag with no tube in it.

If you have no pastry bag and still wish to pipe cookies, make a large cone from parchment paper, as in the illustrations below.

The cone in the illustrations is small—it is intended for streaking chocolate on a cake or cookies and only needs to hold about a tablespoon of melted chocolate. To make a cone large enough to pipe cookies, diagonally cut a 12- × 18-inch piece of parchment paper in half to make two 12- × 18- × 21-inch triangles. A triangle this size is comfortable for piping cookie doughs. And the best part is: no cleanup.

To use the paper cone as a replacement for a pastry bag, cut the end off about ½ inch up from the point and drop in a piping tube, plain or star. After filling the cone with the cookie batter, I usually like to reinforce the area around the tube with tape, since the paper has a tendency to tear.

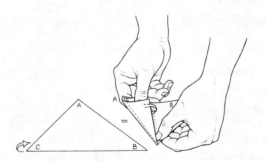

To make a parchment cone, start with a right triangle of parchment paper. Using the area opposite the right angle as the point of the cone, curl the larger side angle around to start the cone.

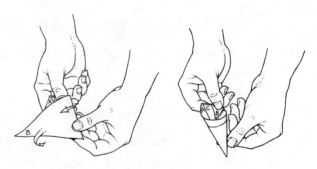

To finish the parchment cone, wind the other angle around the cone and fold the edge into the cone to secure it.

CHOCOLATE CHIP COOKIES

8 tablespoons (1 stick) unsalted butter, softened
¼ cup light or dark brown sugar
¼ cup granulated sugar
1 egg
1¼ cups bleached all-purpose flour
⅛ teaspoon baking soda (divide ¼ teaspoon in
    half on a plate or other flat surface)
1 cup (one 6-ounce bag) chocolate chips

Two cookie sheets or jelly-roll pans lined with
parchment or foil

FORTY-EIGHT TO SIXTY 2-INCH COOKIES

What may be just about everyone's favorite cookie starts this group of recipes. These may be made the traditional way—as drop cookies—or also as refrigerator (slice and bake) cookies. See the Variations at the end of the recipe for this.

For these cookies to be successful, take care not to overbeat the dough.

1. Set racks at the middle and upper thirds of the oven and preheat to 375 degrees.

2. In a bowl, beat the butter with the sugars to mix, then beat in the egg until smooth.

3. Mix the flour and baking soda together and stir into the butter mixture, then stir in the chocolate chips.

4. Drop the batter on the prepared pans in ¾-inch mounds. Leave room for the cookies to spread.

5. Bake for 12 to 15 minutes, or until the cookies are firm and golden.

6. Slide the paper from the pans onto racks to cool the cookies.

SERVING: Serve these cookies as dessert.

STORAGE: Heap the cookies in a tin or tight-lidded plastic container at room temperature.

VARIATIONS

CHOCOLATE CHUNK COOKIES: Cut 6 ounces dark chocolate coarsely and use it instead of the chips.

WHITE (OR MILK) CHOCOLATE CHUNK COOKIES: Cut 6 ounces white (or milk) chocolate coarsely and use it instead of the chips.

NUT CHIP COOKIES: Add 1½ cups coarsely chopped pecans, walnuts, or macadamias to the dough along with the chips.

CHOCOLATE CHIP REFRIGERATOR COOKIES: Divide the dough in half, then form each half into a cylinder, about 12 inches long and about ¾ inch in diameter on a piece of parchment paper. Wrap in plastic and chill or freeze. Slice the cookies, arrange them on the pans, and allow to come to room temperature before you bake them, as above.

CHRIS GARGONE'S CHOCOLATE CHEWS

8 ounces semisweet chocolate

3 ounces unsweetened chocolate

8 tablespoons (1 stick) unsalted butter

3 eggs

1¼ cups sugar

2 teaspoons vanilla extract

⅔ cup bleached all-purpose flour

½ teaspoon baking powder

¼ teaspoon salt

1½ cups (about 9 ounces) chocolate chips

1½ cups (about 6 ounces) chopped walnuts

1½ cups (about 6 ounces) chopped pecans

Three cookie sheets lined with parchment or foil

ABOUT 60 COOKIES

These rich cookies, a little like freestanding brownies, are the creation of Chris Gargone, the talented pastry chef of Remi, one of New York's more popular Italian restaurants. Before you start, a word of caution: chews are addictive.

1. Set racks at the upper and lower thirds of the oven and preheat to 325 degrees.

2. Place the chocolates and butter in a bowl or the top of a double boiler and place over hot, not simmering, water. Stir occasionally until the chocolate and butter have melted. Cool.

3. In a bowl, whisk the eggs and sugar until lightened. Whisk in the chocolate mixture and vanilla.

4. Combine the flour, baking powder, and salt. Stir into the chocolate mixture. Stir in the chocolate chips and nuts.

5. Drop tablespoon-size cookies onto the prepared pans. Bake for 12 to 15 minutes, until the cookies are slightly firm and cracked.

6. Cool on the pans.

SERVING: Chews are so rich, they are best on their own. Or try making them half size and serving them with ice cream for a really rich treat.

STORAGE: Keep chews at room temperature in a tin or tight-lidded plastic container, or freeze them, packed between sheets of wax paper, for longer storage.

LACE COOKIES

¼ cup bleached all purpose flour
⅔ cup (about 3 ounces) ground almonds or
   pecans
½ cup sugar
8 tablespoons (1 stick) unsalted butter
2 tablespoons heavy cream

Two cookie sheets or jelly-roll pans, heavily buttered

ABOUT 36 COOKIES

These delicate and original cookies are like a sweeter version of French tuiles. Try not to make too many at once or the baking and cooling may become rushed, and you may lose some cookies because they'll harden on the pan.

1. Set racks at the upper and lower thirds of the oven and preheat to 375 degrees.

2. Combine all the ingredients in a saucepan and bring to a boil over low heat, stirring constantly.

3. Drop batter in half teaspoonfuls, well apart, on the pans.

4. Bake for about 5 minutes, until the cookies are well colored and simmer on the pan.

5. Remove the pan from the oven and immediately lift the cookies from the surface with a spatula and drape over a rolling pin so they cool curved.

6. Allow to cool and crisp.

SERVING: Lace cookies are great with a simple fruit dessert, or fruit sherbet.

STORAGE: Keep leftover lace cookies in a tin—moisture will make them soggy. Consume leftovers as soon as possible (not usually a difficulty).

VARIATIONS

Substitute walnuts or hazelnuts for the almonds or pecans.

FRENCH CURRANT DISKS
(PALETS AUX RAISINS DE CORINTHE)

8 tablespoons (1 stick) unsalted butter, softened
½ cup sugar
1 teaspoon vanilla extract
2 eggs
1 cup bleached all-purpose flour
¾ cup currants

Two cookie sheets or jelly-roll pans covered with parchment or foil

72 TO 84 COOKIES

This standard French cookie is light and delicate. The currants add a note of richness.

1. Set racks at the upper and lower thirds of the oven and preheat to 350 degrees.

2. In a bowl, beat the softened butter and add the sugar in a stream. Continue beating until the butter/sugar lightens. Add the vanilla, then the eggs, one at a time. Beat until smooth after each addition. Stir in the flour and currants.

3. Drop ½-inch mounds of batter on the prepared pans. Bake the cookies for about 12 minutes, or until they have spread and browned lightly at the edges.

4. Slide the paper from the pans onto racks to cool the cookies.

SERVING: These are so delicate, I think of them more as a teatime cookie than a dessert.

STORAGE: Keep in a tin or tight-lidded plastic container.

FRENCH HAZELNUT BOULDERS
(ROCHERS AUX NOISETTES)

¾ cup whole hazelnuts

4 egg whites

Pinch of salt

1 cup sugar

¼ teaspoon ground cinnamon

1 teaspoon dark rum or a sweet liqueur

Two cookie sheets or jelly-roll pans lined with parchment or foil

ABOUT 60 COOKIES

These delicate and fragile cookies get their name from their irregular shape. They may also be made with other nutmeats.

1. Roast the hazelnuts in one layer on a jelly-roll pan at 350 degrees for about 15 minutes. Allow them to cool slightly, then rub them in a towel to loosen and remove the skins. After removing the hazelnuts from the oven, lower the temperature to 250 degrees; set racks at the upper and lower thirds. Crush the hazelnuts coarsely with the bottom of a saucepan.

2. In a bowl, whip the egg whites with the salt until they are white and opaque, then gradually and slowly beat in the sugar. Whip the meringue until very stiff. Dissolve the cinnamon in the liqueur and fold it into the meringue, then fold in the hazelnuts.

3. Spoon or pipe the meringue onto the prepared pans in irregular mounds. Bake for about 45 minutes, until the cookies are crisp but still very pale.

4. Cool the cookies on the pans.

SERVING: These are great as an after-dinner cookie with espresso.

STORAGE: Keep in a tin or tight-lidded plastic container, or else they will soften and become soggy.

HINT FOR SUCCESS: Beat in the sugar very slowly or the meringue will fall and liquefy.

VARIATIONS

Omit the cinnamon; substitute chopped toasted walnuts or pecans for the hazelnuts.

BAR COOKIES

Baked as a single giant cookie in a square or rectangular pan, bar cookies are cut into portions after being baked and cooled. They may be made from rich cake batters as in the case of brownies, perhaps the ultimate bar cookie. Or they may be a thin layer of a dough or cake batter with a rich topping, often containing nuts.

Practical when you need to prepare a lot of cookies with a minimum of effort, they may be cut into squares, rectangles, or diamonds.

For best results in handling and cutting bar cookies, follow these steps:

+ Allow to cool completely in the pan before unmolding.

+ After removing the paper or foil on which the bars baked, trim the edges.

+ Use a ruler to mark the cuts, so that the resulting bars are of uniform size.

+ Use a sharp serrated knife to cut bars, making sure to cut all the way through both the topping and base for the neatest results.

CHOCOLATE PECAN SQUARES

COCOA COOKIE DOUGH

12 tablespoons (1½ sticks) unsalted butter, softened

¾ cup granulated sugar

3 egg yolks

⅓ cup non-alkalized unsweetened cocoa powder

1½ cups bleached all-purpose flour

CHOCOLATE PECAN FILLING

½ cup light corn syrup

1 cup light brown sugar

4 tablespoons unsalted butter

½ cup heavy cream

4 ounces semisweet chocolate, coarsely chopped

2 tablespoons dark rum (optional)

3 cups (about 12 ounces) toasted pecans, coarsely chopped

One 13 × 9 × 2-inch baking pan, lightly buttered and lined with foil

ABOUT TWENTY-FOUR 2-INCH SQUARES

These easy bars are also excellent when almonds, hazelnuts, or walnuts are substituted for the pecans.

1. To make the dough: beat the butter and sugar with a hand mixer set at medium speed, or in a heavy-duty mixer fitted with the paddle attachment, until it is soft and pale in color. Add the yolks, one at a time, beating well between each addition. Continue to beat until the mixture is light and very smooth. Sift together the cocoa and flour several times to break up any lumps. Fold into the butter mixture thoroughly with a rubber spatula.

2. Scrape the dough into the prepared pan and spread it evenly over the bottom. Use an offset metal spatula, or press it in with floured fingertips. Chill the dough while you prepare the filling.

3. Set a rack at the lowest level of the oven and preheat to 350 degrees.

4. To make the filling, mix the corn syrup and brown sugar together well in a saucepan. Place on medium heat and stir occasionally until the syrup comes to a boil. Add the butter and cream and return to a boil. Simmer, stirring occasionally, for 2 minutes, or until the syrup forms a thread when a spoonful is dropped into a cup of iced water—about 230 degrees on a candy thermometer. Remove from the heat and stir in the chocolate. Whisk smooth, add the optional rum, and stir in the hazelnuts.

5. Pour the filling onto the dough and, if necessary, smooth the top with a metal spatula. Bake the pastry for about 30 minutes, or until the dough is firm and baked through and the filling is just beginning to bubble.

6. Cool on a rack to room temperature.

7. To unmold the pastry, place a cookie sheet or cutting board on the pan and turn it over. Remove the pan and peel away the foil. Place a cutting board on the exposed pastry and turn right side up. Remove the cookie sheet or board and trim away ⅛ inch around the edge. Cut into 2-inch squares.

STORAGE: Keep the squares tightly covered at room temperature.

HINT FOR SUCCESS: Be careful not to overcook the filling—if you see that the temperature has exceeded 230 degrees, remove the pan from the heat, add a tablespoon of water, return the mixture to a boil, and watch the thermometer carefully. Adding the water "uncooks" the syrup so that it becomes less dense.

VARIATION

Substitute other nuts, or a combination of nuts for the pecans, above.

CARAMEL HAZELNUT DIAMONDS

1 recipe Sweet Dough for a two-crust pie (page 149)

CARAMEL HAZELNUT FILLING

⅔ cup light corn syrup

1¼ cups light brown sugar

4 tablespoons unsalted butter

½ cup heavy cream

2 teaspoons vanilla extract

1 tablespoon dark rum

3½ cups (about 14 ounces) toasted, skinned, and chopped hazelnuts

One 10½ × 15½-inch jelly-roll pan, buttered and lined with parchment or foil

FORTY-TWO TO FORTY-EIGHT 2-INCH DIAMONDS

These chewy—and addictive—diamonds are perfect for a big party—they are fast to prepare and are as good as they are easy.

1. Prepare and chill the dough.

2. On a floured surface roll the dough out into a 12 × 17-inch rectangle. Drape the dough over the rolling pin, then place it in the pan. Press the dough well against the bottom and sides and fold the excess back into the pan and form it into a high fluted edge. Refrigerate while you prepare the filling.

3. Set a rack at the lower third of the oven and preheat to 350 degrees.

4. For the filling, mix the corn syrup and sugar together well in a saucepan over medium heat. Stir occasionally until the syrup comes to a boil, then add the butter and cream and return to a boil. Simmer for 3 minutes, stirring occasionally. Remove from the heat and stir in the vanilla and rum.

5. Place the chopped hazelnuts in a heatproof mixing bowl. Pour the cooked filling over them and mix together well. Pour the filling over the dough in the pan and spread it even with a metal spatula.

6. Bake for about 30 minutes until the edges of the dough are pale golden and the filling is set and a deep golden color. Turn the pan occasionally to make sure the dough and filling bake evenly.

7. Remove the pan from the oven and cool it to room temperature on a rack. Wrap the pan in plastic wrap and chill overnight.

8. To unmold, run a small, sharp knife between the crust and the sides of the pan. Place the pan on low heat for a few seconds, then place a cookie sheet over the top and invert. Remove the baking pan and replace it with a cutting board. Turn right side up, remove the cookie sheet, and trim away the edges of the pastry. Cut into 2-inch diamonds.

STORAGE: Keep the cookies in a tin or tight-lidded plastic container between sheets of wax paper.

FUDGY BROWNIES

10 ounces semisweet chocolate
¾ pound (3 sticks) unsalted butter
6 eggs
2 cups granulated sugar
1 cup dark brown sugar
2 teaspoons vanilla extract
½ teaspoon salt
2 cups cake flour
3 cups (about 12 ounces) coarsely chopped
walnuts, plus extra for topping (optional)

One 10½ × 15½-inch jelly-roll pan, buttered and lined with parchment or wax paper

ABOUT THIRTY-SIX 2-INCH BROWNIES

This version of the American classic is particularly rich and moist.

1. Cut the chocolate and butter into 1-inch pieces and place in a dry bowl or the top of a double boiler. Set over a pan of hot water and stir occasionally until melted.

2. Meanwhile, combine the eggs with the sugars, vanilla, and salt and whip on medium speed in a mixer bowl until light. Stir in the chocolate mixture and sift over and fold in the flour. Stir in the 3 cups of nuts.

3. Spread the batter in the prepared pan and scatter more chopped nuts on the surface, if desired.

(continued)

4. Bake at 375 degrees for about 40 minutes, until the brownies are firm but still moist.

5. Cool in the pan on a rack. Cut into 2-inch squares to serve.

SERVING: Serve as cookies, of course, or cut the brownies into 3-inch squares and serve topped with ice cream for a lavishly rich dessert.

MARYLAND BROWNIES

2 ounces unsweetened chocolate, coarsely chopped
8 tablespoons (1 stick) unsalted butter
2 large eggs
1 cup sugar
½ cup bleached all-purpose flour
1 cup (about 4 ounces) chopped walnuts or pecans

One 8-inch square baking pan, buttered and the bottom lined with parchment or wax paper

SIXTEEN 2-INCH BROWNIES

I always think of these as the original brownies. The recipe comes from a collection of recipe cards bought by a friend at a yard sale on Cape Cod. From the information on the backs of the cards and other scraps of paper included with the cards, the recipes would seem to have originally been collected in Baltimore, Maryland, hence the name.

STORAGE: Keep the brownies tightly wrapped in plastic at room temperature, or wrap in a single layer and freeze.

VARIATION

Flavor the brownies with 1 tablespoon instant espresso coffee dissolved in 1 tablespoon water, adding it with the vanilla extract.

1. Set a rack at the middle level of the oven and preheat to 350 degrees.

2. Bring a small pan of water to a boil and remove from the heat. Combine the chocolate and butter in a heatproof bowl and place over the water, stirring occasionally until melted. Remove from the water and cool.

3. In a bowl, whisk the eggs and sugar by hand until just combined. With a rubber spatula, fold in the chocolate mixture, then the flour, and finally the nuts. Do not overmix.

4. Pour the batter into the prepared pan and bake until the brownies are slightly puffed and set, 25 to 30 minutes.

5. Let cool in the pan on a rack. When completely cool, unmold and cut into 2-inch squares.

SERVING: These are rich and moist; a dessert in themselves.

STORAGE: Keep brownies tightly covered at room temperature or wrap in plastic and freeze.

HINT FOR SUCCESS: Avoid overmixing the batter or the brownies will be cakey, not moist.

CHOCOLATE WALNUT SQUARES

1½ cups (about 6 ounces) coarsely chopped
    walnut pieces
½ cup bleached all-purpose flour
2 eggs
Pinch of salt
1 tablespoon dark rum
¼ cup sugar
½ cup dark corn syrup
3 ounces bittersweet or semisweet chocolate,
    finely chopped
3 tablespoons butter

*One 8-inch square pan, buttered and the bottom
lined with a square of parchment or wax paper*

SIXTEEN 2-INCH SQUARES

When *Cook's* magazine editors thought a chocolate walnut pie would be too heavy for an article on chocolate desserts to appear in a summer issue, I suggested to the food editor Pam Anderson that she add a little flour to the filling and bake it in a square pan, for a brownielike result. Months later, much to my surprise, when the issue finally appeared, these chocolate walnut squares were pictured on the cover!

1. Set a rack at the middle level of the oven and preheat to 350 degrees.

2. Combine the walnuts and flour and set aside. In a medium bowl, whisk the eggs with salt and rum.

3. In a saucepan, stir the sugar and corn syrup well to mix. Place over low heat and bring to a boil. Remove from the heat and add the chocolate and butter. Allow to stand for 3 or 4 minutes, then whisk smooth.

4. Whisk the chocolate mixture into the egg mixture. Stir in the walnuts and flour.

5. Pour the batter into the prepared pan and bake for about 35 minutes, until set and firm.

6. Cool in the pan on a rack. Unmold and cut into 2-inch squares.

SERVING: Serve the squares as a cookie—they are especially good with tea.

STORAGE: Keep the squares tightly covered at room temperature or wrap and freeze for longer storage.

VARIATION

Substitute pecans or toasted chopped almonds for the walnuts.

BETTY SHAW'S HERMITS

8 tablespoons (1 stick) unsalted butter

1 cup dark brown sugar, firmly packed

2 large eggs

½ cup unsulfured molasses

½ cup buttermilk

2 cups bleached all-purpose flour

1 teaspoon baking soda

1 teaspoon ground cinnamon

¼ teaspoon ground cloves

¼ teaspoon grated nutmeg

¼ teaspoon salt

1½ cups raisins

1½ cups (about 6 ounces) chopped walnuts or
   pecans

*One 10½ × 15 ½-inch jelly-roll pan, buttered and
lined with parchment or wax paper*

ABOUT THIRTY-SIX 2-INCH SQUARES

Betty Shaw, a great baker from Fort Worth, Texas, recently shared this recipe for a favorite cookie. Using pecans for these makes them "real Texan."

1. Set a rack at the middle level of the oven. Preheat to 350 degrees.

2. In an electric mixer, beat together the butter and brown sugar on medium speed until smooth, about 3 minutes. Add the eggs, one at a time, and beat until each is incorporated, scraping the bowl occasionally with a rubber spatula. Combine the dry ingredients and add to the butter mixture. Mix at low speed. By hand, fold in the raisins and nuts.

3. Pour the batter into the prepared jelly-roll pan and bake for about 15 minutes or until the center is set.

4. Let cool in the pan on a rack. When completely cool, cut into 2-inch squares.

SERVING: Serve the hermits as a cookie.

STORAGE: Keep hermits tightly covered at room temperature or wrap in plastic and freeze.

ROLLED COOKIES

Though rolled cookies may be as fragile and tender as any other type of cookie, sometimes they fall short of being as delicate as they might. The reason is simple—bakers often fear that delicate doughs may stick while being rolled and are consequently too generous with the flour both on the work surface and on the dough. Also cookies, cut into shapes—whether they be round or novelty shapes—generate scraps. Rerolling the scraps may also toughen them somewhat, though it doesn't have to. Observe the following precautions for rolled cookies:

* After mixing the dough for rolled cookies, refrigerate ¼-inch-thick pieces of dough between sheets of plastic wrap—this is a way of having the dough almost "prerolled" and can help eliminate many of the problems associated with rolling soft, delicate doughs.

* Roll small pieces of dough at a time—this prevents the dough from softening just because it takes a long time to roll a large piece. It also means that the dough will need less flour and be easier to cut.

* Always keep the work surface and the dough floured, but use pinches of flour, rather than handfuls—the dough will absorb any amount of flour you place on or under it.

* Rather than reroll the scraps, form them into a cylinder and refrigerate them. After they have chilled, slice and bake them, rather than reroll. Or if you do choose to reroll the dough, cut it into squares or rectangles to avoid generating more scraps. Remember: the more you roll the dough, the tougher it becomes.

SCOTTISH SHORTBREAD

½ **pound (2 sticks) unsalted butter, softened**
½ **cup sugar**
2½ **cups bleached all-purpose flour**

Two cookie sheets or jelly-roll pans lined with parchment or wax paper

ABOUT TWENTY-FOUR 2- TO 2½-INCH COOKIES

This recipe is an adaptation of one given me by Peggy Pinckley, owner of the former Parisian Pantry in Springfield, Missouri, and a native of Scotland.

1. Set racks at the middle and upper thirds of the oven and preheat to 325 degrees.

2. Beat the butter in a mixer with a paddle until soft and light. Beat the sugar in a stream and continue beating for 5 to 10 minutes, until the mixture is very light and pale. Stir in the flour by hand just until it's absorbed—no more or the dough will toughen.

3. Turn the dough out onto a floured surface and drop pinches of flour onto the dough. Press the dough out with your hands, then roll over it very gently once or twice with a rolling pin until it is about ½ inch thick. Cut with floured cutters and transfer the cut pieces to the prepared pan.

To use a shortbread mold to shape, press the mold into the floured dough and cut around it. Transfer the cutout to the prepared pan and chill for about 1 hour until firm. Bake as above.

4. Bake the shortbread for about 15 minutes, until it is *very* lightly colored.

5. Cool the shortbread on a rack.

SERVING: Shortbread was made to be served with tea, though it is also a wonderful accompaniment to fruit desserts.

STORAGE: Keep the shortbread in a tin or a tight-lidded plastic container. Freeze for storage of longer than a few days.

HINTS FOR SUCCESS: See general hints for rolled cookies (page 241).

CINNAMON STARS
(CHURER ZIMTSTERNE)

1½ cups (about 8 ounces) whole unblanched
    almonds
1½ teaspoons ground cinnamon
1 teaspoon grated lemon zest
2 large (about ¼ cup) egg whites
Pinch of salt
1½ cups confectioners' sugar
1 teaspoon water

*Two cookie sheets or jelly-roll pans lined with
parchment or foil*

ABOUT 36 COOKIES

In all Germanic cultures, these are one of the
most popular Christmas cookies. This version is
from Chur, the gateway city to the Grisons, south-
eastern Switzerland's high mountains.

1. Place the almonds in a food processor fitted
with a metal blade. Pulse repeatedly until they are
finely ground. Add the cinnamon and lemon zest,
pulse twice, then set aside.

2. In a clean, dry bowl, whip the egg whites with
the salt until they're firm, then gradually whip in
the confectioners' sugar. Remove ⅓ cup of the
meringue to a bowl and reserve it, covered, at
room temperature.

3. Add the remaining meringue, about ⅔ cup, to
the almonds in the work bowl and pulse
repeatedly until the mixture forms a firm dough.
Dust your work surface with confectioners' sugar,
and with your hands press the dough out about ¼
inch thick.

4. Cut with a star-shaped cutter and place on the
prepared pans immediately after cutting. Moisten
the cutter frequently with water so the dough
releases easily. Press the scraps back together and
continue cutting cookies until all the dough has
been used.

5. Stir the teaspoon of water into the reserved
meringue to liquefy it and brush or spread it over
the surface of each of the stars. Allow to dry for
1 hour before baking.

6. Set racks at the middle and upper thirds of
the oven and preheat to 300 degrees.

7. Bake the stars for 10 to 15 minutes, or until
they are firm but still moist.

8. Cool them on the pans.

STORAGE: You can store these stars indefinitely
in a tin with a tight-fitting lid.

CHOCOLATE ALMOND SPICE COOKIES
(BASLER BRUNSLI)

1½ cups sugar

1½ cups (about 8 ounces) whole unblanched
  almonds

6 ounces semisweet chocolate

1½ teaspoons ground cinnamon

½ teaspoon ground cloves

2 large (about ¼ cup) egg whites

*Two cookie sheets or jelly-roll pans covered with
parchment or foil*

ABOUT 42 COOKIES

These chocolate cookies are a great specialty of Basel, in northern Switzerland, near the French border. There are many versions made with cocoa powder. These, made with chocolate, are more tender and flavorful, I think.

1. Place the sugar and almonds in a food processor fitted with a metal blade. Pulse repeatedly until the nuts are finely ground. Do not overprocess or allow the mixture to become warm.

2. Chop the chocolate finely into small pieces and add to the processor. Pulse until the chocolate is finely ground and mixed with the almonds and sugar. Add the remaining ingredients and pulse rapidly, until a fairly stiff dough forms.

3. Cover the work surface with sugar and press the paste out with your hands about ¼ inch thick.

4. Cut the cookies into hearts, stars, and cloverleaf shapes and place on the prepared pans. Press the scraps back together and continue cutting cookies until all the dough has been used. Allow to dry several hours, uncovered, at room temperature.

5. Set racks at the middle and upper thirds of the oven and preheat to 300 degrees.

6. Bake the cookies for 10 to 15 minutes, or until they are slightly expanded but still feel rather soft—they will become firmer as they cool. Do not overbake or they will be *very* hard.

7. Cool on pans.

SERVING: Serve the *Brunsli* as a dessert with tea or coffee.

STORAGE: Keep cookies in a tin or other airtight container.

SWISS BUTTER MAILAENDERLI

DOUGH

½ pound (2 sticks) unsalted butter, softened

½ cup sugar

1 teaspoon vanilla extract

3 egg yolks

2½ cups bleached all-purpose flour

Egg wash: 1 egg well beaten with a pinch of salt

Two cookie sheets or jelly-roll pans lined with parchment or foil

A 2- to 2½-inch cookie cutter

ABOUT FORTY-EIGHT 2-INCH COOKIES

These delicate cookies are called in Swiss dialect "Little Milanesi"—probably because they were originally based on an Italian cookie.

1. For the dough, beat the butter and sugar by machine on medium speed until very soft and light. Beat in the vanilla and the yolks and continue beating until smooth and shiny, about 3 more minutes. Stop the mixer, sift over the cake flour, and with a rubber spatula fold in by hand. Scrape the dough onto a piece of plastic wrap, cover with another piece of wrap, and with your hands press about ½ inch thick. Chill the dough until firm, about 1 hour, although it will keep for up to 2 days.

2. Set racks at the upper and lower thirds of the oven and preheat to 325 degrees.

3. On a lightly floured surface, roll the dough out about ¼ inch thick. Dip the tines of a fork in flour, then lightly pull the back of the tines down the dough to make parallel grooves. Use floured cutters to cut the dough into hearts, stars, or any simple 2- to 2½-inch shapes. Place each cookie as soon as it is cut onto a prepared pan. Rather than rerolling the scraps, shape into a cylinder and chill.

4. After all the cookies have been cut, carefully brush on the egg wash, brushing in the direction of the grooves. Slice the cylinder into ¼-inch wafers and arrange on the pans. Egg-wash, but do not groove the surfaces.

5. Bake the cookies for about 20 minutes, until golden and just baked through.

6. Cool on pans.

SERVING: Serve the cookies with a custardy or fruit dessert or for tea.

STORAGE: Pack in tins between wax paper for storage.

COOKIES & SMALL PASTRIES

DECORATED GINGERBREAD COOKIES

DOUGH

4 cups unbleached all-purpose flour
1 tablespoon ground ginger
2 teaspoons ground cinnamon
1 teaspoon salt
½ teaspoon grated nutmeg
½ teaspoon ground cloves
½ teaspoon baking soda
½ pound (2 sticks) unsalted butter
⅔ cup light or dark brown sugar
2 large eggs
⅔ cup unsulfured molasses

ICING

1 pound confectioners' sugar
3 large egg whites
1 drop lemon juice or vinegar
Food coloring

Raisins, currants, nutmeats, colored sugar
  sprinkles, and other decorations

Three or four cookie sheets lined with parchment or foil

ABOUT 60 LARGE COOKIES

Resist the urge to add more flour to this soft dough—better to have patience and chill it until it may be easily rolled. The bonus is delicate and tender cookies—and the scraps reroll perfectly, making cookies just as tender as the first ones to be rolled.

1. For the dough, add the dry ingredients (except sugar) to a mixing bowl and stir well to combine.

2. Beat the butter and sugar by machine and beat in the eggs, one at a time. Continue beating until the mixture is smooth. Beat in half the flour mixture, then stop and scrape the bowl and beater(s). Beat in the molasses, scrape again, and beat in the remaining flour mixture, just until combined.

3. Divide the dough into several pieces and press each piece into a rectangle about ¼ inch thick between 2 sheets of plastic wrap. Chill the dough for at least 1 hour or until firm.

4. Set racks in the middle and upper thirds of the oven. Preheat the oven to 350 degrees.

5. Roll the dough, one piece at a time, on a floured surface, just to make the dough flat and even, but not much thinner. Cut with floured cutters and arrange on the pans an inch or two apart, to make room for expansion during baking. Repeat with the remaining dough. Reroll the scraps immediately; or press together, chill, and reroll later.

6. Bake the cookies for about 10 minutes, until firm when pressed with a fingertip.

7. Cool the cookies on pans. Meanwhile, for the icing, combine the confectioners' sugar and egg whites in a mixing bowl and beat by machine until combined. Add the lemon juice or vinegar and continue beating until fluffy.

8. Divide the icing into several small bowls and add the coloring. Keep plastic wrap pressed against the surface of the icing to prevent a crust from forming. Use a paper cone, page 228, or the snipped end of a plastic bag to pipe icing on the cookies.

9. Use the raisins and other decorative ingredients to accent the icing.

SERVING: Aside from being good to eat, decorated cookies make great Christmas tree decorations: make a small hole about 1 inch down from the top of the cookies as soon as they come out of the oven. After the cookies cool and are decorated, pull the string or narrow ribbon through the hole, then knot.

STORAGE: Keep the cookies between layers of wax paper in a tin.

HINT FOR SUCCESS: Keep the decorations simple—the more elaborate they are, often the less appetizing they look.

VARIATION

Cut round cookies and sandwich them with some heated apricot jam.

BERNESE "LICKS"
(BERNER LECKERLI)

DOUGH

½ cup honey

½ cup dark brown sugar, firmly packed

½ cup granulated sugar

2 large eggs

1 teaspoon finely grated orange zest

2 cups (10 to 11 ounces) whole unblanched
    hazelnuts

2½ cups bleached all-purpose flour

½ teaspoon baking soda

1¼ teaspoons ground coriander

1 teaspoon ground cinnamon

¾ teaspoon grated nutmeg

¾ teaspoon ground ginger

Confectioners' sugar for finishing

*Two cookie sheets or jelly-roll pans lined with
parchment or foil*

42 TO 48 COOKIES

A great specialty of Berne, the capital of Switzerland, these cookies will last, and even improve, if kept for several months in a tin.

1. Combine the honey, sugars, eggs, and orange zest in a heatproof mixing bowl and whisk over a pan of simmering water until lukewarm. Grind the hazelnuts in a food processor and stir into the egg mixture. Combine all the remaining ingredients and stir in to form a soft dough.

2. Turn the dough out onto a floured surface and cover with a towel. Allow to rest for 5 minutes.

3. Roll the dough ¼ inch thick and cut with a rectangular or heart-shaped cutter.

4. Place the cookies on the prepared pans and allow to dry at room temperature, about 1 hour.

5. Set racks at the middle and upper thirds of the oven and preheat to 325 degrees.

6. Bake for about 20 minutes, until the cookies are no longer shiny-looking and beginning to become firm.

7. Cool the cookies on pans, then dust lightly with the confectioners' sugar.

SERVING: Serve the cookies as part of an assortment of cookies with tea or coffee.

STORAGE: Store indefinitely in a tin or other tightly sealed container.

REFRIGERATOR COOKIES

The original "slice and bake" cookies, refrigerator cookies are made from doughs that need to chill before being formed and baked. For the best refrigerator cookies remember:

+ Form the dough into a cylinder on wax or parchment paper, or press it into a small pan to be cut into rectangular bars before slicing.

+ Always chill the dough until it is firm, to avoid having the cookies distort in shape while being cut.

+ Rotate the cylinder while cutting, so it doesn't continuously get pressed from the same direction.

+ Bake the cookies while they are still cool.

VANILLA SABLÉS

8 tablespoons (1 stick) unsalted butter, softened
¼ cup sugar
Pinch of salt
1 egg yolk
½ teaspoon vanilla extract
1 cup plus 2 tablespoons bleached all-purpose
　　flour

Two cookie sheets or jelly roll pans lined with parchment or foil

ABOUT 36 COOKIES

These cookies may be varied infinitely with additions of nuts and/or dried and candied fruits to the dough.

Sablé means "sandy" in French, referring to the crumbly texture of the cookies.

1. In a mixer bowl, beat the butter with the sugar and salt until the mixture is very light, about 5 minutes on medium speed. Beat in the yolk, then the vanilla extract. Remove from the mixer. Sift the flour over and stir in.

2. Shape the dough into an 8-inch-long cylinder in a sheet of parchment paper. Chill until firm.

(continued)

COOKIES & SMALL PASTRIES

3. Set racks at the middle and upper thirds of the oven and preheat to 325 degrees.

4. Slice the cylinder of dough every ¼ inch and arrange the slices on the prepared pans.

5. Bake for 18 to 20 minutes, until the cookies are firm and very light golden.

6. Cool on the pans.

STORAGE: Store the cookies in a tin or other tightly sealed container.

VARIATIONS

Moisten the outside of the cylinder with egg white and roll in cinnamon sugar or coarse sugar before slicing and baking.

Add 6 ounces (1½ cups) chopped nuts to the dough before shaping.

Add ½ pound very green blanched pistachios to the dough before shaping.

Add ¼ pound each rinsed and quartered candied cherries and chopped nuts to the dough before shaping.

CHOCOLATE SABLÉS

4 tablespoons unsalted butter, softened
⅓ cup sugar
Pinch of salt
1 egg
¼ teaspoon baking soda
1 tablespoon milk
1 cup bleached all-purpose flour
¼ cup non-alkalized cocoa powder

Two cookie sheets or jelly-roll pans lined with parchment or foil

ABOUT 36 COOKIES

Use this dough to make a chocolate version of sablés, or combine it with Vanilla Sablé dough to make pinwheel and checkerboard cookies, below.

1. In a mixer bowl, beat the butter with the sugar and salt until the mixture is very light, about 5 minutes on medium speed. Add the egg and beat until smooth. Combine the baking soda with the milk and beat in. Remove from the mixer and sift over and stir in the flour and cocoa.

2. Shape the dough into an 8-inch-long cylinder in a sheet of parchment paper. Refrigerate until firm.

3. Set racks at the middle and upper thirds of the oven and preheat to 325 degrees.

4. Slice cylinder of dough every ¼ inch and arrange the cookies on the prepared pans.

5. Bake for 18 to 20 minutes, until the cookies are firm and no longer shiny-looking.

6. Slide the paper from the pans onto racks to cool the cookies.

VARIATIONS

PINWHEEL COOKIES: Cut a cylinder of Vanilla Sablé dough (page 249) and one of chocolate in half and roll each into a 4 × 18-inch rectangle. Paint the chocolate dough with a beaten egg and place the vanilla dough over it. Roll tightly from the long end. Repeat with the other half of each log. Refrigerate, slice, and bake. Repeat with the remainder of each log.

CHECKERBOARD COOKIES: Roll a cylinder of Vanilla Sablé (page 249) and one of Chocolate Sablé dough into a 6-inch square. Paint the vanilla dough with a beaten egg and cover with the square of chocolate dough. Cut the dough into 2 rectangles, egg-wash one, and top with the other to make 4 alternating layers; refrigerate. Cut the dough into strips as wide as one layer is thick (about ¼ inch). Egg-wash the strips and stack 4 strips high. Alternate direction of colors as you stack. Refrigerate, slice, and bake.

PIPED COOKIES

Piping is supposed to make forming the cookies easier, not more difficult. If you have never tried piping before, it is a simple matter to pick up a plastic pastry bag and a ½-inch star and plain tubes. With these three implements you can pipe almost any cookies that exist.

Review the techniques for piping Pâte à Choux (page 367) for information on filling and holding the bag for piping different shapes of dough.

MACAROONS

½ **pound canned almond paste**
⅔ **cup granulated sugar**
¼ **cup confectioners' sugar**
2 **large egg whites**

Two cookie sheets or jelly-roll pans lined with parchment

ABOUT 34 COOKIES

Though macaroons are always made with prepared almond paste in the United States, in Europe it is more common to make macaroon paste from almonds and sugar crushed in a special machine called a *broyeuse* in French and a *raffinatrice* in Italian. It is like a giant pasta machine with a pair of rollers that may be set at varying distances to adjust the fineness of the material that passes through.

1. Set a rack at the middle level of the oven and preheat to 375 degrees.

2. Break the almond paste into 1-inch pieces. Combine with the sugars in the bowl of a mixer with the paddle attachment. Mix on the slowest speed to crumble together the almond paste and sugars. Pour in the egg whites in 3 or 4 additions, beating well between each addition. Scrape down the bowl frequently as you are adding the egg whites.

3. If possible, leave time to pack the macaroon paste into a plastic container and allow it to age overnight in the refrigerator before baking.

4. Use a plain tube with a ½- to ¾-inch opening (Ateco #7 or #8) to pipe ¾- to 1-inch macaroons on the prepared pans. Leave 1 inch around each macaroon.

5. Moisten the surface of the macaroons with a wet towel and sprinkle with granulated or confectioners' sugar. Bake immediately for 15 to 20 minutes, until they're well puffed and golden.

6. Cool the macaroons. When cool, remove them from the paper by turning the paper over and moistening the back of the paper, then peel it off.

SERVING: Serve the macaroons with or as dessert.

STORAGE: Store the macaroons in a tin between layers of wax paper.

VARIATIONS

CHOCOLATE MACAROONS: Add ¼ cup sifted unsweetened cocoa powder with the sugars.

PINE NUT MACAROONS: Cover the moistened macaroons with pine nuts, shaking away the excess before baking.

MACAROON CRESCENTS: Add ½ cup flour to the macaroon paste along with the sugars. Decrease the egg whites to 2. Form the paste into a cylinder by hand and cut into 24 pieces. Roll the pieces into cylinders, point ends slightly, roll in egg wash, then in crushed sliced almonds or pine nuts. Place on the pan and curve the cylinders into crescent shapes.

GOMMÉS: This name derives from the fact that these French macaroons were washed over with a glaze made from gum arabic after baking. Decrease the egg whites to 2 in the macaroon paste. Pipe with a star tube in the same shapes as Spritz cookies (see below) and decorate with almonds or candied fruit. Allow to dry for several hours, then bake at 450 degrees just until lightly colored, about 5 minutes. Brush over with heated corn syrup as soon as they come out of the oven.

ALMOND BUTTER SPRITZ COOKIES

¼ **pound almond paste**
1¼ **cups confectioners' sugar**
½ **cup eggs (2 large eggs and 1 yolk, usually)**
½ **pound (2 sticks) unsalted butter, softened**
3 **cups cake flour**

Two or three cookie sheets or jelly-roll pans lined with parchment or foil

ABOUT SEVENTY-TWO 2-INCH COOKIES

The name of these cookies derives from the verb "to squirt," which Germans use to describe piping with a pastry bag and tube.

1. Set racks on the top and lower thirds of the oven and preheat to 325 degrees.

2. In a bowl, soften the almond paste with the confectioners' sugar and half the eggs. Beat in the butter gradually, then gradually add the remaining eggs. Cream all of the ingredients until light. Add the cake flour all at once and mix until all the elements adhere. Do not overmix.

(continued)

3. Pipe ½-inch shapes onto the prepared pans with a ½-inch star tube (Ateco #4).

4. Bake for about 15 minutes.

5. Cool on the pans.

VARIATIONS

Use these suggestions for piping Spritz cookie dough:

SHELL: Use a ½-inch star tube (Ateco #4) to pipe a straight shell with a fairly blunt point. Dip the pointed edge in melted chocolate after baking. It may then be dipped in white or milk chocolate shavings, chopped blanched pistachios, or crushed toasted sliced almonds.

BOW: Pipe two straight shells, pointed ends facing and overlapping slightly, as above. Cover the juncture with a quarter candied cherry.

STAR: Pipe stars with a ½-inch star tube (Ateco #4). Indent the center and fill with thick jam before baking. Or indent, bake empty, and fill with reduced jam or melted chocolate after baking.

SPIRAL: Pipe a spiral with a ⅛-inch (Ateco #4) plain or ¼-inch star tube (Ateco #2). Dust lightly with cocoa before baking if desired.

ROSETTE: Pipe rosettes with a ½-inch star tube (Ateco #4). Before baking, decorate with quarter candied cherry, off center.

BAR: Pipe a 2-inch finger with a ½-inch star tube (Ateco #4).

WREATH: Pipe a circle with a ½-inch star tube (Ateco #4). Decorate the overlapped area with a piece of candied fruit.

S: Pipe tight S-shapes with a ½-inch star tube (Ateco #4).

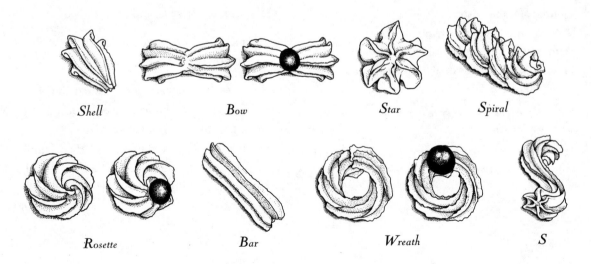

Shell   *Bow*   *Star*   *Spiral*

Rosette   *Bar*   *Wreath*   *S*

SANDWICH COOKIES

Though any disk- or finger-shaped cookie may be made into a sandwich, the following recipes are for rich nut cookies with delicate fillings. Two rules apply to making perfect sandwich cookies:

+ Be sure to make the cookies a uniform size, or they look unattractive when sandwiched.

+ Don't overdo the filling—the cookies need only enough to hold them together.

ALMOND BUTTER DISKS

BATTER

8 tablespoons (1 stick) unsalted butter, softened
½ cup sugar
Grated zest of 1 lemon
1 tablespoon dark rum
2 egg whites
1 cup (about 4 ounces) ground almonds
6 tablespoons flour

FILLING

⅔ cup apricot preserves
1 tablespoon dark rum

Two cookie sheets or jelly-roll pans lined with parchment

Twenty-four to thirty-six 2-inch sandwiches

These delicate almond wafers are just as good by themselves as sandwiched.

1. Set racks at the middle and upper thirds of the oven and preheat to 350 degrees.

2. In a bowl, beat the softened butter and add the sugar in a stream. Continue beating until the butter whitens. Beat in the lemon zest and rum, then the egg whites, one at a time, beating until smooth after each addition. Combine the almonds and flour and by hand stir them into the batter.

3. Pipe the batter onto the prepared pans in 1-inch mounds using a ½-inch plain tube (Ateco #6). Bake the cookies for 12 to 15 minutes, or until they're firm and golden.

(continued)

4. To make the filling, bring the preserves and the rum to a boil in a small pan over medium heat, stirring occasionally. Strain the glaze into another small pan and return it to a boil. Paint the filling onto the bottoms of the cookies while it is still very hot.

5. Cool the cookies upside down (filling up) on the paper and sandwich them together after they have cooled.

STORAGE: Store the cookies in a tin or other tightly sealed container between layers of wax paper.

VARIATIONS

HAZELNUT BUTTERSCOTCH SANDWICHES: Substitute hazelnuts for the almonds, and light or dark brown sugar for the granulated sugar.

APRICOT WALNUT DISKS: Substitute walnuts and ½ teaspoon ground cinnamon for the almonds, above.

DOUBLE CHOCOLATE PECAN SANDWICHES

BATTER

8 tablespoons (1 stick) unsalted butter, softened
½ cup sugar
2 egg whites
¼ cup bleached all-purpose flour
2 tablespoons non-alkalized cocoa powder
1 cup (about 4 ounces) ground pecans

CHOCOLATE FILLING (GANACHE)

½ cup heavy cream
6 ounces bittersweet or semisweet chocolate
1 tablespoon dark rum or bourbon

Pecan halves for decorating the cookies

Two cookie sheets or jelly-roll pans lined with parchment or foil

ABOUT 48 COOKIES

These rich chocolate sandwiches are just as good made with almonds or walnuts.

1. Set racks in the middle and upper thirds of the oven and preheat to 350 degrees.

2. In a bowl, cream the butter until it's light. Beat in the sugar in a stream and continue to beat until the mixture whitens. Add the egg whites, one at a time, and continue beating until very creamy. Sift the flour and cocoa powder together several times, then combine with the ground pecans and stir into the batter.

3. Using a pastry bag fitted with a ½-inch plain tube (Ateco #6), pipe or spoon 1-inch-diameter cookies onto the prepared pans.

4. Bake for about 10 minutes, until firm and no longer shiny. Remove the paper from the pans and cool the cookies.

5. To make the filling, in a saucepan heat the cream until hot to the touch. Chop the chocolate fine and off the heat stir into the cream. Stir until smooth. Strain into a mixing bowl and allow to cool at room temperature until thickened. Beat the ganache by hand for a minute, beating in the rum or bourbon in a stream. Spoon the ganache into a pastry bag fitted with a ¼-inch plain tube (Ateco #4).

6. Turn half the cookies over so that the flat side is up. Pipe a dab of the ganache onto each flat surface. Top with the other cookies. Press them together well.

7. Pipe a tiny dab of filling onto the top of each cookie. Press a small pecan half into that filling. Or streak the cookies with melted chocolate and sprinkle with a pinch of ground pecans.

SERVING: Serve the cookies as dessert.

STORAGE: Store in a tin in a cool place—they only keep a day or so because of the filling.

LINZER EYES
(LINZER AUGEN)

DOUGH

12 tablespoons (1½ sticks) unsalted butter,
    softened

½ cup sugar

1 cup (about 4 ounces) ground blanched
    almonds

2 cups unbleached all-purpose flour

Egg wash: 1 egg beaten with a pinch of salt

Blanched sliced almonds

12 ounces (about 1 generous cup) apricot or
    raspberry preserves

¼ cup water

Confectioners' sugar for sifting

Two cookie sheets or jelly-roll pans lined with parchment or foil

FIFTEEN 4-INCH COOKIES

These delicate layered cookies are a dessert in themselves. They are made from an almond shortbread sandwiched with apricot or raspberry preserves, then finished with more preserves. Be careful not to overbake the dough or the Linzer augen will be hard and dry.

1. In a bowl, beat the butter until light and soft, then beat in the sugar. Continue beating until very light. Stir in the ground almonds, then the flour.

2. Turn the dough out onto a piece of plastic wrap, flatten and wrap. Refrigerate until firm, about 1 hour.

3. Set racks at the middle and upper thirds of the oven and preheat to 350 degrees.

4. Flour the dough and work surface very lightly and roll the dough out ¼ inch thick. Use a fluted cutter to cut into 3- to 4-inch rounds. Transfer to the prepared pans and with a 1-inch plain cutter cut a circle out of half the rounds.

5. Paint the cut rounds with the egg wash and sprinkle with the sliced almonds. Bake for about 15 minutes, keeping them very pale. Let cool.

6. Combine the preserves and water and bring to a boil over medium heat, stirring occasionally. Strain into another pan and simmer the glaze until it is sticky.

7. Sift confectioners' sugar over the almond-coated tops. Paint the bottoms with the glaze and stick the tops to them. Fill in the openings with more glaze.

SERVING: Serve the cookies for dessert or tea.

STORAGE: Keep the cookies in a tin or other tightly sealed container.

VARIATION

Substitute seedless raspberry preserves or another favorite flavor for the apricot preserves.

Different from sandwich cookies, filled cookies are baked with a filling. The one rule that makes for successful filled cookies:

> ✦ Never stretch the dough around the filling. It is far better to leave a tiny gap than to stretch and have the dough crack or pull away from the filling.

✦ *FIG BARS*

SWEET PASTRY DOUGH

2 cups all-purpose flour
⅓ cup sugar
¼ teaspoon salt
½ teaspoon baking powder
8 tablespoons (1 stick) cold unsalted butter
2 large eggs

FIG FILLING

1 pound dried Calimyrna figs
1 cup water
¼ cup honey
¼ cup sugar
1 teaspoon lemon juice
Pinch of ground cinnamon

Two cookie sheets or jelly-roll pans lined with parchment or foil

ABOUT 24 COOKIES

This cookie, which was introduced at the turn of the century, has remained one of the most popular of all American cookies ever since.

1. To make the dough, stir the dry ingredients together in a mixing bowl to combine. Cut the butter into 8 or 10 pieces and rub into the dry ingredients until there are no large pieces of butter visible. Be careful that the mixture remains cool and powdery. Beat the eggs together lightly and with a fork stir them into the dough until it masses together.

2. Turn the dough out onto a floured surface and knead lightly until it is smooth. Form into a rectangle about 1 inch thick and wrap in plastic. Refrigerate the dough until it is firm, about 1 hour.

3. To make the filling, stem the figs and dice them. Combine with the remaining ingredients in a nonreactive saucepan. Bring to a simmer over low heat and allow to simmer for about 5 minutes, until slightly thickened. Cool and puree in a food processor. If the filling is still somewhat thin after cooling and pureeing, cook for a few minutes longer to thicken.

4. Set racks in the middle and upper thirds of the oven and preheat to 350 degrees.

5. To form the fig bars, divide the dough into 4 pieces and form each into a 12-inch-long cylinder. Flatten the cylinder and roll it into a 4 × 12-inch rectangle. Moisten the dough with water. Spoon a quarter of the filling in a strip about 2 inches wide down the center of the dough, then bring the edges of the dough up and join them over the filling. Press down slightly with the palm of your hand to make the filled rectangle about 1½ inches wide. Place seam side down on the prepared pan. Repeat with the remaining dough and filling, arranging 2 bars on each pan.

6. Bake for 15 to 20 minutes, until the dough is a deep golden brown.

7. Cool on pans and then slice into 2½-inch lengths.

STORAGE: Keep the cookies in a tin or other airtight container between layers of wax paper.

SHERI PORTWOOD'S SOUR CREAM DOUGH

1½ cups bleached all-purpose flour
¼ teaspoon salt
12 tablespoons (1½ sticks) cold unsalted butter
½ cup sour cream

ABOUT 22 OUNCES OF DOUGH, ENOUGH FOR 36 TO 48 MINIATURE PASTRIES

This recipe comes from my friend Sheri Portwood, a Dallas caterer. She uses it for Rugelach (page 261).

After it is baked, this sour cream dough has a light, flaky texture similar to puff pastry.

1. Combine the flour and salt in the work bowl of a food processor and pulse several times.

2. Cut the butter into 15 to 20 pieces and add to the work bowl. Pulse repeatedly, about 20 times in all, to reduce the mixture to a fine powder. Open the cover and check the consistency occasionally to avoid overprocessing and turning the mixture into a paste.

3. Add the sour cream to the work bowl and pulse 5 or 6 times more, or until the dough forms a coherent ball. Don't overprocess.

4. Remove the dough from the work bowl to a floured surface and press it into a 6-inch square. Wrap in plastic and refrigerate.

STORAGE: Keep the dough in the refrigerator for up to 2 days, or double-wrap in plastic and freeze for up to several weeks.

RUGELACH

1 recipe Sour Cream Dough (page 200)

FILLING

½ cup currants or raisins
⅔ cup light brown sugar
½ cup (about 2 ounces) finely chopped walnut
    pieces
½ teaspoon cinnamon

Two large cookie sheets or jelly-roll pans covered with parchment paper or foil

ABOUT THIRTY-SIX 2-INCH PASTRIES

One of the most popular little pastries in the New York area, rugelach (pronounced rug-luh or rug-guh-luh) has as many variations as there are bakers who prepare it. Basically, it is made from a sour cream or cream cheese dough rolled thin and sprinkled with sugar (white or brown); cinnamon; raisins or currants; and nuts, usually walnuts. Then the variations begin: a layer of apricot jam, a few chocolate chips, some melted butter brushed on the dough—the list goes on and on.

This version owes its existence to suggestions from my editor, Susan Friedland, friends Sheri Portwood and Kyra Effren in Dallas, and Richard Sax and Jeffrey Steingarten in New York.

1. Divide the dough into thirds and shape each piece into a rough circle. Roll each out to about 10 inches, place on a plate or pan, and refrigerate while you prepare the filling.

2. For the filling, place the currants in a saucepan and cover with water. Bring to a boil over low heat. Drain and cool. In a separate bowl, combine the remaining filling ingredients.

3. Set a rack at the middle level of the oven and preheat to 350 degrees.

4. Remove one circle of dough at a time from the refrigerator, place it on your work surface, and paint with water. Scatter a third of the filling over the dough, then a third of the currants. With a pastry wheel cut the dough into 12 wedges and roll each up from the edge to the point.

5. Arrange the pastries on one of the baking pans; repeat with the remaining circles of dough, filling, and currants. Place 18 pastries on each pan.

6. Bake the rugelach for about 30 minutes, checking them often. Some of the sugar always leaks out and puddles around the rugelach, and if it is unattended it may burn. If the bottoms are beginning to become dark before the entire pastry seems baked through, lower the temperature 25 degrees and slide another pan under the one on which the pastries are baking.

7. When the pastries are done, cool them briefly on the pan, then remove to racks to cool.

(continued)

SERVING: Serve the rugelach as a snack or a cookie.

STORAGE: Keep the rugelach in a tin in a cool place for up to 1 week.

HINTS FOR SUCCESS: If some of the filling falls out while you are rolling the rugelach—and it is inevitable that it will—pick it up from the work surface and return it to the bowl so you can place it on the next piece of dough. If there is some filling left over after you have covered the 3 pieces of dough, remove the currants and sprinkle the filling over the tops of the rugelach.

VARIATIONS

Spread each piece of dough with a tablespoon of apricot or seedless raspberry jam before sprinkling on the filling.

Add 4 ounces semisweet chocolate, chopped, to the filling.

HAMANTASCHEN

1 recipe Cookie Dough (page 207)

FILLING

One 12-ounce box pitted prunes

½ cup water

¼ cup sugar

1 teaspoon grated lemon zest

Two large cookie sheets or jelly-roll pans covered with parchment paper or foil

ABOUT TWENTY-FOUR 2-INCH PASTRIES

This traditional Jewish pastry is always made for the feast of Purim, before Passover. Purim is the feast of lots and commemorates the victory of the Jews over Haman, a Persian who had cast lots to determine the day on which all the Jews in Persia would be slaughtered. Haman's efforts were thwarted when Mordecai, cousin of Queen Esther, convinced her to persuade her husband, King Ahasuerus, not to permit Haman to carry through his plans.

The tricorn shape of the pastry is said to recall the shape of Haman's hat, though the name literally means "Haman's pockets." There is also a theory that the name derives from the German *Mohntaschen,* or poppy-seed pockets. Whatever the name means, the pastries are excellent any time of the year. The version here uses a prune filling, and there are variations following the recipe for apricot and poppy-seed fillings.

1. Prepare and chill the dough.

2. To make the filling, combine the prunes, water, and sugar in a nonreactive saucepan. Bring to a simmer over low heat and continue to simmer for about 15 minutes, until the prunes are plump and have absorbed most of the liquid. Remove from the heat, cool slightly, and add the lemon zest. Puree the mixture in a food processor or blender. Let cool.

3. Set a rack at the middle level of the oven and preheat to 350 degrees.

4. To form the pastries, divide the dough in half and roll out each half on a floured surface to form a 10-inch square. Use a floured 2½- to 3-inch cutter to cut the dough into circles. Arrange the dough on the prepared pans as it is cut. Repeat with the second half of the dough.

5. One pan at a time, use a flexible pastry brush to paint the dough with water. Then place about 1 teaspoon of the filling in the center of each circle of dough. Turn 3 sides of the dough up against the filling. Pinch the corners gently so they hold together firmly. Repeat with the remaining filling and dough.

6. Bake the pastries for about 20 minutes, or until they are a light golden color. Cool the Hamantaschen on the pans.

SERVING: Serve the Hamantaschen as a snack or a cookie.

STORAGE: Keep the Hamantaschen in a tin in a cool place for up to 1 week.

HINT FOR SUCCESS: If you use your fingertips to place the filling on the dough, rinse and dry your hands before you shape the pastries or they will have unappetizingly vivid fingerprints on them.

VARIATIONS

APRICOT HAMANTASCHEN: Substitute dried apricots for the prunes in the recipe above.

POPPY-SEED HAMANTASCHEN: Substitute a half-recipe of poppy-seed filling (page 428) for the prune filling, above.

7
CAKES

There is (hardly) anyone who would refuse a piece of cake. Cake is always welcome, whether at tea, or, depending on the cake, at breakfast, lunch, or dinner, or in between.

Cakes, of course, are also associated with life's milestones. Birthdays, christenings, graduations, confirmations, bar (and bas) mitzvahs, engagements, showers (wedding and baby), weddings, and anniversaries, as well as most holidays throughout the year, are celebrated with special cakes. Cakes need not be difficult or complicated to prepare, but when an extra-special cake is required to mark an extra-special occasion, its elaborateness often matches the event's importance. Such special-occasion cakes may be composed of cake layers, a flavoring and moistening syrup, filling(s), frosting or icing, and decorations. To attempt to make a cake of this complexity from start to finish all in one day is madness. For the sake of your sanity, it is best to do as professional bakers do: allow several days for the preparation of all the component parts and only assemble the cake on the day it is to be served. Some cakes taste better if they are assembled the day before, though any elaborate finishing or decoration should be done on the day the cake will be served to avoid accidents that may invariably occur.

Make sure butter and eggs are at room temperature or the batter may separate and cause the baked cake to be rough textured. If you have forgotten to remove them from the refrigerator in time, place the eggs in a bowl of warm tap water for 5 minutes; the butter will warm up sufficiently while you are beating it.

The following is a list of the types of cakes in this chapter.

BASIC CAKE LAYERS: These are all cakes that, though they may be very good unadorned, are all used as an element in a more elaborate cake presentation, including an icing, and sometimes even a filling and moistening syrup.

PLAIN CAKES: These are loaf cakes, pound cakes, and other cakes that require little or no finishing after baking. Though these are not elaborate, this category includes some of the best-tasting cakes because their simplicity allows the delicacy of fine ingredients to be tasted unobscured by other elements (fillings, frostings, etc.) added later. Angel food cakes are also included here.

NUT CAKES: These are cakes made with ground nuts to bind and enrich them. They may be simple and served like the plain cakes, above, or complex and finished into more elaborate presentations.

CAKES MADE WITH FRESH FRUIT: These cakes usually consist of a rich batter spread thinly in a pan, then topped with fresh fruit and often also a crumb or other topping.

FRUITCAKES AND OTHER CAKES MADE WITH DRIED FRUIT: These cover a spectrum from the elaborate fruit and nut–studded Christmas fruitcake flavored with spices and marzipan to simple raisin or currant loaf cakes.

LAYER CAKES: These are cakes with multiple layers stacked with a filling. Some may use the layers above, and others use layers unique to their preparations.

CHOCOLATE CAKES: Though not a category according to technique of mixing or assembly, these cakes are a mixture of layered and nonlayered rich cakes.

ROLLED CAKES: These are cakes spread with a filling and rolled into a log shape.

CHEESECAKES: Cream cheese and other cheese-based batters are baked on bases made of baked pastry dough or slices of baked cake layers.

GÉNOISE

This practical, all-purpose sponge cake is quick and easy to prepare and may be used in a variety of circumstances. It works well as a layer or rolled cake and may also be used in conjunction with cheesecakes, instead of a pastry dough base, or even as a plain cake, with a simple frosting. Many recipes for génoise call for folding in butter at the end—a practice I think often accounts for overmixing and consequently ruining the batter. The butter does contribute extra richness and moisture, but the same thing can be accomplished by using a combination of whole eggs and extra yolks, as in the recipe below.

PLAIN OR WHITE GÉNOISE

½ **cup cake flour**
¼ **cup cornstarch**
3 large eggs plus 3 large egg yolks
¾ **cup sugar**
Pinch of salt

One 9 × 2-inch-deep round pan or a 9-inch springform pan, buttered, bottom lined with a disk of parchment or wax paper

ONE 9 × 2-INCH-DEEP ROUND LAYER

Use this cake layer in any of the recipes that call for it in this chapter. Though this calls for a round cake layer, see variations at the end of the recipe for instructions on preparing a rectangular sheet.

1. Set a rack in the middle level of the oven and preheat to 350 degrees.

2. Combine the cake flour and cornstarch and stir well to mix. Sift once and set aside. Whisk the eggs and yolks in the bowl of an electric mixer. Whisk in the sugar in a stream, then the salt.

3. Place the bowl over a pan of simmering water and gently whisk until the egg mixture is lukewarm. Whip by machine on high speed until the egg mixture is cold and increased in volume.

4. Remove the bowl from the mixer and sift the cake flour mixture over the egg mixture, in 3 or 4 additions, folding it in with a rubber spatula. Pour the batter into the prepared pan and smooth the top evenly with a spatula.

5. Bake the layer for about 25 minutes, until well risen and firm to the touch.

6. Loosen the layer from the sides of the pan and invert to a rack; immediately re-invert to a rack so that the cake layer cools on the paper.

STORAGE: Double-wrap the layer in plastic wrap and refrigerate it for several days or freeze for several months.

HINT FOR SUCCESS: Only heat the eggs and sugar to lukewarm or they will not whip to as great a volume and the cake will not rise well.

VARIATIONS

CHOCOLATE GÉNOISE: Substitute ⅓ cup cake flour, ⅓ cup cornstarch, ¼ cup unsweetened cocoa powder, and a pinch of baking soda for the cake flour and cornstarch above.

GÉNOISE SHEET: Bake the batter at 400 degrees in a 10½ × 15½ × 1-inch pan buttered and lined with a piece of parchment or wax paper. The cake will bake in 10 to 15 minutes—be careful not to overbake, especially if the layer is for making a rolled cake.

CLASSIC WHITE CAKE

12 tablespoons (1½ sticks) unsalted butter, softened

1½ cups sugar

2 cups bleached all-purpose flour

2 teaspoons baking powder

¼ teaspoon salt

¾ cup (about 6 large) egg whites

¾ cup milk

2 teaspoons vanilla extract

Two 9-inch-diameter × 1½-inch-deep layer pans, or one 13 × 9 × 2-inch pan, buttered, bottom(s) lined with parchment or wax paper

TWO 9-INCH-DIAMETER × 1½-INCH-DEEP LAYERS, OR ONE 13 × 9 × 2-INCH LAYER

The fine moist crumb of this cake complements any type of filling and frosting—the perfect celebratory cake.

1. Set a rack at the middle level of the oven and preheat to 350 degrees.

2. In a large mixing bowl, beat the butter and sugar for about 5 minutes, until light and fluffy.

3. In another bowl, stir together the flour, baking powder, and salt. Set aside.

4. In a third bowl, combine the egg whites, milk, and vanilla extract. Add a third of the dry ingredients to the butter mixture, then add half the milk mixture. Continue to alternate, beginning and ending with the dry ingredients. Scrape the bowl and beater often.

(continued)

5. Pour the batter into the prepared pan(s) and smooth the top with a metal spatula. Bake the cake(s) for 25 to 30 minutes, or until a toothpick inserted in the center emerges clean.

6. Cool in the pan on a rack for 5 minutes, then turn out onto a rack, remove the paper, and let cool completely.

STORAGE: To store, rinse the pan(s) and return the cake(s) to them. Wrap tightly in plastic wrap and refrigerate for up to 1 week, or freeze for up to 2 months.

HINT FOR SUCCESS: Make sure all the ingredients are at room temperature for ease of mixing.

DEVIL'S FOOD CAKE

3 ounces unsweetened chocolate, coarsely chopped
⅓ cup water
2 large eggs
8 tablespoons (1 stick) unsalted butter, softened
1½ cups dark brown sugar, firmly packed
2 cups bleached all-purpose flour
1½ teaspoons baking powder
½ teaspoon baking soda
¼ teaspoon salt
¾ cup sour cream

Two 9-inch-diameter × 1½-inch-deep layer pans, or one 13 × 9 × 2-inch pan, buttered, bottom(s) lined with parchment or wax paper

TWO 9-INCH-DIAMETER × 1½-INCH-DEEP LAYERS, OR ONE 13 × 9 × 2-INCH LAYER

This is the cake that delights kids of all ages.

1. Set a rack at the middle level of the oven and preheat to 350 degrees.

2. Place the chocolate and ⅓ cup water in a medium-sized heatproof bowl over a pan of hot, but not simmering, water. Stir occasionally until the chocolate melts. Remove from the heat, cool slightly, and whisk in the eggs.

3. In a large mixing bowl, beat the butter and sugar for about 5 minutes, until fluffy. Beat in the chocolate and egg mixture. Scrape the bowl and beaters and continue beating until smooth.

4. Stir together the dry ingredients. Beat half the flour mixture into the batter and scrape the bowl and beaters. Beat in the sour cream, then the remaining flour mixture.

5. Pour the batter into the prepared pan(s) and smooth the top with a metal spatula. Bake the cake(s) for 25 to 30 minutes, or until a toothpick inserted in the center emerges clean.

6. Cool in the pan(s) on a rack for 5 minutes, then turn out onto a rack, remove the paper, and let the cake cool completely.

STORAGE: To store, rinse the pan(s) and return the cake(s) to it (them). Wrap tightly in plastic wrap and refrigerate for up to 1 week, or freeze for up to 2 months.

FILLING AND ICING A CAKE

Though there are many techniques for filling and frosting a cake, they all have one common goal: to cover the cake neatly and efficiently. Many professional cake decorators use a turntable. The cake is placed in the center of the turntable and the icing is applied to the sides of the revolving cake. Other bakers hold and turn the cake on one hand and spread the icing with a spatula held in the other. Both of these methods work well and easily but require practice.

If you only intend to finish a few cakes a year, by far the easiest method is to put the cake on the serving platter and spread on the frosting from the top down, as in the following instructions:

1. For a single-layer cake, turn the cake upside down on the serving platter so that its flat bottom is up.

2. Brush all excess crumbs off the cake, platter, and work surface.

3. If you wish, cover the platter with thin strips of wax paper inserted under the edge of the cake to keep it free of drips. Pull the strips of paper away after the cake is frosted. (Or, turn the cake over onto a piece of stiff cardboard, roughly ¼ inch larger all around than the cake, then slide the frosted cake from the cardboard to the platter. This method is better if you wish to finish the side of the cake with nuts or other solids.)

4. To frost with ganache and buttercream, apply a thin layer over the cake with an offset metal icing spatula. Spread the frosting first on top, then on the sides to seal the outside of the cake and prevent the cake's crust from crumbing up into the frosting. Chill the cake for 10 minutes to set this first coat.

If you are frosting a two-layer cake, place one layer on the platter, bottom side down. Spread a ½-inch layer of the frosting over the top of this layer. Place the second layer on the frosting, bottom side up. Proceed with steps 3 or 4, above.

5. To put the final coat on the cake, place 4 or 5 dabs of the frosting on the top of the cake. Use the spatula to join the dabs and cover the top of the cake. Spread from the center outward so excess frosting falls down the sides of the cake.

6. To finish the sides, hold the spatula handle upward, blade about ⅛ inch away from the side of the cake, and spread any frosting already on the side of the cake smooth. Add more dabs of frosting to the sides of the cake if necessary, so it is covered evenly. Finish the top by spreading any icing standing up around the edge of the cake evenly in toward the center. Hold the spatula at a slight slant across the top of the cake.

7. If you with to press toasted nuts, shaved chocolate, or other solids onto the side of a cake, do so immediately. Hold the cake with one hand and tilt toward the nuts or chocolate. Bring the cake directly against them. Use your other hand to press nuts onto the cake. Use a spatula to press the chocolate so it doesn't melt against your hand.

MIXING AND MATCHING CAKES AND FROSTINGS

Yου are the best judge of what kind—and flavor—of frosting to use with the cake you have baked. Though it's fun to experiment, you may wish to try one of the combinations suggested on page 330. Or, follow these simple guidelines for frosting flavors that go well with each of the cakes:

CHOCOLATE CAKE: Vanilla, most all liqueurs and liquors, chocolate, coffee, orange, raspberry. *Beware of*: lemon, herb liqueurs (anisette).

WHITE CAKE: Chocolate, coffee, all fruit flavors. *Beware of*: strong liqueur and liquor flavors that would completely mask the flavor of the cake.

NUT CAKE: Any corresponding nut flavor (amaretto for almonds, etc.), chocolate, coffee. *Beware of*: fruit flavors, except with almond.

CAKE FINISHING

Finishing off a cake can be easy and fun if you follow a few simple preliminary rules to make the process neat, efficient, and above all, quick.

1. Make sure the cake layers are completely cooled—chilled is better.

2. Have all the ingredients and equipment ready so you won't be searching through a drawer with icing-covered hands.

3. Tear a dozen paper towels off the roll before you start—they make little clean-up tasks easier.

4. Before you start, brush all loose crumbs off the cake surface and work surface.

MOIST, BUTTERY NUT CAKE

12 tablespoons (1½ sticks) unsalted butter, softened

1½ cups light brown sugar, firmly packed

3 large eggs

2 cups bleached all-purpose flour

1 cup (about 4 ounces) ground nuts

1 teaspoon baking powder

1 teaspoon baking soda

1 cup milk or buttermilk

Two 9-inch-diameter × 1½-inch-deep layer pans, or one 13 × 9 × 2-inch pan, buttered, bottom(s) lined with parchment or wax paper

TWO 9-INCH-DIAMETER × 1½-INCH-DEEP LAYERS, OR ONE 13 × 9 × 2-INCH LAYER

Whether you make this cake with almonds, pecans, walnuts, or hazelnuts, it never fails to please.

1. Set a rack at the middle level of the oven and preheat to 350 degrees.

2. In a large mixing bowl, beat the butter and sugar for about 5 minutes, until light and fluffy. Beat in the eggs, one at a time, beating well and scraping the bowl and beater after each addition.

3. Combine the flour with the ground nuts, baking powder, and baking soda. Add a quarter of the flour mixture to the butter mixture, then add a third of the milk. Repeat, beginning and ending with the flour mixture. Scrape the bowl and beater often.

4. Pour the batter into the prepared pan(s) and smooth the top with a metal spatula. Bake the cake(s) for 25 to 30 minutes, or until a toothpick inserted in the center emerges clean.

5. Cool in the pan(s) on a rack for 5 minutes, then turn out of the pan(s) onto a rack, remove the paper, and let the cake cool completely.

STORAGE: To store, rinse the pan(s) and return the cake(s) to it (them). Wrap tightly in plastic wrap and refrigerate for up to 1 week, or freeze for up to 2 months.

Though the name conjures thoughts of foods that would be less than appetizing, plain cakes are actually among some of the best ones you can make. They fall into my favorite category of "mix-bake-eat" baked goods and need no fancy or time-consuming finishes to make them good. These are the cakes that you bake when you want to have something to offer last-minute guests, or to indulge yourself and your family with a sweet treat.

ANGEL FOOD CAKE

1¼ cups (10 or 11 large) egg whites
Pinch of salt
1 cup sugar
2 teaspoons lemon juice
2 teaspoons vanilla extract
1 cup self-rising cake flour

One 10-inch loose-bottomed tube pan

ONE 10-INCH CAKE

Though angel food cake has been popular since the middle of the nineteenth century, it is only in our current fat-conscious world that it has achieved an important place among other richer cakes. It is only a little tricky to prepare—make sure the egg whites are not overwhipped and your angel food cake will be perfect every time. This recipe calls for self-rising cake flour—a little insur-

ance against overwhipping and overmixing that would cause the egg whites to deflate and the cake to rise poorly.

Make sure you use a 10-inch tube pan with a removable bottom (easy to find in hardware stores) for this cake. Because the pan is not greased, it would be impossible to remove the cake from another type of pan.

1. Set a rack at the middle level of the oven and preheat to 325 degrees.

2. In a mixing bowl, whip the egg whites and salt with a hand or table-model mixer on medium speed until they are white and opaque and beginning to hold their shape. Increase the speed to high and whip in ½ cup of the sugar slowly, about a tablespoonful at a time, until the whites hold a soft, glossy peak. Beat in the lemon juice and vanilla extract.

3. Stir the remaining ½ cup of sugar and all the flour together in a bowl. Then in 3 or 4 additions, sift them over the egg whites and fold each addition in with a rubber spatula before sifting the next.

4. Scrape the batter into the ungreased pan and level the top of the batter. Bake the cake for 35 to 45 minutes, until it is well colored and springs back when gently pressed with a fingertip.

5. To cool, turn the pan over and insert the neck of a bottle into the tube so the pan is hanging. (Don't worry; the cake won't fall out.) Allow to cool completely.

6. When cool, turn cake right side up and insert a knife between the cake and the pan and run it gently around the side of the pan to loosen the cake. Remove the pan. The cake will still be attached to the base; loosen it the same way, turn it over onto a platter, and remove the base.

SERVING: Serve with whipped cream or a compote (page 279).

STORAGE: Cover the cake with plastic wrap and keep it at room temperature or in the refrigerator. To freeze the cake, wrap well and freeze for up to 1 month.

HINT FOR SUCCESS: See Perfect Whipped Egg Whites (page 278).

VARIATIONS

ORANGE ANGEL FOOD CAKE: Add 1 teaspoon finely grated orange zest and 2 teaspoons orange extract instead of the vanilla extract.

GINGER ANGEL FOOD CAKE: Add 2 teaspoons ground ginger, sifting it in with the sugar and cake flour.

SPICY ANGEL FOOD CAKE: Add 1 teaspoon ground cinnamon, ½ teaspoon grated nutmeg, ½ teaspoon ground ginger, and ¼ teaspoon ground cloves, sifting in the spices along with the sugar and cake flour.

COCOA ANGEL FOOD CAKE: Add 2 tablespoons cocoa powder and a pinch of baking soda to the sugar and flour mixture.

PERFECT WHIPPED EGG WHITES

Although whipping egg whites is not difficult, many home bakers have trouble with the process. Be sure to observe these simple rules and your egg whites and angel food cakes will always be perfect.

1. Separate eggs when they are cold—the white is thicker and flows slowly from the shell, making it less likely that the yolk will scrape against the jagged shell and break. Then, let the whites warm to room temperature. Or, warm them, stirring, over a pan of warm water.

2. Make sure there are *no* traces of yolk in the whites. Fat prevents egg whites from absorbing air, so the whites will whip partially or not at all, ruining the texture of the cake.

3. For the same reason, make sure that all vessels and utensils for separating and whipping the whites are clean, dry, and free of grease.

4. Add the sugar slowly, after the whites have begun to hold their shape. Adding the sugar too early makes the whites sticky and soft.

5. Don't overwhip. It is better to have egg whites a little underwhipped than overwhipped. Overwhipped whites have a dry, gritty texture and folding other ingredients into them requires so much effort to rid the batter of these firm lumps of egg white that the whites deflate completely.

6. Fold other ingredients gently, but thoroughly, into the whites. Use a rubber spatula and scrape all the way down to the bottom while cutting across the diameter of the bowl. The dry ingredients tend to reach the bottom quickly and will stay there unless you deliberately scrape them up and into the batter.

7. Finally, put the batter into the pan and the pan into the oven immediately after mixing. If the batter waits too long before baking, it will fall.

Although there are a lot of rules, the process itself is quick and simple.

COMPOTES TO SERVE WITH ANGEL FOOD CAKE

Serving some fruit along with it considerably dresses up an angel food cake and does not add any fat to the dessert.

Cranberry Compote

One 12-ounce bag cranberries, rinsed and
　　drained
⅔ cup sugar
½ cup strained orange juice
1 teaspoon grated orange zest
2 tablespoons orange liqueur

1. Combine all the ingredients in a nonreactive saucepan. Over low heat, bring to a simmer, and cook, stirring occasionally, until slightly thickened, about 5 minutes.

2. Cool, then refrigerate, covered, until needed.

VARIATIONS

RASPBERRY COMPOTE: Substitute two 10-ounce packages frozen raspberries, thawed, for the cranberries. Omit the orange zest and juice. Substitute raspberry liqueur or kirsch for the orange liqueur.

STRAWBERRY COMPOTE: Substitute 2 pints strawberries, rinsed, hulled, and sliced, for the cranberries, above. Use the orange flavoring as in the cranberry compote, above, or flavor as for the Raspberry Compote variation, above.

EASY POUND CAKE

½ pound (2 sticks) unsalted butter, softened
1 cup sugar
4 eggs
¼ teaspoon salt
Pinch of ground mace
1½ teaspoons vanilla extract
¼ cup milk
¾ teaspoon baking powder
2 cups cake flour

One 8½ × 4½ × 2¾-inch loaf pan, buttered, bottom lined with parchment or wax paper

ONE 8½-INCH LOAF

Mace, the outer covering of a nutmeg, is the traditional flavoring for pound cake.

1. Set a rack at the middle level of the oven and preheat to 325 degrees.

2. In a bowl, beat the butter with the sugar until soft and light. Beat in 3 of the eggs, one at a time. Beat in the salt, mace, and vanilla extract.

3. In a separate bowl, combine the remaining egg with the milk.

4. In a third bowl, stir the baking powder into the flour and sift once. Beat a third of the flour into the butter/sugar/egg mixture. Beat in half of the milk, then the flour again, and continue until everything is incorporated—5 additions—beginning and ending with the flour.

5. Fill the pan about five-sixths full. Bake the pound cake at 325 degrees for about 1 hour, or until it is well risen and colored, cracked on the surface, and a thin knife inserted in the thickest part of the cake emerges clean.

6. Cool on a rack in the pan. Unmold, remove the paper, wrap, and cut on the following day.

SERVING: With a sharp serrated knife, cut the cake into ¾-inch slices. Pound cake makes a good accompaniment to any fruit compote, fruit salad, ice cream, or sherbet.

STORAGE: Wrap the cake tightly in plastic wrap and store at a cool room temperature or in the refrigerator. If refrigerated, bring to room temperature before serving. Or freeze the cake for several weeks. Defrost it unwrapped and loosely covered with a towel at room temperature before serving.

HINT FOR SUCCESS: Be sure that the butter and eggs are at room temperature or the batter may separate while you are mixing and the cake will have a rough, irregular texture instead of a smooth, tender one.

VARIATIONS

VANILLA BEAN POUND CAKE: Omit the mace. Split and scrape out the seeds of a vanilla bean. Add the seeds to the butter and egg mixture and omit the vanilla extract.

ORANGE POUND CAKE: Omit the mace. Add the finely grated zest of a medium navel orange to the butter and egg mixture and substitute orange extract for the vanilla extract.

LEMON POUND CAKE: Omit the mace. Add the finely grated zest of a large lemon to the butter and egg mixture and add 2 teaspoons lemon extract instead of 1½ teaspoons vanilla.

HONEY SPICE POUND CAKE: Decrease the sugar in the butter and egg mixture to ¾ cup and add ¼ cup honey and the finely grated zest of 1 large lemon to the butter and egg mixture. Omit the vanilla extract. Stir ½ teaspoon each ground cinnamon, ground cloves, and grated nutmeg into the flour before it is added to the butter and egg mixture.

GINGER POUND CAKE: Substitute 2 teaspoons ground ginger for the spices in the Honey Spice Pound Cake variation, above. Prepare the recipe with honey and sugar or only with sugar.

FRESH GINGER POUND CAKE: Substitute 1 tablespoon grated fresh ginger for the spices in the Honey Spice Pound Cake variation, above, and prepare the recipe with honey or sugar.

CHOCOLATE SOUR CREAM POUND CAKE

3 ounces unsweetened chocolate, cut into chunks

1 cup bleached all-purpose flour

¼ teaspoon baking powder

¼ teaspoon baking soda

¼ teaspoon salt

8 tablespoons (1 stick) unsalted butter, softened

1 cup sugar

2 large eggs

1 teaspoon vanilla extract

½ cup sour cream

CHOCOLATE PECAN GLAZE

¼ cup water

¼ cup light corn syrup

¾ cup sugar

8 ounces bittersweet chocolate, finely cut

½ cup (2 ounces) lightly toasted pecan halves

One 8½ × 4½ × 2¾-inch pan, buttered, bottom lined with parchment or wax paper

ONE 8½ × 4½ × 2-INCH CAKE, ABOUT 10 SLICES

This chocolate classic has a deep chocolate flavor and a real pound cake texture.

1. Set a rack at the middle level of the oven and preheat to 325 degrees.

2. Place the chocolate in a small heatproof bowl over hot, but not simmering, water. Stir occasionally as the chocolate melts; cool.

3. In another bowl, stir the flour, baking powder, baking soda, and salt well to combine; set aside.

4. Beat the butter and sugar in a bowl with an electric mixer until light and fluffy, about 2 minutes. Beat in the cooled chocolate, then the eggs, one at a time, and the vanilla.

5. With a rubber spatula, stir half the flour mixture into the chocolate and butter, then stir in the sour cream. Stir in the remaining flour.

6. Scrape the batter into the prepared pan and smooth the top. Bake for 45 to 50 minutes, until the cake is well risen and a toothpick inserted in the center of the cake emerges clean.

7. Cool in the pan on a rack for 10 minutes, then remove from the pan and cool completely.

8. To make the glaze, combine the water, corn syrup, and sugar in a small saucepan. Place over low heat and cook, stirring occasionally, until the syrup comes to a full boil. Remove from the heat, add the chocolate, and allow to stand for 2 minutes so the chocolate melts. Whisk smooth and pour over the top of the cooled cake. Allow the excess glaze to drip down the sides.

9. Quickly decorate with the pecan halves while the glaze is still wet.

SERVING: With a sharp serrated knife, cut the cake into ¾-inch slices. Serve with ice cream.

STORAGE: Wrap in plastic and store at a cool room temperature or in the refrigerator. If refrigerated, bring to room temperature before serving.

MARBLE SPICE CAKE

2¼ cups cake flour

2 teaspoons baking powder

10 tablespoons (1¼ sticks) unsalted butter, softened

1 cup sugar

¼ teaspoon salt

2 large eggs, at room temperature

½ cup milk

2 tablespoons unsulfured molasses

1 teaspoon ground cinnamon

½ teaspoon freshly grated nutmeg

½ teaspoon ground cloves

One 9-inch springform pan, 3 inches deep; or a 9-inch round layer pan, 2 inches deep, buttered, bottom lined with a disk of parchment or wax paper

ONE 9-INCH CAKE, 8 TO 10 SERVINGS

After I adapted this recipe from a 1930s cake flour pamphlet, I tried several of the variations, listed at the end of the recipe, and they work just as well. Basically an old-fashioned 2-egg cake, this is a perfect quick cake to make for a birthday or any other special occasion because it is easy to prepare; it always turns out light, moist, and flavorful; and doesn't necessarily need a frosting to finish it off.

1. Set a rack at the middle level of the oven and preheat to 350 degrees.

2. In a small bowl, stir the cake flour and baking powder together well to combine.

3. In a large mixing bowl, cream the butter until soft and light. Use a hand mixer set at medium speed or a heavy-duty mixer fitted with the paddle, if you have one. Gradually beat in the sugar and salt and continue beating for about 5 minutes, until very light. Beat in the eggs, one at a time, continuing to beat until the mixture is smooth and fluffy.

4. Sift half the cake flour mixture over the butter mixture, then stir it in by hand. Stir in the milk thoroughly, scraping the side of the bowl, then sift over and stir in the remaining cake flour mixture. Beat the batter for a few seconds by hand to ensure that everything is thoroughly incorporated.

5. Divide the batter in half and stir the molasses and spices thoroughly into one half.

6. Spoon alternating tablespoons of the two batters into the prepared pan. Use the point of a table knife to run a zigzag through the batters to marble them. Bake the cake for about 35 minutes, or until it is well risen and a skewer inserted in the center of the cake emerges clean.

7. Cool in the pan on a rack for 5 minutes, then remove the pan side and slide the cake from the pan bottom to the rack to cool. If the cake was baked in a layer pan, turn it over onto a rack, remove the pan and paper, then turn the cake right side up onto another rack to cool.

SERVING: Serve the cake with a dusting of confectioners' sugar and pass a bowl of sweetened whipped cream. Or finish the cake by spreading the outside with whipped cream or Caramel Icing (page 310).

STORAGE: Keep the cake tightly wrapped (or under a cake dome if iced) at room temperature. If the cake is covered with whipped cream, refrigerate leftovers loosely covered with plastic wrap.

VARIATIONS

These are one-flavor cakes so omit steps 5 and 6 and continue on to 7.

MOLASSES SPICE CAKE: Add double quantities of the spices to the cake flour. Increase the molasses to ¼ cup and add it to the batter with the milk. Bake as for the marble cake, above.

CITRUS-FLECKED CAKE: Omit the molasses and spices. Add 1 teaspoon each finely grated lemon and orange zests and ½ teaspoon each lemon and orange extracts to the batter along with the eggs. Bake as for the marble cake, above.

GINGERBREAD

2 cups bleached all-purpose flour
2 teaspoons baking powder
½ teaspoon baking soda
½ teaspoon salt
2 teaspoons ground ginger
1 teaspoon ground cinnamon
8 tablespoons (1 stick) unsalted butter, softened
¼ cup sugar
1 large egg
⅔ cup unsulfured molasses
⅔ cup milk or water

One 8 × 8 × 2-inch pan, buttered, bottom lined
with a square of parchment or wax paper

ONE 8-INCH CAKE, ABOUT SIXTEEN 2-INCH SQUARES

Descendants of ancient ceremonial breads, used by the Romans in the celebration of fertility rites and weddings, gingerbreads are related to many other preparations such as the Italian *panforte,* the French *pain d'épices,* and even English fruitcake.

Good gingerbread is easy to prepare, and benefits from aging for a day or two after baking. Of course, make sure the spices you use are as fresh as possible and the gingerbread will have a strong, clean flavor.

1. Set a rack at the middle level of the oven and preheat to 350 degrees.

2. In a mixing bowl, stir the dry ingredients, except sugar, together well.

3. In another bowl, beat the butter and sugar until light and fluffy, by hand or by machine on medium speed. Beat in the egg, and continue beating until smooth.

4. In a small bowl, stir the molasses and milk together and add to the butter mixture with the dry ingredients. Fold the batter together with a rubber spatula.

5. Scrape the batter into the prepared pan. Bake the gingerbread for 35 to 45 minutes, until well risen and firm in the center.

6. Cool in the pan for 5 minutes, then unmold to a rack to cool completely.

SERVING: This cakelike gingerbread is great served as a dessert with a baked apple, or for breakfast with butter or cream cheese. Or serve with whipped cream or applesauce, or both. It is a great tea cake and perfect after a light lunch.

STORAGE: Keep wrapped in plastic at room temperature, or freeze, wrapped, for up to a month.

HINT FOR SUCCESS: Make sure the butter and sugar mixture is smooth and soft before continuing with the recipe, or the cake will not have a smooth texture.

NUT CAKES

The nut cake layers on page 275 are meant to be used as components of more elaborate cakes, though they are also excellent as plain cakes with just a dusting of confectioners' sugar. The following nut cakes, the gugelhupf and the financier, are Viennese and French versions of a rich nut cake to serve as a coffee cake, or as a dessert for a very casual meal.

HAZELNUT GUGELHUPF

½ cup (about 2 ounces) whole natural hazelnuts
⅓ cup raisins
1¼ cups cake flour
6 large eggs, separated
⅔ cup sugar
Grated zest of 1 lemon
1 teaspoon vanilla extract
¼ cup hazelnut oil

One 1½- or 2-quart gugelhupf or Bundt pan, buttered and floured

ONE 9-INCH GUGELHUPF, 8 TO 10 SERVINGS

Any nuts may be used for this, though the hazelnut version is the classic Viennese one. It adds flavor to finish this cake with a nut oil, such as the hazelnut oil used here (walnut and almond oils are also available in specialty stores). If you have trouble finding these oils, use the equivalent amount of melted, clarified butter (melted butter that has had all the foam and liquid removed).

1. Set a rack at the middle level of the oven and preheat to 350 degrees.

2. Place hazelnuts in food processor and pulse to grind finely. In a bowl, stir together the raisins, hazelnuts, and cake flour and set aside.

3. Beat 5 of the egg yolks with ⅓ cup of the sugar, the lemon zest, and the vanilla extract until the eggs are light. Beat in the oil.

4. In a clean, dry bowl with clean, dry beaters, whip all the egg whites until they are opaque, then whip in the remaining ½ cup of sugar in a stream. Continue whipping until the whites hold a firm peak.

5. Fold the whites into the yolk mixture, then fold in the flour mixture.

6. Pour the batter into the prepared pan. Bake for about 45 minutes, until the cake is well risen and the point of a knife inserted between the side and the tube emerges clean.

7. Unmold the cake immediately and cool on a rack.

SERVING: Serve alone for tea or breakfast or with ice cream or whipped cream for dessert.

STORAGE: Store covered at room temperature or wrap and freeze. Defrost and allow to come to room temperature before serving.

BUTTER ALMOND FINANCIER

1 cup (about 5 ounces) whole almonds, plus ¼ cup (about 1 ounce) sliced, blanched almonds
1½ cups sugar
1 cup bleached all-purpose flour
10 tablespoons (1¼ sticks) unsalted butter
2 tablespoons dark rum
2 teaspoons vanilla extract
1 cup (about 8 large) egg whites
Pinch of salt
Confectioners' sugar for dusting

One 10-inch springform or layer pan, buttered, bottom lined with a disk of parchment or wax paper

ONE 10-INCH CAKE, 8 TO 10 SERVINGS

The name of this traditional French dessert probably comes from its richness. It is an unusual batter where ground almonds, sugar, and flour and a large quantity of melted butter are folded into egg whites which have been beaten with sugar. Of course, the egg whites fall and liquefy as the butter is folded in, but the financier rises well, nonetheless.

1. Set a rack at the middle level of the oven and preheat to 350 degrees.

2. Place the whole almonds and ¾ cup of the sugar in a food processor and pulse until the mixture is finely ground. Transfer to a bowl and stir in the flour.

3. In a saucepan, melt the butter, and add the rum and vanilla extract. Set aside to cool slightly.

4. In a clean, dry bowl, whip the egg whites with the salt until they form a very soft peak. Add the remaining ¾ cup of sugar in a very slow stream, whipping constantly. Continue whipping the egg whites until they hold a soft peak.

5. Alternately fold the almond and butter mixtures into the egg whites, a third at a time. Begin with the almond mixture and end with the butter.

6. Pour the batter into the prepared pan. Smooth the top and sprinkle with the sliced almonds.

7. Bake the financier for about 50 minutes, until it's well risen and golden. The center of the cake should feel firm when pressed with the palm of the hand.

(continued)

8. Cool the financier briefly on a rack and remove the pan and paper. If some of the almonds on the surface fall off, replace them on the cake. Dust very lightly with confectioners' sugar.

SERVING: Serve the financier for tea or with fruit as a dessert after a meal.

STORAGE: Keep the financier covered, at room temperature, or double-wrap in plastic and freeze for up to 2 months.

VARIATIONS

HAZELNUT FINANCIER: Substitute 1 cup whole unblanched hazelnuts for the almonds, above.

ALMOND AND HAZELNUT FINANCIER: Use ½ cup whole blanched almonds and ½ cup whole unblanched hazelnuts instead of 1 cup almonds, above.

BROWN BUTTER FINANCIER (Financier au Beurre Noisette): Melt the butter over medium heat in a 2- to 3-quart pan. After the butter has melted, continue cooking it until it foams and darkens slightly. Carefully pour the hot browned butter into a dry heatproof bowl. Allow to cool to lukewarm before using. The brown butter is good with almonds, hazelnuts, or a combination.

PISTACHIO FINANCIER: Bring 1½ cups very green, unsalted pistachios to a boil and drain them. Rub off the skins and place the blanched nuts on a jelly-roll pan. Bake them at 300 degrees for 7 or 8 minutes to dry but not color them. Use the blanched pistachios instead of the almonds, above. Substitute kirsch for the rum.

CAKES WITH FRESH AND DRIED FRUIT

Adding fruit to a cake while it is baking can make for wonderful changes in texture and flavor. The fruit may be dried—as in a fruitcake or the pureed fig filling of a Linzertorte. Or it may be fresh fruit, such as berries melting between a moist buttermilk cake and a crisp crumb topping. When buying fruit for cake baking, choose unblemished and ripe fresh fruit. Taste dried and candied fruit to see that it is sweet and moist—avoid all dried-out or bitter dried or candied fruit.

FIG AND ORANGE LINZERTORTE

FIG FILLING

2 cups (about 12 ounces) dried white
    (Calimyrna) figs
½ cup orange juice
¼ cup honey
¼ teaspoon ground cinnamon

LINZER DOUGH

1½ cups bleached all-purpose flour
1½ cups (about 6 ounces) walnut pieces, finely
    ground
⅔ cup granulated sugar
½ teaspoon ground cinnamon
½ teaspoon grated nutmeg
½ teaspoon ground cloves
1 teaspoon baking powder

12 tablespoons (1½ sticks) cold unsalted butter
1 egg plus 1 egg yolk
1 teaspoon grated orange zest

Confectioners' sugar for dusting

One 9-inch springform or 2-inch-deep layer pan, buttered and lined with a disk of parchment or wax paper

ONE 9-INCH CAKE, ABOUT 12 SERVINGS

I gave a recipe for a classic Linzertorte, like the one prepared at Demel's pastry shop in Vienna, in my first book. This recipe is similar to the traditional variety, but it replaces the standard almonds or hazelnuts with walnuts and the jam, usually raspberry, with a filling made from dried figs flavored with orange and honey.

(continued)

1. To make the filling, stem and dice the figs and combine with the remaining ingredients in a nonreactive saucepan. Bring to a simmer and cook over low heat, stirring occasionally, until the figs are soft and the mixture is thickened, about 15 minutes. Stir often as the filling thickens so it doesn't scorch. Cool and puree in a food processor.

2. Set a rack at the middle level of the oven and preheat to 350 degrees.

3. To make the dough, combine the dry ingredients in a mixing bowl. Rub in the butter evenly, making sure the mixture does not become pasty. Whisk the egg, yolk, and orange zest together, and stir into the other ingredients. Continue to stir until a soft dough forms.

4. Spread two thirds of the Linzer dough in the bottom of the prepared pan. Evenly spread the filling over the dough, keeping it about ½ inch from the edge.

5. Place the remaining dough in a pastry bag fitted with a ½-inch plain tube (Ateco #6). Pipe 4 lines of the dough, spaced equidistantly, over the filling. Pipe 4 more lines diagonally across the first ones. With the remaining dough, pipe a circle of small spheres around the rim of the cake.

6. Bake the Linzertorte for 45 minutes, until the center is firm when gently pressed with a fingertip.

7. Cool in the pan on a rack. Unmold and dust lightly with the confectioners' sugar immediately before serving.

SERVING: Serve the torte in wedges for tea or as a dessert after a light meal.

STORAGE: Keep loosely covered at room temperature for up to several days, or wrap tightly in plastic and freeze for up to several months.

HINT FOR SUCCESS: If you prefer not to pipe the lattice and border of dots on the torte, chill the dough and divide it into 12 pieces. Roll each into a pencil-thick strand and make the lattice on the top with these. Use 4 of the strands to make the edge.

VARIATION

Substitute pecans for a definitely nontraditional Linzertorte.

❖

LINZERTORTE

Most of us think of a Linzertorte as a pastry or tart, but not as a cake. The real Viennese version of this cake (yes, *torte* means "cake" in German) has a moist cakey texture, not at all like the French-influenced versions of the cake that use a pastry dough that is rolled out and fairly crisp after baking.

FRESH RASPBERRY LINZERTORTE

DOUGH

1½ cups bleached all-purpose flour
1 cup (about 4 ounces) blanched almonds, ground
¾ cup granulated sugar
¼ teaspoon ground cloves
1 teaspoon baking powder
12 tablespoons (1½ sticks) unsalted butter
1 egg plus 1 egg yolk
1 teaspoon grated lemon zest
1 teaspoon vanilla extract

FINISHING

⅓ cup raspberry preserves
2 baskets raspberries
⅓ cup (about 1½ ounces) toasted sliced almonds
Confectioners' sugar for dusting

One 9-inch springform or 2-inch-deep layer pan, buttered and lined with a disk of parchment or wax paper

ONE 9-INCH CAKE, ABOUT 8 SERVINGS

The flavor combination of nuts and spice in a buttery cake such as this is one of my favorites. Here the Linzer dough is baked without the traditional jam filling and then used as a base for raspberry preserves and a topping of fresh berries.

1. Set a rack at the middle level of the oven and preheat to 350 degrees.

2. To make the dough, mix all the dry ingredients in a bowl. Rub in the butter finely by hand. In a small bowl, whisk the egg and yolk together with the lemon zest and vanilla extract and stir into the dough with a fork—the dough will be very soft.

3. Spread two thirds of the dough evenly in the pan. Place the remaining dough in a pastry bag fitted with a ½-inch plain tube (Ateco #6) and pipe a border of dots around the edge.

4. Bake for 25 to 30 minutes, until the cake is well colored and firm, but not dry. Cool in the pan. Unmold and slide or invert onto a platter.

5. To finish, spread the preserves on top of the cooled cake, avoiding the raised border formed by the dots of dough. Arrange the raspberries on the preserves. Decorate the edge with the almonds and dust lightly with the confectioners' sugar.

SERVING: Serve a little whipped cream with the Linzertorte.

STORAGE: Keep the finished dessert at room temperature for up to several hours. For advance preparation, bake the cake base early in the day, then finish with the preserves and fruit several hours before serving. The cake base may be refrigerated for several days or frozen for several months.

HINT FOR SUCCESS: Avoid having the butter too soft or overmixing and melting it into the dry ingredients, or the baked cake will have a tough, rather than a tender texture.

APRICOT CRUMB CAKE

CAKE

8 tablespoons (1 stick) unsalted butter
¾ cup sugar
1 egg plus 3 egg yolks
1 teaspoon grated lemon zest
1 teaspoon vanilla extract
1¼ cups bleached all-purpose flour
1 teaspoon baking powder

TOPPING

1¼ cups bleached all-purpose flour
½ cup sugar
¼ teaspoon ground cinnamon
8 tablespoons (1 stick) unsalted butter
1½ to 2 pounds (about 12 medium) apricots

One 10-inch springform pan, buttered and lined with a disk of parchment or wax paper

ONE 10-INCH ROUND CAKE, 8 TO 10 SERVINGS

This good all-purpose crumb cake can be made with any juicy fresh fruit. Try substituting prune plums or pitted cherries for the apricots.

1. Set a rack at the middle level of the oven and preheat to 350 degrees.

2. For the cake batter, in a large mixing bowl, cream the butter until soft and light. Use a hand mixer set at medium speed or a heavy-duty mixer fitted with the paddle, if you have one. Gradually beat in the sugar and continue beating for about 5 minutes, until very light. Add the egg and continue beating until lighter. Add the yolks, one at a time, beating after each addition and scraping the bowl and the paddle occasionally. Beat in the lemon zest and vanilla. Sift the flour and baking powder together several times, then stir into the batter.

3. To make the topping, mix the flour, sugar, and cinnamon in a bowl. Melt the butter and stir it in evenly. Rub the mixture to coarse crumbs by hand.

4. Rinse, halve, and pit the apricots. Spread the batter evenly in the prepared pan. Arrange the apricot halves, leaving a margin of ½ inch around the edge, cut side up on the batter, but don't press them in. Scatter the crumbs evenly over the apricots and the batter.

5. Bake the cake for 50 to 60 minutes, until the crumbs are well colored and the cake is firm and no longer liquid in the center.

6. Cool the cake in the pan, then run a knife around the edges to loosen it from the pan. Remove pan side and slide from base to a platter. Dust the cake lightly with the confectioners' sugar.

SERVING: Serve the cake for breakfast, brunch, or tea, or as a dessert for a casual lunch.

STORAGE: Keep loosely covered at room temperature. Wrap in plastic and refrigerate for several days or freeze for up to several months. Defrost and reheat the cake at 300 degrees for about 15 minutes, and cool before serving.

HINT FOR SUCCESS: Taste the apricots to make sure they are ripe—really underripe apricots are painfully sour.

VARIATIONS

PINEAPPLE CRUMB CAKE: Substitute 1 pineapple, peeled, cored, quartered in the length, and sliced, for the apricots, above. Arrange the pineapple slices in concentric circles and slightly overlapping on the cake batter.

PLUM CRUMB CAKE: This is perfect in the late summer and early fall when the first Italian or prune plums come to market. Substitute 12 prune plums, rinsed, halved, and pitted, for the apricots, above.

CRUMB CAKES

These crumb cakes have a layer of fruit trapped between a cake layer below and crisp, crumb topping. Though a crumb cake need not have the addition of fruit, it dresses up the presentation and lightens and moistens what might ordinarily be a dry cake.

BLUEBERRY CRUMB CAKE SQUARES

CAKE

½ pound (2 sticks) unsalted butter, softened

1½ cups granulated sugar

3 eggs plus 3 egg yolks

2 teaspoons vanilla extract

¼ cup milk or buttermilk

2½ cups bleached all-purpose flour

2 teaspoons baking powder

1 quart blueberries, rinsed, picked over, and
  dried

CRUMB TOPPING

2 cups bleached all-purpose flour

⅓ cup granulated sugar

⅓ cup brown sugar

½ teaspoon ground cinnamon

¼ teaspoon grated nutmeg

12 tablespoons (1½ sticks) unsalted butter,
  melted

One 10 × 15-inch jelly-roll pan, buttered

FIFTEEN 3-INCH CAKE SQUARES

These are easy to make for a crowd and have the same delicate texture as the larger crumb cakes.

1. Set a rack at the middle level of the oven and preheat to 350 degrees.

2. For the cake batter, in a large mixing bowl, beat the butter and sugar until they're soft and light. Add the 3 eggs one at a time, beating well after each addition. Beat in the vanilla. In another bowl, stir the yolks into the milk. Sift together the flour and baking powder and stir into the batter in 3 additions, alternating with the yolks and milk, beginning and ending with the flour. Spread the batter in the prepared pan.

3. Scatter the blueberries evenly over the batter, and press them in gently.

4. To make the crumbs, mix the dry ingredients in a bowl. Stir in the melted butter. Rub the mixture to coarse crumbs by hand. Scatter the crumbs over the berries as evenly as possible.

5. Bake the cake for 50 to 60 minutes, until the batter is firm and the crumbs are well colored.

6. Cool the cake in the pan on a rack. Cut the cooled cake into fifteen 3-inch squares. Remove the squares from the pan to a platter.

SERVING: Serve the cake squares as a casual dessert—they're great for a picnic.

STORAGE: Keep loosely covered at room temperature.

VARIATION

CHERRY CRUMB CAKE SQUARES: Substitute 4 cups pitted sour cherries for the blueberries.

BEST AND EASIEST BANANA CAKE

CAKE

12 tablespoons (1½ sticks) unsalted butter, softened
½ cup light brown sugar, firmly packed
½ cup granulated sugar
3 large eggs
1 teaspoon vanilla extract
1 teaspoon baking powder
½ teaspoon baking soda
2½ cups cake flour
1 cup mashed, not pureed, bananas (2 large bananas, 6 to 7 ounces each)
¾ cup milk or buttermilk

WHIPPED CREAM

1 cup heavy cream
2 tablespoons granulated sugar
½ teaspoon vanilla extract, or 1 tablespoon dark rum

One 9 × 13 × 2-inch pan, buttered, bottom lined with parchment or wax paper

ONE 13 × 9 × 1½-INCH CAKE, ABOUT TWENTY-FOUR 2-INCH SQUARES

To achieve a vivid banana flavor the secret is to mash, not puree, the bananas.

1. Set a rack at the middle level of the oven and preheat to 350 degrees.

2. For the cake batter, in a large mixing bowl, cream the butter until it's soft and light. Use a hand mixer set at medium speed or a heavy-duty mixer fitted with the paddle, if you have one. Gradually beat in the sugars and continue beating for about 5 minutes, until very light. Beat in the eggs, one at a time, beating smooth between each addition, scraping the bowl and beater(s) occasionally. Beat in the vanilla. In another bowl, stir the baking powder and soda into the cake flour and sift over the butter and egg mixture. Stir in the bananas and milk to mix. Beat by machine on low speed for 2 minutes, scraping the bowl and beater(s) several times.

3. Scrape the batter into the prepared pan and bake for about 35 minutes, until the cake is well risen and a skewer inserted in the center emerges clean.

4. Cool the cake in the pan for 10 minutes, then cover with a rack and remove the pan and paper. Immediately turn the cake right side up and finish cooling.

5. To make whipped cream, combine all the ingredients in a bowl and whip until the cream holds a very soft peak.

SERVING: Serve squares or slices of cake with a spoonful of the cream on the side.

STORAGE: Keep the cake loosely covered at room temperature, or wrap tightly in plastic and refrigerate for several days or freeze for several months.

OXFORD FRUITCAKE

8 ounces each dates, dried figs, and mixed candied fruit

4 ounces each candied cherries and candied pineapples

8 ounces each dark raisins, golden raisins, and currants

4 ounces each walnut halves, pecan halves, and whole almonds

½ cup dark rum or brandy, plus extra for the cake

2¼ cups unbleached all-purpose flour

1 teaspoon ground cinnamon

1 teaspoon freshly grated nutmeg

1 teaspoon salt

1 teaspoon baking powder

½ teaspoon baking soda

½ teaspoon ground cloves

½ pound (2 sticks) unsalted butter

1 cup dark brown sugar

4 large eggs

MARZIPAN TOPPING

1 pound almond paste

One 1-pound box (4 cups) confectioners' sugar, plus extra for dusting work surface

1 cup light corn syrup

One 11 × 17-inch pan, buttered and lined with parchment paper

ONE 11 × 17-INCH CAKE, ABOUT FORTY 2-INCH SQUARES

This has been my favorite fruitcake since I first tasted it when I was in my teens. The recipe is adapted from one given to me by Daphne Giles, the British sister-in-law of my childhood friend, Noel Giles. Daphne comes from Newbury, near Oxford, and prepared this every year for Noel's Christmas Day birthday.

1. Pick over the dates for pits and cut them into ½-inch pieces. Stem and cut the figs into ½-inch pieces. Rinse all the candied fruit in cold water and cut the pineapple in ½-inch pieces. Combine with the remaining fruit and nuts and toss with ½ cup rum or brandy. The mixture may be left covered with plastic wrap for several days at this point.

2. When you're ready to bake the cake, set a rack at the middle level of the oven and preheat to 300 degrees.

3. For the cake batter, sift the flour with the other dry ingredients (except brown sugar) and set aside. Beat the butter until light, then beat in the brown sugar. Continue beating until lighter. Beat in a third of the flour mixture, then 2 of the eggs, and continue alternating until all are combined, ending with the flour mixture. Pour the batter over the fruit and nuts and fold thoroughly together.

4. Press the batter into the prepared pan. Place a piece of parchment or foil over the batter and press it so it adheres well. Bake for about 1 hour, until the cake is firm and no longer wet.

5. Cool the fruitcake in the pan, sprinkle with rum, and wrap in cheesecloth which has been moistened with rum. Wrap the cake in plastic and foil and age the fruitcake for several weeks, if you wish.

6. For the topping, combine the almond paste, sugar, and ⅓ cup of the corn syrup in a food processor fitted with the metal blade. Pulse repeatedly, 10 or 12 times in all, to form a dough. Remove from the work bowl and knead until smooth. Double-wrap in plastic and store until needed at room temperature.

7. To cover the fruitcake with the marzipan, bring the remaining corn syrup to a boil in a small saucepan. Brush half the hot corn syrup on the fruitcake. On a surface dusted with confectioners' sugar, roll half the marzipan to the size of the fruitcake. Lift and place the marzipan on the fruitcake, pressing to adhere. Invert the fruitcake to a clean surface and repeat with the remaining corn syrup and marzipan. Trim the edges and cut the fruitcake into 2-inch squares.

SERVING: Serve the fruitcake as you would a confection or candy: after a meal with coffee, or as an occasional refreshment.

STORAGE: You may keep the fruitcake for several months before finishing it with the marzipan. Though it should keep well at room temperature, especially since it has been well doused with alcohol, I still prefer to refrigerate it. To keep the marzipan-covered fruitcake fresh, individually wrap the squares in plastic wrap.

HINT FOR SUCCESS: Don't overbake the cake or it will be inedibly dry and may become bitter if the abundant sugar in the candied fruit begins to caramelize.

IRISH CURRANT CAKE

½ pound (2 sticks) unsalted butter, softened
1½ cups sugar
1 teaspoon salt
2 large eggs
One 10-ounce box (about 1¾ cups) currants
4½ cups unbleached all-purpose flour
2 teaspoons baking powder
2 teaspoons baking soda
1½ cups buttermilk or milk

*Two 8½ × 4½ × 2¾-inch loaf pans, buttered and
lined with parchment or buttered wax paper*

TWO 8½ × 4½ × 2¾-INCH LOAVES

Ellen Giles, the mother of my childhood friend Noel, made this cake every week for her family. Noel and I would devour great slabs of it thickly spread with sweet butter, accompanied by cups of strong Irish tea. The Gileses were from Toome Bridge, County Antrim, in Northern Ireland—along with this recipe I also acquired something of an Antrim accent during my years of friendship with the Giles family.

1. Set a rack at the middle level of the oven and preheat to 350 degrees.

2. In a large mixing bowl, beat the butter until soft and light with a hand mixer set at medium speed or in a heavy-duty mixer fitted with the paddle. Gradually beat in the sugar and salt and continue beating for about 5 minutes, until very light. Beat in the eggs, one at a time, continuing to beat until the mixture is smooth and fluffy.

3. Place the currants in a small bowl and toss them with 2 tablespoons of the flour. In another bowl, stir the baking powder and baking soda into the remaining flour to mix. Stir half the flour into the butter and egg mixture, then stir in the buttermilk. Stir in the remaining flour, then stir vigorously or beat by machine on the lowest speed for about 1 minute, until well mixed. Stir in the floured currants well.

4. Scrape the batter into the prepared pans and smooth the top. Bake for about 1¼ hours, until the cakes are well risen and a deep golden color. A skewer or thin knife plunged into the center of the cakes should emerge clean.

5. Cool in the pans on a rack. Unmold the cooled cakes and peel away the paper.

SERVING: Serve the currant cake in ½-inch slices for breakfast, brunch, or tea. Although in my youth I spread the slices with butter, I no longer do that today.

STORAGE: Wrap the cake tightly in plastic wrap and store at room temperature for several days. Freeze the cake, wrapped, for longer storage—up to 2 months.

VARIATION

Substitute dark or golden raisins or a mixture for half or all of the currants.

LAYER CAKES

Layer cakes are made from cake layers (see pages 270 to 275) stacked with fillings. The layers may be baked separately or one layer may be sliced into separate horizontal layers after baking and cooling.

Some of the recipes here utilize the layers referred to above, while others rely on special layers used just for the assembly of a particular cake. Feel free to experiment with different layers and fillings—guidelines for this are given on page 330, in the section on celebration cakes.

GUSTAV KLIMT TORTE

CAKE

12 tablespoons (1½ sticks) unsalted butter
1 cup sugar
9 eggs, separated
Grated zest of 1 lemon
1 teaspoon vanilla extract
2 cups (about 8 ounces) ground hazelnuts
⅔ cup dry breadcrumbs

FILLING

1 cup raspberry preserves

GLAZE

1 cup sugar
⅓ cup water
⅓ cup corn syrup
8 ounces semisweet chocolate, finely cut

One 10-inch round pan, buttered, bottom lined with parchment or wax paper

ONE 10-INCH ROUND CAKE, ABOUT 12 SERVINGS

Many of the great hotels and pastry shops in Vienna have specialties they refer to as "shipping cakes"—ones that are capable of being shipped from Vienna to anywhere in the world. Needless to say, these cakes need to stay moist and palatable for the long time it takes them to arrive at their destinations—so they are the ideal make-ahead cakes.

This cake, named for the turn-of-the-century Viennese Secession artist, is a specialty of the Cafe im Park at the Vienna Hilton. I am indebted to Hermann Reiner, former executive chef at the Vienna Hilton, for sharing this recipe with me when he was chef at Windows on the World.

1. Set a rack at the middle level of the oven and preheat to 350 degrees.

2. For the cake batter, in a bowl, beat the butter until it's soft and light, then beat in ½ cup of the sugar until the mixture whitens. Beat in the yolks, one at a time, then the lemon zest and vanilla. Stir the hazelnuts and crumbs in by hand.

(continued)

3. Beat the egg whites until they're white and opaque using medium speed. Increase the speed, then beat in the remaining ½ cup of sugar in a stream. Continue to beat until the whites hold a firm peak. Stir a quarter of the whites into the batter, then fold in the remaining whites.

4. Pour the batter into the prepared pan and bake for about 50 minutes, or until the cake is well risen and firm. Unmold to a rack to cool.

5. Trim the cake if necessary. Slice the cake into 2 layers and place one of the layers, cut side up, on a cardboard. Spread the layer with raspberry preserves and top with the second layer, cut side down.

6. To make the chocolate glaze, bring the sugar, water, and corn syrup to a boil. Take care that all the sugar crystals are dissolved. Off the heat, stir the cut chocolate into the syrup and stir until the chocolate melts and the glaze is smooth.

7. Place the cake on a rack over a jelly-roll pan and pour the freshly made glaze over it. Allow the glaze to set before removing the cake from the rack.

SERVING: Serve the cake with whipped cream.

STORAGE: Keep the cake loosely covered at room temperature. For longer storage, keep the cake in a tightly sealed plastic container or tin.

VARIATIONS

Substitute walnuts, or even pecans, for the hazelnuts.

LEMON MACAROON CAKE

CAKE LAYER

¾ **pound almond paste**

¾ **cup sugar**

5 large eggs

12 tablespoons (1½ sticks) unsalted butter

1 cup cake flour

FILLING

2 cups milk

⅓ **cup sugar**

Zests of 2 lemons, stripped with a vegetable peeler and left, as much as possible, in strips

⅓ **cup strained lemon juice**

¼ **cup cornstarch**

4 egg yolks

Pinch of salt

12 tablespoons (1½ sticks) unsalted butter

FINISHING

1½ cups (about 4 ounces) toasted sliced almonds

Confectioners' sugar for dusting

One 10-inch round pan, buttered and lined with parchment or wax paper

ONE 10-INCH CAKE, 12 TO 15 SERVINGS

The bittersweet flavor of this almond paste–based cake complements the slight acidity of the lemon perfectly. Small portions are in order—this is a rich cake.

1. Set a rack at the middle level of the oven and preheat to 325 degrees.

2. For the cake, cut the almond paste into 1-inch cubes and place in a mixing bowl with the sugar and 1 egg. Beat with a paddle (if you have one) on low speed until smooth. Beat in the butter and continue to beat until light, at least 5 minutes. Then beat in the remaining eggs, one at a time, scraping the bowl and paddle or beater frequently. Sift over the cake flour and fold in with a rubber spatula.

3. Scrape the batter into the prepared pan and bake for 35 to 45 minutes, until the cake is well colored and firm.

4. Turn out onto a rack, remove the paper, turn right side up, and cool completely.

5. To make the filling, combine the milk, sugar, and zests in a nonreactive saucepan. Place over low heat and bring to a simmer. Remove from the heat and allow to steep while preparing the remaining ingredients. Pour the lemon juice into a bowl and whisk in the cornstarch, then the yolks and salt. Remove the zests from the milk and bring the milk to a boil. Whisk a third of the boiling milk into the starch mixture, then return the remaining milk to a boil. Whisk the starch mixture into the boiling milk and continue to cook and whisk until thickened and boiling. Remove from the heat and whisk in the butter. Scrape the filling into a nonreactive bowl, press plastic wrap against the surface, and chill.

(continued)

6. To assemble the cake, slice the cooled cake into 2 layers. Beat the filling with an electric mixer until it is light, then spread half over one layer. Top with the remaining layer and cover the top and sides of the cake with the filling. Press the almonds into the sides and top of the cake. Dust lightly with the confectioners' sugar just before serving.

SERVING: Serve the cake in small wedges.

STORAGE: Keep the cake loosely covered in the refrigerator. Wrap and refrigerate leftovers.

HINT FOR SUCCESS: After adding the butter, let the batter mix for as long as possible before continuing for a light, fine-textured cake.

TRADITIONAL LAYER CAKES

Though I hesitate to use the term "old-fashioned" to describe a particular type of cake, these layer cakes would easily fit into that category. These are all homey and simple cakes, most finished with a simple boiled icing or whipped cream. In the cases where the filling is more elaborate, it still imparts that comforting homey flavor and texture to the cake.

STRAWBERRY SUNBURST CAKE

2 recipes Plain Génoise (page 270), baked in 9-inch round pans

FILLING

2 pints strawberries
½ cup sugar
1 tablespoon lemon juice
1 tablespoon kirsch
2 tablespoons cornstarch

SYRUP

⅔ cup water
½ cup sugar
2 tablespoons lemon juice
2 tablespoons kirsch

MERINGUE

¾ cup (about 6 large) egg whites
1 cup sugar

FINISHING

Toasted sliced almonds
1 pint strawberries

ONE 9-INCH CAKE, 12 TO 15 SERVINGS

This is an ideal hot-weather cake because it contains neither whipped cream nor buttercream. Also the fruit filling and the meringue covering are light. Make it when strawberries are at their peak.

1. Bake and cool the cake layers.

2. To make the filling, rinse, hull, and slice the 2 pints strawberries. Place a quarter of the berries in a saucepan with the sugar and bring to a boil. In a bowl, combine the lemon juice, kirsch, and cornstarch, and off the heat stir into the strawberry mixture. Return to a boil, stirring, and cook for 2 minutes. Remove from the heat, cool, and stir in the remaining sliced berries.

3. To make the syrup, combine the water and sugar in a small pan, bring to a boil, and cool. Stir in the lemon juice and kirsch.

4. To make the meringue, combine the egg whites and sugar in a medium-sized, heatproof bowl. Whisk over simmering water until the egg whites are hot and the sugar is dissolved. Off the heat, beat at medium speed until the meringue is cold and risen in volume, but not dry.

5. Place one of the cake layers on a cardboard and brush with half of the syrup. Spread with the filling. Repeat with the second layer and remaining syrup. Spread the cake with the meringue and pipe a border of meringue on the cake, using a ½-inch star tube, such as Ateco #4.

6. Place the cake, still on the cardboard, on a cookie sheet. Place in a preheated 400 degree oven for 3 to 4 minutes just to color the meringue. Remove from the oven and cool.

7. To decorate the cake, rinse, hull, and slice the remaining berries. Arrange the slices in concentric circles from the outside in.

(continued)

SERVING: Cut the cake with a sharp, thin knife to avoid dislodging the strawberry decoration on the top.

STORAGE: Keep the cake loosely covered at room temperature until time to serve. Wrap and

refrigerate leftovers. They will keep until the next day.

HINT FOR SUCCESS: In making the meringue, be sure the egg whites have become hot (about 130 degrees), or they will not whip up well.

AMBROSIA CAKE

1 recipe Classic White Cake (page 271), baked in two 9 × 1½- to 2-inch round pans

AMBROSIA FILLING

4 large oranges
1 cup sweetened shredded coconut
1 tablespoon white rum

WHIPPED CREAM

2 cups heavy cream
3 tablespoons sugar
2 teaspoons vanilla extract

1 cup toasted sweetened coconut

ONE 9-INCH CAKE, 12 TO 15 SERVINGS

Ambrosia, a traditional southern dessert made from coconut and oranges, is a delicious and easy celebration cake.

1. Bake and cool the cake layers.

2. To make the ambrosia filling, cut all the peel and pith from the oranges, then halve from stem to blossom end and slice them. In a bowl,

combine with the shredded coconut and rum and refrigerate for several hours to blend the flavors.

3. To assemble the cake, in a bowl, whip the cream with the sugar and vanilla, until it holds firm peaks. Drain the ambrosia, reserving the liquid. Place one cake layer on a platter or cardboard and moisten with half the reserved liquid. Spread with the whipped cream and arrange half the ambrosia over it. Spread a thin layer of whipped cream over the fruit, then top with the other layer. Sprinkle the top layer with the remaining reserved liquid then spread the remaining whipped cream all over the outside of the cake. Neatly arrange the remaining drained ambrosia on the top of the cake. Press the toasted coconut into the sides of the cake.

SERVING: Use a sharp, thin knife to cut the cake to avoid dislodging the fruit on the top.

STORAGE: Refrigerate the cake until serving time. Wrap and refrigerate leftovers for a day or so.

HINT FOR SUCCESS: Have the cream, bowl, and beater(s) cold before whipping the cream, or it may separate and not be smooth in taste or appearance.

MICHELLE TAMPAKIS'S CARROT CAKE

CAKE

4 eggs

2 cups light brown sugar

½ teaspoon salt

1 cup vegetable oil

½ cup milk

3½ cups cake flour

1½ teaspoons baking powder

¾ teaspoon baking soda

1 teaspoon ground cinnamon

½ teaspoon grated nutmeg

½ teaspoon ground ginger

¼ teaspoon ground cloves

5 cups grated carrots (about 12 medium)

1 cup (about 4 ounces) walnut pieces

CREAM CHEESE ICING

4 tablespoons unsalted butter

½ pound cream cheese, at room temperature

1 cup confectioners' sugar

1 teaspoon vanilla extract

One 9 × 13 × 2-inch pan, buttered and lined with parchment or wax paper

ONE 6 × 9½-INCH CAKE, ABOUT 12 SERVINGS

This excellent carrot cake is easy to prepare and keeps moist for several days; it also freezes well.

1. Set a rack at the middle level of the oven and preheat to 350 degrees.

2. For the cake batter, in a bowl, combine the eggs, sugar, salt, vegetable oil, and milk and beat on medium speed for 30 seconds. In another bowl, sift together the dry ingredients. Stop the mixer, add the dry ingredients, and beat on low speed until absorbed. Remove from the mixer and fold in the carrots and nuts.

3. Spread the batter evenly in the prepared pan, and bake for 30 to 40 minutes, until the cake is firm, but not dry. Cool in the pan.

4. To make the icing, beat the butter (with a paddle if you have one) at medium speed until soft and light. Beat in the cream cheese and continue beating until very smooth. Add the sugar and vanilla and beat until smooth. Continue beating for about 5 more minutes to aerate. Use immediately.

5. To finish the carrot cake, remove the paper from the cake and transfer the cake to a cutting surface. Cut the cake in half to make two 9 × 6½-inch layers. Place one on a plate, cover with icing, then top with the other layer and cover the cake with the rest of the icing.

SERVING: This is a good cake for a picnic or a casual brunch or lunch.

STORAGE: Keep the cake loosely covered at room temperature until serving time. Wrap in plastic and refrigerate leftovers for two days. For advance preparation, wrap and freeze the cake layer for up to several months before finishing.

(continued)

HINT FOR SUCCESS: Only mix the ingredients until combined—avoid overbeating, or the cake will have a fluffy and dry, rather than a dense and moist, texture.

COCONUT LAYER CAKE

CAKE

8 tablespoons (1 stick) unsalted butter

1 cup sugar

2 large eggs

2 teaspoons vanilla extract

½ teaspoon lemon extract

¼ teaspoon salt

1½ teaspoons baking powder

½ teaspoon baking soda

1⅔ cups bleached all-purpose flour

½ cup sour cream

One 7-ounce package (2 cups) sweetened grated coconut

BUTTERCREAM

1 cup canned coconut cream

2 eggs

½ pound (2 sticks) unsalted butter

2 tablespoons white rum

2 teaspoons vanilla extract

One 7-ounce package (2 cups) sweetened grated coconut

Two 9-inch layer pans (1½ inches deep), buttered, bottoms lined with parchment or wax paper

ONE 9-INCH CAKE, ABOUT 12 SERVINGS

Leave the cake as a single layer and just ice the top.
You may also bake the cake in two 9-inch round pans.

This is a favorite cake of my friend, Brooklyn-based teacher of Italian cooking, Anna Amendolara Nurse.

1. Set a rack at the middle level of the oven and preheat to 325 degrees.

2. For the cake, in a bowl, beat the butter with the sugar until light. Beat in the eggs, one at a time, beating until smooth after each addition. Beat in the vanilla and lemon extracts. In another bowl, mix the salt, baking powder, and soda into the flour. Beat half the flour mixture into the butter mixture and continue to beat until smooth. Beat in the sour cream, then the coconut, and finally the remaining flour mixture.

3. Divide the batter evenly between the prepared pans. Bake for about 25 minutes, until the cakes are well risen and firm in the center.

4. Cool in the pans for 5 minutes, then unmold onto a rack, remove the paper, and let cool completely.

5. To make the buttercream, bring the coconut cream to a boil in a small saucepan over low heat. Meanwhile, beat the eggs together in a bowl. Beat the boiling coconut cream into the eggs and return the mixture to the pan. Cook over low

heat, stirring constantly, until the mixture is slightly thickened. Strain into a bowl and cool to room temperature. In another bowl, beat the butter until soft and light. Beat in the cooled coconut mixture, a little at a time, beating until smooth after each addition. Beat in the rum and vanilla a little at a time.

6. To finish the cake, arrange a cake layer on a plate, cover with the coconut buttercream, top with the other layer, and cover the top and sides of the cake with the coconut buttercream. Press the grated coconut all over the cake.

SERVING: Serve the cake at room temperature for maximum flavor.

STORAGE: Keep the cake loosely covered at room temperature until serving time. Wrap in plastic and refrigerate leftovers for two days.

HINT FOR SUCCESS: Don't overcook the coconut cream and eggs, or they will curdle. If they do, pour the hot, curdled mixture into a blender and puree it at high speed until smooth.

VARIATION

Toast the coconut lightly at 300 degrees for about 10 minutes, stirring often, for the outside of the cake. Cool before applying to the cake.

DACQUOISE AND MERINGUE LAYER CAKES

These unusual cakes are typical of a traditional French cake, called a "dacquoise." Made by combining a stiff meringue with ground nuts and flavoring, these cake layers are piped or spread on cookie sheets. After they are baked, they have a crisp and tender texture that makes them an ideal foil for a rich filling such as a buttercream.

Dacquoise was introduced to New York in the early 1970s by the late Gino Cofacci, a former architect and longtime companion of James Beard. For about ten years Cofacci operated a wholesale baking company out of the Greenwich Village brownstone that now houses the James Beard Foundation. The company supplied many of New York's finest restaurants with exquisite pastries and desserts. In 1974 or '75, I went to meet Gino with the idea of working with him and visited his "laboratoire de patisserie" (where usually only French was spoken) and saw him prepare the famous dacquoise. His "labo" was really the front room of his third-floor brownstone apartment, surprisingly outfitted with a large Hobart mixer, several forced-convection ovens, and all the other paraphernalia needed to produce his pastries and desserts.

GINO COFACCI'S HAZELNUT AND ALMOND DACQUOISE

DACQUOISE LAYERS

1 cup (3½ ounces) skinned hazelnuts
1 cup (3½ ounces) blanched almonds
1 cup sugar
2 tablespoons cornstarch
¾ cup (about 6 large) egg whites
Pinch of salt
¼ cup sugar
2 teaspoons vanilla extract
¼ teaspoon almond extract

COFFEE BUTTERCREAM

¾ cup milk
½ cup sugar
4 egg yolks
¾ pound (3 sticks) unsalted butter, softened
3 tablespoons instant espresso coffee powder
    dissolved in 1 tablespoon warm water

Confectioners' sugar for finishing

Three jelly-roll pans or cookie sheets lined with parchment or foil, a 10-inch circle drawn on each piece of paper

MAKES ONE 10-INCH CAKE, ABOUT 12 SERVINGS

This dacquoise recipe and variations are adapted from Cofacci's recipe that appeared in *The Pleasures of Cooking,* a magazine once published by Carl Sontheimer when he owned Cuisinarts, Inc.

1. Set racks in the upper and lower thirds of the oven and preheat to 350 degrees.

2. For the dacquoise, place the nuts in the work bowl of a food processor fitted with a steel blade and pulse repeatedly until they're coarsely ground and the largest pieces are about ⅛ inch across. Place the nuts in a small roasting pan or on a jelly-roll pan and toast for about 10 minutes, stirring several times until golden. Cool the ground nuts and lower the oven temperature to 300 degrees. In a bowl, combine the nuts with 1 cup sugar and cornstarch and stir well to mix.

3. Next, combine the egg whites and salt in the bowl of an electric mixer and whip on low speed until white and opaque, about 2 minutes. Increase the speed and beat in the ¼ cup sugar in a stream, continuing to beat until the whites hold a firm peak, but are not dry. Beat in the extracts and remove the egg whites from the mixer.

4. With a rubber spatula, fold the ground nut mixture into the whites until they're thoroughly combined.

5. Using a pastry bag fitted with a ½-inch plain tube (Ateco #6), pipe the meringue on the prepared pans into spiral disks, as in the illustration.

6. Bake the layers for 1 to 1¼ hours, until they are golden and firm. Cool on the pans on racks.

Pipe the meringue into spiral disks, holding the pastry bag perpendicular to the pan and about an inch above it.

7. While the layers are baking, prepare the buttercream filling. Combine the milk and sugar in a medium nonreactive saucepan and bring to a simmer over low heat. Whisk the yolks in a bowl and whisk the hot milk into the yolks. Return the mixture to the pan and cook briefly over low heat until thickened—do not overcook the cream or it will scramble. Immediately pour the thickened cream into a mixer bowl and whip on medium speed until cooled. Whip in the butter, then the instant coffee dissolved in water. Continue whipping until the buttercream is smooth and fluffy.

8. To assemble, place one of the layers on a platter or cardboard and spread with a third of the buttercream. Place another layer on the buttercream and spread with another third of the

buttercream. Place the last layer on and spread the remaining buttercream on the sides of the cake, leaving the top bare. Chill to set the buttercream and dust lightly with confectioners' sugar immediately before serving.

SERVING: Cut into wedges with a sharp serrated knife—a dacquoise is a great dessert for a fancy occasion.

STORAGE: Refrigerate the dessert loosely covered until an hour or so before serving time. Or wrap in plastic and refrigerate for several days or freeze for several weeks. Bring to room temperature before serving.

HINT FOR SUCCESS: See Perfect Whipped Egg Whites (page 278).

VARIATIONS

CHOCOLATE PECAN DACQUOISE: Replace the almonds and hazelnuts with 2 cups pecan pieces. Add to the filling 6 ounces chocolate melted over a pan of hot water with 4 tablespoons milk and cool. Pipe 12 rosettes of the chocolate buttercream on top of the cake and top each with a pecan half.

PISTACHIO RASPBERRY MERINGUE: Replace the almonds and hazelnuts with 2 cups blanched unsalted pistachios. Omit the coffee from the filling and flavor with 2 tablespoons lemon juice. Scatter a ½-pint basket of raspberries between the layers when assembling the dessert, and another on the top.

OLD-FASHIONED SPICE CAKE WITH BOILED ICING

CAKE

16 tablespoons (2 sticks) unsalted butter,
softened

1 cup dark brown sugar

1 cup granulated sugar

2½ teaspoons baking powder

1 teaspoon each ground cinnamon, cloves,
ginger, and freshly grated nutmeg

½ teaspoon salt

2⅔ cups bleached all-purpose flour

5 large eggs

1 cup milk

BOILED ICING

2 large (¼ cup) egg whites

1½ cups granulated sugar

⅓ cup water

Two 9 × 2-inch round pans, buttered, bottoms lined
with parchment or wax paper

ONE 9-INCH CAKE, ABOUT 12 SERVINGS

Though spice cake usually conjures up images of New England farm kitchens, it reminds me more of the cinnamon- and clove-scented pastries prepared by my Italian grandmothers.

1. Set a rack at the middle level of the oven and preheat to 350 degrees.

2. For the cake, in a large mixing bowl, beat the butter and sugars for about 5 minutes, until light and fluffy. In another bowl, stir the baking powder, spices, and salt into the flour. Set aside. In a small bowl, combine the eggs and milk. Beat a third of the flour mixture into the butter mixture, then beat in half the liquid. Repeat, beginning and ending with the flour mixture. Scrape the bowl and beater often.

3. Pour the batter into the prepared pans and smooth the top with a metal spatula. Bake the cake for 25 to 30 minutes, or until a toothpick inserted in the center emerges clean.

4. Cool in the pan on a rack for 5 minutes, then turn out onto a rack, remove the paper, and cool completely.

5. To make the icing, combine all the ingredients in a medium-sized heatproof bowl and place over a pan of simmering water. Whisk constantly until hot, then off the heat beat by machine until the icing is cooled and stiff.

6. Spread the icing between the layers and over the top and sides of the cake.

SERVING: Serve small wedges of this sweet cake.

STORAGE: Keep the cake loosely covered at room temperature until serving time. Wrap in plastic and refrigerate leftovers for several days.

HINT FOR SUCCESS: Heat the icing slowly, whisking gently. If you whisk air into the mixture while it is heating, the sugar may not dissolve completely and it will make a gritty icing.

CHOCOLATE PASTRY CAKE

1 recipe Chocolate Génoise (page 271), baked in a 9-inch round pan

CHOCOLATE DOUGH

3 cups unbleached all-purpose flour

½ cup non-alkalized unsweetened cocoa powder

⅓ cup sugar

Pinch of salt

¼ teaspoon baking soda

¾ pound (3 sticks) unsalted butter

4 to 6 tablespoons cold water

ORANGE LIQUEUR SYRUP

⅔ cup sugar

⅓ cup water

⅓ cup orange liqueur

GANACHE

1¼ pounds (20 ounces) semisweet chocolate

1½ cups heavy cream

6 tablespoons unsalted butter

Six 10 ½ × 15 ½-inch jelly-roll pans lined with parchment paper

ONE 9-INCH CAKE, ABOUT 12 SERVINGS

This dessert was created by Albert Kumin for the opening of Windows on the World in 1976 and became one of their signature desserts. This recipe is close to the original, but uses my recipes for the different component parts.

1. Cool the génoise.

2. To make the dough, place the flour in a mixing bowl and sift the cocoa powder over it. Stir in the sugar, salt, and baking soda. Cut the butter into small pieces, then rub it into the dry ingredients until no pieces show, leaving the mixture cool and powdery. Stir in only enough water so that the dough holds together. Press the dough together, then wrap it in plastic and chill.

3. To make the syrup, in a saucepan, bring the sugar and water to a boil. Cool and stir in the orange liqueur.

4. To make the ganache, cut the chocolate into small pieces. In a saucepan, bring the cream and butter to a boil and remove from the heat. Add the chocolate and allow to stand for 2 minutes. Whisk smooth and cool.

5. Set racks at the middle and lower thirds of the oven and preheat to 350 degrees.

6. Divide the chilled chocolate dough into thirds and roll each to fit a prepared pan. Pierce the dough all over with a fork, cover each piece with another piece of paper, then another pan.

7. Bake at 325 degrees until the layers are dry and crisp, about 30 minutes. Bake in several batches if necessary.

(continued)

8. Remove the baked sheets to a cutting board and cut into three 9-inch circles. Use the trimmings to patch together a fourth 9-inch circle. Crumble the scraps and reserve.

9. To assemble, beat the ganache on medium speed for 1 minute, until light. Slice the génoise into 3 layers. Dot a piece of cardboard with a bit of ganache, then place one of the chocolate pastry circles on it. This is so it won't slide. Construct the cake this way from the bottom: pastry, ganache, génoise, syrup; ganache, pastry, ganache, génoise, syrup; ganache, pastry, ganache, génoise, syrup; ganache, pastry. Cover the top and sides of the cake with the ganache. Press the crumbs into the ganache around the top and sides of the cake.

SERVING: Serve small wedges of this rich cake.

STORAGE: Keep the cake loosely covered at room temperature until serving time. Wrap in plastic and refrigerate leftovers for up to a week.

HINT FOR SUCCESS: Don't be concerned if the pastry layers break while you are putting them in place on the cake—just patch them into as complete layers as possible.

FANCY CHOCOLATE CAKES

This catchall term refers to some rich cakes using chocolate layers or chocolate fillings. Some of them are mainstays of the Viennese baking tradition where rich cakes with batters enhanced with ground nuts are the rule.

VIENNESE "SADDLE OF VENISON" CAKE (REHRÜCKEN)

CAKE

6 ounces semisweet chocolate

12 tablespoons (1½ sticks) unsalted butter

⅔ cup sugar

8 large eggs, separated

1⅓ cups (about 5 ounces) blanched or unblanched ground almonds

⅔ cup dry breadcrumbs

1 teaspoon ground cinnamon

GLAZE

1 cup currant jelly

ICING

⅓ cup water

1 cup sugar

⅓ cup light corn syrup

8 ounces semisweet chocolate

FINISHING

½ cup slivered almonds

Two 10-inch Rehrücken pans, or one 10-inch round pan, buttered and floured

TWO 10-INCH REHRÜCKENS, OR ONE 10-INCH ROUND CAKE (SEE VARIATIONS, BELOW), 12 TO 15 SERVINGS

Typical of the Viennese love of the absurd, this rich chocolate almond cake is baked in a ridged, semi-cylindrical pan. After the chocolate icing is poured over the unmolded cake, it is stuck with pieces of slivered almond. Thus, it resembles a tied, larded, and sauced roast.

For any of you who might not have the mold, this is equally delicious baked in a 10-inch round pan and served as an unwhimsical cake.

1. Set a rack at the middle level of the oven and preheat to 350 degrees.

2. To make the cake batter, cut the chocolate into fine pieces and place in a small bowl over hot water to melt, stirring occasionally. Set aside to cool. Beat the butter with ⅓ cup of the sugar until the mixture is soft and light, then beat in the chocolate, then the yolks, one at a time. In a small bowl, combine the almonds, crumbs, and cinnamon and stir them in. In a clean, dry bowl with clean, dry beaters, beat the egg whites until they hold a very soft peak, then beat in the remaining ⅓ cup of sugar in a slow stream. Continue to beat the whites until they hold a firm peak. Stir a quarter of the whites into the batter, then fold in the rest with a rubber spatula.

3. Pour the batter into the prepared pan(s) and bake for about 40 minutes, until the cake is well risen and firm. Unmold the cakes onto a rack to cool.

4. For the glaze, bring the currant jelly to a boil over medium heat. Lower the heat and simmer until the jelly is sticky and slightly thickened. Paint this glaze over the cooled cakes.

5. To make the chocolate icing, combine the water, sugar, and corn syrup in a saucepan and bring to a boil over low heat, stirring to dissolve the sugar completely. While it cooks, cut the chocolate into fine pieces. Remove the pan from the heat, add the chocolate, and allow to stand for a minute. Whisk smooth.

6. Position the cakes on a rack with a jelly-roll pan under them. Pour the icing over the cakes. Repair any uncovered areas with the icing that has dripped into the pan. Remove the cakes to platters before the icing has a chance to harden or it will crack.

7. Insert the pieces of slivered almonds in rows, at an angle, down the length, all over the cake.

SERVING: Serve the Rehrücken with whipped cream.

STORAGE: Keep the cake loosely covered at room temperature until serving time. Wrap and refrigerate leftovers.

HINT FOR SUCCESS: If the batter becomes firm before it is time to fold in the egg whites, place the mixing bowl in a pan or bowl of warm water and stir until the batter is again soft and smooth.

VARIATIONS

CHOCOLATE ALMOND CAKE: Bake the Rehrücken batter in a 10-inch round pan, 2 inches deep, for about 40 minutes. Glaze and finish as above.

CHOCOLATE ALMOND PASSOVER CAKE: Substitute matzo meal for the breadcrumbs in the cake and honey for the corn syrup in the glaze. To make a nondairy version, substitute parve margarine for the butter.

SWISS CHOCOLATE TRUFFLE CAKE
(TRUFFELTORTE)

1 recipe Rehrücken batter without cinnamon
   (page 313)

TRUFFLE FILLING

24 ounces (1½ pounds) semisweet chocolate
2 cups heavy cream
3 tablespoons unsalted butter
3 tablespoons light corn syrup

Unsweetened cocoa powder for finishing

*One 11 × 17-inch jelly-roll pan, buttered and lined
with a sheet of parchment or wax paper*

TWO 3½ × 8-INCH RECTANGULAR CAKES

An adaptation of the truffle cake from the famous Sprungli pastry shop in Zurich. This dessert is easy to make in advance and, as it makes two cakes, one may be used immediately and the other refrigerated or frozen for later use.

1. Set a rack at the middle level of the oven and preheat to 350 degrees.

2. Spread the cake batter on the pan and bake for about 20 minutes, or until firm. Slide the cake layer from the pan to a rack to cool.

3. To make the filling, cut up the chocolate into fine pieces and set aside. Combine the remaining ingredients in a pan and bring to a boil. Remove from the heat, add the chocolate, and allow to stand for 5 minutes. Whisk smooth and strain into a bowl. Refrigerate until thickened. Immediately before using the filling, whisk gently by hand to lighten slightly.

4. To assemble the cakes, cut the baked layer into 6 layers, each about 3½ × 8 inches. Place 2 of the layers on 4 × 8½-inch pieces of cardboard to make handling easier. Spread each with a thin layer of filling. Cover each with another layer, and cover those with filling. Place the last layer on each cake and mask the sides with a thin layer of filling. Divide the remaining filling in half and place half on the top of each cake. Smooth the filling into a wedge shape on top of each cake; slant the short ends upward toward the center of the cake. Chill the cakes to set the filling, and dust very lightly with cocoa powder before serving.

SERVING: Serve the cake in thin slices.

STORAGE: Chill the cakes to set the filling, then keep the cakes loosely covered in the refrigerator until serving time. Wrap in plastic and refrigerate leftovers. The cakes may be wrapped and frozen for a month after the filling has set.

HINT FOR SUCCESS: If the filling becomes too firm to spread before the cakes are finished, warm the bowl of filling in a bowl of warm water, stirring constantly, to make it smooth again.

CHOCOLATE MOUSSE CAKE WITH RASPBERRY EAU-DE-VIE

CAKE

12 ounces semisweet or bittersweet chocolate

½ cup sugar

⅓ cup water

½ pound (2 sticks) unsalted butter

4 eggs

2 tablespoons framboise (raspberry eau-de-vie) or liqueur

FINISHING

1 cup heavy cream

2 tablespoons sugar

1 basket fresh raspberries (optional)

One 8 × 1½ or 2-inch-deep pan, buttered, bottom lined with a disk of parchment or wax paper

ONE 8-INCH CAKE, ABOUT 12 SERVINGS

This unusual cake batter may be made in other flavors by changing the liqueur. Though not a layer cake, I include it here because it is a rich dessert cake.

1. Set a rack at the middle level of the oven and preheat to 300 degrees.

2. For the cake batter, cut the chocolate finely and set it aside. Combine the sugar and water in a saucepan and bring to a boil over low heat, stirring occasionally to make sure all the sugar crystals dissolve. Remove the syrup from the heat and stir in the butter and chocolate. Cover the pan and allow it to stand for 5 minutes. Whisk smooth. In a bowl, whisk the eggs and framboise until liquid, and whisk in the chocolate mixture in a stream. Be careful not to overmix.

3. Pour the batter into the pan and place the cake pan in a larger, shallow pan (a small roasting pan, for instance). Carefully pour 1 inch of warm water into the larger pan. Bake for about 45 minutes, until the batter is set and slightly dry on the surface.

4. Remove the cake pan to a rack to cool to room temperature in the pan. When cool, cover with plastic wrap. Refrigerate the dessert in the pan. To unmold, run a knife between the cake and the pan and immerse the bottom of the pan in hot water to loosen the cake. Invert onto a platter and remove the paper.

5. To finish, whip the cream with the sugar until it holds a soft peak. Spread the whipped cream over the top of the dessert. Edge the top with the raspberries, if desired.

SERVING: Serve small wedges with additional whipped cream, if you wish.

STORAGE: Keep the cake loosely covered and refrigerated until serving time. Wrap in plastic and refrigerate leftovers.

VARIATIONS

Substitute a liqueur, other spirit, or 2 tablespoons vanilla extract for the framboise.

ROLLED CAKES

I remember the first time I followed instructions—from a magazine, I think—to make a rolled cake. There was a step that required rolling up the cake in a towel while it was still warm to "train" it. Of course, compressing the warm cake in a towel did nothing to improve its texture, which was ultimately damp and uninvitingly chewy.

The following recipes include no towels or other unnecessary steps. To make a perfect rolled cake, one thing is important—don't overbake the layer, which of course would make it dry and difficult to roll. Aside from that, position the cooled layer on a large sheet of parchment or wax paper, fold the close end of the layer over about ½ inch, then lift the paper to roll up the cake. It's almost automatic. The last step of tightening the roll by squeezing it between the folded-over paper with a board or cookie sheet ensures a tight, cylindrical roll, as in the illustration.

Tighten the roll by squeezing it between the folded paper with a board or cookie sheet.

HAZELNUT MARSALA ROLL

1 recipe Moist, Buttery Nut Cake (page 275),
    made with unblanched hazelnuts, baked in a
    10½ × 15½-inch pan

MARSALA WHIPPED CREAM

1½ cups heavy cream

3 tablespoons sugar

¼ cup imported sweet Marsala, such as Florio or
    Pellegrino

1 tablespoon dark rum

¼ cup (about 1 ounce) toasted skinned hazelnuts,
    coarsely chopped

ONE 12- TO 14-INCH ROLL, ABOUT 10 SERVINGS

This was a popular dessert during the first year the Cellar in the Sky at Windows on the World was open. This dessert originated with Barbara Kafka, who planned the menus, though my recipe is a bit more elaborate.

If you wish, you may substitute another sweet, fortified wine for the Marsala, or use a liqueur to flavor the whipped cream.

1. Cool the nut cake layer.

2. To make the Marsala whipped cream, in a bowl, combine all the ingredients and whip by machine until the cream is firm enough to hold its shape, but not grainy.

3. To assemble the roll, slide a cookie sheet under the cake layer. Place a sheet of parchment or wax paper over the layer, then cover with another cookie sheet. Turn everything over together, remove the first cookie sheet, and peel away the paper. Replace with a clean piece of paper and the cookie sheet, and turn over again. Remove the top pan and paper and slide the remaining cookie sheet out from under the layer. The layer is now just on a clean paper. Position it so the long sides are top and bottom.

4. Spread the layer with half the Marsala whipped cream, using a metal spatula. Fold over 1 inch of the long edge closest to you. Then use the paper to ease the layer into a tight roll. After it is rolled, center the roll on the paper, tightly wrap the paper around it, and twist the ends of the paper to seal. Refrigerate the roll and the remaining filling for about 1 hour.

5. To finish the roll, unwrap it and turn it out of the paper onto a platter or board, seam side down. Spread smoothly with the remaining whipped cream and strew with the chopped hazelnuts. Trim the ends of the roll diagonally for neatness.

SERVING: Cut diagonal slices to serve.

STORAGE: Refrigerate the cake until immediately before serving.

CHOCOLATE MOCHA WALNUT ROLL

1 recipe Moist, Buttery Nut Cake (page
    275), made with walnuts, baked in a
    10 ½ × 15 ½-inch pan

MOCHA GANACHE

1 cup heavy cream
⅓ cup strong brewed coffee
12 ounces semisweet chocolate, finely chopped
4 tablespoons unsalted butter, softened
2 tablespoons dark rum

Walnut halves for decorating

ONE 12- TO 15-INCH-LONG ROLL, ABOUT
10 SERVINGS

The slight bitterness of the walnuts combines with the chocolate and coffee to make a rich but not excessively sweet cake.

1. Cool the nut cake layer.

2. To make the ganache, in a saucepan, bring the cream and coffee to a boil. Remove from the heat and add the chocolate. Stir once to mix, and set aside for 5 minutes. Add the butter and rum and whisk smooth. Pour into a bowl, cover with plastic wrap, and cool until thickened and beginning to set. If the ganache is needed immediately, place the bowl over a bowl of cold water and stir with a rubber spatula, scraping the inside of the bowl to avoid lumps, until the ganache is cool and slightly thickened. Do not cool too much or it will solidify. If it does, break the ganache into pieces and warm it for a few seconds at a time over warm water, stirring vigorously with a rubber spatula, until the ganache is smooth and of spreading consistency.

3. To assemble the roll, slide a cookie sheet under the cake layer. Place a sheet of parchment or wax paper on the top surface of the layer, then another cookie sheet. Turn everything over, remove the first cookie sheet, and peel away the paper. Replace with a clean piece of paper and the cookie sheet, and turn over again. Remove the top pan and paper and slide out the cookie sheet from under the layer. The layer is now just on a piece of clean paper. Position the layer with the long sides top and bottom.

4. Spread the layer with half the ganache, using a metal spatula. Fold over 1 inch of the long edge closest to you. Then use the paper to ease the layer into a tight roll. After it is rolled, center the roll on the paper, wrap the paper tightly around it, and twist the ends of the paper to seal. Refrigerate the roll for about 1 hour, but leave the remaining ganache at room temperature, or it will solidify.

(continued)

5. To finish the roll, unwrap it and turn it out of the paper onto a large platter or board, seam side down. Spread smoothly with the remaining ganache, then run a fork all over the ganache to give the roll a grooved appearance. Place the walnut halves on top of the roll to delineate the portions. Trim the ends of the roll diagonally for a neat appearance.

6. Refrigerate the roll until about 30 minutes before serving, then remove from the refrigerator so that the ganache softens slightly.

SERVING: Cut diagonal slices to serve.

STORAGE: Refrigerate the cake until immediately before serving.

CHOCOLATE CHESTNUT BÛCHE DE NOËL

1 recipe Chocolate Génoise (page 271), baked in
   a 10½ × 15½-inch jelly-roll pan

BUTTERCREAM

¾ pound (3 sticks) unsalted butter
1½ cups sweetened chestnut spread (Faugier
   brand)
2 tablespoons white rum
2 teaspoons vanilla extract

MARZIPAN

¼ pound almond paste
1 cup confectioners' sugar
2 to 3 tablespoons light corn syrup

FINISHING

Unsweetened cocoa powder
Confectioners' sugar

ONE 12- TO 15-INCH-LONG ROLL, ABOUT
10 SERVINGS

There are many flavor and presentation variations for this traditional French Christmas log. I like this one because the chocolate cake and chestnut buttercream are not excessively sweet together. Also, the marzipan decorations can be prepared well in advance and kept loosely covered until needed.

1. Cool the génoise layer.

2. To make the buttercream, in a bowl, beat the butter by machine until soft and light, then beat in the chestnut spread until smooth. Gradually beat in the rum and vanilla and continue beating until the buttercream is very light and smooth, 4 or 5 minutes.

3. Turn the génoise layer over and peel away the paper. Cover with a piece of fresh paper, turn over again so the cake is on the clean paper, long sides top and bottom, and spread with half the buttercream. Use the paper to roll from the long side nearest you into a tight cylinder. Wrap the paper tightly around the roll and twist the ends together. Refrigerate the cake while preparing the marzipan. Reserve the remaining buttercream refrigerated for the outside of the buche.

4. To make the marzipan, combine the almond paste, confectioners' sugar, and 2 tablespoons of the corn syrup in a food processor and pulse only 5 or 6 times, until the mixture is coarse and crumbly in appearance. *Do not overprocess.* Remove from the work bowl, and knead smooth, adding up to 1 tablespoon more corn syrup if the mixture seems dry. Wrap in plastic until needed.

5. To make marzipan mushrooms, roll the marzipan into a cylinder and slice into 1-inch lengths. Roll half the lengths into balls. Press the cylinders against the balls to attach them, flatten one side of the balls slightly, and form mushrooms. Smudge with cocoa powder.

6. Remove the rolled cake from the refrigerator and unwrap. Trim the edges diagonally, cutting one of the edges about 2 inches away from the end. Position the roll on a platter and place the uncut end of the 2-inch piece about two thirds along the top side of the roll. Cover the bûche with the remaining buttercream, making sure to curve up the protruding branch on the top, leaving the three cut ends unfrosted. Streak the buttercream with a fork or decorating comb. Decorate with the mushrooms. Dust the platter and bûche sparingly with confectioners' sugar "snow."

SERVING: Cut diagonal slices to serve.

STORAGE: Refrigerate the cake until immediately before serving.

CHOCOLATE SOUFFLÉ ROLL

CAKE

6 ounces semisweet chocolate
3 tablespoons orange liqueur, rum, or water
2 tablespoons unsalted butter
5 large eggs, separated
Pinch of salt
⅓ cup sugar

WHIPPED CREAM

1 cup heavy whipping cream
1 tablespoon liqueur (optional)

1 basket fresh raspberries

One 10½ × 15½-inch jelly-roll pan, buttered and lined with buttered parchment or wax paper

ONE 15-INCH ROLL, ABOUT 10 SERVINGS

Loosely based on James Beard's recipe for chocolate roll, this is a perfect dessert to prepare on short notice.

1. Position a rack at the middle level of the oven and preheat to 350 degrees.

2. Cut the chocolate finely and combine it with the liqueur or water and the butter in a heatproof bowl. Place the bowl over a pan of hot, but not simmering, water and stir occasionally until the chocolate is melted and the mixture is smooth. Beat in the yolks, one at a time.

3. In another bowl, beat the egg whites with the salt until they are just beginning to hold a very soft peak, then beat in the sugar in a slow stream, beating faster. Stir a quarter of the egg whites into the chocolate batter, then fold the chocolate batter into the remaining egg whites.

4. Pour the batter into the prepared pan and smooth the top. Bake the layer for about 15 minutes, until firm to the touch.

5. Remove the pan from the oven and loosen the cake with a small, sharp knife. Pulling on the paper, slide the layer onto the work surface to cool, about 20 minutes.

6. To finish the roll, slide a pan or cookie sheet under the layer. Cover the layer with a clean piece of parchment or wax paper and another pan, invert the cake between the pans. Lift off the top pan and peel off the paper stuck to the layer. Replace with a clean paper and replace the pan. Invert again and remove the top pan and paper.

7. Whip the cream with the liqueur, if desired, until it holds a firm peak. Spread the cream on the layer with a metal spatula. Roll the layer by picking up the long edge of the paper and easing the layer into a curve. Continue lifting the paper to roll the layer, and roll it directly onto a platter, seam side down. Trim the edges of the roll. Serve with a garnish of raspberries or other fresh fruit.

SERVING: Cut the roll into diagonal slices with a sharp serrated knife.

STORAGE: Refrigerate, loosely covered with plastic wrap, until ready to serve. Tightly cover and refrigerate leftovers.

Each of the following frostings will make enough to finish either a rectangular or round cake, although the frosting on the rectangular cake will be thicker than that on the round ones.

GANACHE

1 cup heavy cream

¼ cup light corn syrup

1 pound (16 ounces) semisweet or bittersweet chocolate, coarsely chopped

4 tablespoons unsalted butter, softened

1 tablespoon fruit liqueur, rum, or brandy (optional)

This classic chocolate filling and frosting of Swiss origin is similar to the center of a chocolate truffle—and just as rich and delicious.

1. In a medium saucepan, combine the cream and corn syrup. Place over medium heat and bring to a boil. Remove from the heat and add the chocolate and butter. Shake the pan and allow to stand for 3 to 4 minutes, then whisk smooth and whisk in the liqueur, if using.

2. Scrape the frosting from the pan to a bowl to cool and thicken. To use immediately, stir it over a bowl of cold water until cooled and of spreading consistency. Or refrigerate and bring back to room temperature before attempting to spread.

3. Before using the frosting, whip it vigorously by hand or briefly with an electric mixer to lighten it slightly. Overwhipping will cause the frosting to separate.

CELEBRATION CAKES

Any of the cake layers (pages 270 to 275) may be used to construct any of these special occasion cakes.

EASY MERINGUE BUTTERCREAM

4 large (½ cup) egg whites
1 cup sugar
Pinch of salt
¾ pound (3 sticks) unsalted butter, softened
Flavoring (see below)

One of the best-tasting buttercreams is also the easiest to prepare. See the end of the recipe for flavoring possibilities.

1. Place the egg whites, sugar, and salt in a medium-sized heatproof mixing bowl over a pan of simmering water, and whisk gently and constantly until the egg whites are hot (about 140 degrees) and the sugar is dissolved, 3 to 4 minutes.

2. Remove from the heat and whip by machine until thick and cooled, about 5 minutes. Beat in the butter and continue beating until the buttercream is smooth and spreadable. Use immediately or refrigerate, covered, for up to 5 days.

3. Before using, bring the buttercream to room temperature and beat smooth by machine.

4. Beat in the flavoring, a little at a time, and continue beating until the buttercream is smooth, about 2 minutes longer (always flavor buttercream immediately before using it).

BUTTERCREAM HINTS: Buttercream needs to be smoothly emulsified if it is going to hold its shape and be easy to spread. Always make sure that the meringue has cooled to room temperature before you add butter. If the meringue is still warm, the butter will melt and the buttercream will be excessively soft. If this happens, stir the soupy buttercream over ice water, then beat by machine until smooth and spreadable.

Sometimes buttercream separates—it will look like soft scrambled eggs. If this happens, briefly immerse the bottom of the mixing bowl in some hot tap water, then beat again until the buttercream is smooth and spreadable.

FLAVORINGS

LIQUEUR: Use 2 to 3 tablespoons liqueur, such as Grand Marnier, or dark or light rum.

LEMON: Use 2 to 3 tablespoons lemon juice.

COFFEE: Use 3 tablespoons instant coffee (espresso, if possible) dissolved in 2 tablespoons water, coffee, or rum.

RASPBERRY: Add ¾ cup thick raspberry puree made by cooking down and straining a 10-ounce package of frozen raspberries.

VANILLA: Use 1 tablespoon of pure vanilla extract.

POPULAR DECORATIONS

All the following decorations are easy to do. For best results, practice making the decoration on a plate or the back of a cake pan before attempting it on the cake.

STREAKING: Use an ounce of chocolate melted with ¼ teaspoon oil. Place in a plastic bag (snip off the corner), squeeze the bottle or paper cone, and streak the top of the cake with parallel lines. Make sure to come completely off the top of the cake, before starting another line, to avoid loops at the edge or side of the cake.

WRITING: Writing Happy Birthday and the birthday person's name on the cake is pretty much obligatory for a birthday cake. Use your regular handwriting, whether cursive or printing, and practice a few times on a cake pan or plate the same size as the cake top, so you can center the message evenly. Use the same tools and material as for STREAKING, above.

ROSETTES: To make a good rosette, hold a pastry bag with a star tube straight up and down about ½ inch above the cake top. Squeeze gently from the top of the bag and describe a letter C with the end of the tube. After completing the rosette, release the pressure and pull away sideways, not upward.

STARS: Hold the bag and star tube as for ROSETTES, above. Squeeze once, to press a star shape from the bag. Release the pressure and pull away straight up from the star.

SHELLS: Hold the bag with a star tube at a 45 degree angle to the top of the cake, with the tube just touching the cake top. Squeeze, pull sideways around the top edge of the cake, and release the pressure in one quick motion to make a pointed shell shape. Start the next shell over the point of the previous one.

BORDERS: A border is an excellent finish for the top or bottom of a cake. Use ROSETTES, SHELLS, or STARS, above. Rosettes and stars may be placed at a distance from each other, or touching, according to your preference.

For further decoration, top a rosette or star with a nutmeat, inverted chocolate chip, large chocolate shaving, or a piece of fresh or candied fruit, if appropriate to the flavors of the cake.

SHAVINGS, NUTS, AND OTHER CRUMBS

One of the easiest ways to give the outside of a cake a finished, professional look, is to coat it with some type of "crumb." These may be sliced or chopped nuts, shaved chocolate, or even (in cases of dire economy) toasted, ground cake or cookie crumbs.

To toast sliced almonds or hazelnuts: Place the sliced nuts on a jelly-roll pan and bake at 325 degrees for 10 to 15 minutes, checking and stirring them often with a metal spatula. After the nuts are golden brown, pour them from the pan onto the work surface to cool. Store toasted nuts in the freezer.

To make sugared sliced nuts: Stir 1 egg white, lightly beaten, into 2 cups sliced almonds or hazelnuts. Stir well to make sure all the nut surfaces are evenly moistened, then stir in 1 cup sugar. Toast as above, stirring often. Also excellent with walnut or pecan halves.

To make toasted chopped nuts: Pulse nutmeats in a food processor until the largest pieces are about ⅛ inch across. Toast as for sliced nuts, above. (For a neater cake, sift away "powdery" nut dust and only use the chunkier pieces of the chopped nuts.)

To make chocolate shavings, use any of the following techniques:

1. Grasp a bar of chocolate with a paper towel (to prevent its melting against the palm of your hand) and grate the chocolate against the coarse side of a box grater.

2. Grate the chocolate with the fine or coarse grating blade of a food processor.

3. Shave a chocolate bar with a vegetable peeler, running it along the narrow edge of the chocolate bar.

4. Scrape a melon-ball scoop or tartelet pan across the flat edge of a chocolate bar.

Whichever method you use, place the shavings on a jelly-roll pan and refrigerate to firm before using.

WHIPPED CREAM

2¼ cups heavy cream
⅓ cup sugar
2 teaspoons vanilla extract

ABOUT 4 CUPS

Cold is the key to successful whipped cream: have bowl, beaters, and especially cream, ice-cold before beginning to whip. In hot weather, place the cream in a mixer bowl and place in the freezer for 10 to 15 minutes before attempting to whip. Or whip the cream by hand in a bowl set over another bowl filled with ice water.

1. In a mixing bowl, combine all the ingredients and whip by hand or by machine, until thick and smooth, about 2 minutes.

2. Store the whipped cream refrigerated until ready to use.

3. Rewhip the cream before using.

VARIATIONS

Flavor whipped cream with a tablespoon of liqueur or a dash of cinnamon or other spice.

❖
CAKE DECORATING

Although dozens of books are published each year on this subject alone, you need not have a degree in cake decorating to produce a great-looking cake. There are many ways to finish a cake without resorting to a pastry bag and tubes, although piping decorations onto a cake can be easy—and fun.

Remember the one cardinal rule of good decorating: use decorations appropriate to the flavors in the cake. Streaking a coffee-frosted chocolate cake with chocolate is appropriate. Piping rosettes of coffee buttercream around the top edge of the cake would also be appropriate. Topping the rosettes with strawberries would not!

DECORATING EQUIPMENT

A visit to a hardware or department store should yield the basics necessary for simple cake decorating. The following is by no means a complete list of all the decorating tools available, but these are the basics you can find and use easily. For a catalogue of simple and elaborate cake decorating equipment, call Sweet Celebrations at (800) 328-6722.

PASTRY BAGS: Plastic or nylon bags are simple to use and clean. A 12-inch bag is easy and comfortable to use for piping decorations on a cake.

COUPLING: A two-piece insert for the tip of a pastry bag. It consists of a plastic tube with a threaded (like a screw) end inserted in the bag. After a tube is placed on the end of the coupling, a plastic ring is screwed around it on the outside. This allows you to change tubes from the outside of the bag.

TUBES: These come in hundreds of shapes and sizes.

PASTRY TUBES are larger and are used without couplings. An open *star tube* has five pointed teeth and may be used for piping whipped cream, buttercream, or ganache. A star tube with many tiny teeth is best used for ganache or buttercream, since they are fairly firm and hold the impression of the small teeth better. Choose a star tube with about a ¼-inch opening for cake decorating.

DECORATING TUBES are small and may be held with a coupling. The opening in the tubes is approximately ⅛ inch or less. *Star tubes, plain tubes* (for streaking or writing), and *drop flower tubes* (to make a flower shape with one squeeze!) are all easy to use.

PARCHMENT PAPER: To make a paper cone for streaking or writing. Wax paper and typing (printer) paper work well, too.

SQUEEZE BOTTLE: A plastic bottle with a screw-on, narrow, pointed top (sometimes used for hair coloring) is an easy way to streak the top of a cake with chocolate or even to write a message on a cake.

PLASTIC FOOD STORAGE BAG: Use a plain food storage bag with a tiny hole cut in one corner to streak or write on a cake.

SPATULAS: Spatulas come in a variety of shapes and sizes. A *straight spatula* with an 8- to 10-inch flexible stainless-steel blade makes frosting a cake easy. A small version with a narrow 3- to 4-inch blade is helpful for tricky spots, such as the corners of a square or rectangular cake. Each of these sizes is also available as an *offset spatula*. These are the easiest of all to use, because the blade has a bend in it making it lower than the handle, the way the blade of a trowel is offset from its handle. Makes smoothing the top of a cake a breeze.

KNIVES: It is practical to use stainless-steel knives for cake finishing, especially if any fruits or fruit juices will be part of the preparation. Carbon steel blades can impart a metallic flavor to acidic foods. A *bread knife* or other *serrated knife* is essential for splitting cakes into layers and may also be used for combing a wavy pattern into the top of the cake and for cutting the finished cake.

GRATERS: Use a *box grater* for chocolate shavings or grating citrus zests. To make chocolate shavings, use either the coarsest or next-to-coarsest openings in the grater. To grate zest, use the round (not the diamond-shaped) openings on the grater.

PEELERS: I prefer a stainless-steel *swivel-bladed peeler*, comfortable to hold and easy to use for making large, curled chocolate shavings.

CARDBOARD CAKE CIRCLES: Corrugated white-top cardboard cake circles or *cake boards* are available at specialty stores and may often be bought from a friendly bakery. They make finishing a cake neater and easier, because they allow you to lift and move the cake easily after it is frosted.

PLATTERS: Use a platter or dish that is completely flat (or has a flat center area the size of the cake). To serve a large rectangular cake, if you don't have a big enough platter, cover the back of a jelly-roll pan or cookie sheet with aluminum foil. Sprinkle the sides of the cake and the exposed foil with confectioners' sugar or cocoa to camouflage the shiny aluminum.

COMBINATIONS FOR CELEBRATION CAKES

Use the following combinations of layers and fillings as guidelines for creating celebration cakes.

I.
WHITE CAKE

1. Ganache (page 323), for a classic chocolate cake.

2. Lemon buttercream (page 324); cover outside of cake with toasted or plain sweetened coconut.

3. Grand Marnier or other orange liqueur buttercream (page 324); decorate with orange slices or candied orange peel.

4. Coffee buttercream (page 324), for a classic mocha cake.

5. Liqueur-flavored whipped cream.

II.
DEVIL'S FOOD CAKE

1. Ganache, for a chocolate lover's cake.

2. Liqueur, orange, or coffee buttercream.

3. Whipped cream, my preference with devil's food.

III.
NUT CAKE

For nut cakes, encrust the outside of the cake with chopped toasted nuts—the same as the ones in the cake batter.

1. Ganache with dark rum added.

2. Rum, brandy, or coffee buttercream.

3. Rum-flavored whipped cream.

CHEESECAKES

Though there are many variations of cheesecakes, they all fall into several simple categories. American-style cheesecakes are usually made with cream cheese and have a prebaked bottom crust of pastry dough or a crumb mixture. These cheesecakes are baked in a pan of water to insulate them from too much bottom heat and have a dense, rich, creamy texture.

European-style cheesecakes are usually made from a curd cheese, such as ricotta or farmer cheese, and are surrounded by a sweet crust and often have a top crust, as well. The surrounding crust accomplishes the same purpose during baking as the water bath and insulates the filling.

CHEESECAKE TECHNIQUE

1. Have all the ingredients at room temperature. Cold ingredients take longer to mix and encourage overbeating. Cold ingredients also often lump during mixing, which also causes overbeating or a less than smooth batter.

2. Mix only until the ingredients are smooth. Overmixing beats the air into the batter and causes it to rise like a soufflé during baking. When the cheesecake cools, the risen center collapses and causes a crater.

3. Avoid overbaking. Remember that the cheesecake becomes firm only after it is cool. The center of a cheesecake can be slightly liquid when it is removed from the oven—retained heat will continue to cook it.

4. *Always* bake American-style cheesecake in a pan of water to diffuse the bottom heat. In an oven with multiple rack settings, place the rack at the middle level.

5. *Never* use a convection oven for American-style cheesecakes. The forced air causes too much coloration and excessive rising, and will result in a fallen center.

6. Immediately after removing American-style cheesecakes from the oven, loosen the top

(continued)

edge from the inside of the pan with the point of a paring knife. The top surface cracks if it contracts while the edge remains stuck to the pan.

7. Cool the cheesecake to room temperature and refrigerate overnight before attempting to unmold. To unmold easily, place the pan on a gas burner for several seconds to warm the bottom slightly; cover the top of the pan with plastic wrap and a cardboard or flat plate and gently turn over. Remove the pan, put another cardboard or a platter on the bottom, and turn right side up. Remove the top cardboard and plastic wrap.

CHEESECAKE CRUST

3 tablespoons unsalted butter, softened
3 tablespoons sugar
1 egg yolk
1 cup bleached all-purpose flour
¼ teaspoon baking powder
⅛ teaspoon salt

ONE BOTTOM CRUST FOR A 9-INCH CHEESECAKE

This recipe produces a crumbly dough meant to be pressed into the bottom of a pan and baked before the cheesecake batter is added to the pan. Use this dough in the cheesecake recipes in this chapter that call for it.

1. In a bowl, cream together the butter and sugar until light and fluffy. Beat in the yolk until smooth.

2. In a separate bowl, combine the dry ingredients and gently fold them into the butter mixture with a rubber spatula. The mixture will be crumbly.

VARIATIONS

CHEESECAKE CRUST WITH ALMONDS: Add ½ cup (about 2¼ ounces) finely chopped sliced or slivered almonds to the dry ingredients, above.

CHEESECAKE CRUST WITH PECANS: Add ½ cup (about 2 ounces) finely chopped pecans to the dry ingredients, above.

NO-FRILLS CHEESECAKE

1 recipe Cheesecake Crust (page 332)

FILLING

2 pounds (32 ounces) cream cheese
1 cup sugar
1 teaspoon vanilla extract
1 teaspoon lemon juice
4 eggs

One 9-inch springform pan, bottom buttered, lined with a round of parchment

ONE 9-INCH CAKE, ABOUT 12 SERVINGS

This is the simplest and, to my mind, the best cheesecake.

1. Set a rack at the middle level of the oven and preheat to 350 degrees.

2. Prepare the dough and place it in the prepared pan. Pat the dough down evenly and firmly to cover the pan bottom. Bake for about 15 to 20 minutes, until the dough is golden and baked through. Lower the oven temperature to 325 degrees.

3. To make the filling, use your mixer's lowest speed. Using a paddle attachment, if your mixer has one, beat the cream cheese smooth, no more than 30 seconds. Stop the mixer and scrape the bowl and beater (or paddle). Add the sugar in a stream, mixing for no more than 30 seconds. Stop and scrape. Add the vanilla, lemon juice, and 1 egg; mix only until absorbed, no more than 30 seconds. Stop and scrape. Add the remaining eggs, one at a time, mixing only until each is absorbed. Stop and scrape after each addition.

4. Wrap aluminum foil around the bottom of the springform pan so it comes at least 1 inch up the sides. Pour the filling into the pan over the crust. Place the pan in a jelly-roll or roasting pan and pour warm water into the pan to a depth of ½ inch.

5. Bake the cheesecake for about 60 minutes, or until lightly colored and firm except for the very center. Remove from the pan of hot water.

6. Remove the foil and cool completely on a rack. Wrap the cheesecake in plastic or foil and chill overnight before unmolding.

SERVING: Serve a few sliced, sugared strawberries or some raspberries with the cheesecake, if you wish, though it is rich and complex enough to need no accompaniment.

STORAGE: If you bake the cheesecake on the day you intend to serve it, keep it loosely covered at a cool room temperature after the cake has cooled. For longer storage, wrap in plastic and refrigerate up to several days. Bring the cheesecake to room temperature for an hour before serving.

SOUR CREAM CHEESECAKE

1 recipe Cheesecake Crust (page 332)

FILLING

1 pound (16 ounces) cream cheese
1 cup sugar
2 cups sour cream
3 eggs
2 teaspoons vanilla extract

One 9-inch springform pan, bottom buttered, lined with a round of parchment

ONE 9-INCH CAKE, ABOUT 12 SERVINGS

Sometimes called "New York" cheesecake, this is a classic of the old-fashioned deli-style cheesecake.

1. Set a rack at the middle level of the oven and preheat to 350 degrees.

2. Prepare the dough and place it in the prepared pan. Pat the dough down evenly and firmly to cover the pan bottom. Bake for about 15 to 20 minutes, until the dough is golden and baked through. Reduce the oven temperature to 325 degrees.

3. To make the filling, your mixer should always be on the lowest speed. Use the paddle attachment, if your mixer has one, to beat the cream cheese smooth, no more than 30 seconds. Stop the mixer and scrape the bowl and beater (or paddle). Add the sugar in a stream, mixing for no more than 30 seconds. Stop and scrape. Add 1 cup of the sour cream; mix only until absorbed, no more than 30 seconds. Repeat with the remaining sour cream. Add the eggs, one at a time, mixing only until each is absorbed. Stop and scrape after each addition. Beat in the vanilla extract last.

4. Wrap aluminum foil around the bottom of the springform pan so it comes at least 1 inch up the sides. Pour the filling into the prepared pan over the crust. Place the pan in a jelly-roll or roasting pan and pour warm water into the jelly-roll pan to a depth of ½ inch.

5. Bake the cheesecake for about 55 minutes, or until lightly colored and firm except for the very center. Remove from the pan of hot water.

6. Remove the foil and cool completely on a rack. Wrap the cheesecake in plastic and chill overnight before unmolding.

SERVING: Serve in wedges after a light meal.

STORAGE: If you bake the cheesecake on the day you intend to serve it, keep it loosely covered at a cool room temperature after the cake has cooled. For longer storage, wrap in plastic and refrigerate up to several days. Bring the cheesecake to room temperature for an hour before serving.

CARAMEL PECAN CHEESECAKE

1 recipe Cheesecake Crust with Pecans
   (page 332)

FILLING

2 pounds (32 ounces) cream cheese
½ cup granulated sugar
½ cup dark brown sugar
4 eggs
2 tablespoons bourbon
1 cup (about 4 ounces) chopped toasted pecans

One 9-inch springform pan, bottom buttered, lined with a round of parchment

ONE 9-INCH CAKE, ABOUT 12 SERVINGS

The flavor of this cheesecake reminds me of fine New Orleans pralines, those wonderful brown sugar and pecan confections that become addictive so easily.

1. Set a rack at the middle level of the oven and preheat to 350 degrees.

2. Prepare the dough and place it in the prepared pan. Pat the dough down evenly and firmly to cover the pan bottom. Bake for 15 to 20 minutes, until the dough is golden and baked through. Reduce the oven temperature to 325 degrees.

3. To make the filling, your mixer should always be set on the lowest speed. Use the paddle attachment, if your mixer has one, to beat the cream cheese smooth, no more than 30 seconds. Stop the mixer and scrape the bowl and beater (or paddle). Add the granulated sugar in a stream, mixing for no more than 30 seconds. Stop and scrape. Repeat with the brown sugar. Add the eggs, one at a time, mixing only until each is absorbed. Stop and scrape after each addition. Add the bourbon, and mix until absorbed. By hand, gently fold in the chopped pecans.

4. Wrap aluminum foil around the bottom of the springform pan so it comes at least 1 inch up the sides. Pour the filling into the prepared pan over the crust. Place the pan on a jelly-roll or roasting pan and pour warm water into the jelly-roll pan to a depth of ½ inch.

5. Bake the cheesecake for about 60 minutes, or until lightly colored and firm except for the very center. Remove from the pan of hot water.

6. Remove the foil and cool completely on a rack. Wrap the cheesecake in plastic and chill overnight before unmolding.

SERVING: Serve in wedges; it needs no accompaniment.

STORAGE: If you bake the cheesecake on the day you intend to serve it, keep it loosely covered at a cool room temperature after the cake has cooled. For longer storage, wrap in plastic and refrigerate up to several days. Bring the cheesecake to room temperature for an hour before serving.

CHOCOLATE ALMOND CHEESECAKE

**1 recipe Cheesecake Crust with Almonds
(page 332)**

FILLING

1½ pounds (24 ounces) cream cheese
¾ cup sugar
8 ounces bittersweet chocolate, melted
2 teaspoons vanilla extract
2 teaspoons almond extract
4 eggs

**½ cup (about 2¼ ounces) toasted, chopped
slivered almonds**

*One 9-inch springform pan, bottom buttered, lined
with a round of parchment*

ONE 9-INCH CAKE, ABOUT 12 SERVINGS

Though it isn't the same recipe, this is based on a memory of a delicious cheesecake that my friend Joseph Viggiani used to make at his Cafe Sandalea in New York.

1. Set a rack at the middle level of the oven and preheat to 350 degrees.

2. Prepare the dough and place it in the prepared pan. Pat it down evenly and firmly to cover the pan bottom. Bake for about 15 to 20 minutes, until the dough is golden and baked through. Lower the oven temperature to 325 degrees.

3. To make the filling, your mixer should always be set on the lowest speed. Use the paddle attachment, if your mixer has one, to beat the cream cheese smooth, no more than 30 seconds. Stop the mixer and scrape the bowl and beater (or paddle). Add the sugar in a stream, mixing for no more than 30 seconds. Stop and scrape. Add the melted chocolate; mix only until absorbed, no more than 30 seconds. Add the vanilla and almond extracts and mix. Add the eggs, one at a time, mixing only until each is absorbed. Stop and scrape after each addition.

4. Wrap the aluminum foil around the bottom of the springform pan so it comes at least 1 inch up the sides. Pour the filling into the prepared pan over the crust. Sprinkle the chopped almonds evenly on top of the filling. Place the pan in a jelly-roll or roasting pan and pour warm water into the jelly-roll pan to a depth of ½ inch.

5. Bake the cheesecake for about 65 minutes, or until lightly colored and firm except for the very center. Remove from the pan of hot water.

6. Remove the foil and cool completely on a rack. Wrap the cheesecake and chill overnight before unmolding.

SERVING: Serve in wedges.

STORAGE: If you bake the cheesecake on the day you intend to serve it, keep it loosely covered at a cool room temperature after the cake has cooled. For longer storage, wrap in plastic and refrigerate up to several days. Bring the cheesecake to room temperature for an hour before serving.

MARBLED CHEESECAKE

1 recipe Cheesecake Crust (page 332)

CHOCOLATE BATTER

1 pound (16 ounces) cream cheese
½ cup sugar
5 ounces bittersweet or semisweet chocolate,
melted
1 teaspoon vanilla extract
3 eggs

PLAIN BATTER

1½ pounds (24 ounces) cream cheese
¾ cup sugar
1 teaspoon vanilla extract
3 eggs

One 9-inch springform pan, bottom buttered, lined with a round of parchment

ONE 9-INCH CAKE, ABOUT 12 SERVINGS

Though this cake is basically simple to achieve, it never fails to impress. The secret to making a really good marbled cheesecake is to use two different batters, each of which will bake to the same consistency, rather than to divide one batter in half and add chocolate to one part.

1. Set a rack at the middle level of the oven and preheat to 350 degrees.

2. Prepare the dough and place it in the prepared pan. Pat the dough down evenly and firmly to cover the pan bottom. Bake for about 15 to 20 minutes, until the dough is golden and baked through. Lower the oven temperature to 325 degrees.

3. To make both batters, your mixer should be set on the lowest speed. Use the paddle attachment, if your mixer has one, to beat the cream cheese smooth, no more than 30 seconds. Stop the mixer and scrape the bowl and beater (or paddle). Add the sugar in a stream, mixing for no more than 30 seconds. Stop and scrape. Add the melted chocolate; mix only until absorbed, no more than 30 seconds. Beat in the vanilla. Add the eggs, one at a time, mixing only until each is absorbed. Stop and scrape after each addition.

To make the plain batter, follow the same procedure as for the chocolate batter, but don't add the chocolate.

4. Wrap aluminum foil around the bottom of the springform pan to come at least 1 inch up the sides. Pour the plain batter into the prepared pan over the crust. Then, with a small ladle, spoon the chocolate batter over the plain one in a pattern of chocolate circles. When all the chocolate batter has been added, use a table knife to swirl the chocolate into the plain, creating a marbled effect. Place the pan in a jelly-roll or roasting pan and pour warm water into the jelly-roll pan to a depth of ½ inch.

5. Bake the cheesecake for about 1¼ hours, or until lightly colored and firm except for the very center. Remove from the pan of hot water.

(continued)

6. Remove the foil and cool completely on a rack. Wrap the cheesecake in plastic and chill overnight before unmolding.

SERVING: Serve in small wedges.

STORAGE: If you bake the cheesecake on the day you intend to serve it, keep it loosely covered at a cool room temperature after the cake has cooled. For longer storage, wrap in plastic and refrigerate up to several days. Bring the cheesecake to room temperature for an hour before serving.

LEMON CHEESECAKE

1 recipe Cheesecake Crust (page 332)

FILLING

1½ pounds (24 ounces) cream cheese
1 cup sugar
1 cup heavy cream
1 teaspoon finely grated lemon zest
3 tablespoons lemon juice
4 eggs

One 9-inch springform pan, bottom buttered, lined with a round of parchment

ONE 9-INCH CAKE, ABOUT 12 SERVINGS

Lemon and cheesecake are a perfect combination.

1. Set a rack at the middle level of the oven and preheat to 350 degrees.

2. Prepare the dough and place it in the prepared pan. Pat the dough down evenly and firmly to cover the pan bottom. Bake for 15 to 20 minutes, until the dough is golden and baked through. Reduce the oven temperature to 325 degrees.

3. To make the filling, your mixer should be set on the lowest speed. Use the paddle attachment, if your mixer has one, to beat the cream cheese smooth, no more than 30 seconds. Stop the mixer and scrape the bowl and beater (or paddle). Add the sugar in a stream, mixing for no more than 30 seconds. Stop and scrape. Add the cream, lemon zest, and lemon juice, and mix only until absorbed, no more than 30 seconds. Add the eggs, one at a time, mixing only until each is absorbed. Stop and scrape after each addition.

4. Wrap aluminum foil around the bottom of the springform pan so it comes at least 1 inch up the sides. Pour the filling into the prepared pan over the crust. Place the pan on a jelly-roll or roasting pan and pour warm water into the jelly-roll pan to a depth of ½ inch.

5. Bake the cheesecake for about 65 minutes, or until lightly colored and firm except for the very center. Remove from the pan of hot water.

6. Remove the foil and cool completely on a rack. Wrap the cheesecake and chill overnight before unmolding.

SERVING: Serve in wedges.

TIRAMISÙ CHEESECAKE

1 recipe Plain Génoise (page 270), baked in a 9-inch round pan

COFFEE-BRANDY SYRUP

¼ cup strong espresso coffee
2 tablespoons sugar
2 tablespoons brandy

MASCARPONE FILLING

1 pound (16 ounces) cream cheese
1 cup sugar
3 eggs
1 pound (about 2 cups) mascarpone cheese

½ teaspoon non-alkalized unsweetened cocoa powder

One 9-inch springform pan, buttered

ONE 9-INCH CAKE, ABOUT 12 SERVINGS

This fun variation on the classic Italian dessert is very much in the spirit of the original—and it eliminates the raw or partially cooked eggs traditionally associated with tiramisù.

STORAGE: If you bake the cheesecake on the day you intend to serve it, keep it loosely covered at a cool room temperature after the cake has cooled. For longer storage, wrap in plastic and refrigerate up to several days. Bring the cheesecake to room temperature for an hour before serving.

1. Cool the génoise.

2. For the syrup, combine the coffee, sugar, and brandy in a small bowl. Set aside.

3. Slice the génoise into 2 layers. Place the bottom of the cake layer in the prepared pan, gently pushing the sides of the cake to meet the sides of the pan. Cut the rest of the cake into ½-inch dice; place in a bowl and sprinkle with the coffee syrup. Set aside.

4. Set a rack at the middle level of the oven and preheat to 325 degrees.

5. To make the filling, your mixer should always be set on the lowest speed. Use the paddle attachment, if your mixer has one, to beat the cream cheese smooth, no more than 30 seconds. Stop the mixer and scrape the bowl and beater (or paddle). Add the sugar in a stream, mixing for no more than 30 seconds. Stop and scrape. Add the eggs, one at a time, mixing only until each is absorbed. Stop and scrape after each addition. In a large mixing bowl, gently soften the mascarpone cheese with a rubber spatula until it is smooth. By hand, fold the cream cheese mixture into the mascarpone cheese.

(continued)

6. Wrap aluminum foil around the bottom of the springform pan so it comes at least 1 inch up the sides. Pour one half of the filling into the prepared pan over the génoise layer. Top the filling with the diced génoise, then pour on the rest of the filling. Through a fine strainer, sprinkle the top of the cake with the cocoa powder. Place the pan in a jelly-roll or roasting pan and pour warm water into the jelly-roll pan to a depth of ½ inch.

7. Bake the cheesecake for about 55 minutes, or until lightly colored and firm except for the very center. Remove from the jelly-roll pan of hot water.

8. Remove the foil and cool completely on a rack. Wrap the cheesecake and chill overnight before unmolding.

SERVING: Serve *small* wedges.

STORAGE: If you bake the cheesecake on the day you intend to serve it, keep it loosely covered at a cool room temperature after the cake has cooled. For longer storage, wrap in plastic and refrigerate up to several days. Bring the cheesecake to room temperature for an hour before serving.

PIZZA DOLCE DI RICOTTA

Sweet Dough for Pies for a one-crust pie (page 149)

FILLING

1 pound or a 15-ounce container whole-milk ricotta cheese

⅓ cup sugar

1 teaspoon lemon zest

¼ teaspoon ground cinnamon, plus extra for top

1 tablespoon white rum

4 eggs

One 9-inch Pyrex pie pan

ONE 9-INCH PIE, ABOUT 8 SERVINGS

This is a traditional southern Italian Easter pie. Though some like to bake it in a deep pan, I like the pie pan because it makes portions smaller and much less rich.

1. Set a rack at the lower third of the oven and preheat to 350 degrees.

2. To make the filling, your mixer should always be set on the lowest speed. Use the paddle attachment, if your mixer has one, to beat the ricotta cheese smooth, no more than 30 seconds. Stop the mixer and scrape the bowl and beater (or paddle). Add the sugar in a stream, mixing for no more than 30 seconds. Stop and scrape. Add the lemon zest, cinnamon, rum, and 1 egg; mix only until absorbed, no more than 30 seconds. Stop and scrape. Add the remaining eggs, one at a time, mixing only until each is absorbed. Stop and scrape after each addition.

3. Lightly flour the work surface and dough. Roll the dough out into a ⅛-inch-thick circle. Fit the dough into the pan, fold under the edge, and flute it. Pour in the filling and sprinkle the top lightly with cinnamon.

4. Bake the tart until the filling is set and the crust baked through, about 40 minutes.

5. Cool on a rack.

SERVING: Serve in wedges.

STORAGE: If you bake the cheesecake on the day you intend to serve it, keep it loosely covered at a cool room temperature after the cake has cooled. For longer storage, wrap in plastic and refrigerate up to several days. Bring the cheesecake to room temperature for an hour before serving.

8

PUFF PASTRY
& CREAM
PUFF PASTRY

❖

Puff pastry is a term used to describe doughs that rise into multiple flaky layers from the pressure of steam built up while they are baking.

Puff pastry contains layers of dough and butter formed by rolling and folding the dough repeatedly.

Sometimes the layers are fairly uneven and randomly distributed as in *quick* or *express puff pastry,* as it is sometimes called. To make this, cubes of butter are added to the flour and other ingredients—much the way a pie dough is made, but large pieces of butter are left unincorporated. When the dough is rolled and folded, the layers form.

In *classic* or *traditional puff pastry,* the layers are of even size and thickness. In the classic recipe a dough that contains very little butter is wrapped around a thick square of butter to form a layered package of dough and butter. After repeated rolling and folding, the finished pastry may have close to a thousand alternating layers of dough and butter in it.

QUICKEST PUFF PASTRY

10 ounces (2½ sticks) cold unsalted butter
½ cup cold tap water
1 teaspoon salt
2 cups unbleached all-purpose flour

ABOUT 1½ POUNDS DOUGH

Although the standard type of quick puff pastry is not very time-consuming, this version, which uses a food processor to mix and adds a technique for rolling, rather than only folding the dough, is much faster.

1. Cut 8 ounces (2 sticks) of the butter into ½- to ¼-inch dice, place on a plate, and refrigerate while preparing the remaining ingredients.

2. Measure the water and stir in the salt to dissolve. Set aside.

3. Coarsely dice the remaining 4 tablespoons (½ stick) of butter. Place the flour in the work bowl of a food processor fitted with a metal blade. Add the 4 tablespoons butter and pulse until the butter is absorbed—about ten to twelve 1-second pulses.

4. Add the chilled butter and pulse once or twice to distribute. Add water and salt mixture and pulse 3 or 4 more times, just until the dough forms a rough ball—do not overprocess.

(continued)

5. Flour the work surface and turn the dough out onto it. Shape the dough into a rough rectangle and place between 2 pieces of plastic wrap. Press the dough with a rolling pin to flatten, then roll back and forth several times with the rolling pin to make a 12 × 18-inch rectangle of dough, as in the illustration.

6. Peel away the top layer of plastic wrap and turn the dough over onto the floured work surface. Peel away the second piece of wrap. Fold the dough in thirds the short way, to make a 4 × 18-inch rectangle, then roll the dough up from one of the 4-inch ends, as in the illustration. Make sure to roll the end under the dough. Press the roll of dough out into a square, wrap in plastic, and refrigerate for 1 hour, or until firm.

STORAGE: Keep the dough refrigerated and use it within 2 to 3 days. Or freeze the dough for up to a month and defrost it in the refrigerator overnight before using.

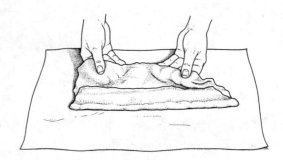

Make a 12 × 18-inch rectangle of dough. Fold the dough in thirds the short way, making a 4 × 18-inch rectangle.

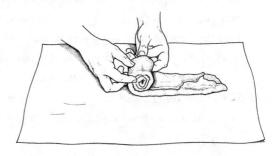

Roll up the dough from one of the 4-inch ends.

CLASSIC PUFF PASTRY

DOUGH

3 cups unbleached, all-purpose flour
¾ cup cake flour
8 tablespoons (1 stick) unsalted butter, softened
1½ teaspoons salt
1 cup very cold water, plus more if necessary

BUTTER LAYER

¼ cup unbleached all-purpose flour
1 pound (4 sticks) cold unsalted butter

ABOUT 2½ POUNDS DOUGH

Supposedly the invention of the seventeenth-century French landscape painter Claude Gellée, also called Claude Lorrain or Le Lorrain, puff pastry always adds a note of luxury to any preparation in which it is used. It turns even the most humble recipe into elegant party fare. The system I use here to create the layers is a short-cut. The 4 double turns or 4-layer turns instead of the classic French system of 6 single or 3-layer turns saves time and effort.

1. To make the dough, place the all-purpose flour in a large bowl and sift the cake flour over it. Stir the flours together thoroughly. Rub the butter in by hand. It should be completely mixed with the flour so no visible pieces remain. Dissolve the salt in the water. Make a well in the center of the flour and pour in the water. Use the tip of a rubber spatula to scrape across the bottom of the bowl through the center of the dough. Rotate the bowl and continue scraping until a ropey dough is formed. Do not apply any pressure to the dough with the spatula. Add more water, a tablespoon at a time, if necessary. Cover the bowl and set it aside while you prepare the butter.

2. To prepare the butter, pour the flour in a mound on the work surface and coat the butter with it. Pound the butter with a rolling pin to render it somewhat plastic. Squeeze the butter with your hands into a solid mass, then shape it into a square 1 inch thick.

3. To form the package of dough, dust the work surface with flour and turn the dough out on it. Press the dough into a rough square about 1 inch thick. Do not be concerned if the dough seems ropey and isn't smooth. Dust the dough with flour and roll out first the 4 corners into flaps, about ⅛ inch thick. Center the square of butter on the dough so that the corners of the square are between the flaps. Fold the flaps over the butter without stretching them. Make sure that all the butter is covered. If some shows through, seal the dough around it by pinching the dough together.

4. To begin rolling the dough, dust flour on the work surface and place the package of dough on it. Dust flour on the dough. With a rolling pin, beginning at the edge of the dough closest to you and working away, gently press (don't roll) the dough in a series of horizontal, very close-together strokes. Continue pressing the dough this way until it is about ⅜ inch thick. As you press, check to see that the surface has adequate flour and dust more on the surface and the dough as needed to prevent sticking. Roll over with an even pressure, once or twice, top to bottom, to make it ¼ inch thick. Take care that the corners remain real 90 degree angles.

5. To fold the dough, fold both the top and bottom ends of the dough in toward the center, then fold again to make 4 layers. The folded package of dough will resemble a book, with a spine on one side and the pages opposite it. Position the package of dough so that the spine is on your left. Dust the surface and the dough with flour and repeat the pressing as before, roll the dough up and down as before, then roll several times right to left so the dough is approximately 9 inches × 18 inches. Check the corners again and fold the dough, both narrower ends in toward the center, then over again as before.

6. To rest the dough, wrap it in plastic wrap and refrigerate it. The ideal resting time is about 1 hour, but the dough may be left longer if necessary, up to 24 hours.

7. To complete the turns, dust the work surface lightly with flour. Unwrap the dough and position it with the spine at your left. If the dough has rested more than 1 hour, it will be very hard. Allow it to soften slightly, until the butter feels flexible when you put hard pressure on the dough with your fingertips. Use a rolling pin to press the dough as in step 4, then dust the surface and the dough with flour and roll it again. Keep the corners even. Fold the dough again so that both ends meet in the center, then fold over again to make 4 layers. Position the dough with the spine on your left and repeat the pressing and rolling once more.

8. To rest the dough before use, wrap it in plastic and refrigerate for at least 4 hours or overnight. During this time the gluten strands which formed during the rolling and folding will relax, and the dough will become less elastic and easier to work with.

STORAGE: To freeze the dough, divide it into 2 or 3 pieces and double-wrap in plastic. Freeze for up to 2 months, then defrost overnight in the refrigerator before using. Puff pastry freezes very well.

Note: To substitute traditional puff pastry for quickest puff pastry in any of the following recipes, use ⅓ batch traditional for ½ batch quickest and ½ batch traditional for ⅔ batch quickest and ⅔ batch traditional for a full recipe of quickest.

PALMIERS

1 cup sugar, plus extra, if needed
½ batch Quickest Puff Pastry (page 345)

Two jelly-roll pans covered with parchment or foil

ABOUT FIFTEEN 3-INCH PASTRIES

One of the world's best-loved pastries is known by a variety of different names: palm leaves, elephant ears, pig's ears, and butterflies are just a few. The simple combination of puff pastry and caramelized sugar creates a sublime dessert flavor. A palmier should be served warm from the oven or at most within a few hours.

This recipe uses a variation on the typical palmier shape—but is also beautiful and just as delicious.

The quantity of sugar is deliberately high. If there is not enough sugar on the dough, the palmiers will be bland. If all the sugar does not stick to the dough, let the dough soften slightly at room temperature before continuing, then sprinkle the sugar on the surface before folding.

1. Scatter ½ cup of the sugar on the work surface and place the dough on it. Scatter another ½ cup of sugar over the dough. Press the sugar into the dough with a rolling pin. Press the pin into the dough gently about every ½ inch.

2. Roll the dough out into a 10-inch square. Turn the dough over often and make sure most of the sugar sticks to it.

3. Following the illustrations on page 350, fold the edges of the dough in toward the middle from the top and bottom. Then fold the rectangle of dough in half, left to right. Finally fold the bottom edge up to the top one. Set aside any remaining sugar on a small plate. Press the dough lightly with the palm of your hand, then chill it for about 30 minutes, or until firm. (The dough may be left until the next day before baking. Do not be alarmed if most of the sugar melts.)

4. Set a rack at the middle level of the oven and preheat to 350 degrees.

5. Slice the folded dough every ⅓ inch and dip the cut sides into the reserved sugar before placing the pastry on the pan. Leave at least 2 inches of space on all sides of each palmier because they spread.

6. Bake for about 20 minutes, until they are well caramelized. If the heat of the oven is uneven, it may be necessary to remove some of the pastries from the pan and return the others to the oven to finish baking. Let the color of the caramelized sugar be your guide; it should be deep amber, not brown.

7. Cool the pastries on a rack and serve them while they are still warm for best flavor.

SERVING: Serve the palmiers as a cookie—with a fruit or custard dessert or with coffee.

STORAGE: Keep the palmiers in an airtight tin or plastic container with a tight-fitting cover.

(continued)

VARIATION

SHOE SOLES: Roll the dough to a 10-inch square in sugar, as for the palmiers, above. With a small plain round cutter, cut the dough into 2- to 3-inch circles. Press the scraps together, reroll quickly, and cut a few more cookies. Place the remaining sugar on the work surface and roll out each piece of dough in it, one at a time, to make ovals about 2 × 4 inches. Arrange the pastries on the pans with about an inch of space all around each. Bake as for palmiers, above.

4 - FINGER PALMIERS

1

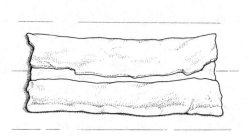

Fold both edges into the center.

2

Fold left to right.

3

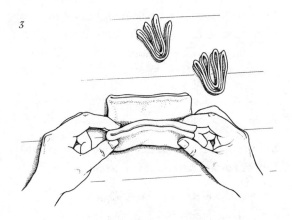

Fold top to bottom.

4

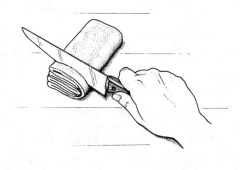

Cut the short edge.

ALMOND AND HAZELNUT TWISTS

½ batch Quickest Puff Pastry (page 345)
Egg wash: 1 egg well beaten with a pinch of salt

FILLING

½ cup sugar
½ teaspoon ground cinnamon
⅓ cup (about 1 ounce) blanched almonds, finely
   chopped but not ground
⅓ cup (about 1 ounce) hazelnuts, lightly toasted,
   skinned, and finely chopped but not ground

One jelly-roll pan lined with parchment or foil

ABOUT TWENTY-FOUR 8- TO 10-INCH PASTRIES

Another simple puff pastry is made richer and fancier by nuts and cinnamon sugar encrusting the dough. Though you may use any nuts, I find this combination of almonds and hazelnuts delicate and flavorful.

1. Place the dough on a floured surface, flour the dough, and roll it out into a 12-inch square. Paint the surface of the dough with the egg wash.

2. In a bowl, combine the sugar, cinnamon, and nuts and spread them evenly over one half of the dough in a 6 × 12-inch rectangle. Fold the other half of the dough over the filling to cover it. Slide onto a pan and refrigerate until the dough is firm, about 15 minutes.

3. Set a rack at the middle level of the oven and preheat to 350 degrees.

4. Remove the dough from the refrigerator and roll out into a 12-inch square. Use a cutting wheel to cut the dough into twenty-four ½-inch-wide strips. Twist each into a corkscrew shape. Press the ends of each twist to the sides of the prepared pan so they stick.

5. Bake the twists for about 20 minutes, until they're well puffed and well caramelized.

6. Remove the pan from the oven and place on a rack to cool for 5 minutes. While the twists are still flexible and before they cool completely, trim off the ends with a sharp knife. If you wish, cut the twists in half to make two 6-inch cookies from each.

SERVING: Serve the twists as a cookie—with a fruit or custard dessert or with coffee.

STORAGE: Keep the twists in an airtight tin or plastic container with a tight-fitting cover.

SWISS PRETZELS

SWEET DOUGH

¾ **cup bleached all-purpose flour**

2 tablespoons granulated sugar

Pinch of salt

¼ **teaspoon baking powder**

3 tablespoons unsalted butter, cold

1 egg yolk

1 teaspoon vanilla extract

2 teaspoons water

½ **batch Quickest Puff Pastry (page 345)**

Egg wash: 1 egg well beaten with a pinch of salt

Confectioners' sugar for finishing

Two cookie sheets or jelly-roll pans lined with parchment or foil

ABOUT SIXTEEN 4- TO 5-INCH PASTRIES

These are not only fast and easy to prepare but also impressive to serve. The use of two different doughs might seem unusual at first, but the result emphasizes the best qualities of each.

1. To prepare the sweet dough by hand, combine the dry ingredients in a medium mixing bowl and stir well to combine. Cut the butter into 1-tablespoon pieces and add to the dry ingredients. Toss once or twice to coat the pieces of butter. Then using your hands or a pastry blender, break the butter into tiny pieces and pinch and squeeze it into the dry ingredients. Occasionally reach down to the bottom of the bowl and mix all the ingredients evenly together. Continue rubbing the butter into the dry ingredients until the mixture resembles a coarse-ground cornmeal and no large pieces of butter remain visible. Beat the egg yolk in a small bowl and add the vanilla extract and water. Pour over the flour and butter mixture. Stir in with a fork until the dough begins to hold together but still appears somewhat dry. Scatter a teaspoon of flour on the work surface and scrape the dough out onto it. Press and knead the dough quickly 3 or 4 times, until it is smooth and uniform.

To prepare the dough in a food processor, combine the dry ingredients in the work bowl of the processor fitted with the metal blade. Pulse 3 or 4 times to mix. Cut the butter into 6 or 8 pieces and pulse about 15 times to form a sandy mixture. Add the yolk, vanilla, and water and pulse until the dough forms a ball. Turn the dough out onto a floured work surface and press into a square. Wrap in plastic and chill briefly.

2. Place the puff pastry dough on a lightly floured surface and flour the dough. Roll into a 12-inch square. Slide the dough onto a floured cookie sheet and paint with the egg wash.

3. Roll the sweet dough out into a 12-inch square and place it on the puff pastry. Press it gently so the two doughs stick together. Chill for a few minutes.

4. Set a rack at the middle level of the oven and preheat to 350 degrees.

5. Remove the dough from the refrigerator and cut it into ¾-inch-wide strips. First corkscrew each strip as for Almond and Hazelnut Twists (page 351); then bend each into a pretzel as in the illustration.

6. Arrange the pretzels well apart on the prepared pans. Bake them for about 20 minutes, until they are a deep golden color and both doughs are baked through.

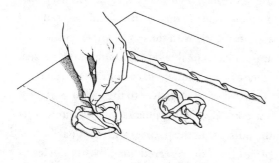

First, twist each strip into a corkscrew shape. Bend each strip into a pretzel.

7. Cool on racks on the pans. Before serving, dust lightly with the confectioners' sugar.

SERVING: Serve the pretzels as a cookie—with a fruit or custard dessert or with coffee.

STORAGE: Keep them in an airtight tin or a plastic container with a tight-fitting lid.

APRICOT PINWHEELS

⅔ batch Quickest Puff Pastry (page 345)

Egg wash: 1 egg well beaten with a pinch of salt

4 large (about ¾ pound total) ripe apricots, rinsed, halved, and pitted

¼ cup (about 1 ounce) blanched sliced almonds

SUGAR ICING

2 cups confectioners' sugar

3 tablespoons water

1 tablespoon unsalted butter

1 tablespoon light corn syrup

1 teaspoon vanilla extract

One jelly-roll pan or cookie sheet lined with parchment or foil

EIGHT 4-INCH PASTRIES

This shape is associated with Danish pastries, but I think a puff pastry pinwheel is both elegant and attractive. The fruits most often used in these pastries are apricots or plums so the icing is necessary to add a bit of sweetness to these ordinarily tart fruits.

1. Place the dough on a floured surface and lightly flour the dough. Roll the dough out into a 12-inch square. Cut the dough into nine 4-inch squares and place eight of them on the prepared pan. With a small fluted round cutter, cut eight 1¼-inch circles out of the remaining square.

2. Set a rack at the middle level of the oven and preheat to 350 degrees.

3. Starting at a corner of one of the squares, cut diagonally in to within an inch of the center. Cut the remaining 3 corners the same way. Repeat with the other 7 squares. Brush the slashed squares lightly with the egg wash. Place an apricot half, cut side down, in the center of each square over the uncut part. Fold every other corner of the dough over to the center of the apricot half, as in the illustration. Carefully brush the outsides of the pastries with the egg wash and place one of the reserved fluted pastry circles over the center of each apricot half. Brush the fluted dough with egg wash and sprinkle with the sliced almonds.

Fold over every other corner of the dough to the center of the apricot half.

4. Bake the pastries for 20 to 25 minutes, until they're deep golden and baked through. Place the pan on a rack to cool.

5. To make the icing, combine all the ingredients in a medium saucepan. Place over low heat and stir constantly, until the icing is lukewarm (about 100 degrees) and has the consistency of heavy cream.

6. Brush or drizzle the icing over the cooled pastries. Allow the icing to dry, then transfer the pastries to a platter.

SERVING: Serve the pastries for breakfast, brunch, or as dessert at a casual lunch or supper. A little whipped cream will dress them up considerably.

STORAGE: These are best on the day they are baked. Keep leftovers at room temperature—reheat briefly before serving.

HINT FOR SUCCESS: To make the pinwheels look the same, when you are folding the corners of the dough inward over the fruit, fold in the same corners on each, as in the illustration on page 354.

VARIATIONS

Substitute plums or even small poached pear halves for the apricots, above.

APPLE DUMPLINGS

BAKED APPLES

**6 small (5 to 6 ounces each) Rome Beauty,
    Granny Smith, or Golden Delicious apples**

½ small lemon

½ cup light brown sugar

½ teaspoon ground cinnamon

**3 tablespoons (about 1 ounce) dark or golden
    raisins or currants**

2 tablespoons unsalted butter

⅓ cup apricot preserves

⅓ cup water

½ batch Quickest Puff Pastry (page 345)

Egg wash: 1 egg well beaten with a pinch of salt

*One small baking pan, such as a 10-inch square or
round one, for baking the apples*

One jelly-roll pan lined with parchment or foil

6 LARGE PASTRIES

After a number of disasters trying to perfect
this recipe for whole apples baked in puff pastry, I
finally hit on a two-part procedure. First, bake the
apples, then chill them and wrap the cold apples
in puff pastry. Bake them just long enough for the
dough to bake through. The results doing it this
way have been uniformly excellent.

Several things are improved by precooking the
apples. They turn out flavorful and sufficiently
sweetened from being cooked with sugar, spices,
and a little apricot preserves. Also, after they are

baked in the pastry, they are always cooked perfectly. If they aren't precooked, they are sometimes only partially cooked when the pastry is
done. And, best of all, when the apples are cooking, the excess juices come out of them (you can
use them to make a sauce to serve with the
dumplings) instead of exuding inside the pastry
and making the dumplings soggy.

1. To make the baked apples, set a rack at the
middle level of the oven and preheat to 350
degrees.

2. Peel and core the apples, leaving them whole.
Rub them all over with the lemon, then place
them in the baking pan. Sprinkle them with the
sugar and cinnamon, making sure that some gets
into the hollow centers. Stuff the raisins or
currants into the centers, then place a small slice
of the butter on each apple. Bring the preserves
and water to a boil in a small pan. Pour around
the apples in the pan, then immediately place the
pan in the oven. After about 10 minutes, baste the
apples every 5 minutes with their juices. The
apples should take about 30 minutes to bake.
They should be tender but not disintegrating.

3. Remove the pan from the oven and place it on
a rack to cool. Baste the apples with the juices in
the pan frequently while they are cooling, then
cover and refrigerate the apples until they are
thoroughly cold, 2 or 3 hours. The apples may be
prepared up to 2 days before forming and baking
the pastries.

4. To form the pastries, remove the apples from
the pan and place them on a rack over the pan to

drain. (Reserve any leftover juices to make a sauce.) Set a rack at the middle level of the oven and preheat to 375 degrees.

5. Place the dough on a floured surface and lightly flour the dough. Roll the dough out into a 10 × 18-inch rectangle. Cut the dough into six 5-inch squares and place them on the prepared pan. Use a small, round, fluted cutter to cut the remaining scrap of dough into six small circles.

6. Brush the squares of dough lightly with the egg wash. Place an apple in the center of each square. (Replace any raisins or currants that might have fallen out of the centers.) Bring each corner of the dough up to the top center of the apple. Pinch the seams of the pastry together, then carefully brush the outside with the egg wash. Place one of the fluted pastry circles on top of each pastry, where the corners join together. Brush the fluted dough with egg wash.

7. Bake the pastries for 20 to 25 minutes, until they're deep golden and baked through.

8. Place the pan on a rack to cool slightly before you serve the apples.

9. While the pastries are baking, strain the reserved juices into a saucepan. Bring to a boil, then remove from the heat and cover. Reheat and serve with the apples.

SERVING: Serve the pastries for brunch or as dessert at a casual lunch or supper. Serve warm or at room temperature with the warmed reserved juices or with whipped cream.

STORAGE: These are best on the day they are baked. Keep leftovers at room temperature—reheat briefly before serving.

VARIATION

Substitute small poached pears for the apples.

APPLE TURNOVERS

⅔ **batch Quickest Puff Pastry (page 345)**

APPLE FILLING

2 pounds (about 4 large) tart apples, such as Granny Smith, Greening, or Northern Spy
⅓ cup granulated sugar
2 tablespoons unsalted butter
¼ teaspoon ground cinnamon

Egg wash: 1 egg well beaten with a pinch of salt
Confectioners' sugar for finishing

One jelly-roll pan or cookie sheet lined with parchment or foil

SIX 5- TO 6-INCH TURNOVERS

The secret of a good turnover is a filling that is both plentiful and flavorful. I think a brief cooking concentrates the flavor of any fruit and also helps get rid of some of the excess water that would make the baked turnovers soggy.

1. Place the dough on a floured surface and lightly flour the dough. Roll it into a 12 × 18-inch rectangle. Slide the dough onto a pan (fold it over a piece of foil or plastic wrap if necessary) and refrigerate it while preparing the filling.

2. To make the filling, peel, halve, and core the apples. Cut the apple halves into ½-inch dice. Place the apples and remaining filling ingredients in a shallow sauté pan over medium heat and quickly bring to a simmer. Cook the apples, tossing or gently stirring frequently, until they are tender and the accumulated juices have begun to

reduce somewhat, 8 or 10 minutes. Scrape the filling into a nonreactive pan and refrigerate it until thoroughly chilled, about 1 hour.

3. Set a rack at the middle level of the oven and preheat to 375 degrees.

4. Remove the dough from the refrigerator and cut it into six 6-inch squares. Paint the perimeter of each square with the egg wash. Place a generous tablespoon of filling off-center on each square, then fold the dough over diagonally to enclose the filling. Quickly transfer the turnovers to the baking pan. Press the edges of the pastry well so they stick together, then carefully brush each turnover with the remaining egg wash. With the point of a small, sharp paring knife, slash a 1-inch vent hole in the top of each turnover.

5. Bake the turnovers for 20 to 25 minutes, until they are well risen, a deep golden color, and the filling is bubbling slightly.

6. Cool briefly on the pan, then remove to a rack to finish cooling. Dust with confectioners' sugar before serving.

SERVING: Serve the pastries for brunch or as dessert at a casual lunch or supper. Serve warm or at room temperature.

STORAGE: These are best on the day they are baked. Keep leftovers at room temperature—reheat briefly before serving.

VARIATIONS

Substitute pears or peeled peaches for apples.

If you wish, drizzle the turnovers with icing from the Apricot Pinwheels (page 354).

BANANA FEUILLETÉS WITH CARAMEL SAUCE

½ batch Quickest Puff Pastry (page 345)

BANANA FILLING

3 large (1¼ to 1½ pounds) bananas
3 tablespoons granulated sugar
2 tablespoons dark rum

CARAMEL SAUCE

1 cup granulated sugar
1 teaspoon water
¾ cup heavy cream

WHIPPED CREAM

1 cup heavy cream
2 tablespoons granulated sugar
1 teaspoon vanilla extract

Confectioners' sugar

Two 10½ × 15½-inch jelly-roll pans, covered with parchment

ABOUT 8 FEUILLETÉS

The flavor of bananas macerated in sugar and rum goes perfectly with caramel and buttery puff pastry. All the elements for this may be assembled the day before, but the puff pastry will taste best if you bake it on the day you plan to serve it. This rich dessert is the perfect ending for either an elegant dinner party or a simple meal.

1. To make the pastry layer, roll the dough out into a 10 × 15-inch rectangle. Place it on one of the paper-covered pans and refrigerate it for an hour.

2. After it has rested for about 40 minutes, set a rack at the middle level of the oven and preheat to 350 degrees.

3. Remove the pastry from the refrigerator and pierce it all over with a fork. Cover with a second piece of parchment and then the second pan and bake for about 30 minutes, until the pastry is deep golden and baked through. Turn the stack of pans and pastry over top to bottom every 8 or 10 minutes to ensure even baking. To prevent warping, cool on a rack between pans.

4. To prepare the filling, peel and cut the bananas into ¼-inch-thick slices. In a non-reactive bowl stir the bananas with the sugar and rum several times to mix, then cover the bowl tightly with plastic wrap and refrigerate until needed.

5. To make the caramel sauce, stir the sugar and water together in a 2-quart saucepan. Place over low heat and allow to melt and caramelize, stirring occasionally. In a separate pan, heat the cream to a simmer. When the caramel is a deep amber color, remove the pan from the heat and add the hot cream, a quarter at a time, from a ladle held at arm's length away from the pan of caramel (it spatters far). After all the cream has been added, stir once, replace the pan on the heat, and allow to come to a full boil. Remove from the heat and pour into a heavy bowl or pan to cool.

6. Shortly before you assemble the dessert, prepare the whipped cream. In a bowl, whip the cream with the sugar and vanilla, cover, and set it aside, refrigerated.

(continued)

7. Use a sharp, round, 3-inch cutter or a cardboard pattern and a sharp paring knife to cut the baked pastry layer into 3-inch circles (you should end up with 16).

8. To assemble, place the caramel sauce in a squeeze bottle—or use a large spoon—and streak the dessert plates with the sauce. Place a pastry in the center of each plate and top with a large spoonful of the bananas. Pipe or spoon a large dollop of whipped cream over the bananas and cover with another pastry. Press it on gently. Dust the surface of the top pastry disk with confectioners' sugar. Pass the remaining whipped cream and caramel sauce in bowls.

SERVING: Serve these as soon as possible after they are assembled. A sweet wine, such as a Sauternes or a French or California late-harvest Riesling would be a wonderful accompaniment to the feuilletés.

STORAGE: Though the desserts cannot be stored, all the elements may be made in advance. If you wish to make the full amount but serve the desserts to fewer people, the leftover caramel sauce will keep well in a jar in the refrigerator—leave it at room temperature for a few hours before you use it. The leftover feuilletés will freeze well wrapped airtight in plastic. Reheat them at 350 degrees for about 5 minutes and let them cool before using them.

HINT FOR SUCCESS: As with all plated desserts, have all the elements ready and at hand before you begin to assemble.

VARIATIONS

Substitute berries or other fruit, such as peaches or nectarines for the bananas.

Use kirsch or framboise as a liqueur with strawberries or raspberries, white rum with peaches or nectarines.

CHOCOLATE RASPBERRY MILLE-FEUILLE

1 recipe Quickest Puff Pastry (page 345)

FILLING

2½ cups heavy cream

6 ounces bittersweet or semisweet chocolate,
    finely cut

3 tablespoons granulated sugar

1 tablespoon raspberry liqueur or framboise
    (raspberry eau-de-vie)

Two ½-pint baskets fresh raspberries

Confectioners' sugar

Cocoa powder

*Six 11 × 17-inch jelly-roll pans lined with
parchment or foil*

**ONE 11- TO 12-INCH SQUARE MILLE-FEUILLE, ABOUT
12 SERVINGS**

A rich and striking variation on the traditional mille-feuille: 3 layers of puff pastry sandwiching cream and fruit. This combines raspberries with chocolate, which is not often paired with puff pastry.

1. Roll the pastry dough out into 3 squares, 11 to 12 inches each. Slide onto pans and refrigerate for about 1 hour, until the pastry dough is firm and rested.

2. For the filling, bring ½ cup of the cream to a boil in a medium saucepan. Remove from the heat and add the chocolate. Allow the chocolate to melt for 2 or 3 minutes, then whisk smooth. Cool to room temperature, but do not refrigerate or the chocolate mixture will harden. In a bowl, whip the remaining cream with the sugar and liqueur and set aside, refrigerated. Pick over the berries if necessary and set aside, refrigerated.

3. Set a rack at the middle level of the oven and preheat to 350 degrees.

4. Pierce the dough all over with a fork and place it on 3 paper-lined pans. Cover each piece of dough with another piece of paper and another pan and bake for about 30 minutes. Turn the stack of pans and dough upside down every 8 minutes or so and watch the dough's progress. Cool the dough between the pans so it doesn't warp.

5. To assemble the filling, remove the whipped cream from the refrigerator and quickly rewhip it, if necessary. Whisk about 1 cup of the whipped cream into the cooled chocolate mixture.

6. Place one of the squares of dough on the back of a pan or cardboard and spread it with half of the chocolate filling. Sprinkle half the raspberries over the filling, then cover with half the whipped cream, spreading it flat and even. Place the second pastry layer on top, press it down well. Repeat with the remaining fillings.

(continued)

7. Place the last layer on the top and press it down well so the mille-feuille is straight. Smooth the fillings at the sides with a spatula and refrigerate for an hour to set the fillings.

8. Cut the mille-feuille into 3 equal strips and stick the trimmings to the filling around the sides of each. Using a *very* sharp serrated knife, cut through them at 1-inch intervals, to make individual portions. Dust confectioners' sugar evenly over the top of each portion, then dust very lightly with the cocoa powder, just to spot the surface.

SERVING: Serve the mille-feuille as the dessert of an elaborate meal. For ease of serving, cut the mille-feuille several hours before serving and keep refrigerated, loosely covered.

STORAGE: Refrigerate leftovers—unfortunately they will become soggy after a few more hours.

HINT FOR SUCCESS: If one of the three layers breaks, use it in the middle; if two break, use them as the middle and bottom.

VARIATION

WHITE CHOCOLATE RASPBERRY MILLE-FEUILLE: Substitute 8 ounces white chocolate for the dark chocolate in the filling.

BISTRO APPLE TART

¼ batch Quickest Puff Pastry (page 345)

COVERING

1 apple, such as Granny Smith, peeled, cored,
    and sliced paper-thin
1 teaspoon sugar

WHIPPED CREAM

½ cup heavy cream
1 tablespoon crème fraîche, or 1 teaspoon yogurt
1 teaspoon sugar
½ teaspoon vanilla extract

GLAZE

2 tablespoons apple jelly or strained apricot
    preserves

One 12 × 15-inch cookie sheet lined with parchment or foil

♦

**ONE VERY THIN 9- TO 10-INCH TART, ABOUT
2 SERVINGS**

This delicate, delicious apple tart is easy to prepare.

To prepare in advance, roll out the crust, cover it with plastic wrap, and refrigerate. Peel, core, and slice the apple keeping the halves intact. Wrap the apple tightly in plastic wrap and refrigerate. About 30 minutes before serving, arrange the apple slices on the crust, sprinkle with sugar, and bake.

1. Press inward on the corners of the puff pastry and shape it as well as you can into an even circle. Place the dough on a lightly floured surface, flour it, and roll it out into a 10-inch circle—the dough will be very thin. Slide it onto a cookie sheet (not the insulated type), cover it with plastic wrap, and refrigerate for at least 1 hour or up to 24 hours.

2. Set a rack at the middle level of the oven and preheat to 450 degrees.

3. Remove the dough from the refrigerator and place a plate or other pattern over it and cut it into an even 10-inch circle. Pierce the dough all over at ½-inch intervals with a fork to prevent it from puffing unnecessarily during baking.

4. For the covering, arrange the apple slices, rounded sides against the outer edge of the dough, beginning about ½ inch in from the edge, in concentric circles. The slices should overlap slightly. Sprinkle with the sugar.

5. Bake the tart for 15 to 20 minutes, until the dough is baked through and the apple slices have colored at the edges.

6. While the tart is baking, whip the cream with the crème fraîche, sugar, and vanilla until the cream forms soft peaks. Scrape into a serving bowl, cover, and refrigerate.

7. Place the jelly in a small pan over low heat and bring to a simmer. Remove the tart from the oven, cool slightly, and paint with the glaze. Serve the tart immediately with the whipped cream.

Note: Adding crème fraîche or yogurt to the whipped cream flavors the cream. You may also want to just use a spoonful of crème fraîche.

CREAM PUFF PASTRY

Cream puff–type pastries, among the oldest fancy pastries being made, are much less popular in the United States than they are in western Europe.

Though *pâte à choux* probably originated in Italy in the late Middle Ages, it was in France that the most delicate creations were made from this dough. Delicate *choux*—little puffs—éclairs, and a host of other cream-filled *choux* pastries have remained part of the standard repertoire of French pastries. And in Italy there are still pastry shops whose main stock consists of different pastries—in all shapes, sizes, and colors—made from *pâte à choux*.

The first time I went to visit my mother's cousins in southern Italy in 1974, their first question to me was: "Can you make desserts and pastries like the ones in pastry shops?" Because I didn't want to be boastful—nor did I want to spend all day every day baking—I modestly said that I knew how to make a few things, but I was really (and it was true) just a beginner.

During the course of my visit I spent a lot of time in the kitchen with my cousin Michele's wife, Pupetta (Dolly). She was an accomplished cook, but constantly asked me questions about how to make various desserts. She was especially curious about *bignè*—cream puffs—the most popular pastry in southern Italy. At every birthday, christening, or other important occasion there are always trays of little pastries, most of them made from cream puff pastry.

I did already know how to prepare that, so I offered to show her. Next morning we shopped for provisions. The shopkeeper at the dairy store asked us curiously what we proposed to do with such a large quantity of butter, eggs, milk, and cream.

Back at the house, to make the pastry cream filling we used the "American" stove, a gas range powered by a large butane tank. The stove was used only about half the time, and only when the large wood-burning stove on which my grandmother had learned to cook seventy-five years before was not in use. When the pastry cream was made and in the refrigerator, we set about preparing the actual *bignè*. Lacking a pastry bag, we formed them with a spoon, large mounds on the foil-covered backs of two roasting pans. We placed them in the oven and went about cleaning up and repeatedly tasting the pastry cream.

Twenty minutes later, we checked the *bignè*. A dismal sight awaited us when we opened the oven. The pastries had puffed slightly, but only slightly, and seemed to have refused to rise any further. They also seemed to have remained substantially raw. By this time, of course, they should have been almost double their original size. We went over the proportions of the recipe again (I was afraid I had not added enough eggs to make the paste rise), but the proportions were right. Just at that moment we heard the telltale shuffle of Zia Maria, a busybody relative, on the steps. We looked at each other and hid the failed *bignè* on the attic stairs, closed the kitchen door, and went into the *soggiorno*, that uniquely Italian combination living and dining room, sat down, and desperately tried to appear nonchalant.

Zia Maria entered and commented on the good smell of something baking. I swallowed hard and said that the pastries wouldn't be ready for hours, but that as soon as they were, we would rush over with some. I hoped we'd have time to prepare a second batch and ward off total disgrace. Satisfied, Zia Maria left after a short visit and Pupetta and I went back to the kitchen and tried to determine the source of the problem. It didn't seem to be in the recipe, so we finally decided to try baking the *bignè* again.

We turned the oven on, but twenty minutes later, it was still cold—the tank of gas was empty. At least we had solved the mystery. We struggled to roll in another tank from the summer kitchen at the back of the house, and within half an hour the *bignè* were finally puffing. Of course they remained a little heavy, but they were nonetheless quite edible. Zia Maria was heard by another cousin to remark that the pastries weren't bad at all considering the fact that they had been made by an American.

To this day, when I see a tray of cream puffs, I still remember the panic of hiding the unrisen ones from Zia Maria, and I smile. I think you will have a much less harrowing experience in preparing these. But if you hear that shuffle on the steps . . .

This dough deserves to be more popular in this country than it is: it is easy to prepare, versatile—it may be used for savory as well as sweet pastries—and relatively foolproof. The buttery flavor of a well-prepared *pâte à choux* container harmonizes with many fillings, from rich custards to fresh fruits.

The only tricky part of baking with *pâte à choux* is to bake it sufficiently. Many people think they don't care for this pastry because they have always had it underdone, so that it comes out heavy and soggy—not appetizing in any type of pastry.

PÂTE À CHOUX
(*CREAM PUFF PASTRY*)

1 cup water
6 tablespoons unsalted butter
¼ teaspoon salt
1 cup unbleached all-purpose flour
4 large eggs

ABOUT 3 CUPS DOUGH, ENOUGH FOR ABOUT 12 TO 18 SMALL PASTRIES

This dough, used to prepare many sweets, is also often used for savory preparations.

1. Combine the water, butter, and salt in a saucepan over medium heat and bring to a boil, stirring occasionally. As soon as it comes to the boil, remove from the heat and sift in the flour, stirring with a wooden spoon to combine smoothly.

2. Return to the heat and cook, stirring constantly, until the paste dries slightly and begins to leave the sides of the pan.

3. Transfer the paste to a bowl and stir with a wooden spoon for 1 minute to cool slightly.

4. Add eggs, one at a time, beating each until it is absorbed before adding the next. Use the pastry immediately.

STORAGE: The *pâte à choux* will puff better in the oven when freshly made. If you must wait before piping and baking, press plastic wrap against the surface of the paste to prevent a skin from forming.

FORMING AND PIPING
PÂTE À CHOUX

Although most people regard using a pastry bag as a big production and a lot of work, piping pastes like *pâte à choux* actually makes the job easier. Also *pâte à choux* piped, rather than dropped from a spoon, has a neater, more uniform appearance.

For small round and oval *choux* and éclairs, hold the pastry bag at a 45 degree angle to the pan, with the bottom end of the tube touching the paper on the pan.

+ For a round *chou*, squeeze once, then stop squeezing and pull away with an upward motion (to avoid leaving a "tail"). Begin the next one about 1½ inches away.

+ For an oval *chou,* the motion is the same as for a round one, but pull the bag about ½ inch toward you, to elongate the shape slightly. Begin the next one about 1½ inches away.

+ For an éclair, the motion is the same as for an oval chou, but keep pulling the bag toward you, maintaining an even pressure from the top, until the éclair is about 3 inches long. Begin the next one about 2 inches away.

+ For other shapes, such as large *choux* and thin coils of the *pâte à choux* (as in pretzels and other composite shapes), hold the bag at a 90 degree angle to the pan, and about an inch above it.

+ For a large *chou*, squeeze with an even pressure until the *pâte à choux* is a large half-sphere 1½ to 2 inches in diameter. Stop squeezing and lift away. If there is a "tail," wet a fingertip with some water or egg wash and smooth away the point.

+ For composite shapes, such as pretzels, polkas, or baskets, allow a stream of the paste, equal in diameter to the opening in the tube, to drop from it. This requires a little practice, but the results are worth it.

PASTRY CREAM

	1½ CUPS	2 CUPS	3 CUPS
MILK	1 cup	1½ cups	2 cups
SUGAR	⅓ cup	½ cup	⅔ cup
EGG YOLKS	3	4	6
SALT	Pinch	Pinch	Pinch
ALL-PURPOSE FLOUR	2½ tbs.	¼ cup	⅓ cup
VANILLA EXTRACT	1 tsp.	1½ tsp.	2 tsp.

1½ TO 3 CUPS PASTRY CREAM, DEPENDING ON THE PROPORTIONS USED

Since pastry cream is a typical filling for *pâte à choux*, I'll give the recipe here and refer to it in the other recipes that call for it. Easy to prepare, pastry cream is a versatile filling—in the recipes that follow you'll see it paired with butter, whipped cream, and all sorts of different flavors.

Because pastry cream must be cold when used, it lends itself well to advance preparation, though it should not be prepared sooner than the day before it is to be used.

Two notes of caution: Since pastry cream is an excellent breeding ground for bacteria of all sorts, make sure all the implements and vessels used for making it are perfectly clean—it spoils easily. Second, always refrigerate pastry cream immediately after it is made to eliminate problems of bacterial multiplication at mid-range temperatures.

1. Combine the milk and half the sugar in a nonreactive saucepan. Whisk once and place over medium heat to come to a boil.

2. Meanwhile, whisk the yolks and salt in a bowl and whisk in the remaining sugar. Sift the flour over the yolks and mix in.

3. When the milk boils, whisk a third of the boiled milk into the egg mixture, whisking constantly. Return the milk to a boil, then pour the hot egg mixture back in in a stream, whisking constantly. Continue whisking until the cream thickens and comes to a boil. Remove from the heat and whisk in the vanilla. Before chilling the pastry cream, recheck the recipe in which it is used for other ingredients to be added before the pastry cream is chilled.

4. Pour the cream into a heatproof glass or stainless-steel bowl or pan. Press plastic wrap directly against the surface of the cream. Chill immediately.

STORAGE: Use the pastry cream by the end of the following day.

SUGAR S's

1 recipe Pâte à Choux (page 366)
Egg wash: 1 egg well beaten with a pinch of salt
1 cup coarse sugar or pearl sugar or coarsely
   crushed sugar cubes

*Two cookie sheets or jelly-roll pans covered with
parchment or foil*

ABOUT THIRTY 2- TO 3-INCH PASTRIES

These sugary little cakes are a popular French way of using *pâte à choux*. The paste is piped onto pans, then brushed with beaten egg and covered with coarse sugar or pearl sugar (see Sources of Supply for obtaining pearl sugar). The result is delightfully crunchy and not too sweet. And because the S's are not filled, not too rich. See variations at the end of the recipe for other ideas for unfilled *pâte à choux*.

1. Set a rack at the middle level of the oven and preheat to 400 degrees. (If two pans will not fit, side by side in the oven, set racks at the upper and lower thirds.)

2. Prepare the *pâte à choux*. Using a pastry bag fitted with a ¼-inch plain tube (Ateco #3), pipe the *pâte à choux* in 2- to 3-inch S shapes. Carefully brush with egg wash and sprinkle with the sugar.

3. Gently knock away the excess sugar by grasping the pan at the top, holding it with the pastry facing you, thumbs firmly against the paper, then quickly rapping the lower edge against the work surface.

4. Bake the pastries about 20 minutes, until they're well risen, crisp, and a deep golden color—some of the sugar on the surface will melt and caramelize.

5. Slide the papers off the pans onto racks to cool.

SERVING: Serve the S's as cookies—they are particularly good as an accompaniment to any soft, custardy dessert.

STORAGE: Keep the S's loosely covered at room temperature. For longer storage, wrap tightly in plastic and freeze. If they were frozen, reheat at 350 degrees for about 5 minutes and cool before serving.

HINT FOR SUCCESS: If you bake the S's on two different racks, change positions several times during the baking so that both pans bake evenly. If the bottom of your oven has a particularly strong heat, use an insulated cookie sheet or slide another pan under the pan in the lower third of the oven.

VARIATIONS

ALMOND PUFFS: Pipe small round *choux* with a ½-inch plain tube (Ateco #6). Egg-wash and sprinkle with sliced almonds, then confectioners' sugar. Bake as above.

SUGAR RINGS, ALMOND RINGS: Pipe 2- to 2½-inch rings, using a ¼-inch tube (Ateco #3). Finish with egg wash and coarse sugar, as with S's, or with almonds and confectioners' sugar, as with the Almond Puffs variation, above.

ITALIAN CREAM PUFFS *FROM* GROTTAMINARDA

(Bignè alla Grottese)

1 recipe Pâte à Choux (page 366)
1 recipe for 3 cups Pastry Cream (page 368)
Confectioners' sugar for dusting

One cookie sheet or jelly-roll pan covered with parchment or foil

TWELVE TO EIGHTEEN 2- TO 2½-INCH PUFFS

These are the subject of my Italian baking adventure, described on page 364. These plain cream puffs are easy to prepare and they deserve to be seen more frequently than they are—try them and I think you'll prepare them often.

1. Set a rack at the middle level of the oven and preheat to 400 degrees.

2. Prepare the *pâte à choux*. Using a pastry bag fitted with a ½-inch plain tube (Ateco #6), pipe twelve to eighteen 2- to 2½-inch-diameter puffs on the prepared pan.

3. Bake the puffs for about 20 minutes, then lower the temperature to 350 degrees and continue baking for 15 to 20 minutes longer, until the puffs are firm, well colored, and crisp. Cool the puffs on a rack.

4. While the puffs are baking, prepare the pastry cream filling.

5. Using a sharp serrated knife, cut across the cooled puffs horizontally, a third of the way from the top, then remove the tops and set aside. Using a pastry bag fitted with the same tube as you used to form the pastries, fill the bottoms with pastry cream. Extend the cream a little above the top. Dust the tops with confectioners' sugar, then replace over the pastry cream at an angle.

SERVING: The *bignè* make a good dessert or teatime pastry.

STORAGE: Unfilled baked *bignè* will keep loosely covered at room temperature for the entire day they are baked if you wish. After more than a day, they will lose some flavor and texture. For longer storage, wrap unfilled pastry tightly in plastic and freeze. If they were frozen, reheat at 350 degrees for about 5 minutes and cool before filling.

The filling may be made up to several days in advance and stored in the refrigerator. Fill the pastries no more than an hour or two before serving to prevent them from becoming soggy.

VARIATIONS

Fill the *bignè* with sweetened whipped cream instead of the pastry cream.

Fill the *bignè* with another flavor pastry cream or a filling of your choice, such as white chocolate filling (page 371) or lemon curd (page 220), mixed with an equal volume of whipped cream.

SNOWBALLS
(BOULES DE NEIGE)

1 recipe Pâte à Choux (page 366)

WHITE CHOCOLATE FILLING

12 ounces white chocolate

1 cup heavy cream

COATING

½ pound white chocolate, coarsely chopped and melted over a pan of hot water

FINISHING

½ pound white chocolate, finely grated into shavings

One cookie sheet or jelly-roll pan covered with parchment or foil

ABOUT TWENTY-FOUR 1-INCH PASTRIES

These are a great way to dress up humble cream puffs. The little puffs are filled with a white chocolate ganache similar to the center of a truffle. Then they are coated in melted white chocolate and rolled in white chocolate shavings—a real treat for lovers of white chocolate.

1. Set a rack at the middle level of the oven and preheat to 400 degrees.

2. Prepare the *pâte à choux*. Use a pastry bag fitted with a ½-inch plain tube (Ateco #6) to pipe about twenty-four 1-inch diameter puffs on the prepared pan.

3. Bake the puffs for about 15 minutes, then lower the temperature to 350 degrees and continue baking for 10 to 15 minutes longer, until the puffs are firm, well colored, and crisp. Cool the puffs on a rack.

4. While the puffs are baking, prepare the filling. Cut the 12 ounces white chocolate into small pieces and set aside. Bring the cream to a boil in a medium saucepan over low heat. Remove from the heat, add the chocolate pieces, and allow to stand for 3 minutes, then whisk smooth. Pour the cream into a heatproof glass or stainless-steel bowl or pan. Press plastic wrap directly against the surface of the cream. Refrigerate for about 1 hour, or until thickened, but not hard. If the filling becomes too firm, bring to room temperature, stirring and mashing occasionally with a rubber spatula, until of spreading consistency. Or stir over a pan of barely warm water to soften it.

5. To fill the *choux,* use a chopstick or the sharp point of a vegetable peeler to make a small hole in the bottom (flat side) of each. Spoon the filling into a pastry bag fitted with a ¼-inch plain tube (Ateco #3). Fill the *choux* and place them, flat side up, on a clean pan.

6. To coat the *choux,* place the pan with the filled *choux* on the work surface. Immediately to its right, place the bowl of melted white chocolate. To its right, place a 9 × 13-inch pan with the shaved white chocolate. Finally, to the right of the shavings, place a clean jelly-roll pan covered with parchment, wax paper, or foil.

(continued)

7. Cover the palm of your right hand with the melted chocolate by dipping it into the bowl. Pick up a *chou* with your left hand and drop it into the palm of your right hand. Roll it around until the pastry is covered with the chocolate. Drop the *chou* into the shavings, at the edge of the pan closest to the edge of the work surface. Use a clean fork (held in your left hand) to roll the *chou* away from you to the other end of the pan. This will coat it with the shaved chocolate. As the *choux* accumulate in the shavings, use your left hand to lift them onto the last empty pan. After all the *choux* are coated, refrigerate them to make sure the chocolate is set.

SERVING: Serve the snowballs as an after-dinner pastry. They would be perfect with coffee after a dessert bowl of fresh fruit.

STORAGE: The snowballs will keep well in the refrigerator for a day. The chocolate coating will seal them and prevent them from absorbing moisture in the refrigerator.

HINTS FOR SUCCESS: Avoid getting any of the filling into the melted chocolate or the moisture in the filling may cause the chocolate to seize and harden. Just dip the palm of your hand into the chocolate and it will remain in good condition.

If you take a long time to coat the *choux,* the chocolate may begin to set before you are finished. Reheat the water over which it melted and replace the bowl over the hot water; stir until the chocolate is melted and smooth.

VARIATIONS

Use sweetened coconut, toasted or untoasted, instead of the grated white chocolate.

Substitute milk or semisweet chocolate for the white chocolate.

COFFEE RUM ÉCLAIRS

1 recipe Pâte à Choux (page 366)

COFFEE PASTRY CREAM

1 recipe for 3 cups Pastry Cream (page 368)
1 tablespoon instant espresso coffee powder
    dissolved in 1 tablespoon water
2 tablespoons unsalted butter, softened

COFFEE ICING

1½ cups confectioners' sugar
2 tablespoons light corn syrup
1 tablespoon instant espresso coffee
1 tablespoon unsalted butter, softened

One cookie sheet or jelly-roll pan covered with parchment or foil

ABOUT TWELVE 4-INCH ÉCLAIRS

Although chocolate éclairs are the traditional popular favorite (instructions for preparing them and several other variations are given at the end of this recipe), I have always been partial to éclairs filled with coffee-flavored cream and covered with coffee icing. Remember, with these you can plan ahead. You can bake the éclair pastry and freeze it on one day, make the filling the next, then reheat, cool, fill, and ice them on the third day. Such a division of labor makes preparing a pastry with many steps, such as this one, easy.

1. Set a rack at the middle level of the oven and preheat to 400 degrees.

2. Prepare the *pâte à choux*. Use a pastry bag fitted with a ½-inch plain tube (Ateco #6) to pipe twelve 4-inch éclairs on the prepared pan.

3. Bake the éclairs for about 20 minutes, then lower the temperature to 350 degrees and continue baking for 10 to 15 minutes longer, until the éclairs are firm, well colored, and crisp. Cool the éclairs on a rack.

4. While the éclairs are baking, prepare the filling. As soon as the pastry cream comes off the heat, whisk in the dissolved coffee and butter. Pour the cream into a heatproof glass or stainless-steel bowl or pan. Press plastic wrap directly against the surface of the cream. Refrigerate immediately.

5. To fill the éclairs, use a chopstick or vegetable peeler to pierce a small hole at each end of the bottom (flat side) of each éclair.

6. Spoon the coffee pastry cream into a pastry bag fitted with a ¼-inch plain tube (Ateco #3) and fill the éclairs. Insert the tube into one of the holes on the bottom of the éclair and squeeze gently until the filling appears in the second hole. Place the éclairs, flat side up, on a clean pan covered with parchment or wax paper.

7. To make the icing, combine all the ingredients in a small, nonreactive saucepan. Place over low heat and stir constantly until the

icing is barely warm, about 100 degrees. Dip a spoon in the icing and let the excess drip off, to see how the icing will coat a surface. If the icing left on the spoon is thin and transparent, add ½ cup more confectioners' sugar and test again. If the icing is too thick, add 1 teaspoon water and test again. Adjust with confectioners' sugar or water until the icing is a good coating consistency.

8. To ice the éclairs, submerge them unpierced (top) ½ inch deep into the icing. Allow the excess icing to drip off by holding the éclair, icing side down, over the pan of icing for 10 to 15 seconds. Turn the éclair icing side up on the empty prepared pan. Repeat with the remaining éclairs, reheating the icing gently if it thickens too much.

9. Arrange the éclairs on a platter to serve.

SERVING: Éclairs make a good dessert or teatime pastry.

STORAGE: You can keep the baked pastry loosely covered at room temperature the entire day they are baked, if you wish. They will have the best flavor and texture if they are served on the day they are baked. For longer storage, wrap tightly in plastic and freeze—reheat at 350 degrees for about 5 minutes and cool before filling.

The filling may be made up to several days in advance and stored in the refrigerator. Fill the pastries no more than 30 minutes to an hour before you serve them so they won't become soggy.

VARIATIONS

Fill the éclairs with sweetened whipped cream instead of the filling, above.

Fill the éclairs with another flavor pastry cream or a filling of your choice, such as white chocolate filling (page 371), or lemon curd (page 220), mixed with whipped cream.

RASPBERRY SHORTCAKES

1 recipe Pâte à Choux (page 366)

RASPBERRY SAUCE

3 cups fresh raspberries, or two 10-ounce
    packages frozen raspberries
½ cup granulated sugar
1 tablespoon raspberry liqueur or framboise
    (raspberry eau-de-vie)

WHIPPED CREAM

1 cup ice-cold heavy cream
2 tablespoons granulated sugar
1 teaspoon vanilla extract

RASPBERRY FILLING

2 cups fresh raspberries

Confectioners' sugar for dusting

*One cookie sheet or jelly-roll pan covered with
parchment or foil*

EIGHT 3-INCH SHORTCAKES

This is a great plated dessert for a fancy dinner party because everything can be made in advance. Of course, the shortcake biscuits used here are really large cream puffs. They are much more delicate than the standard baking powder biscuit used for shortcakes.

See the Variation at the end of the recipe for substituting other fruit.

1. Set a rack at the middle level of the oven and preheat to 400 degrees.

2. Prepare the *pâte à choux.* Use a pastry bag fitted with a ½-inch plain tube (Ateco #6) to pipe about eight 3-inch puffs. Hold the bag an inch above the pan with the tip pointed straight down. As each puff is completed, release the pressure and twist the bag away to avoid leaving a point at the top of the puff. Crisscross the top of each puff with the back of the wet tines of a fork to press it down slightly.

3. Bake the puffs for about 20 minutes, then lower the temperature to 350 degrees and continue baking for 15 to 20 minutes longer, until the puffs are firm, well colored, and crisp. Cool the puffs on a rack.

4. While the puffs are baking, prepare the raspberry sauce. Bring the raspberries and sugar to a simmer in a medium nonreactive saucepan over low heat. Cook for about 10 minutes, until slightly thickened. Cool, puree in a food processor or blender, and press the puree through a strainer or food mill to remove the seeds. Add the raspberry liqueur or eau-de-vie and chill the sauce. (If the sauce seems thin after straining, cook again and reduce until it gets thick.)

5. To make the whipped cream, combine all the ingredients in a bowl and whip by hand or machine until the cream holds a soft peak. Cover and refrigerate the cream until needed. If necessary, rewhip the cream briefly by hand just before you use it.

(continued)

6. Just before you assemble the desserts, place the raspberries in a mixing bowl and fold in ⅓ cup of the raspberry sauce.

7. When you are ready, cover the dessert plates with the sauce. Cut a puff in half horizontally and place the bottom half in the center of the plate. Fill with the raspberries. Top the raspberries with a spoonful of whipped cream. Place the other half of the puff on top of the whipped cream. Dust the top with confectioners' sugar. Repeat with the other puffs. Serve immediately.

SERVING: Serve with a dessert wine such as a Sauternes or a French or California late-harvest Riesling.

STORAGE: Though the desserts themselves don't stand up well if prepared in advance, all the component parts may be made in advance. The sauce and puffs will keep several days in the refrigerator or several months in the freezer. Keep the sauce in a plastic container with an airtight cover. Keep the puffs in a plastic bag. Reheat the puffs in a single layer on a cookie sheet at 375 degrees for about 10 minutes, and cool before assembling the dessert.

Whipped cream may be prepared in the morning and refrigerated, tightly covered, then rewhipped according to the instructions in the recipe.

HINTS FOR SUCCESS: When you assemble the dessert, do the same step to each plate before doing the next. Cover all the plates with sauce, place the bottoms of the puffs on each plate. It will take less time and the desserts will be more uniform in appearance.

VARIATION

PEACH AND RASPBERRY SHORTCAKES: Substitute 4 or 5 yellow or white peaches, peeled and sliced, for the raspberries. Fold the raspberry sauce into the peaches as with the raspberries, above. Or use a combination of sliced peaches and whole raspberries, bound with the raspberry sauce.

POLKAS

PASTRY DOUGH FOR BASES

1¼ cups bleached all-purpose flour
2 tablespoons granulated sugar
¼ teaspoon salt
¼ teaspoon baking powder
6 tablespoons cold unsalted butter
1 large egg

1 recipe Pâte à Choux (page 366)

Egg wash: 1 egg well beaten with a pinch of salt

FRENCH CUSTARD FILLING

1 recipe for 2 cups Pastry Cream (page 368)

Confectioners' sugar for dusting

One large cookie sheet or jelly-roll pan covered with parchment or foil

ABOUT TWELVE 3-INCH PASTRIES

These are old-fashioned French pastries. The typical polka has a pastry cream filling, but it makes a versatile container for many types of fillings; see the Variations at the end of the recipe for other ideas. They are especially pretty when made into baskets, as in Strawberry Baskets, below.

My guess is that the name derives from that period in the mid-nineteenth century when there were many émigrés from eastern Europe in Paris, since there is also a small pastry called a mazurka—another Polish dance like the polka.

1. To make the dough, stir the dry ingredients together well in a mixing bowl. Rub in the butter (or pulse the dry ingredients and butter in a food processor) until the mixture is a fine meal. Add the egg and stir or pulse until the dough forms a ball. Knead the dough gently on a lightly floured work surface 5 or 6 times. Form the dough into a square, then wrap and refrigerate it while you prepare the *pâte à choux*.

2. Set a rack at the middle level of the oven and preheat to 400 degrees.

3. Remove the dough from the refrigerator and on a lightly floured surface, roll it into a 9 × 12-inch rectangle. Cut into twelve 3-inch circles and arrange them with about 2 inches of space on all sides on the pan. Pierce the dough several times with a fork and paint lightly with the egg wash.

4. Use a pastry bag fitted with a ¼-inch plain tube (Ateco #3) to pipe a border of the *pâte à choux* around the perimeter of each circle of dough.

5. Bake for 20 to 25 minutes, until the dough bases and *pâte à choux* are baked through and deep golden. Cool on the pan on a rack.

6. While the pastries are baking, make the filling. Scrape it into a small heatproof glass or stainless-steel bowl. Press plastic wrap against the surface of the cream and refrigerate until cold.

(continued)

7. To assemble the pastries, pipe or spoon the pastry cream into the wells of the pastries. Dust with confectioners' sugar just before serving.

SERVING: Polkas make a good dessert or teatime pastry.

STORAGE: You can keep the baked bases loosely covered at room temperature for the entire day they are baked, if you wish. They will have the best flavor and texture if they are served the day they are baked.

The filling may be made up to several days in advance and stored airtight in the refrigerator. Fill the pastries no more than 30 minutes before you serve them so they don't become soggy.

VARIATIONS

Place a spoonful of jam or preserves on the bottom of the bases before adding the pastry cream.

Fill the bases with sweetened whipped cream and decorate with a half-strawberry or a few raspberries, if you wish.

Fill the bases with another flavor pastry cream or a filling of your choice, such as chocolate filling (page 323), or even lemon curd (page 220).

STRAWBERRY BASKETS: When you pipe the *pâte à choux* around the pastry, set aside ¼ cup. Put the reserved dough into a pastry bag fitted with a ¼-inch plain tube, the same as you used for the bases. On a paper or foil-lined pan, pipe 12 U shapes about 3 inches tall and about 2 inches wide. Bake with the bases. Fill the bases with 1 pint strawberries, rinsed, hulled, sliced, and macerated in 2 tablespoons sugar and a tablespoon of kirsch. Cover the berries with a spoonful or rosette of sweetened whipped cream. Insert U's as basket handles, pressing them well into the whipped cream. Dust lightly with confectioners' sugar before serving.

SAVORY PUFF PASTRIES

Not only are puff pastries the most delicate of all small, savory pastries, they are practical, too. They lend themselves well to advance preparation. They may be frozen formed and unbaked, and baked on the day they are served. Some of the pastries here, such as the cheese straws and cheese palmiers, may be frozen after they are baked and then reheated before serving.

CHEESE STRAWS

1 recipe Quickest Puff Pastry (page 345)
Egg wash: 1 egg well beaten with a pinch of salt
1 cup finely grated Parmigiano-Reggiano
½ teaspoon salt
1 tablespoon sweet Hungarian paprika

Two jelly-roll pans lined with parchment paper or foil

SIXTY TO SEVENTY-TWO 6-INCH STRAWS

Called *paillettes* (little straws) in French, these straws used to be the classic accompaniment to clear soups, such as consommé. Nowadays, clear soups have all but disappeared from menus, even in France, and the cheese straw has found a new place as an accompaniment to cocktails. With drinks before dinner, it is enough to serve a few cheese straws, a bowl of olives, and maybe another of toasted almonds or pecans.

1. On a floured surface roll the chilled pastry dough into a 12 × 18-inch rectangle. Paint the dough with the egg wash. Cover the right half of the dough (a 9 × 12-inch rectangle) with the cheese, salt, and paprika. Fold the left side of the dough over to cover the cheese, then press with a rolling pin to make the layers of dough stick together. Slide onto a cookie sheet and refrigerate for 10 minutes.

2. Preheat the oven to 375 degrees.

3. Remove the dough from the refrigerator and roll it out again into a 12 × 18-inch rectangle. Using a pizza wheel, cut the dough into 36 strips, each ½ × 12 inches. Twist each into a corkscrew shape and place on the pan, press the ends of the straws so they stick to the sides of the pan.

4. Bake the straws for about 20 minutes, until they are pale golden and beginning to color. Remove the pan from the oven and immediately trim the straw ends, then cut the straws in half, to make 6-inch lengths.

(continued)

SERVING: Serve the straws at room temperature, with drinks, soup, or even with salad.

STORAGE: Keep leftover straws in a tightly sealed tin or plastic container.

VARIATION

CARAWAY SALT STICKS: Substitute 1 tablespoon kosher salt and 2 tablespoons caraway seeds for the cheese, salt, and paprika, above.

PARMESAN AND PAPRIKA PALMIERS

½ batch Quickest Puff Pastry (page 345)
Egg wash: 1 egg well beaten with a pinch of salt
1 cup grated Parmesan cheese
½ teaspoon salt
1 tablespoon sweet Hungarian paprika

Two cookie sheets or jelly-roll pans lined with parchment or foil

ABOUT TWENTY-FOUR 3-INCH PALMIERS

The paprika between the layers of dough makes these pungent pastries look as attractive as they taste.

1. On a floured surface, roll the puff pastry dough to a 9 × 12-inch rectangle. Paint the dough with the egg wash.

2. Sprinkle evenly with the cheese, salt, and paprika.

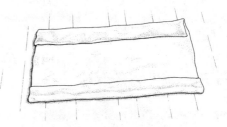

From the top and bottom, fold the edges of the dough about one third of the way toward the middle.

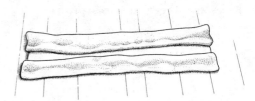

Fold over the edges again toward the middle.

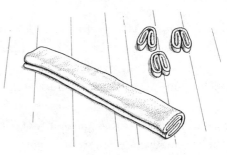

Fold over again at the center. Cut the short edge to make palmiers.

3. Fold the outer 1½ inches of each long end in toward the center, as in the illustration on page 380. Repeat so the folds meet at the center, then fold in half at the center line. Wrap in plastic and chill until firm.

4. Set racks at the upper and lower thirds of the oven and preheat the oven to 350 degrees.

5. Cut the dough into ½-inch slices and arrange, cut sides up and down, on the prepared pans, leaving about 2 inches of space around each palmier on all sides.

6. Bake for about 20 minutes, until the palmiers are golden and crisp. Cool on the pans and serve at room temperature or reheated.

SERVING: Serve the palmiers at room temperature, with drinks, soup, or even with salad.

STORAGE: Keep leftover palmiers in a tightly sealed tin or plastic container.

MOZZARELLA AND PROSCIUTTO TURNOVERS

½ batch Quickest Puff Pastry (page 345)
Egg wash: 1 egg well beaten with a pinch of salt
¼ cup shredded mozzarella
¼ cup minced prosciutto
2 tablespoons chopped flat-leaf parsley
Freshly ground black pepper

Two cookie sheets lined with parchment

ABOUT 30 TURNOVERS

These turnovers are a perfect fancy little hors d'oeuvre and can be made ahead. I have frozen these successfully for up to a week before baking them. If you decide to freeze them, don't brush the outside with egg wash until just before you bake them; the egg wash becomes freezer-burned very easily.

1. Roll the pastry out into a 12 × 18-inch rectangle. Slide onto a pan and refrigerate for about 1 hour, until the dough is firm and rested.

2. Use a floured, round, 2½-inch cutter to cut out the dough. Arrange the cut dough on the prepared pans, about 1 inch apart.

3. In a bowl, stir together the cheese, ham, parsley, and pepper.

4. Brush the egg wash lightly on the dough and arrange the filling over half of each circle of dough.

5. Fold the empty side of the dough over the filling and seal the edges well with your fingertips. Seal again by pressing around the rim with the back of the tines of a fork. Dip the fork in flour so it doesn't stick. Arrange the turnovers about 1 inch apart on the prepared pan. Refrigerate the turnovers loosely covered with plastic wrap until 30 minutes before serving.

6. Set a rack in the upper third of the oven and preheat to 375 degrees. Egg-wash the tops of the turnovers and bake for about 20 minutes, until they're well colored and crisp.

7. Cool the pastries on the pans and reheat to serve.

SERVING: Reheat the turnovers at 350 degrees for about 10 minutes to serve them warm.

STORAGE: Refrigerate or freeze leftovers and reheat before serving.

HINT FOR SUCCESS: Make sure the edges are well sealed or the turnovers will open while they are baking.

VARIATIONS

Substitute cooked ham or another cured meat for the prosciutto.

Any firm cheese may be substituted for the mozzarella.

9
SWEET YEAST-RISEN BREADS & PASTRIES

Yeast-risen desserts and pastries are among the most popular of all baked goods. They probably originated in eastern Europe, which would explain why the French identify the art of preparing them as *Viennoiserie* (Viennese goods) as distinct from *boulangerie* or "bread making." These delicacies range from such breakfast items as brioches, croissants, and Danish pastries, through the holiday treats such as panettone, to fancy little dessert babas and savarins. Although each has its own flavor and texture, they share a common origin as enriched and sometimes manipulated bread dough.

The enrichments involve taking the simple bread dough (flour, water, yeast, and salt) and adding such rich ingredients as butter, eggs, and sugar. Manipulation occurs when further processes, such as rolling and folding the dough to create layers, are done.

Croissant dough, in which bread and puff pastry meet head-on, is used to make the most delicate of all yeast-risen pastries. A dough that is very much like a simple bread dough is allowed to rise in the refrigerator; then the dough has softened butter spread on it and it is rolled and folded to make the layer of butter thinner and to increase the amount of layers in the dough, causing the croissants to have their characteristic flakiness after baking.

Brioche dough is made by adding butter, sugar, and eggs to enrich, sweeten, and tenderize the bread dough. Danish pastry combines both enrichment and manipulation, since it is made from a rich briochelike dough, into which butter is rolled and folded, as for croissant dough.

In other examples of this type of pastry, the baba and the panettone, for instance, only the yeast is a reminder that they were once prepared from leftover bread dough.

BRIOCHES

Brioche, often associated with French baking, is really Viennese in origin. It found its way to France some time between 1775 and 1825. Marie Antoinette's famous remark, "Let them eat cake," is variously stated in French as "Let them eat the bread stuck to the inside of the oven," or "Let them eat brioche." The pastry may or may not have appeared in France by then, but the ill-fated monarch was an Austrian Hapsburg, and so may have been familiar with the specialty of her homeland. During the last half of the nineteenth century, the brioche became the rage in France. It made the reputations and fortunes of the great pastry shops of Paris, including the now-defunct Maison Felix.

Since that time, brioches of all types appear throughout the French repertoire. Breakfast may begin with a *brioche à tête*—a small cake with a tiny spherical "head" baked in a flared, fluted pan—or any one of a number of rolls dusted with flour or coarse sugar granules before baking.

Brioche dough is also used to make *pains aux raisins*—little buns for which a sheet of dough is spread with an almond filling, sprinkled with raisins, and sliced before baking. This last variation is the closest the French get to what we would recognize as a Danish pastry.

Loaves, braids, and crowns (like giant doughnut shapes) are usually reserved for the *goûter,* or French afternoon tea, though we Americans would be most likely to serve them for breakfast or brunch.

Although it takes a long time to make brioche dough, it does not require a lot of work or complicated procedures. You can also make the dough one day and form and bake the brioche, whatever type you choose, on the next day.

Many of the recipes for rich yeast doughs in this chapter call for making a sponge using the yeast, all or some of the liquid, and some of the flour in the recipe. This then rises quickly, so the yeast has an opportunity to multiply freely before it encounters such rich ingredients as butter and eggs, or refined sugar, all of which slow down its growth and lengthen the rising time.

Using a sponge to leaven a yeast dough is probably eastern European in origin. Many doughs from this region are made in this manner. An eastern European origin is also suggested by the fact that in French the sponge is called a *poolish* or *pouliche,* probably a corruption of *polnish,* the German word for Polish.

If you wish to prepare other yeast dough recipes with this method, warm ½ cup of the liquid from the recipe and dissolve the yeast in it. Add ¾ cup of the flour and stir it in smoothly. Cover and allow to rise for 30 minutes. Of course, you must remember to subtract the amounts of liquid and flour when you incorporate the remaining amounts with the sponge into the dough.

My method for mixing the ingredients in brioche dough differs from the traditional French procedure in which the butter is added last. I have found that this can cause the elastic structure of the dough to break down and get quite messy if you are mixing the dough by hand. I, therefore, mix the butter, sugar, salt, eggs, and flour as for a cake batter, and add the sponge last. This makes the dough fast and easy to mix, whether you do it by hand or with a machine. (If you choose to mix the dough by machine, use a heavy-duty mixer with the paddle attachment.)

◆ BRIOCHE DOUGH

SPONGE

1 cup milk

5 teaspoons (2 envelopes) active dry yeast

1½ cups unbleached all-purpose flour

DOUGH

12 tablespoons (1½ sticks) unsalted butter, softened

6 tablespoons sugar

1 teaspoon salt

3 large eggs plus 1 large egg yolk

2¼ cups unbleached all-purpose flour

ABOUT 2½ POUNDS DOUGH, ENOUGH TO MAKE TWO OF ANY OF THE BRIOCHE RECIPES THAT FOLLOW

1. To make the sponge, in a small saucepan over low heat, heat the milk until it feels just warm, about 110 degrees. Pour the milk into a small bowl. Whisk in the yeast, then stir in the flour. Cover the bowl with plastic wrap and set aside at room temperature for about 30 minutes, until the sponge is well risen. Make sure, however, that it doesn't take you more than 30 minutes to make the dough

because the sponge must be incorporated into the dough as soon as it is fully risen. If the sponge rises too long it can develop a sour taste.

2. To mix the dough by hand, place the butter in a large mixing bowl and beat it with a heavy wooden spoon until it is soft and light. Beat in the sugar and salt and one of the eggs. Continue beating until smooth. Beat in a third of the flour until it is absorbed. Beat in another egg, then another third of the flour. Finally, beat in the remaining egg and the yolk, and after they are absorbed, beat in the remaining flour. Add the sponge, scraping it from its bowl with a rubber spatula, and continue beating until the dough is smooth and elastic and a uniform color, about 5 minutes.

To mix the dough by machine, use a heavy-duty mixer fitted with the paddle attachment on medium speed, and follow the same procedure as for hand mixing, above. After adding the sponge, beat the dough for about 2 minutes.

3. Cover the bowl with plastic wrap and allow the dough to rise until it doubles in bulk, up to 1 hour. If you have mixed the dough by hand, punch down the dough 2 or 3 times while it is rising to make it more smooth and elastic.

4. Butter a 4-quart mixing bowl and turn the risen dough into it. Press the dough well to deflate it and turn it upside down so that the top is now buttered. Cover the bowl tightly with plastic wrap and refrigerate. The dough will continue to rise in the refrigerator until the butter solidifies again, 2 to 3 hours.

5. Remove the dough from the refrigerator and turn it out onto a floured work surface. Press well to deflate the dough and shape it into a 6-inch square, about 2 inches thick. Use the dough immediately for one of the recipes that follow, or refrigerate it.

STORAGE: The dough can be refrigerated up to 24 hours before using it.

If you choose to keep the dough in the refrigerator for any length of time, be sure that it is well wrapped in plastic to avoid its forming a crust. I usually slide the wrapped dough into a large plastic bag and close the bag by folding the excess under before replacing on the refrigerator shelf.

HINTS FOR SUCCESS: Be careful not to heat the milk beyond 110 degrees before adding the yeast, or the yeast will die.

Remember that the sponge must be incorporated as soon as it is fully risen.

Check the dough occasionally after refrigerating it the first time. Deflate the dough if it is getting too close to the top of the bowl and refrigerate until it is cold and firm.

EASY FOOD PROCESSOR BRIOCHE LOAF

½ **cup milk**

2½ **teaspoons (1 envelope) active dry yeast**

2¼ **cups unbleached all-purpose flour**

6 **tablespoons unsalted butter**

3 **tablespoons sugar**

½ **teaspoon salt**

2 **large eggs**

One 8½ × 4½ × 2¾-inch loaf pan, buttered, bottom lined with a piece of buttered wax paper or parchment

ONE 8½-INCH-LONG LOAF, 6 TO 8 SERVINGS

This relatively quick (about 20 minutes of preparation, 90 minutes for rising and baking) brioche loaf can be made even more efficiently if you prepare the dough in the evening, allow the loaf to rise in the refrigerator, and bake the loaf the next morning.

If you mix the dough and place it in a bowl to rise instead of in a loaf pan, you may deflate and chill the dough and use it in any of the recipes calling for a half-batch of the full-process brioche dough (beginning on page 391).

1. In a small saucepan over low heat, heat the milk until it is just warm, about 110 degrees. Remove from the heat and pour into a small bowl. Whisk in the yeast, then stir in 1 cup of the flour. Cover the bowl with plastic wrap and set aside at room temperature while preparing the other ingredients. The sponge may even begin to rise slightly before you add it to the dough.

2. Cut the butter into 6 or 8 pieces and combine with the sugar and salt in the work bowl of a food processor, fitted with the metal blade. Pulse at 1-second intervals until the mixture is soft and smooth, scraping the inside of the bowl several times to ensure even mixing. Add the eggs, one at a time, and process until smooth. If the mixture appears curdled, continue to process for about 1 minute longer, until it looks smoother. (It may remain somewhat curdled in appearance.) Add the remaining 1¼ cups of flour, then scrape the milk-yeast-flour mixture from its bowl with a rubber spatula. Pulse at 1-second intervals until the ingredients form a soft, smooth dough. Then process continuously for 15 seconds.

3. Remove the work bowl from the base and remove the blade. Turn the dough out onto a generously floured work surface and fold it over on itself several times to make it more elastic. Press the dough into a rough rectangle, about 9 × 5 inches. Fold each side about 1 inch in toward the center and press firmly to seal. Then starting at the top—a short side—of the rectangle, fold the top half of dough toward the middle. Fold the bottom of the dough up past the seam and pinch to seal. Place the dough in the prepared pan, seam side down. Press the top of the dough firmly with the palm of your hand so it flattens and fills the pan evenly. Cover the pan with a piece of buttered plastic wrap or a towel and allow the dough to rise to about 1 inch above the rim of the pan, about 1 hour.

4. About 40 to 45 minutes after placing the dough in the pan to rise, set a rack in the middle level of the oven and preheat to 350 degrees.

5. Using the corner of a razor blade or the point of a sharp knife held at a 90 degree angle to the top of the loaf, cut a slash from about 1 inch before the end of the loaf down the middle of the top, to 1 inch before the end. Bake the loaf for about 40 minutes, until it is well risen and a deep golden color.

6. Place the pan on a rack to cool for about 5 minutes. Then turn the loaf out of the pan and let it finish cooling on its side on the rack to prevent the loaf from compressing as it cools.

SERVING: Serve in thin slices with jam or preserves but no butter. Stale brioche makes excellent toast or French toast.

STORAGE: Use immediately or cool completely, wrap tightly in plastic wrap, and refrigerate or freeze. Bring to room temperature, or reheat and cool before serving.

HINT FOR SUCCESS: Be careful not to heat the milk beyond 110 degrees before adding the yeast, or the yeast will die.

VARIATIONS

Scatter ½ cup dark or golden raisins, currants, chopped toasted nuts, or a combination of raisins and nuts onto the dough after you transfer it to the floured work surface. Continue to fold the dough over on itself until the raisins and/or nuts are evenly distributed throughout the dough. Shape the dough as above.

BRIOCHE ROLLS
(PETITS PAINS BRIOCHÉS)

½ recipe Brioche Dough (page 387), or a full
   recipe of Easy Food Processor Brioche Loaf
   dough (page 389), risen in a bowl, deflated,
   and chilled

Egg wash: 1 egg well beaten with a pinch of salt

*Two 10½ × 15½-inch jelly-roll pans or 12 × 15-
inch cookie sheets lined with parchment or buttered
wax paper*

ABOUT TWELVE 4-INCH-LONG ROLLS

These plain, oval brioches make an excellent breakfast or brunch bread. The variation that follows the recipe is for an amusingly shaped sweet loaf topped with a wide ribbon of sugar.

1. On a lightly floured surface, press the half batch of brioche dough into an 8-inch square. With a knife or bench scraper, cut the square into four 2 × 8-inch rectangles. First mark, then cut each rectangle the long way into 3 equal pieces, making 12 pieces of dough in all.

2. One at a time, round the pieces of dough into even spheres: place a piece of dough on an unfloured part of the work surface and cup your hand over the piece of dough. The top of the dough should touch the palm of your hand. Pressing gently on the dough, move your hand in a circle, rotating the dough under your hand, as in the illustration on page 85. As the pieces of dough are rounded, arrange them on the work surface. Cover the rolls with a towel and allow them to rest for 5 minutes.

3. To finish the rolls, go back and forth over each with the palm of your hand to elongate it slightly. Then, with both palms, go back and forth over the short ends to point the ends slightly. As the rolls are finished, place them, one at a time, 2 inches apart on the work surface.

4. Carefully brush each roll with the egg wash. Arrange the rolls on the pans, leaving plenty of room between them to allow them to expand during rising and baking. Cover with buttered plastic wrap. Allow the rolls to rise until doubled in bulk, up to 1 hour.

5. About 40 minutes after the rolls have been put to rise, set racks in the lower and upper thirds of the oven and preheat to 375 degrees.

6. Bake the rolls for about 20 minutes, or until they are well risen and a deep golden color. Test by lifting one from the pan; if it feels light for its size, it is baked through.

7. Cool the rolls on a rack.

STORAGE: Keep loosely covered at room temperature if you are serving them within a few hours. For longer storage, refrigerate or freeze, tightly wrapped in plastic wrap. Warm the rolls at 375 degrees for 7 or 8 minutes before serving.

SERVING: Serve the rolls for breakfast, brunch, or tea with jam or preserves, but no butter.

HINTS FOR SUCCESS: After dipping the brush in the egg wash, draw it against the rim of the bowl to remove excess wash, to avoid having the egg wash puddle under the rolls.

To ensure even baking, move the bottom pan to the upper rack and vice versa at least once during baking.

VARIATIONS

To make a single loaf from the rolls, arrange them in a row, long sides just touching, on a pan covered with parchment or buttered foil. Carefully spoon ¼ cup granulated sugar down the middle of the loaf in a 1-inch-wide strip. Allow to rise, and bake as for the rolls, above.

BRIOCHES AU SUCRE: Leave the rolls round; after they have risen, brush them with egg wash and sprinkle with pearl sugar or crushed sugar cubes.

BRIOCHE ROLLS WITH LITTLE "HEADS"
(BRIOCHES À TÊTE)

½ recipe Brioche Dough (page 387) or 1 recipe Easy Food Processor Brioche Loaf dough (page 389), risen in a bowl, deflated, and chilled

Egg wash: 1 egg well beaten with a pinch of salt

20 fluted brioche pans, about 2½ inches in diameter at the top and 1¼ inches deep, buttered

One 10½ × 15½-inch jelly-roll pan or a 12 × 15-inch cookie sheet

ABOUT 20 *BRIOCHES À TÊTE*, **DEPENDING ON THE SIZE OF THE MOLDS**

The *brioche à tête* is the classic brioche shape. Each roll baked in a flared, fluted pan is crowned with a small, spherical head or topknot. The little pans are not difficult to find in department and kitchenware stores. They may also be ordered by mail (see Sources of Supply). The ones I use are about 2½ inches in diameter and 1¼ inches deep. Unfortunately, sizes are not standardized and the molds you purchase may have different dimensions.

Use this simple rule to determine the correct amount of dough for a given size mold: the dough before shaping should fill the mold by no more than two thirds so it can expand during rising and baking. It requires some practice to shape brioches—do not be discouraged if in your first batch of *brioches à tête* the heads lean a bit to one side or another.

1. Arrange the brioche pans so they are 1½ inches apart on the jelly-roll pan or cookie sheet.

2. On a lightly floured surface, use your hands to press out the dough into an 8 × 10-inch rectangle. With a knife or bench scraper, cut the dough into four 2 × 10-inch pieces. First mark, then cut each piece into five 2-inch squares, making 20 pieces of dough in all.

3. One at a time round the pieces of dough into even spheres: place a piece of dough on an unfloured part of the work surface and cup your hand over the piece of dough. The top of the dough should touch the palm of your hand. Pressing gently on the dough, move your hand in a circle, rotating the piece of dough under your palm, as in the illustration on page 85. As the pieces of dough are rounded, arrange them on the work surface.

4. To form the heads, place a rounded piece of dough on its side. Place the side of your hand a third of the way over down the former top (rounded side) and press. Roll the side of your hand back and forth once to form the head. Be careful not to sever it at the neck. See the illustration. Stand the brioche upright again, head on top, and use both index fingers to press down through to the bottom of the piece of dough, first on one side of the head, then on the other. Make 4 indentations in all, as in the illustration. Place each formed *brioche à tête* in a pan and press down the area around the head well.

5. Carefully brush each brioche with the egg wash. Make sure none of the egg wash touches the inside surface of the pan; it might cause the brioche to stick. Cover with buttered plastic wrap.

(continued)

To form the heads, place a rounded piece of dough on its side. Place the side of your hand one third of the way down from the former top (rounded side) and press. Roll the side of your hand back and forth once to form the head. Be careful not to sever it at the neck.

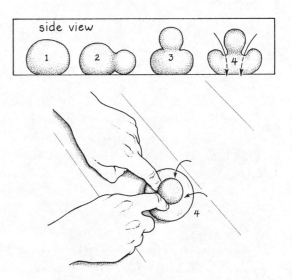

Stand the brioche upright again, head on top, and use both index fingers to press down to the bottom of the piece of dough, first on one side of the head, then on the other. Make four indentations in all.

6. Allow the brioches to rise until doubled in bulk, up to 1 hour.

7. About 40 minutes after the rolls have been put to rise, set racks in the lower and upper thirds of the oven and preheat to 375 degrees.

8. Bake the brioches for about 20 minutes, until they are well risen and a deep golden color. Test by lifting one from the pan. If it feels light for its size, it is baked through.

9. Cool for 5 minutes in the pans, then lift the brioches from the pans to a rack to cool.

SERVING: Serve the rolls for breakfast, brunch, or tea with jam or preserves, but no butter.

STORAGE: Keep the rolls loosely covered at room temperature if you are serving them within a few hours. For longer storage, freeze, tightly wrapped in plastic in a single layer so you don't dislodge the heads. Warm the rolls at 375 degrees for 7 or 8 minutes before serving, and serve warm or cooled.

HINT FOR SUCCESS: After dipping the brush in the egg wash, draw it against the rim of the bowl to remove any excess and to prevent the egg wash from puddling against the sides of the pans and under the rolls.

USING RAISINS AND CANDIED FRUIT

Many recipes for yeast-risen specialties call for dark or golden raisins, currants, or candied fruit. I like to blanch (bring to a single boil and drain) all these fruits before using them. Dried fruit can become hard and too dry, especially if you have had it on hand for several months before using it. Candied fruit sometimes has a clinging sticky syrup, or may have a slightly bitter flavor if it has not been sufficiently blanched during the manufacturing process.

Place raisins, currants, or candied fruit in a saucepan and cover with cold water. Bring to a boil over medium heat and drain. Arrange the blanched fruit in one layer on paper towels or a clean kitchen towel and allow to drain while you prepare the rest of the recipe.

If you wish to keep a supply of preplumped rum- or brandy-soaked raisins or currants on hand, blanch and drain them as above, then pack them fairly tightly into a glass jar with a tight-fitting lid, such as a canning jar. Pour on dark rum or brandy, close the jar, and refrigerate it for up to several months.

Try the same procedure with pitted, quartered prunes, but soak them in Armagnac after blanching them. Always blanch dried or candied fruit before soaking it in liquor. Blanching restores enough moisture so that the fruit will not soak up too much liquor and have a strong alcohol taste.

SWISS ALMOND AND RAISIN FILLED BRIOCHE CAKE
(BRIOCHE SUISSE)

1 recipe Brioche Dough (page 387)

ALMOND FILLING

1½ cups (about 6 ounces) whole blanched almonds

¾ cup granulated sugar

1 teaspoon almond extract

4 large egg whites (½ cup)

1 teaspoon grated lemon zest

¾ cup seedless raspberry or strained apricot preserves

½ cup raisins or currants

Confectioners' sugar for dusting

One 12-inch-diameter × 2-inch-deep cake pan, buttered, bottom lined with parchment or buttered wax paper cut to fit

ONE 12-INCH CAKE, 8 TO 10 SERVINGS

This cake, popular in Switzerland and France, is made by lining a pan with brioche dough and filling it with spirals of more brioche dough spread with an almond filling. Though the traditional Swiss recipe calls for scattering raisins on the almond filling, I prefer to spread it with some colorful raspberry preserves which also give a sharp flavor contrast. If you wish, you may substitute 12 ounces of canned almond paste for the almonds, sugar, and almond extract in the filling.

1. Divide the brioche dough unevenly into two pieces, one two thirds of the dough and the other one third. Lightly flour the work surface and the dough and roll the smaller piece into an 18-inch circle. Fold the dough into quarters, and transfer to the prepared pan, putting the point in the center. Unfold the dough, pressing it well into the bottom and side of the pan. Let the excess dough hang over the top edge. Cover loosely with plastic wrap and refrigerate while you continue the preparation.

2. Roll the remaining dough into an 8 × 18-inch rectangle. Fold the dough in half the long way, slide the 4 × 18-inch dough onto a cookie sheet, cover with plastic wrap, and refrigerate while you prepare the filling.

3. To make the filling, place the almonds in a saucepan and cover them with water. Bring to a boil over medium heat. As soon as they come to a boil, drain the almonds and place them in the work bowl of a food processor. Process the almonds until they are reduced to a paste. Add the sugar and pulse several times to mix. Add all the remaining filling ingredients.

4. Remove the rectangle of dough from the refrigerator and unfold it on the work surface. Spread the dough evenly with the filling, using a small offset metal spatula. Stir the preserves to soften them, then spread them evenly over the filling with a spatula. Sprinkle with the raisins.

(continued)

5. Begin at one of the long ends and roll the filling up in the dough to form a roll about 18 inches long. If the dough has softened during the spreading and rolling, cut the roll in half, slide both pieces onto a pan and refrigerate until firm, about 15 minutes. Mark the top of the roll at 1½-inch intervals, then cut through with a sharp, thin knife, making 12 separate rolls. Or wrap a piece of thin string around the roll at each mark and pull the ends of the string across each other to slice the roll. As you cut the rolled dough, arrange the pieces on the work surface. After they are all cut, adjust the shape from the side, if necessary, so that each piece is circular.

6. Remove the dough-lined pan from the refrigerator and pierce the surface of the dough all over with a fork at 1-inch intervals. Arrange the rolls, cut side up, in the dough-lined pan. Place 3 rolls in the center, and 9 around them, positioning the 9 midway between the 3 in the center and the side of the pan. Cover the pan with buttered plastic wrap and allow the dough to rise until the spaces between the rolls are filled in, up to 1 hour.

7. About 40 minutes after putting the cake to rise, set a rack at the middle level of the oven and preheat to 350 degrees.

8. Immediately before baking, use the point of a small knife to trim away the excess dough at the top edge of the pan just below the inside edge of the pan. Bake the cake for about 45 minutes, until the dough is firm and baked through and a deep golden color.

9. Place the pan on a rack until cool enough to handle, then cover with a plate and invert onto the plate. Remove the pan and paper and replace with a cooling rack. Invert the cake onto the rack and remove the plate. Just before serving dust the cake with confectioners' sugar.

SERVING: Serve the cake for breakfast or brunch, cutting it into wedges.

STORAGE: Keep loosely covered at room temperature if serving the cake within a few hours. If not, wrap tightly in plastic wrap and refrigerate or freeze. Reheat at 350 degrees for about 10 minutes, and serve warm or at room temperature.

HINT FOR SUCCESS: Don't skimp on the refrigerator time needed to firm the dough. It makes the process of handling this soft dough much easier.

VARIATIONS

Scatter 4 ounces semisweet or bittersweet chocolate, finely cut, on the preserves before rolling up the dough.

Instead of the raspberry preserves, bring 1 cup raisins or currants to a boil, drain, and cool, then scatter them on the almond mixture.

BRIOCHE BEESTING CAKE
(NID D'ABEILLES/ BIENENSTICH)

½ recipe Brioche Dough (page 387)

ALMOND BRITTLE TOPPING

6 tablespoons unsalted butter
¼ cup honey
¼ cup sugar
1 cup (about 4 ounces) sliced blanched almonds

PASTRY CREAM FILLING

1 cup milk
¼ cup sugar
2 tablespoons cornstarch
4 large egg yolks
2 teaspoons vanilla extract
1 tablespoon kirsch (optional)
8 tablespoons (1 stick) unsalted butter, softened

One 10-inch-diameter × 2-inch-deep cake pan, or one 9- or 10-inch-diameter × 3-inch-deep springform pan, buttered, bottom lined with parchment or buttered wax paper cut to fit.

ONE 10-INCH CAKE, 10 TO 12 SERVINGS

The French call this cake "Bee's Nest" and the Swiss, Austrians, and Germans call it "Bee's Sting." The risen, unbaked dough is covered with a mixture of almonds, honey, sugar, and butter, which, when it is baked, caramelizes to a rich color and crunchy texture. After the cake cools, it is split and filled with a buttery pastry cream. This is a perfect brunch dish; it's a bit too rich for breakfast and too substantial to be the dessert in any but the lightest meal.

1. To form the dough, fold it over on itself several times on a lightly floured surface and form it into a sphere, rounding it so that the outside skin of the dough is smooth and seamless. Cover the rounded piece of dough with a towel and allow to rest for 5 minutes. Then press the dough evenly into the prepared pan and pierce it at 1-inch intervals with a fork. Cover the pan with a towel and allow the dough to rise at room temperature until the dough is half again larger in bulk, about 30 minutes. Uncover the dough and refrigerate it for 20 minutes.

2. Immediately after you refrigerate the dough, set a rack at the middle level of the oven and preheat to 350 degrees.

3. To make the topping, combine all the ingredients except the almonds in a small saucepan. Place the pan over low heat and bring the mixture to a boil, stirring constantly. Stir in the almonds, then remove the pan from the heat, and pour the topping into a buttered, heatproof bowl and cool it to room temperature.

4. After the dough has chilled for 20 minutes, remove it from the refrigerator and, using the back of a spoon or a small offset metal spatula, spread the almond topping evenly. Bake for about 30 minutes, until the topping is well caramelized and the dough is firm and baked through.

(continued)

5. Remove the pan to a rack to cool for 10 minutes, then loosen the topping from the sides of the pan by inserting the point of a small sharp knife ½ inch down between the topping and the side of the pan. Unmold the cake, remove the paper, and cool it right side up on a rack.

6. While the cake is baking, prepare the filling: combine ¾ cup of the milk and the sugar in a nonreactive saucepan over low heat. Whisk once to mix in the sugar and bring to a boil. Meanwhile, whisk the remaining milk and the cornstarch thoroughly in a small mixing bowl and whisk in the yolks. Whisk in the boiled milk in a stream and return the mixture to the pan. Replace the pan over low heat and whisk constantly as the cream thickens and comes to a boil, about 2 minutes. Allow the cream to boil, whisking constantly for about 30 seconds. Remove from the heat and whisk in the vanilla and kirsch if used.

7. Divide the butter into 8 pieces and whisk into the cream one piece at a time. Pour the cream into a bowl, scrape the sides of the bowl clean with a rubber spatula, and press plastic wrap against the surface of the cream to prevent a skin from forming. Refrigerate the cream until cold, about 2 hours.

8. Remove the cream from the refrigerator and whisk by hand until smooth, about 10 seconds. To fill the cake, slice it in half horizontally using a sharp serrated knife. Place the bottom layer on a platter and, using a small offset metal spatula, spread the layer evenly with the filling. Cut the top of the cake into 10 or 12 wedges and rearrange them on top of the cake, fitting them closely together. (Precutting the top eliminates pressure when the cake is cut and prevents the filling from oozing out.)

SERVING: Serve the cake unadorned or with a few berries on the side.

STORAGE: Keep the cake at a cool room temperature for no more than a few hours before it is served. Cover leftovers with plastic wrap and refrigerate. Serve leftovers within 36 to 48 hours of filling the cake.

HINTS FOR SUCCESS: After pressing the dough into the pan, be sure to pierce it through or the cake may rise unevenly during baking.

Check the cake several times while it is baking: if the top is not well caramelized after 20 minutes, move the pan to a rack at the upper third of the oven to give it stronger top heat.

VARIATION

BRIOCHE CRUMB CAKE: Substitute 1 recipe Crumb Topping (page 292), for the almond brittle topping. Egg-wash the top of the cake before applying the crumb topping. When you unmold the cake, some of the crumb topping may fall off. Gather it up and replace it on the cake.

ITALIAN CHRISTMAS BREAD
(PANETTONE)

SPONGE

½ **cup milk**

2½ **teaspoons (1 envelope) active dry yeast**

¾ **cup unbleached all-purpose flour**

DOUGH

8 **tablespoons (1 stick) unsalted butter, softened**

½ **teaspoon salt**

⅓ **cup sugar**

1 **teaspoon finely grated lemon zest**

2 **teaspoons vanilla extract**

1 **tablespoon white rum**

3 **large eggs plus 3 large egg yolks, at room temperature**

3 **cups unbleached all-purpose flour**

½ **cup (about 3 ounces) each diced candied orange peel, dark raisins or currants, and golden raisins**

2 **tablespoons unsalted butter, melted, for finishing**

One 9-inch-diameter × 3-inch-deep springform pan, buttered and floured

ONE 9-INCH CAKE, 8 TO 10 SERVINGS

In Italy, panettone is the traditional Christmas bread—offered when friends drop in throughout the holiday season, served for breakfast Christmas morning, and sometimes filled with pastry cream or chocolate to make a fancy dessert.

Though in Italy panettone is prepared in some pastry shops, most often, even there, it comes from the same industrial bakeries that market their panettoni in the United States—Motta, Alemagna, and Tre Marie, to name a few.

Panettone, whether prepared in a pastry shop or a factory, is usually made with a type of sourdough known as *lievito madre* or *lievito naturale* (mother yeast or natural yeast) rather than the manufactured yeast which is a by-product of beer making. *Lievito madre* is a combination of flour, water, and a natural yeast-rich source, such as grape skins or hops, which cause fermentation. Enzymes and acids that form during the fermentation of the *lievito madre* (but not when manufactured yeast is used) retard staling, moisture loss, and mold.

The following recipe is for a *panettone alla casalinga*, or home-style panettone made with yeast. Though it is not difficult to prepare, do take the following precautions. Make sure all ingredients are at room temperature; cold butter or eggs may cause the dough to "break" or separate, and make a coarse-textured panettone. Be careful not to let the dough overferment, either after it is mixed or in the pan, or the panettone will fall when it is baked. Test for doneness with a thin knife or skewer after about 40 minutes—overbaked panettone is lethally dry.

1. To make the sponge, in a small saucepan over a low flame, heat the milk until it is just warm,

(continued)

about 110 degrees. Remove from the heat and pour into a small bowl; whisk in the yeast. Stir in the flour until smooth. Cover the bowl tightly with plastic wrap and allow the sponge to rise at room temperature for about 30 minutes.

2. To make the dough, use a heavy-duty mixer fitted with the paddle, and beat the butter until it is soft and light, then add the salt, sugar, lemon zest, vanilla, and rum. Continue beating until light and smooth, about 5 minutes.

3. Combine the eggs and yolks and beat a third into the butter mixture; continue to beat until the mixture is smooth. On the lowest speed, add a third of the flour and beat until it is absorbed. Scrape the sides of the bowl and paddle and add another third of the egg mixture, then another third of the flour. Finally, add the remaining egg mixture. Beat until smooth, then scrape the bowl and beat in the remaining flour until it is absorbed. Scrape the sponge into the mixer bowl and beat on the lowest speed for about 5 minutes, until the dough is smooth and slightly elastic. Beat in the candied peel and raisins.

4. Butter a bowl and turn the dough out into it. Turn the dough so the top is buttered. Cover the bowl tightly with plastic wrap and allow the dough to rise at room temperature for up to 1½ hours, or until doubled in bulk.

5. Stir the dough with a rubber spatula to deflate it and scrape it into the prepared pan. Butter a

piece of plastic wrap and drape loosely over the pan, buttered side in. Allow the dough to rise again at room temperature for about 1 hour, or until it reaches the top of the pan.

6. When the dough has almost reached the top of the mold, set a rack in the middle level of the oven and preheat to 375 degrees.

7. When the dough has risen completely, uncover and place in the oven. Bake for about 20 minutes, until the dough is well risen and deeply colored, then cover the top loosely with a piece of aluminum foil and continue baking for 20 to 30 minutes longer, or until a thin knife inserted in the center emerges without any dough clinging to it.

8. Cool in the pan on a rack for 5 minutes, remove the side of the pan, and slide the panettone off the pan base to a rack. Paint it all over with the melted butter and allow it to cool completely.

SERVING: Serve for breakfast, brunch, or tea. It also makes good French toast.

STORAGE: Wrap cooled panettone in several layers of plastic wrap to retain maximum freshness. Panettone may be frozen for 1 month. Leftover, slightly dry panettone makes excellent toast.

HINT FOR SUCCESS: Watch the dough carefully when it is rising in the pan. If it rises too much, it will fall when it is baked.

IRISH YEAST-RISEN TEA CAKE
(BARM BRACK)

SPONGE

¾ **cup milk**

½ **cup water**

About 4 teaspoons (1½ envelopes) active dry
    yeast

1½ cups unbleached all-purpose flour

DOUGH

1½ cups golden raisins

½ **cup currants**

½ **cup diced candied orange or lemon peel, or a**
    combination

6 tablespoons unsalted butter, softened

⅓ **cup sugar**

1 teaspoon salt

½ **teaspoon ground cinnamon**

¼ **teaspoon freshly grated nutmeg**

⅛ **teaspoon ground cloves**

⅛ **teaspoon ground allspice**

2 large eggs

3 cups unbleached all-purpose flour

Two 8-inch-diameter × 2-inch-deep cake pans,
buttered, bottoms lined with a piece of parchment or
buttered wax paper cut to fit

TWO 8-INCH CAKES, ABOUT 20 GENEROUS SERVINGS

Though I had read recipes for barm brack (*barmbrack* translated from the Irish language means "speckled cake") over the years, I was never tempted to make it until I tasted it. My friend Sandy Leonard had just returned from a trip to Ireland laden with baked goods, among them several versions of this cake. It is pleasantly moist and tender, like a lean version of panettone, which it resembles in flavor, preparation, and appearance.

This version is adapted from *Maura Laverty's Traditional Irish Cook Book, Volume 1: Bread and Cakes* (Anvil Books, 1985), a souvenir from Sandy.

1. To make the sponge, in a small saucepan over a low flame, heat the milk and water until just warm, about 110 degrees. Pour into a small bowl, whisk in the yeast, and stir in the flour. Cover the bowl with plastic wrap and allow the sponge to rise at room temperature for 30 minutes, or until doubled in bulk.

2. For the dough, combine the raisins, currants, and candied peel in a saucepan, cover with water, and bring to a boil over medium heat. Drain the fruit and spread it in a single layer on paper towels to cool and dry slightly while preparing the dough.

3. To mix the dough by hand, in a bowl, beat the butter with the sugar, salt, and spices until it's soft and smooth. Beat in the eggs, one at a time, then continue beating until they're smooth and light. Stir in the sponge and the flour. Place the dough on a lightly floured surface and knead it until it is smooth and elastic, about 10 minutes.

To make the dough in a mixer, use a heavy-duty mixer fitted with the paddle and beat the butter with the sugar, salt, and spices until it's soft and smooth. Beat in the eggs, one at a time, then

SWEET YEAST-RISEN BREADS & PASTRIES

continue beating until they're smooth and light. Beat in the sponge and the flour. Continue to mix until the dough is smooth and elastic, about 5 minutes.

To mix the dough in a food processor, place the butter, sugar, salt, spices, and eggs in the work bowl fitted with a metal blade. Pulse 10 or 12 times at 1-second intervals to mix smooth. Remove the metal blade and attach a plastic blade; add the sponge and flour and pulse to form a dough. Process for 15 seconds.

4. Place the dough in a buttered bowl and cover with buttered plastic wrap, butter side down. Allow the dough to rise at room temperature until the dough is doubled in bulk, about 1 hour.

5. Punch the dough to deflate, and turn it out onto a lightly floured surface. Distribute the fruit on the dough and knead it in evenly by continuing to fold the dough over onto itself. Cover with plastic wrap or a dry towel and allow to rest for 30 minutes.

6. Place half the dough in each prepared pan and press to make the tops flat and even. Cover the pans with buttered plastic wrap or a dry towel and allow the tea cakes to rise at room temperature until doubled, up to 1 hour.

7. Once the cakes have begun to puff, set a rack at the middle level of the oven and preheat to 400 degrees.

8. When the cakes are completely risen, bake them for about 45 minutes, or until well risen and golden brown. Test by inserting a thin knife or skewer near the center, which should emerge without any raw dough clinging to it.

9. Cool on racks for 5 minutes, then unmold and place back on the racks to cool completely.

SERVING: In Ireland, slices of barm brack are thickly buttered and served with tea. We might use less butter or none at all. Stale barm brack makes excellent toast and French toast.

STORAGE: Keep loosely covered at room temperature on the day they are baked. For longer storage, wrap in plastic and refrigerate or freeze. Defrost at room temperature before serving.

HINT FOR SUCCESS: Use a good-quality candied peel or more currants.

VARIATIONS

BARA BRITH: The Welsh version of barm brack is molded in loaf pans. Divide the dough for barm brack, above, in half and press each piece into a 10 × 6-inch rectangle. Fold in the short ends, then roll the dough, from the top down, several times, to make a tight roll. Press each formed piece of dough into a buttered 8½ × 4½ × 2¾-inch (6-cup) loaf pan. Allow to rise and bake as above.

SELKIRK BANNOCK: The Scottish version is molded as a free-form round loaf. Omit currants from the dough, above, and make up the quantity with more candied peel. After the dough rests, divide it in half, form each half into a round loaf, and place it on a cookie sheet covered with parchment or buttered wax paper. Cover and allow to rise. Before baking, brush with egg wash made by beating 1 egg with a pinch of salt. Bake as above.

VIENNESE YEAST-RISEN TEA CAKE
(WIENER GUGELHUPF)

SPONGE

½ cup milk

2½ teaspoons (1 envelope) active dry yeast

½ cup unbleached all-purpose flour

DOUGH

1 cup golden raisins

12 tablespoons (1½ sticks) unsalted butter, softened

½ cup granulated sugar

¼ teaspoon salt

1 teaspoon finely grated lemon zest

1 teaspoon vanilla extract

1 large egg plus 2 egg yolks

2 cups unbleached all-purpose flour

Confectioners' sugar for finishing

One 1½-quart to 2-quart gugelhupf mold or Bundt pan

ONE 8- TO 9-INCH-DIAMETER GUGELHUPF,
10 SERVINGS

This popular Austrian cake (also called "kugelhopf" and prepared in Alsace as well as Germany) probably migrated to France with Stanislaw Leszczynski, the exiled king of Poland who set up court in Nancy, capital of the Lorraine. The king was a legendary baker and he is credited variously with having introduced the baba (page 407) and the savarin (page 410) to France. Perhaps his interest in bread was passed on to his daughter Maria, who married Louis XV and became queen of France.

A mold with a central tube is essential to the baking of this delicate and easy-to-prepare yeast-risen cake. Though gugelhupf molds are fairly easy to find in kitchenware shops and department stores, you may substitute a Bundt pan. But if you do, note that it probably will have a much larger capacity, so make sure that the dough does not rise too much or the resulting gugelhupf will have a foul, yeasty taste. Or double the recipe—that will fill a standard 3-quart Bundt pan perfectly.

1. Thickly butter the gugelhupf mold with soft, but not melted, butter. Remember to butter the rim of the mold and the top of the central tube.

2. To make the sponge, heat the milk to lukewarm, about 110 degrees, in a small saucepan over a low flame. Pour the milk into a bowl and whisk in the yeast. Stir in the flour smoothly and cover the bowl with plastic wrap. Allow the sponge to rise at room temperature for 30 minutes, until the sponge is more than doubled in bulk.

3. For the dough, cover the raisins with water in a saucepan and bring to a boil. Drain and cool.

4. To make the dough, in a heavy-duty mixer, with the paddle attachment, beat the butter with the sugar on medium speed until soft and light. Beat in the salt, lemon zest, and vanilla. Beat in the egg and continue beating until smooth, then beat in the yolks, one at a time, beating the batter smooth after each addition. Beat in the flour, then the sponge, and beat the dough smooth. Add the raisins and mix gently to incorporate.

To mix the dough in a food processor, combine all the ingredients except the flour, sponge, and raisins in the work bowl fitted with the metal blade. Pulse to form a paste, then allow the machine to run continuously for 30 seconds. Remove the metal blade and attach a plastic blade; add the flour and sponge and pulse until a soft dough has formed. Allow the machine to run continuously for 15 seconds. Add the raisins and pulse 2 or 3 times to distribute them throughout the dough. Scrape the dough into a buttered bowl and cover with plastic wrap. Allow the dough to rise at room temperature until the dough has doubled, up to 1½ hours.

5. Deflate the dough and distribute large spoonfuls of it evenly around the mold. Smooth the top of the dough with the back of a spoon to make it flat and even. Cover loosely with buttered plastic wrap or a dry towel. At room temperature, allow the dough to rise until it fills the mold (or half fills the Bundt pan), up to 1½ hours.

6. When the gugelhupf is almost completely risen, set a rack at the lower third of the oven and preheat to 375 degrees.

7. Bake the gugelhupf for about 45 minutes, until it is a deep golden brown and a thin knife blade inserted between the side of the mold and the central tube emerges without any wet dough clinging to it.

8. Unmold to a rack to cool. Sprinkle lightly with confectioners' sugar before serving.

SERVING: Serve the gugelhupf for breakfast, brunch, or tea.

STORAGE: Keep the gugelhupf loosely covered with plastic wrap on the day it is baked. For longer storage, cover tightly with plastic wrap and refrigerate or freeze. Let the gugelhupf come to room temperature, loosely covered, before serving.

HINT FOR SUCCESS: To butter the mold as thickly as possible, chill it for 15 minutes, then use a pastry brush to give it a ⅛-inch-thick coating of soft butter.

VARIATIONS

Scatter sliced almonds on the buttered surface of the mold before adding the dough.

See page 286 for a non-yeast-risen version of gugelhupf.

SWISS BUTTER BRAID
(BUTTERZOPF)

SPONGE

½ **cup milk**

2½ **teaspoons (1 envelope) active dry yeast**

¾ **cup unbleached all-purpose flour**

DOUGH

2 **large eggs plus 1 egg yolk**

½ **cup sugar**

¼ **teaspoon salt**

6 **tablespoons unsalted butter, melted**

2 **cups unbleached all-purpose flour**

One cookie sheet or jelly-roll pan covered with parchment or foil

ONE 15-INCH BRAID, ABOUT 20 GENEROUS SLICES

The typical Sunday breakfast bread of Switzerland, the *butterzopf* or *tresse au beurre* was one of the treats I looked forward to every week during my apprenticeship in Zurich in the early 1970s. Armand, the hotel pastry chef, would arrive early every Sunday to prepare the braids. While they were baking, he would invariably become distracted and the bottoms would burn. It became a weekly tradition that some time around eight o'clock every Sunday morning we would hear the raspy sound of Armand's grater scraping away the burned part from the bottoms of the braids.

1. To make the sponge, heat the milk until it is lukewarm, about 110 degrees, in a small saucepan over a low flame. Pour the milk into a bowl and whisk in the yeast. Stir in the flour until the mixture is smooth. Cover the bowl with buttered plastic wrap and allow the sponge to rise at room temperature for about 30 minutes, until the sponge has more than doubled in bulk.

2. To make the dough, whisk the eggs and yolk together in a mixing bowl. Remove 2 tablespoons of the egg mixture to a small bowl, cover with plastic wrap, and reserve for glazing the top of the braid before baking. Into the large portion, whisk the sugar, salt, and the melted butter, one ingredient at a time, beating to combine well between each addition. Next, using a wooden spoon or rubber spatula, stir in the flour, then the sponge. Beat the dough with a wooden spoon until it is smooth and elastic, about 2 minutes. You can also use a heavy-duty mixer with the paddle attachment on low speed, but the dough is too firm for a hand mixer or food processor.

3. Cover the bowl with plastic wrap and allow the dough to rise at room temperature until the dough has doubled, about 1 hour.

4. Turn the dough out onto a lightly floured work surface, flour the dough, and press it to deflate it. Shape it into a rough rectangle and cut the rectangle into 3 equal pieces. Roll each piece into a cylinder about 16 inches long, flouring them lightly if they are sticky.

(continued)

5. Place the 3 cylinders of dough on the prepared pan and braid them loosely. Pinch each end together and turn it under the braid. For best results, begin braiding in the middle, toward one end; then turn the pan around and braid from the middle to the other end. This makes a braid of uniform width. If you start to braid at one end, the loaf will be wider at the beginning and narrower at the end because the strands get stretched during braiding, as in the illustration on page 77.

6. Cover the braid loosely with buttered plastic wrap or a dry towel and allow it to rise at room temperature until the braid has doubled in bulk, about 1 hour.

7. Before the braid is completely risen, set a rack at the middle level of the oven and preheat to 375 degrees.

8. Just before putting the bread into the oven carefully paint it with the reserved beaten egg. Bake the braid for about 30 minutes, making sure that it does not color too deeply. If the loaf is a deep golden brown after only a short time, cover it loosely with aluminum foil for the remainder of the baking time. The braid is done when it feels firm when pressed and sounds hollow when tapped on the bottom.

9. Slide the braid onto a rack to cool.

SERVING: Serve the braid warm or at room temperature. To reheat, place the braid on a cookie sheet and cover loosely with aluminum foil. Bake in a preheated 350 degree oven for about 10 minutes.

STORAGE: On the day it is baked, keep the braid loosely covered at room temperature, or refrigerate or freeze it wrapped in plastic.

HINT FOR SUCCESS: Don't braid the loaf too tightly or it will split unattractively while it is baking.

VARIATIONS

After mixing the dough, knead in 1½ cups raisins, currants, diced dried or candied fruit, or a combination.

BRIOCHE BRAID: Use a half-recipe of Brioche Dough (page 387) to make the braid, if you wish.

ORANGE BABAS MARCELLA

SPONGE

½ cup milk

2¼ teaspoons (1 envelope) active dry yeast

¾ cup unbleached all-purpose flour

DOUGH

3 eggs

2 tablespoons sugar

½ teaspoon salt

1 teaspoon finely grated orange zest

8 tablespoons (1 stick) unsalted butter, melted
    and cooled

1½ cups unbleached all-purpose flour

⅓ cup chopped candied orange peel

ORANGE SYRUP

3 cups water

2 cups sugar

3 large oranges

½ cup high-quality orange liqueur, such as
    Cointreau or Grand Marnier

APRICOT GLAZE

⅓ cup Orange Syrup, above

1 cup apricot preserves

WHIPPED CREAM

1 cup heavy whipping cream

2 tablespoons sugar

FINISHING

Candied orange peel

Three 12-cavity miniature muffin pans, buttered

ABOUT THIRTY-SIX 2-INCH BABAS, 18 TO
24 SERVINGS (SEE NOTE)

A baba should be a buttery, yeast-risen cake, low in sugar, soaked in a seasoned syrup to flavor it and make it moist. Unfortunately, what most pastry shops prepare are rather large, fine-textured babas that develop an unattractively sodden texture after they are soaked, in what is usually a syrup flavored with inferior liqueurs or fruit juices. So, most people look at a baba and flee.

These babas are quite different from those described above. They are tiny, so their rich sweetness is a pleasant mouthful; they are a bit coarse-textured, so they don't become soggy after being soaked; and the syrup is flavored with orange liqueur and orange juice, which contributes a fresher taste than the usual rum and spices. The recipe for a traditional *baba au rhum* is included as a variation, below.

I first made these babas for a dinner at the James Beard House in New York in honor of Marcella and Victor Hazan, the Italian food experts. The dessert was a selection of miniature pastries, including the babas. I held my breath as the dessert was served (I was sitting next to Marcella and she had only played with most of the food that night). But after tasting the baba she leaned over and said, "Can you send me the recipe for these babas, I love their coarse texture." I enjoyed my dessert after that.

1. To make the sponge, in a small saucepan over a low flame, heat the milk until it is just warm, about 110 degrees. Remove from the heat and pour into a small bowl. Whisk in the yeast, then stir in the flour. Cover the bowl with plastic wrap

and set aside at room temperature for about 20 minutes, until the sponge is well risen.

2. To make the dough, combine all the ingredients except the flour and candied orange peel in the bowl of a heavy-duty mixer fitted with the paddle attachment. Beat on medium speed until mixed, about 15 seconds. Add the flour and sponge and beat again, scraping the bowl and paddle often, until the dough is smooth and elastic, about 2 minutes. Beat in the candied orange peel.

To mix the dough in a food processor, use the metal blade and combine all the ingredients except the flour and candied orange peel. Pulse 6 to 8 times at 1-second intervals to mix smoothly. Add the sponge and flour and pulse again 10 to 12 times to mix. The dough will not form a ball. Process the dough continuously for 15 seconds, then add the candied orange peel. Pulse 2 or 3 times to mix it in without chopping it further.

3. Place half the dough at a time in a pastry bag fitted with a ½-inch plain tube (Ateco #6). (Using a pastry bag to fill the pans makes this job much easier.) Position the tube about 1 inch above one of the cavities in the pan and squeeze about 2 tablespoons of the dough into it, filling it about half full. Using a buttered spatula or finger, sever the dough from the end of the tube. Repeat until all the cavities are filled, refilling the bag with the remaining dough when the first batch is finished. Or fill the pans with a tablespoon, pushing the dough off the spoon with your finger.

4. Cover the filled pans with buttered plastic wrap, buttered side down, and allow the babas to

rise at room temperature until they're doubled, up to 1 hour.

5. After they have begun to rise visibly, set a rack at the middle level of the oven and preheat to 375 degrees.

6. Bake the babas for about 20 minutes, or until they are well puffed, a deep golden brown, and when lifted feel light for their size. Unmold onto a rack to cool.

7. To make the syrup, combine the water and sugar in a large nonreactive saucepan. Use a stainless vegetable peeler to strip the zest from the oranges in large pieces. Add to the pan and bring the syrup to a boil over medium heat. Remove from the heat, cover, and allow the zests to steep in the syrup for 5 minutes. Remove the zests with a slotted spoon. Squeeze and strain the juice from the oranges and add to the syrup. Return the syrup to a boil and add the orange liqueur. Remove and reserve ⅓ cup syrup to make the glaze later on.

8. To soak the babas, place 6 at a time in the saucepan and push them down into the syrup with the back of a skimmer or slotted spoon. As soon as they appear to inflate slightly, remove them from the syrup to a rack set over a platter or nonreactive pan to drain. Repeat with the remaining babas. Reheat the syrup several times if necessary (if the syrup is not boiling hot, it will not penetrate completely). Cool the babas while preparing the glaze.

9. To make the glaze, combine the reserved ⅓ cup of syrup with the preserves in a small saucepan. Bring to a boil over low heat, stirring occasionally. Allow to simmer for 2 or 3 minutes, until slightly thickened, then strain into a bowl to remove the pulp. Using a soft pastry brush, paint the babas with the glaze. Allow the glaze to cool and set, then arrange the babas on a platter.

10. To finish the babas, in a bowl, whip the cream with the sugar until it holds soft peaks. Use a pastry bag fitted with a ½-inch star tube (Ateco #4) to pipe a rosette or spoon a dollop of the cream onto each cooled baba. Top the rosette with a piece of candied orange peel.

SERVING: Serve the babas alone or as part of an assortment of small pastries.

STORAGE: Keep the babas refrigerated until you serve them. If you prepare them more than 2 hours in advance, do not finish with the whipped cream. Or, decorate the glazed babas with the candied orange peel and serve a spoonful of whipped cream next to the babas on the plate.

Note: Thirty-six babas seems like an enormous quantity, but the babas are tiny—and the recipe does not call for large quantities of ingredients. If you wish, prepare all the components—the babas, syrup, and glaze—and freeze them. Finish in several batches.

VARIATION

TRADITIONAL *BABA AU RHUM:* Omit the orange zest and substitute currants for the candied orange peel in the dough. Omit the orange peel, juice, and liqueur from the syrup. To the boiling syrup add 2 cloves, 2 cinnamon sticks, ¾ cup dark rum, and 1 tablespoon anisette. Bring to a boil and strain. Omit the candied orange peel decoration on the finished babas.

STRAWBERRY SAVARIN

1 recipe dough for Orange Babas Marcella (page 407), without the orange zest and candied orange peel

KIRSCH SYRUP

3 cups water

2 cups sugar

½ cup kirsch

2 tablespoons lemon juice

APRICOT GLAZE

⅓ cup Kirsch Syrup, above

1 cup apricot preserves

WHIPPED CREAM

1 cup heavy whipping cream

2 tablespoons sugar

FINISHING

2 pints strawberries, rinsed, hulled, and sliced

One 10-inch ring mold, 2-quart capacity, buttered and floured

ONE 10-INCH SAVARIN, ABOUT 10 SERVINGS

A *savarin,* named for the great early-nineteenth-century French philosopher of the table, Jean-Anthelme Brillat-Savarin, is a large cake made from the same dough as for Orange Babas Marcella (but without the orange flavoring), but baked in a ring mold. It has an old-fashioned quality. After the savarin is soaked with flavored syrup and glazed, the center is filled with fruit or whipped cream, which is served with each slice of cake. In this version, strawberries are paired with a kirsch-flavored syrup, a classic combination. Feel free to vary the fruit and flavorings. During the winter, try sliced oranges with an orange-flavored syrup, or poached pears, with some pear eau-de-vie added to the poaching syrup.

1. Spoon the dough into the prepared mold and level the top of the dough with a rubber spatula. Cover the pan with buttered plastic wrap or a dry towel. Allow the savarin to rise until doubled in bulk, up to 1 hour.

2. Once the savarin has begun to puff, set a rack at the middle level of the oven and preheat to 375 degrees.

3. Bake the fully risen savarin for about 30 minutes, or until high and a deep golden brown. Turn the savarin out onto a rack and lift off the mold. Cool.

4. To make the syrup, combine the water and sugar in a large nonreactive saucepan. Bring the syrup to a boil and add the kirsch and lemon juice. Reserve ⅓ cup of the syrup to make the glaze later on.

5. Soak the savarin by placing it on a deep round serving platter. Ladle the boiling hot syrup into the center of the savarin first so it can begin soaking the bottom, then continue to ladle the syrup all over the savarin. Occasionally tip the excess syrup that accumulates in the bottom of the platter back into the pan. The savarin is

sufficiently soaked when it appears to have swelled or puffed. If the savarin does not seem sufficiently soaked through, reheat the remaining syrup and repeat step 5.

6. To make the glaze, combine the reserved ⅓ cup of syrup with the preserves in a small saucepan. Bring to a boil over low heat, stirring occasionally. Allow to simmer for 2 or 3 minutes, until slightly thickened. Strain into a bowl to remove the pulp, then use a soft pastry brush to paint the glaze onto the savarin. Allow the glaze to cool and set.

7. Keep the savarin in the refrigerator until about 1 hour before you serve it. To assemble, whip the cream with the sugar until it holds soft peaks, and place in a serving bowl. Fill the center of the savarin with the berries.

SERVING: Serve slices of the savarin with a spoonful each of the strawberries and the whipped cream on the side.

STORAGE: Keep refrigerated until you plan to serve it.

HINT FOR SUCCESS: Make sure the syrup is boiling hot or the savarin will remain dry in the center.

VARIATIONS

RASPBERRY SAVARIN: Substitute raspberries for the strawberries. For the syrup, use ⅓ cup kirsch and 2 tablespoons framboise (raspberry eau-de-vie).

MIXED FRUIT SAVARIN (SAVARIN AUX FRUITS): Fill the center of the savarin with 3 cups mixed cut fruit macerated in the leftover soaking syrup.

CROISSANTS

Legend has it that the Turkish army was tunneling under the city walls of Vienna or Budapest one night in the seventeenth century. The bakers, being the only ones awake, heard the enemy, sounded the alarm, and saved the city. As a reward, the bakers were allowed to create a pastry to commemorate the event, and they chose to bake a crescent, the shape which adorned the Ottoman flag.

Croissants (the French name for the crescent-shaped roll—the German name is *Gipfel*), which are as popular in northern and eastern Europe as they are now in the United States, are thought of as primarily French. That's probably because the French-style croissant has that buttery, flaky quality we associate with the best of this kind of pastry. Swiss, Viennese, and other versions are a bit more bread-like and less flaky. In France, yeast-risen croissants, such as these, are known as *croissants de boulanger* (bread baker's croissants) and they may be prepared plain, with fillings, or as *pains au chocolat,* rectangular packages of croissant dough containing a slender bar of chocolate. Other filled croissants which may be made from non-yeasted puff pastry are somewhat less light than the yeasted type. The puff pastry croissants are usually referred to as *croissants de pâtissier* (pastry-cook's croissants).

Croissants are special for me professionally, because they were the first recipe I ever taught. In the late 1970s, Harriet Reilly taught a class in brioche and croissant baking that was held at 6:30 weekday mornings at Bill Liederman's first cooking school on Madison Avenue. Bill made a change in the schedule, and asked me to teach the class on Saturday mornings, beginning in February 1979. For that first class, Harriet gave me her recipe for croissants, which Lydie Marshall of La Bonne Cocotte cooking school had given her. I have used it since, with only minor adjustments. This recipe has been baked successfully by at least five thousand students since that first class in 1979, and was the subject of an article in the April 1983 issue of *Cuisine* magazine.

Croissants require no more work than making a batch of puff pastry. The process may be interrupted at several stages and made to fit into your schedule. One word of advice: if you are planning to serve home-baked croissants for a special occasion, form them well in advance, bake them, freeze them, and reheat them for the party. You will then be free for other party preparations.

CROISSANT DOUGH

DOUGH

1½ cups milk

4 teaspoons (about 1½ envelopes) active dry
   yeast

3½ cups unbleached all-purpose flour

4 tablespoons sugar

1½ teaspoons salt

BUTTER LAYER

3 tablespoons unbleached all-purpose flour

¾ pound (3 sticks) cold unsalted butter

ABOUT 2½ POUNDS DOUGH, ENOUGH FOR ABOUT
24 MEDIUM CROISSANTS

1. For the dough, in a small saucepan over a low
flame, heat the milk until it feels just warm, about
110 degrees. Remove from the heat and pour into
a small bowl. Whisk in the yeast and set aside.

2. Combine the flour, sugar, and salt in a 3- to
4-quart mixing bowl and stir in the milk/yeast
mixture with a rubber spatula. Beat by hand for
about 15 seconds, or until fairly smooth in
appearance. The dough will be soft and sticky.
Scrape the sides of the bowl clean with a spatula,
cover tightly with plastic wrap, and refrigerate for
4 to 12 hours.

   To mix the dough in a food processor, place
the dry ingredients in a work bowl fitted with a
metal blade and pulse several times just to
combine. Add the milk/yeast mixture and pulse
8 or 10 times at 1-second intervals, until the dry
ingredients are evenly moistened. Process
continuously for 10 seconds, transfer the dough

to a mixing bowl (you may need the help of a
scraper), cover, and refrigerate for 4 to 12 hours.

3. To prepare the butter layer, which will be
incorporated into the dough, scatter the
3 tablespoons of flour over the work surface.
Remove the butter from the refrigerator, unwrap
it, and roll the sticks of butter in the flour to coat
them. Pound the butter with a rolling pin, gently
at first, turning it often to keep it coated with
flour. The butter should become soft and
malleable, but should not begin to melt. Press the
butter occasionally with your fingertip to check
its consistency—it should be cool and pliable.
Flour your hands with any flour left on the work
surface (or up to 1 tablespoon additional flour)
and quickly knead the butter into a solid mass.
Set the butter aside for a moment while you
prepare the dough. If the room is warm,
refrigerate the butter.

4. Scrape the work surface clear of any bits of
butter stuck to it, and flour it lightly. Remove the
dough from the refrigerator. Turn the dough out
of the bowl onto the work surface in one piece,
using a rubber spatula. Make sure the dough
doesn't fold over on itself, or it may become too
elastic to roll. Lightly flour the top of the dough,
and using the palm of one hand, press and pull it
into a 6 × 12-inch rectangle, short ends at the
top and bottom.

5. Divide the softened butter into 8 fairly equal
pieces and press each quickly between the palms
of your hands to flatten it. Distribute the flattened
pieces of butter in a 6 × 9-inch rectangle over the
bottom two thirds of the dough.

6. Fold the top (unbuttered) third of the dough down over the middle (buttered) third to enclose the butter. Then fold the bottom (buttered) third up over the other layers, to make 5 dough and butter layers. You will be folding as you would a business letter.

7. Position the dough on the work surface so that the fold is on your left. Lightly flour the work surface and dough and, using a rolling pin to press rather than to roll, flatten the dough ½ inch thick by gently pressing a series of horizontal lines into the dough. Now you will roll, but be careful not to squeeze out the butter from between the layers. Quickly roll over the middle of the dough, being careful to stay away from the edges, and make a 12 × 24-inch rectangle.

8. Fold the two narrow ends of the dough up toward the middle, leaving a ½-inch space in the middle, then fold over again at that ½ inch to make 4 layers.

9. Repeat step 7. Wrap the dough loosely in plastic wrap, then slide it into a large plastic bag to allow room for expansion, and refrigerate it.

STORAGE: Use the dough 2 to 24 hours after preparing it. For longer storage, double-wrap in plastic and freeze. Defrost the dough overnight in the refrigerator before shaping the croissants.

HINTS FOR SUCCESS: Choose a cool day to prepare this dough. Because both the dough and butter are fairly soft, a hot kitchen can turn the process into a nightmare.

If the butter begins to melt while you are softening it, sandwich it between 2 pieces of plastic wrap and press it out to about ¼ inch thick. Refrigerate the butter until it firms slightly, then use it immediately.

CROISSANTS

½ recipe Croissant Dough (page 413)
Egg wash: 1 egg well beaten with a pinch of salt

*Two 10½ × 15½-inch jelly-roll pans lined with
parchment (Cookie sheets will not do for croissants
because some of the butter melts during baking and
might leak onto the bottom of the oven and burn.)*

TWELVE 5-INCH CROISSANTS

Though you may choose to use an entire batch
of dough to prepare plain croissants, I have given
the recipe for plain croissants as well as the variations—Almond Croissants and *pains au
chocolat*—in half-batches. This is to make it easier
should you wish to prepare more than one kind
from a single batch of dough.

1. Lightly flour the work surface and the dough,
then using a rolling pin, press the dough out into
a 6 × 12-inch rectangle using gentle horizontal
strokes. Keep a fine dusting of flour on both the
work surface and dough to prevent the dough
from sticking. Add more flour if necessary. Roll
the pin back and forth gently over the dough,
without pressing too hard or rolling over the
edges, until you have created a 12-inch square.
As you roll, slide your hands under the dough
and allow it to spring back to a smaller size, if
necessary, to prevent it from stretching and
distorting after it is cut. If the dough becomes soft
and sticky while you are rolling, slide it onto a
floured cookie sheet and refrigerate for about 10
minutes, or until it is firm.

2. Use a pastry wheel to cut the dough into two
6 × 12-inch strips. Gently stretch the top right
and bottom left corners of the dough outward to
slant the sides, as in the illustration on page 416.
Then mark each strip into 6 triangles with a
4-inch base. After the dough is marked, cut it
with the pastry wheel into 12 triangles. If your
kitchen is warm, refrigerate the triangles of dough
for a few minutes, or until they are firm.

3. To form the croissants, gently stretch the base
of each triangle out until all 3 sides of the triangle
are approximately the same length. Fold about
½ inch of the stretched side and press it with your
fingertips to seal. Using your left hand, grasp the
point of the triangle and stretch it to elongate
about 3 inches more. Meanwhile, use your right
hand to press the folded side and roll it up into a
croissant. Make sure when you are finished
rolling that the point is on the bottom. Arrange 6
croissants with 2 inches between them on all
sides, on each pan. Curve each into the crescent
shape. Cover the pans with plastic wrap or dry
towels and allow the croissants to rise at room
temperature until doubled in bulk, up to 1½
hours. When the croissants are fully risen they
will appear light and slightly puffed, but won't be
more than twice their original size.

4. About 20 minutes before the croissants are
fully risen, set racks at the upper and lower thirds
of the oven and preheat to 375 degrees.

(continued)

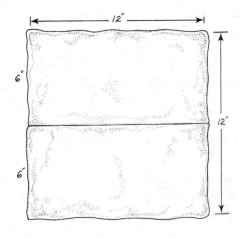

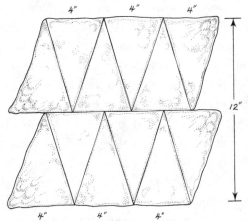

Using a pastry wheel, cut the dough into two 6 × 12-inch strips. To slant the sides, gently stretch the top right and bottom left corners of the dough outward. Next, mark each strip into six triangles, each with a 4-inch base. After the dough is marked, cut it with the pastry wheel into twelve triangles.

5. Carefully brush the risen croissants with the egg wash, making sure that the egg wash does not puddle under the pastries. Bake the croissants for about 25 minutes, or until they are well risen, a deep golden color, and feel light for their size when lifted from the pan.

6. Immediately remove them to racks to cool.

SERVING: Serve the croissants with jam or marmalade, but no butter, for breakfast, brunch, or tea. Croissants are too rich to serve as a dinner roll.

STORAGE: Keep cooled croissants loosely covered at room temperature on the day they are baked. For longer storage, pack croissants in plastic bags, seal tightly, and freeze. To reheat frozen croissants, remove them from the plastic bags, place them on cookie sheets, and bake at 375 degrees for about 10 minutes.

HINTS FOR SUCCESS: Refrigerate the dough any time that it becomes soft during the rolling and shaping. You will be more than compensated for the extra time by how much easier the dough will be to handle.

Be patient with the final rising. The chilled dough occasionally takes its time before it will begin to rise again. Be careful not to bake underrisen croissants—they will be tough and chewy.

Paint croissants with egg wash and bake them as soon as they are completely risen. If they rise too long, they may collapse when they are baked.

ALMOND CROISSANTS (CROISSANTS AUX AMANDES): To make 12 croissants, beat ¼ pound almond paste with 1 egg white until smooth. (If you don't have almond paste, in a food processor fitted with the metal blade, process together until smooth ½ cup [about 2 ounces] whole blanched almonds, ½ cup sugar, ½ teaspoon almond extract, and the 1 egg white.) Place about 2 teaspoons of the filling across the base of each triangle before beginning to roll it up. Sprinkle risen, egg-washed croissants with sliced almonds before baking them. Heat ¼ cup light corn syrup to a simmer and as soon as you remove the hot croissants from the oven brush them with the syrup. Cool as for plain croissants, above.

CHOCOLATE CROISSANTS
(PETITS PAINS AU CHOCOLAT)

½ recipe Croissant Dough (page 413)
4 ounces semisweet chocolate, coarsely chopped, or 24 bâtonnets au chocolat
Egg wash: 1 egg well beaten with a pinch of salt

Two 10½ × 15½-inch jelly-roll pans lined with parchment (Don't use cookie sheets for pains au chocolat *because some of the butter melts during baking and might leak onto the bottom of the oven and burn.)*

TWELVE 2 × 3-INCH *PAINS AU CHOCOLAT*

These rectangular pastries made from croissant dough and filled with chocolate are a typical after-school snack for French children. It is now possible to obtain the tiny chocolate bars (*bâtonnets au chocolat*) especially made for filling *pains au choco-lat* here in the United States; see Sources of Supply.

1. Lightly flour the work surface and the dough. Use a rolling pin to press the dough in gentle horizontal strokes into a 6 × 12-inch rectangle. Keep a fine dusting of flour on both the work surface and the dough to prevent the dough from sticking. If necessary, add more flour. Without pressing too hard or rolling over the edges, roll the dough gently into a 10 × 18-inch rectangle. To prevent the dough from getting stretched, which would distort it after it is cut, slide your hands under the dough and allow it, if necessary, to spring back to its smaller size. If the dough becomes soft and sticky while you are rolling, slide it onto a floured cookie sheet and refrigerate it for about 10 minutes, or until it is firm.

2. Use a pastry wheel to cut the dough into two 5 × 18-inch strips. Cut each strip into six rectangles, each 3 × 5 inches.

3. Place the chocolate or *bâtonnets* across the middle of each rectangle, about 2½ inches from

one of the 3-inch sides. Fold the 3-inch sides in over the chocolate, overlapping the edges slightly. Invert the *pains au chocolat* onto the prepared pans, leaving about 2 inches around each pastry in all directions. Cover with plastic wrap or clean towels and allow the *pains* to rise at room temperature until doubled in bulk, up to 1½ hours.

4. About 20 minutes before the *pains au chocolat* are fully risen, set racks at the upper and lower thirds of the oven and preheat to 375 degrees.

5. Carefully brush the risen *pains au chocolat* with the egg wash, making sure that the egg wash does not puddle under the pastries. Bake for about 25 minutes, or until they are well risen, a deep golden color, and feel light for their size when lifted from the pan.

6. Immediately remove the *pains au chocolat* to racks to cool.

SERVING: Serve with coffee or tea for breakfast, brunch, or tea.

STORAGE: Keep cooled *pains au chocolat* loosely covered at room temperature on the day they are baked. For longer storage, pack in plastic bags, seal tightly, and freeze. To reheat frozen *pains au chocolat,* remove from the plastic bags, place on cookie sheets, and bake at 375 degrees for about 10 minutes. Serve warm or cooled.

HINTS FOR SUCCESS: Refrigerate the dough any time that it becomes soft during the rolling and shaping. You will be more than compensated for the extra time by how much easier the dough will be to handle.

Be patient with the final rising. The chilled dough occasionally takes its time before it will begin to rise again. Be careful not to bake underrisen croissants—they will be tough and chewy.

Paint croissants with egg wash and bake them as soon as they are completely risen. If they rise too long, they may collapse when they are baked.

In Scandinavia, Danish pastry is known as *Viennabrød,* or "Vienna bread," and in Vienna as *Plunder,* or "lumber," because of the stacked layers of dough and butter. I think the name we use derives from the fact that the bakers of Copenhagen excel beyond all others in the preparation of this type of pastry, and it was they who made its international reputation.

If you have had only commercial Danish pastry, you will be surprised by the complexity and richness of the flavor of the homemade variety. In these recipes the buttery quality of the dough is enhanced, never obscured, by the fillings, all of which are fairly quick to prepare. Each of the variations that follow the dough recipe calls for one third the dough, so that you can bake three varieties from every batch or freeze part of the dough to use later.

DANISH PASTRY DOUGH

DOUGH

1 cup milk
5 teaspoons (2 envelopes) active dry yeast
4½ cups unbleached all-purpose flour
½ cup sugar
1 teaspoon salt
½ teaspoon ground cinnamon
4 tablespoons cold unsalted butter
3 eggs

BUTTER LAYER

⅓ cup unbleached all-purpose flour
14 ounces (3½ sticks) cold unsalted butter

ABOUT 3 POUNDS DOUGH

This dough is similar to both brioche and croissant doughs, and is actually a combination of the two. The recipe is freely adapted from *Wiener Süss-speisen* (Viennese Sweets) by Eduard Mayer.

1. For the dough, in a small saucepan over a low flame, heat the milk just until it feels warm, about 110 degrees. Pour it into a small bowl, and whisk in the yeast. Set aside.

2. Place the dry ingredients in the bowl of a food processor fitted with a metal blade; pulse several times just to combine. Add the 4 tablespoons of butter and pulse 6 or 8 times, until the butter is absorbed and the mixture looks powdery. Add the eggs and yeast mixture and continue to pulse until the dough forms into a ball. If the dough refuses to form a ball, add up to 3 tablespoons of

flour, a tablespoon at a time, pulsing once or twice after each addition.

To mix by hand, combine the dry ingredients in a bowl and stir well to mix. Rub in the butter by hand, being careful to leave the mixture cool and powdery. Beat the eggs into the yeast mixture and add to the bowl. Stir vigorously with a rubber spatula until the dough forms.

3. Cover the bowl with plastic wrap and allow the dough to rest for 5 minutes. Turn the dough out onto a floured surface (you may need the help of a scraper) and fold the dough over on itself 6 or 8 times. Sprinkle with up to 3 tablespoons more flour if the dough is very soft. Wrap the dough in plastic wrap and refrigerate for from 1 to 8 hours.

4. To prepare the butter layer to be incorporated into the dough, scatter the flour on the work surface. Remove the butter from the refrigerator, unwrap it, and roll the butter in the flour to coat it. Pound the butter with a rolling pin, gently at first. Turn it often to keep it coated with flour. The butter should become soft and malleable, but not begin to melt. Press the butter occasionally with your fingertip to check its consistency—it should be cool and pliable. Flouring your hands with any flour left on the work surface (or up to 1 tablespoon additional flour), quickly knead the butter into a solid mass and set it aside for a moment. If the room is warm, refrigerate the butter.

5. Scrape off any bits of butter stuck to the work surface and flour it lightly. Remove the dough from the refrigerator and turn the dough out in one piece onto the surface using a rubber spatula.

Make sure the dough does not fold over onto itself or it may become too elastic to roll. Lightly flour the top of the dough and, using the palm of one hand, press and pull it into a 6 × 12-inch rectangle.

6. Divide the softened butter into 8 fairly equal-sized pieces and press each quickly between the palms of your hands to flatten it. Distribute the flattened pieces of butter in a 6 × 9-inch rectangle over the bottom two thirds of the dough.

7. Fold the top (unbuttered) third of the dough down over the middle (buttered) third. Then fold the bottom (buttered) third up over the other layers to make a 5-layered package of dough and butter.

8. Position the dough on the work surface so that the fold is on your left. Lightly flour the work surface and dough and, with a rolling pin, press a series of horizontal lines in the dough to flatten it gently. You don't want the butter to squeeze out the sides or the dough to become thinner at the edges, so when the dough is approximately ½ inch thick, roll it, without rolling over the edges, to make a 12 × 24-inch rectangle. Fold the two narrow ends of the dough to within ¼ inch of the middle, leaving a ½-inch space between their ends. Fold over again at the space to make 4 layers.

9. Repeat step 8. Loosely wrap the dough in plastic wrap, then slide it into a large plastic bag, to allow room for it to expand.

STORAGE: Keep the dough refrigerated for 2 to 24 hours after preparing it. If you want to keep it longer, or use only part of the dough, freeze it. Allow it to rest in the refrigerator for several hours, then remove it from the refrigerator, deflate it by pressing it gently with the palms of your hands, and cut off the amount you wish to freeze. Double-wrap that portion in plastic wrap and freeze it for up to several weeks. Defrost the frozen dough in the refrigerator overnight before using it.

HINT FOR SUCCESS: Refrigerate the dough any time that it becomes soft during the rolling and shaping. You will be more than compensated for the extra time by how much easier the dough will be to handle.

Be patient with the final rising. The chilled dough occasionally takes its time before it will begin to rise again. Be careful not to bake underrisen croissants—they will be tough and chewy.

Paint croissants with egg wash and bake them as soon as they are completely risen. If they rise too long, they may collapse when they are baked.

DANISH WALNUT BRAID

WALNUT FILLING

1½ cups (6 ounces) walnut pieces
⅔ cup milk
¼ cup granulated sugar
1 tablespoon butter
¼ cup dry breadcrumbs
2 teaspoons vanilla extract
½ teaspoon ground cinnamon

⅓ recipe Danish Pastry Dough
    (page 419)
Egg wash: 1 egg well beaten with a
    pinch of salt

CINNAMON ICING

¾ cup confectioners' sugar
1 teaspoon ground cinnamon

1 tablespoon milk or water
1 teaspoon vanilla extract

One 12 × 15-inch cookie sheet lined with parchment paper

ONE 4 × 12-INCH BRAID, ABOUT 10 SERVINGS

This large braid is easier and quicker than forming individual Danish pastries. Though the beautifully woven top of the pastry looks complicated, it is not difficult to do.

The walnut filling for the braid is particularly Viennese. If you wish, substitute another filling listed in the Variations at the end of the recipe. Poppy seed is my favorite.

1. To make the filling, place the walnut pieces in the work bowl of a food processor fitted with the steel blade. Pulse 5 or 6 times at 1-second

SWEET YEAST-RISEN BREADS & PASTRIES

intervals. Remove ¼ cup of the chopped walnuts and set aside for finishing the braid. Continue to pulse the remaining walnuts until they are finely ground, but not pasty. Combine the milk, sugar, and butter in a heavy nonreactive saucepan and bring to a simmer over low heat. Add the ground walnuts and breadcrumbs and cook, stirring constantly, until the filling thickens, 1 to 2 minutes. Remove from the heat, add the vanilla and cinnamon, and scrape the filling into a bowl to cool.

2. Lightly flour the work surface and the dough and roll the dough into a 12-inch square. Slide the dough onto the prepared cookie sheet, cover it with plastic wrap, and refrigerate it until the filling has cooled to room temperature.

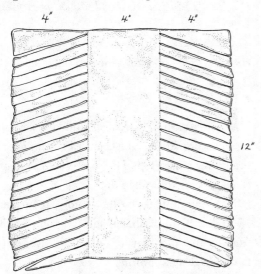

Mark but don't cut the chilled dough into three sections, each 4 inches wide and 12 inches long. Slash downward diagonally through the two outermost sections at 1/2-inch intervals.

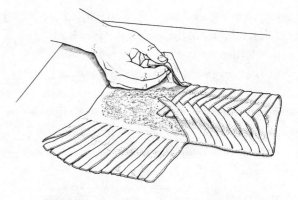

Fold the slashes over the center filled section one at a time, alternating strips of dough from first one side then the other.

3. Remove the pan of dough from the refrigerator. Mark but don't cut the chilled dough into 3 sections, each 4 inches wide and 12 inches long. Slash through the 2 outermost sections diagonally downward at ½-inch intervals, as in the illustration at left. Spread the cooled filling over the center (unslashed) section. Fold the slashes one at a time over the center filled section, alternating a strip of dough from first one side then the other, as in the illustration above. Cover with a dry towel or plastic wrap and allow the braid to rise at room temperature until the braid puffs slightly, up to 30 minutes.

4. Meanwhile, set a rack in the middle level of the oven and preheat to 400 degrees.

5. Paint the braid with the egg wash. Draw the brush against the rim of the bowl to remove excess wash, to avoid having the egg wash puddle under the braid. Sprinkle the braid with the reserved chopped walnuts. Bake the braid for about 20 minutes, until it is well risen and a deep golden color.

6. Slide the braid, still on the paper, onto a rack to cool.

7. To make the icing, combine all the ingredients in a small saucepan. Stir with a wooden spoon until smooth and place over low heat, stirring constantly, until the icing is warm, about 110 degrees. Drizzle the icing from the end of a metal spoon into the braid in an irregular pattern. Slide the braid off the paper onto a platter or cutting board.

SERVING: Serve for breakfast, brunch, or tea or as dessert with a light lunch or late supper.

STORAGE: Keep the braid loosely covered at room temperature on the day it is baked. For longer storage, do not ice the braid. Wrap it tightly in plastic wrap after it has cooled. Refrigerate for several days or freeze. Reheat the braid at 325 degrees for about 15 minutes, then cool and apply the icing.

HINT FOR SUCCESS: If the dough begins to soften and become sticky while you are rolling it or forming the braid, slide it onto a cookie sheet and refrigerate for 10 minutes, or until it is firm again.

VARIATIONS

DANISH PECAN OR HAZELNUT BRAID: Substitute pecan pieces or toasted, skinned hazelnuts for the walnuts in the filling, above.

DANISH POPPY-SEED BRAID: Substitute poppy-seed filling (page 428), for the walnut filling, above. Sprinkle the egg-washed braid with poppy seeds before baking. Omit the cinnamon from the icing.

DANISH ALMOND BRAID: Use the filling for Brioche Suisse (page 395), with or without the raisins or currants, instead of the walnut filling, above. Sprinkle the egg-washed braid with sliced almonds. Omit the cinnamon from the icing.

DANISH CRESCENTS

⅓ recipe Danish Pastry Dough (page 419)

FILLING

⅓ cup (about 1½ ounces) whole blanched
    almonds
⅓ cup granulated sugar
½ teaspoon almond extract
1 egg white
¼ teaspoon ground cinnamon
3 ounces finely chopped semisweet or bittersweet
    chocolate

TOPPING

Egg wash: 1 egg well beaten with a pinch of salt
½ cup (about 2 ounces) sliced almonds
Confectioners' sugar

*Two 10½ × 15½-inch jelly-roll pans, or two
12 × 15½-inch cookie sheets, lined with parchment
paper*

Twelve 5- to 6-inch pastries

The filling for these crescents incorporates one of my favorite combinations of flavors: chocolate, cinnamon, and nuts. If you wish, you can substitute ½ cup almond paste for the almonds, sugar, and almond extract in the filling.

1. Lightly flour the work surface and the dough. Using a rolling pin, press the dough with gentle horizontal strokes, until it is a 6 × 12-inch rectangle. Keep a fine dusting of flour on both the dough and the work surface to prevent the dough from sticking. Add more flour to both if necessary. Roll out the dough in back-and-forth strokes, without pressing too hard or rolling over the edges, so the butter doesn't squeeze out and the dough remains an even thickness, until it is a 12-inch square. Slide the dough onto a cookie sheet, cover it with plastic wrap, and refrigerate it while you prepare the filling.

2. To make the filling, combine the almonds and sugar in the work bowl of a food processor fitted with a steel blade. Pulse until finely ground. Add the remaining ingredients, except the chocolate, and continue to pulse until the mixture becomes smooth, but is still firm. Scrape the filling into a bowl and stir in the chocolate with a rubber spatula.

3. Remove the dough from the refrigerator. Using a pastry wheel, cut the dough into 2 strips, each 6 × 12 inches. Gently stretch the top right and bottom left corners of the dough outward to slant the sides, as in the illustration on page 416. Then mark each strip into 6 triangles having a 4-inch base. After marking the dough, cut through it with the pastry wheel. You will have 12 triangles of dough. If the room is warm, refrigerate the dough for a few minutes, or until it is firm.

4. To form the pastries, gently stretch the base of each triangle outwards, until all 3 sides of the triangle are approximately the same in length. Place about 2 teaspoons of the filling along the base of each triangle, about ½ inch in from the bottom, then fold the stretched sides over the filling and press with your fingertips to seal. Using your left hand, grasp the point of the triangle and stretch it about 3 inches more, while pressing and rolling the folded side with your right. Roll up the triangle, making sure that when you have finished, the point is on the bottom.

5. Arrange 6 pastries, with 2 inches of space on all sides, on each pan, and curve each into a crescent shape. Cover the pastries with plastic wrap or clean towels and allow them to rise at room temperature until they begin to puff slightly, up to 30 minutes.

6. Meanwhile, set racks in the upper and lower thirds of the oven and preheat to 400 degrees. Carefully brush the risen pastries with egg wash, making sure that the egg wash does not puddle under them. Sprinkle the pastries with sliced almonds.

7. Bake for about 20 minutes, or until the pastries are well risen and a deep golden color, and feel light for their size when lifted from the pan.

8. Immediately remove to racks to cool.

9. Dust the crescents lightly with confectioners' sugar just before serving.

SERVING: Serve the pastries for breakfast, brunch, or tea. They need no accompaniment.

STORAGE: Keep cooled pastries loosely covered at room temperature on the day they are baked. For longer storage, pack in plastic bags, seal tightly, and freeze. To reheat frozen pastries, remove from the bags and bake on cookie sheets at 375 degrees for about 10 minutes.

HINT FOR SUCCESS: Refrigerate the dough to firm it any time that it becomes soft during the rolling and shaping. The extra time it takes is more than compensated for by the increased ease of handling.

VARIATIONS

Use about a third of any of the fillings for Danish Walnut Braid (page 421) for these pastries.

DANISH CHEESE POCKETS

⅓ recipe Danish Pastry Dough (page 419)

CHEESE FILLING

½ pound farmer cheese or cream cheese

3 tablespoons granulated sugar

1 teaspoon vanilla extract

1 teaspoon finely grated lemon zest

1 egg yolk

¼ cup golden raisins

Egg wash: 1 egg well beaten with a pinch of salt
Confectioners' sugar

Two 10½ × 15½-inch jelly-roll pans, or two
12 × 15½-inch cookie sheets, lined with parchment
paper

TWELVE 3- TO 4-INCH PASTRIES

These pastries may be varied almost infinitely by using different fillings. Try the poppy-seed filling on page 428, or the almond filling on page 417.

1. Lightly flour the work surface and the dough and use a rolling pin to press the dough in gentle horizontal strokes, into a 6 × 12-inch rectangle. Keep a fine dusting of flour on both the work surface and dough to prevent the dough from sticking. Add more flour if necessary. Roll the rolling pin over the dough in back-and-forth strokes, without pressing too hard or rolling over the edges (so the butter won't squeeze out and the dough remains an even thickness), to make a 12 × 16-inch rectangle. Slide the dough onto a cookie sheet, cover it with plastic wrap, and refrigerate it while you prepare the filling.

2. To make the filling, combine the cheese, sugar, vanilla, and lemon zest in the work bowl of a food processor fitted with a steel blade. Pulse to mix. Add the yolk and pulse again, just until smooth. Scrape the filling into a bowl and stir in the raisins.

3. Remove the dough from the refrigerator. Use a pastry wheel to cut the dough into twelve 4-inch squares and arrange 6 squares on each prepared pan. Paint each square of dough sparingly with egg wash. Spoon or pipe a generous tablespoon of the filling onto the center of each square.

4. To form the pastries, grasp opposite corners and pull them toward each other over the filling and overlap them so they overlap by about ½ inch. Pinch well to seal. Repeat with the other 2 corners to form roughly square pastries. Cover the pastries with plastic wrap or clean towels and allow them to rise at room temperature until they begin to puff slightly, up to 30 minutes.

5. Meanwhile, set racks in the upper and lower thirds of the oven and preheat to 400 degrees.

6. Carefully brush the risen pastries with egg wash, making sure that the egg wash does not puddle under them. Bake for about 20 minutes, or until the pastries are well risen, a deep golden color, and feel light for their size when lifted from the pan.

7. Immediately remove to racks to cool.

8. Dust the pockets lightly with the confectioners' sugar just before serving.

SERVING: Serve the pastries for breakfast, brunch, or tea. They need no accompaniment.

STORAGE: Keep cooled pastries loosely covered at room temperature on the day they are baked. For longer storage, pack in plastic bags, seal tightly, and freeze. To reheat frozen pastries, remove them from the bags and bake on cookie sheets at 375 degrees for about 10 minutes.

HINT FOR SUCCESS: Refrigerate the dough any time it becomes soft during the rolling and shaping. The extra time is more than compensated for by the increased ease of handling.

VARIATIONS

To vary the shape of the pastries, pinch only 2 of the corners together to make an open elongated diamond shape.

If you wish, after brushing the pastries with the egg wash, sprinkle them (either shape) with slivered or sliced almonds.

The pastries may be drizzled with the icing on page 421 (omit the cinnamon).

POPPY SEEDS AND POPPY-SEED FILLING

Poppy seeds, which are often sprinkled on breads and pastries, make a delicious filling for Danish pastries and the traditional Jewish pastry, Hamantaschen. Filling made from the blue-black poppy seeds adds a striking visual note to many pastries.

These seeds are from the *Papaver somniferum*, the same poppy from which opium is derived, but are completely harmless. The drug is a concentration of the juices that exude from the slashed seed pod. (The red and orange garden and wild poppies are of a different, non-opium-bearing species.) To make a poppy-seed filling, the seeds must first be ground. In areas with a significant eastern European population, ready-ground seeds may be purchased. They may also be ordered by mail (see Sources of Supply). But if you have no access to ground poppy seeds, do what I do: grind them in a small electric coffee or spice mill. Unfortunately, neither a food processor nor a blender does as good a job of grinding the seeds. Clean out the mill by grinding a few pieces of stale bread in it, then wipe the inside of the grinder and the cover with a damp paper towel or cloth. Grind about ¼ cup poppy seeds at a time, pulsing the mill on and off, until the seeds are a fine powder. Don't be concerned if they become pasty—poppy seeds are rich in natural oil and will cake up in the mill after they have been sufficiently ground.

If you have no coffee mill, cook the filling as described in the alternate method, then puree the cooked mixture in a blender—it will taste the same, but will lack the vivid color of a filling made with ground seeds.

One note of caution: Always be sure to taste poppy seeds before you purchase them. They easily turn rancid and bitter tasting.

Poppy-Seed Filling

1 cup poppy seeds
1 cup milk
¼ cup sugar
1 tablespoon unsalted butter
¼ cup dry breadcrumbs
½ cup dark raisins (optional)
½ teaspoon ground cinnamon

About 1½ cups filling

1. Grind the poppy seeds in a coffee or spice mill, about ¼ cup at a time.

2. Combine the milk, sugar, and butter in a heavy nonreactive saucepan over low heat and bring to a boil. Add the ground poppy seeds all at once and stir smooth with a wooden spoon. Continue to cook, stirring occasionally, until the mixture becomes fairly thick and you can easily see the bottom of the pan while stirring.

3. Remove from the heat and stir in the remaining ingredients.

ALTERNATE METHOD—FOR UNGROUND POPPY SEEDS

1. Place the poppy seeds in a saucepan and cover them with 3 cups water. Bring to a boil, remove from the heat, cover the pan, and allow the seeds to soak for 1 hour.

2. Drain all the water off the soaked seeds and add the milk, sugar, and butter. Bring to a boil over low heat, stirring occasionally, and cook as in step 2, above.

3. Puree the filling in a blender, half at a time, making sure that most of the seeds are reduced to a paste. Transfer the pureed mix-ture to a bowl and stir in the remaining ingredients.

STORAGE: Pack the filling into a bowl or plastic container, cover with plastic wrap, and refrigerate. You may keep the filling several days before using, or freeze for longer storage. Defrost the filling in the refrigerator before using.

VARIATIONS

Add ½ cup coarsely ground walnuts or hazelnuts to the filling along with the breadcrumbs.

To make an uncooked filling with poppy seeds, add 1 cup of them (ground or not, as you wish) to an almond filling, such as the one for Brioche Suisse (page 395).

DANISH SNAILS

⅓ recipe Danish Pastry Dough (page 419)

FILLING

3 tablespoons unsalted butter
¼ cup granulated sugar
1 teaspoon ground cinnamon
1 cup (about 4 ounces) walnut pieces
1 cup raisins or currants

ICING

¾ cup confectioners' sugar
1 tablespoon water
1 teaspoon vanilla extract

Two 10½ × 15½-inch jelly-roll pans, or two 12 × 15½-inch cookie sheets, lined with parchment paper

TWELVE 3- TO 4-INCH ROUND PASTRIES

These rolled buns made of Danish pastry are a fast and easy way to use Danish pastry. Feel free to vary the type of nut used.

I usually make one (or several) of the variations at the end of the recipe, not because they are better, but because they are more interesting looking than the snails.

1. Lightly flour the work surface and the dough and use a rolling pin to press the dough with gentle horizontal strokes, into a 6 × 12-inch rectangle. Keep a fine dusting of flour on both the work surface and dough to prevent the dough from sticking. Add more flour, if necessary. Use back-and-forth strokes, without pressing too hard or rolling over the edges (so the butter doesn't squeeze out and the dough remains an even thickness), to roll the dough into a 12-inch square. Slide the dough onto a cookie sheet, cover it with plastic wrap, and refrigerate it while you prepare the filling.

2. To make the filling, combine the butter, sugar, and cinnamon in the work bowl of a food processor fitted with the steel blade and pulse until well mixed and smooth. Add the walnuts and pulse until the nuts are finely chopped, but not ground. Scrape the filling into a bowl and stir in the raisins.

3. Remove the dough from the refrigerator and spread it evenly with the filling, using a small offset metal spatula. Beginning at the end closest to you, roll up the dough around the filling. Seal the roll by pinching the long edge against the cylinder. Cut the dough into 12 slices and arrange them, cut side down, on the prepared pans. Flatten each pastry slightly with the palm of your hand. Cover the pan with plastic wrap or clean towels and allow the pastries to rise at room temperature until they begin to puff slightly, up to 30 minutes.

4. Meanwhile, set racks in the upper and lower thirds of the oven and preheat to 400 degrees.

5. Bake for about 20 minutes, or until the pastries are well risen and a deep golden color, and feel light for their size when lifted from the pan.

6. Immediately remove to racks to cool.

7. To make the icing, combine all the ingredients in a small saucepan. Stir with a wooden spoon until smooth and place over low heat, stirring constantly, until the icing is warm, about 110 degrees. Drizzle or brush the icing on the cooled pastries.

SERVING: Serve the pastries for breakfast, brunch, or tea. They need no accompaniment.

STORAGE: Keep the cooled pastries loosely covered at room temperature on the day they are baked. For longer storage, do not ice the pastries. Pack in plastic bags, seal tightly, and freeze. To reheat frozen pastries, remove from the bags and bake on cookie sheets at 375 degrees for about 10 minutes. Cool, and apply the icing.

HINT FOR SUCCESS: Refrigerate the dough to firm it any time that it becomes soft during the rolling and shaping. The extra time it takes is more than compensated for by the increased ease of handling.

VARIATIONS

Use other nuts in place of the walnuts.

Replace half the raisins with finely diced candied orange peel and prepare the icing with orange juice instead of water.

Add 1 teaspoon grated lemon zest to the filling and omit the cinnamon. Prepare the icing with lemon juice instead of water.

DANISH ROLLS: After cutting the dough into 12 slices, use a chopstick or the narrow handle of a wooden spoon to press down hard along the top of the rounded, uncut, side of each slice. This will make the cut sides squeeze face upward, as in the illustration below.

DANISH FANS: After cutting the snails, begin about ¼ inch in from the rounded edge and make 2 vertical cuts all the way through the dough, each about a third of the way in from a cut edge, as in the illustration at right. Open the fans out as

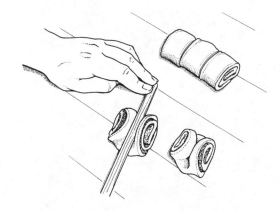

After cutting the dough, use a chopstick or the narrow handle of a wooden spoon to press down hard along the top of the rounded, uncut side of each slice. This will squeeze the cut sides upward.

you place them on the pans. Finish as for the Danish snails, above.

DANISH SCROLLS: Instead of rolling the dough from one end, roll 2 opposite sides of the dough in to the center. Cut and finish as for the snails, above.

DANISH FIGURE-EIGHTS: Roll the dough as for the Danish Scrolls variation, above. Place the scrolls on the pans, then lift one of the ends and turn it over to make a fat S shape. Finish as for the snails, above.

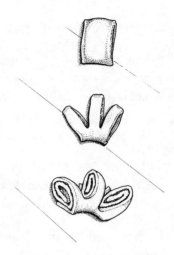

Begin about 1/4 inch in from the rounded edge and make two vertical cuts all the way through the dough, each about one-third of the way in from a cut edge. Open the fans out as you place them on the pans.

DANISH KNOTS

½ recipe Danish Pastry Dough (page 110)

FILLING

3 tablespoons unsalted butter, softened
¼ cup light brown sugar
½ teaspoon ground cinnamon
1 cup raisins or currants

CRUMB TOPPING

4 tablespoons unsalted butter
¼ cup light brown sugar
⅔ cup unbleached all-purpose flour
½ teaspoon ground cinnamon

Egg wash: 1 egg well beaten with a pinch of salt
Confectioners' sugar

Two 10½ × 15½-inch jelly-roll pans, or two 12 × 15½-inch cookie sheets, lined with parchment paper

EIGHTEEN 2 × 4-INCH PASTRIES

These knots enclose a buttery filling between 2 layers of dough, a horizontal version of Danish Snails (page 430). The crumb topping is an American addition and its crispness makes a gentle contrast to the tender pastry. The variation, Danish Pretzels, below, is one of the most attractive looking of all pastries.

1. Lightly flour the work surface and the dough and use a rolling pin to press the dough with gentle horizontal strokes, until it is a 6 × 12-inch rectangle. Keep a fine dusting of flour on both the work surface and dough to prevent the dough from sticking. Add more flour if necessary. Roll the dough using back-and-forth strokes, without pressing too hard or rolling over the edges (so the butter doesn't squeeze out and the dough remains an even thickness) to form a 12 × 18-inch rectangle. Lightly flour the top of the dough, fold it in half to make it easier to handle, slide the dough onto a cookie sheet, cover it with plastic wrap, and refrigerate it while preparing the filling.

2. To make the filling, in a bowl, beat the butter, sugar, and cinnamon together until smooth. Set aside.

3. To make the crumb topping, melt the butter and stir in the remaining ingredients. Allow the topping to rest for 5 minutes, then break it into ¼-inch crumbs with your fingertips.

4. Remove the dough from the refrigerator, unfold it, and spread the filling, using an offset metal spatula, onto one long half (a 9 × 12-inch rectangle) of the dough. Sprinkle the filling evenly with the raisins or currants. Fold the unfilled side of the dough over the filling, press well, and roll out to a 12-inch square. Using a pastry wheel, cut the dough into three strips, each 4 × 12 inches. Cut each strip into six 2 × 4-inch rectangles.

5. Make a 2-inch slash along the center of the 4-inch length of each rectangle, as in the illustration on page 434. Pass one of the short ends of the pastry through the slash and arrange it on the prepared pan. Repeat with the remaining pastries. Cover the pastries with

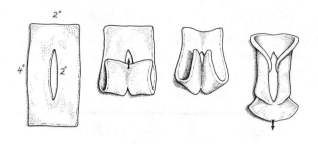

Make a 2-inch slash along the center of the 4-inch length of each rectangle. Pass one of the short ends of the pastry through the slash.

plastic wrap or clean towels and allow them to rise at room temperature until they begin to puff slightly, up to 30 minutes.

6. Meanwhile, set racks in the upper and lower thirds of the oven and preheat to 400 degrees.

7. Brush the pastries with the egg wash. Draw the brush against the rim of the bowl to remove excess wash, to avoid having the egg wash puddle under the pastries. Sprinkle evenly with the crumb topping. Bake for about 20 minutes, or until the knots are well risen and a deep golden color, and feel light for their size when lifted from the pan.

8. Immediately remove to racks to cool.

9. Just before serving, dust lightly with the confectioners' sugar.

SERVING: Serve the pastries for breakfast, brunch, or tea. They need no accompaniment.

STORAGE: Keep cooled pastries loosely covered at room temperature on the day they are baked. For longer storage, pack the pastries in plastic bags, seal tightly, and freeze. To reheat frozen pastries, remove from the bags and bake on cookie sheets at 375 degrees for about 10 minutes.

HINT FOR SUCCESS: Refrigerate the dough any time it becomes soft during the rolling and shaping. The extra time it takes is more than compensated for by the increased ease of handling.

VARIATION

DANISH PRETZELS: After filling the dough and rerolling it to a 12-inch square, cut the dough into twelve 1-inch strips. Holding the top steady and rotating the bottom, twist each strip into a corkscrew (see Swiss Pretzels, page 352). Shape each twisted strip of dough into a pretzel. Arrange the pastries facedown on the prepared pans, cover, and allow to rise. Paint with egg wash and sprinkle with crumb topping or sliced almonds. Bake as for Danish Knots, above. Cool and dust with confectioners' sugar or drizzle with icing (page 430).

SOURCES OF SUPPLY

EQUIPMENT

BRIDGE KITCHENWARE
214 East 52nd Street
New York, NY 10022
Telephone: (212) 688-4220
Catalogue available ($3.00, refundable with first order)
Tart pans, tartlet pans, brioche molds, and assorted pastry equipment and cookware.

LAMALLE KITCHENWARE
36 West 25th Street, 6th floor
New York, NY 10010
Telephone: (212) 242-0750
       (800) 660-0750
Catalogue available ($3.00)
Tart pans, tartlet pans, brioche molds, and assorted pastry equipment and cookware.

NEW YORK CAKE AND BAKING DISTRIBUTORS
(FORMERLY THE CHOCOLATE GALLERY)
56 West 22nd Street
New York, NY 10010
Telephone: (212) 675-2253
Catalogue available ($3.00)
Eighty-page catalogue offers a full line of pans, decorating equipment, and chocolate.

SUR LA TABLE
Pike Place Farmers Market
84 Pine Street
Seattle, WA 98101
Telephone: (206) 448-2244
       (800) 243-0852
General and baking catalogues available
Tart pans, tartlet pans, brioche molds, and assorted pastry equipment and cookware.

SWEET CELEBRATIONS
(FORMERLY MAID OF SCANDINAVIA)
7009 Washington Avenue South
Edina, MN 55439
Telephone: (800) 328-6722
Catalogue available
Wide variety of decorating supplies, including chocolate.

WILLIAMS SONOMA
100 North Point Street
San Francisco, CA 4133
Telephone: (800) 541-2233
Catalogue available
Tart pans, tartlet pans, brioche molds, and assorted pastry equipment and cookware.

WILTON INDUSTRIES, INC.
2240 West 75th Street
Woodridge, IL 60517
Telephone: (708) 936-7100
       (800) 323-1717
Catalogue available
Bakeware and baking and decorating products.

FOOD PRODUCTS

BALDUCCI'S
424 Sixth Avenue
New York, NY 10011
Telephone: (212) 673-2600
       (800) 572-7041
Catalogue available ($3.00, refundable with first order)
Food products of all kinds. Chickpea flour and chestnut spread available through catalogue, but not listed in it.

THE COOK SHOP
7251 SW 57 Court
Miami, FL 33143
Telephone: (305) 667-5957
No catalogue
  Canned guava shells.

GREAT VALLEY MILLS
1774A County Line Road
Barto, PA 19504
Telephone: (800) 688-6455
Catalogue available
  Organic flour.

MAISON GLASS
111 East 58th Street
New York, NY 10022
Telephone: (212) 755-3316
Catalogue available
  Faugier chestnut spread.

MOZZARELLA COMPANY
2944 Elm Street
Dallas, TX 75226
Telephone: (214) 741-4072
             (800) 798-2954
Product list available
  Ricotta and mozzarella cheeses.

PAPRIKAS WEISS
1546 Second Avenue
New York, NY 10028
Telephone: (212) 288-6117
Catalogue available
  Ground poppy seeds, pearl sugar, and baking equipment.

RAYMOND HADLEY CORPORATION
P.O. Box 492A
Spencer, NY 14883
Telephone: (607) 589-4415
             (800) 252-5220
Product list available
  Semolina, cornmeal, corn flour. Other flours not listed, including chickpea flour, may be available upon request.

ROBERT IS HERE FRUIT STAND
19200 South West 344 Street
Homestead, Florida 33034
Telephone: (305) 246-1592
Catalogue available for jellies and jams
  Meyer lemons in season.

TODARO BROTHERS
555 Second Avenue
New York, NY 10016
Telephone: (212) 679-7766
Catalogue available
  Semolina and corn flour.

WHITE LILY FOODS COMPANY
P.O. Box 871
Knoxville, TN 37901
Telephone: (615) 546-5511
Brochure available
  White Lily self-rising flour.

BIBLIOGRAPHY

Akerstrom, Jenny. *The Princesses Cook Book.* New York: Albert Bonnier Publishing House, 1936.

Bachman, Walter. *Swiss Bakery & Confectionery.* London: Maclaren & Sons Limited, 1949.

Barker, William. *The Modern Pâtissier.* New York: Arco, 1978.

Beard, James. *The Fireside Cook Book.* New York: Simon & Schuster, Inc., 1949.

———. *James Beard's American Cookery.* Boston, Toronto: Little, Brown & Company, 1972.

Bradley, Alice. *Desserts.* Boston: M. Barrows & Co., 1930.

Calvel, Raymond. *La Boulangerie Moderne.* Paris: Eyrolles, 1980.

———. *Le Goût du Pain.* Paris: Éditions Jérôme Villette, 1990.

Chaboissier, D. *Le Compagnon Pâtissier.* 2 vols. Paris: Éditions Jérôme Villette, 1983.

Child, Julia. *From Julia Child's Kitchen.* New York: Alfred A. Knopf, 1975.

Coria, Giuseppe. *Profumi di Sicilia.* Palermo: Vito Cavallotto, 1981.

Correnti, Pino. *Il Libro d'Oro della Cucina e dei Vini di Sicilia.* Milan: Mursia, 1986.

Couet, A., and E. Kayser. *Pains Spéciaux et Décorés.* Paris: Éditions St-Honoré, 1989.

Cunningham, Marion. *The Fannie Farmer Baking Book.* New York: Alfred A. Knopf, 1984.

Darenne, E., and E. Duval. *Traité de Pâtisserie Moderne.* Paris: Flammarion, 1974.

David, Elizabeth. *English Bread & Yeast Cookery.* New York: Viking Press, 1980.

D'Ermo, Dominique. *The Modern Pastry Chef's Guide to Professional Baking.* New York: Harper & Row, 1962.

Dubois, Urbain. *La Pâtisserie d'Aujourd'hui.* Paris: Dixième, 1925.

Escudier, Jean-Noël. *La Véritable Cuisine Provençale et Niçoise.* Toulon: Provencia, 1964.

Faccioli, Emilio. *L'Arte della Cucina in Italia.* Torino: Giulio Einaudi, 1987.

Fance, Wilfred James. *The Students' Technology of Breadmaking and Flour Confectionery.* London, Henley & Boston: Routledge & Kegan Paul, 1966.

———. *The New International Confectioner.* London and Coulsdon: Virtue & Company, 1981.

Francesconi, Jeanne Carola. *La Cucina Napoletana.* Naples: Del Delfino, ND.

Grasdorf, Erich, and Pia Gruber. *Zurcher Rezepte.* Zurich: AT Verlag, 1993.

Heatter, Maida. *Maida Heatter's Book of Great American Desserts.* New York: Alfred A. Knopf, 1985.

Hilburn, Prudence. *A Treasury of Southern Baking.* New York: HarperPerennial, 1993.

Jacob, Heinrich Eduardo. *6000 Jahre Brot.* Hamburg: Rowohlt, 1954.

Killeen, Johanne, and George Germon. *Cucina Simpatica: Robust Trattoria Cooking from Al Forno.* New York: HarperCollins Publishers, 1991.

Laverty, Maura. *Full & Plenty: Breads & Cakes,* vol. 1. Dublin: Anvil Books, 1985.

Masterton, Elsie. *The Blueberry Hill Menu Cookbook.* New York: Thomas Y. Crowell Company, ND.

Mayer, Eduard. *Wiener Süss-speisen.* Linz, Austria: Trauner Verlag, 1982.

McBride, Mary Margaret. *Mary Margaret McBride Encyclopedia of Cooking.* Evanston: Homemakers Research Institute, 1959.

McCully, Helen, and Eleanor Noderer. *Just Desserts.* New York: Ivan Obolensky, Inc., 1961.

Modesto, Maria de Lourdes. *Cozinha Tradicional Portuguesa.* São Paulo: Lisbon, 1982.

Parloa, Maria. *Home Economics.* New York: The Century Company, 1898.

Pasquet, Ernest. *La Pâtisserie Familiale.* Paris: Flammarion, 1974.

Peck, Paula. *The Art of Fine Baking.* New York: Simon & Schuster, 1961.

Pellaprat, Henri-Paul. *Les Desserts, Pâtisserie, et Entremets.* Paris: Jacques Kramer, 1937.

Platt, June. *June Platt's Party Cook Book.* Boston: Houghton Mifflin Company, 1936.

———. *June Platt's Plain and Fancy Cook Book.* Boston: Houghton Mifflin Company, 1941.

Poilâne, Lionel. *Guide de l'Amateur du Pain.* Paris: Robert Laffont, 1987.

Pyler, E. J. *Baking Science and Technology,* Third Edition, vols. 1 and 2. Merriam: Sosland Publishing Company, 1988.

Richards, Paul. *Cakes for Bakers.* Chicago: Baker's Helper Company, 1932.

Richemont Craft School. *Swiss Confectionary.* Lucerne: Richemont, 1985.

Richemont, École Professionelle. *La Boulangerie Suisse.* Lucerne: Richemont, 1983.

Seranne, Ann. *The Complete Book of Home Baking.* New York: Doubleday & Company, 1950.

Standard, Stella. *Our Daily Bread.* New York: Bonanza Books, ND.

Strause, Monroe Boston. *Pie Marches On.* New York: Ahrens Publishing Company, Inc., 1951.

Sultan, William J. *Modern Pastry Chef,* vols. 1 and 2. Westport, CT: AVI, 1977.

Viard, J. M. *Le Compagnon Boulanger.* Paris: Éditions Jérôme Villette, ND.

Wakefield, Ruth Graves. *Ruth Wakefield's Toll House Tried & True Recipes.* New York: M. Barrows & Company, 1937.

Wallace, Lily Haxworth. *The New American Cook Book.* New York: American Publishers' Alliance, 1942.

Wennberg, G. L. *Desserts, Pastries and Fancy Cakes.* Copenhagen: Ivan Forlag, 1964.

Witzelsberg, Richard. *Das Oesterreichische Mehlspeisen Kochbuch.* Vienna: Verlag Kremayr & Scheriau, 1979.

Wolcott, Imogene. *All About Home Baking.* New York: General Foods Corporation, 1933.

———. *Great Baking Begins with White Lily Flour: A Collection of Treasured Southern Baking Recipes.* Des Moines: Meredith Publishing, 1982.

———. *The New England Yankee Cook Book.* New York: Coward-McCann, Inc., 1939.

INDEX

INDEX